PRISONERS OF AMERICA'S WARS

STEPHANIE CARVIN

Prisoners of America's Wars

From the Early Republic to Guantanamo

Columbia University Press
New York

Columbia University Press
Publishers Since 1893
New York   Chichester, West Sussex
Copyright © 2010 Stephanie Carvin
All rights reserved

Library of Congress Cataloging-in-Publication Data

Carvin, Stephanie, 1978–
    Prisoners of America's wars : from the early republic to Guantanamo / Stephanie Carvin.
        p. cm.
    Includes bibliographical references.
    ISBN 978-0-231-70156-3 (alk. paper)
    1. United States—History, Military. 2. Prisoners of war—United States—History.
    3. Prisoners of war—Legal status, laws, etc.—United States—History. 4. Prisoners of
    war—History. 5. Prisoners of war—Legal status, laws, etc.—History. 6. War (Inter-
    national law)—History. I. Title.

    E181.C44 2010
    355.00973—dc22

                                    2010010232

∞

Columbia University Press books are printed on permanent and durable acid-free paper.
This book is printed on paper with recycled content.
Printed in India

c 10 9 8 7 6 5 4 3 2 1

References to Internet Web sites (URLs) were accurate at the time of writing.
Neither the author nor Columbia University Press is responsible for URLs
that may have expired or changed since the manuscript was prepared.

ABSTRACT

Prisoners of war have been a significant feature of virtually every conflict that the United States has engaged in since its revolutionary beginnings. Today visitors to Washington will frequently see a black POW flag flying high on government buildings or war memorials and monuments in silent memory. This act of fealty towards prisoners reflects a history where they have frequently been a rallying point, a source of outrage and a problem for both military and political leaders. This is as true for the 2003 Iraq War as it was for the American Revolution.

Yet, the story of prisoners in American wars (both enemies taken and soldiers captured) helps to reveal much about the nation itself; how it fights conflicts and its attitudes towards laws of war. A nation born out of an exceptional ideology, the United States has frequently found itself faced with the contradictory imperatives to be both exemplary and secure, resulting in situations that were sometimes ironic and sometimes tragic. At the same time as American diplomats might be negotiating a treaty at The Hague, American soldiers might be fighting against a bloody insurrection where it seemed that few or no rules applied.

The complex relationship between America, prisoners of war and international law is not one entirely based on exemplary culture or carnage, but on a blend of ideology, historical experience and national imperatives that has challenged presidents from Washington through to Obama. By taking a historical approach, this book demonstrates that the challenges America faced regarding international law and the war on terror were not entirely unique or unprecedented, despite the claims made by the Bush administration or its policies, as claimed by its critics. Rather, to be properly understood, such dilemmas must be contextualized within the long history of those prisoners captured in American wars.

CONTENTS

ACKNOWLEDGMENTS

This book comes out of a (now heavily modified) PhD completed at the London School of Economics in 2006. There are many people who were instrumental in the completion of both projects and to whom I am greatly in debt. I would first like to thank my PhD supervisor, Chris Brown, who was everything a PhD student ever needed in an adviser–someone who knew how to bring out the strengths in a candidate and overcome obstacles. I would also like to thank the staff and my fellow graduate students at the International Relations Department at the LSE while I was there, particularly Kirsten Ainley and Kim Hutchings for their support over the years. Departmental Manager Hilary Parker also helped me navigate the maze that doing a PhD can sometimes become.

I am also very fortunate to work in the young and vibrant Department of Politics and International Relations at Royal Holloway, University of London. I owe a great deal of thanks to my colleagues who have provided much support over the years, particularly Andrew Chadwick and Nathan Widder who have been excellent and understanding department heads since my arrival in 2006. In addition, I would like to thank the administrative staff, Marilyn Corrigan, Lisa Dacunha and Brenda Wareham, for their assistance over the years.

This book would not have been possible without the time and support of many individuals who took time to talk with me, answer my questions and share their both their knowledge and experience. In particular, I would like to thank the many lawyers of the US Department of Defense (both JAGs and civilians) who answered the questions of a persistent Canadian postgraduate student. Of these individuals, I would like to give special thanks to W. Hays Parks who, for over five years, has been an invaluable help whether it be over email or a pub lunch. Aside from working in this area, he has made an enormous contribution to the literature on the laws of war and how they are understood (as well as participating in many of the conferences which wrote and designed the treaties which are applicable today.) I would also like to thank Richard Jackson, Michael N. Schmitt and Gary Solis.

Several UK military lawyers (active and retired) also helped answer my questions and provided me with valuable insights on the laws of war, including William Boothby, Charles Garraway, and Stephen Haines (who was also my colleague for three years in the academic world). Additionally, I would like to thank Christopher Greenwood who allowed me to sit in on his law of armed conflict seminar and answer questions regarding the US legal system during his office hours while he was teaching at the LSE, and Sir Adam Roberts who also helped answer several questions and occasionally provide feedback on a few elements of the book. Susan Breau and Jason Ralph have also been very supportive during the various stages of this project.

I have, over the years, received numerous comments on various chapters and versions of this book. I would like to particularly thank Michael Cox and Nick Wheeler who examined my PhD thesis and provided excellent feedback on it at the same time. Peter C. Wilson assisted me with early draft chapters and in coordinating international relations theory seminars where students could present our material. More recently, Justin Anderson has provided excellent feedback and been a great sounding board for ideas as this project reached its conclusion.

Michael Dwyer at Hurst & Co Publishers has helped me bring the book from a .doc file to a book and I am very grateful for his assistance. I would also like to acknowledge the reviewers of this manuscript who played a significant role in shaping the final copy.

While I was a postgraduate student in London, I was fortunate enough to live in the wonderful environment provided by Goodenough College. It twice provided me bursaries and provided the ideal environment in which to write and complete my graduate studies. I met many friends while living there over the course of four years. Of these "Goodenoughers", I would like to thank Kristine Alexander, Sarah Duff, Carina Fourie and Jane McGaughey for their friendship and support. I would also like to thank Michael J. Williams who has been an excellent fellow student, colleague and, most importantly, friend over the years.

Finally, I would like to thank my family, Thomas, Darcy, Christopher Carvin and my Grandmother (or as I know her, Baba) who, for almost a decade, supported me in university and graduate school. It is hard to express just

ACKNOWLEDGMENTS

how wonderful and important their love and support have been over the years and it is to them that this book is dedicated.

Stephanie Carvin
London/Washington October 2009

INTRODUCTION

THE POLITICS OF THE LAWS OF WAR

In his controversial book on the 1991 Gulf War, Anthony Swofford describes the following scene:

The instructor breaks in. "Hey, gents, can we talk about the rifles? It's not news that this war is gonna be all-American. I'm here to teach you how to kill people and disable vehicles with your new toy. By the way, you all know you can't hit a human target with a fifty-caliber weapon, right? It's in the Geneva Convention. So you hit the gas tank on their vehicle, and they get blown the hell up, but you can't target some lonely guard or a couple of towlies in an OP calling in bombs. You'll have to get closer with the forty or call in your own bombs."

"We can't shoot people with this thing? Fuck the Geneva Convention" a sniper from the Fifth Marines says.

Dickerson says, "You fuck the Geneva Convention and I'll see you in Leavenworth. That's like shooting a nun or a doctor. Where'd we find this retard?"[1]

Perhaps it is a little crude, but Swofford's narration illustrates a debate over restraint in warfare that has challenged the United States from its inception. What are the obligations to one's enemy? Can killing be done humanely? When a cause is just why should a nation hold back its armies?

Of course, these are the questions that challenge all nations (or perhaps, more correctly, all conscientious nations) with armies that find their interests and security challenged by military threats. Yet in the case of the United States, the influence of its founding ideologies, its expanding empire and the sheer scale of its military engagements abroad have, throughout its history, prompted a lot of soul searching on these questions by soldiers, lawyers and philosophers alike. There is no doubt that America's global position and even its global role are unique. But what are the implications of this for the way it conducts its military affairs abroad–if any?

1

With the possible exception of Vietnam, the debates on this issue have traditionally been held behind closed doors in the Pentagon, or at international conferences in Geneva, The Hague and San Remo. Certainly before the 1990s the moral complexities and practical dilemmas of the laws of war had not caught much media attention or scrutiny. It is true that citizens in America and throughout the world were familiar with the Geneva Conventions–if only through clichéd World War II movies or through television programmes like *Hogan's Heroes*. However, debates over whether killing an enemy with 0.50 calibre ammunition constituted an inhumane practice under the laws of war, or the obligations of a defender with regard to placing munitions factories in a populated area, or the legality of using white phosphorus, etc. largely escaped public notice.

True, there was some attention given to the laws of war as the conduct of the wars following the break-up of Yugoslavia came under media scrutiny. However, it was after the publication of pictures of prisoners in orange jumpsuits, blindfolded and strapped to stretchers at Guantánamo Bay's Camp Delta, in January 2002 that this rapidly changed. The assertion by the Bush administration that the Geneva Conventions could not, and should not, apply to a "war on terror" put the Conventions in the spotlight and under a new media scrutiny. The result was to generate what seemed to be a largely uninformed debate in the popular press about the Geneva Conventions and the laws of war. Are there such things as unlawful combatants? Did the rules apply if the Taliban did not wear a distinctive mark? How could the laws of war possibly apply to terrorists?

As the attention switched from Afghanistan to Iraq, the focus on the laws of war somewhat diminished in favour of a debate over the legality of the 2003 Iraq invasion. Yet the laws of war still attracted some significant media attention. Certainly this was the case when US soldiers were captured by Iraqi troops in March 2003 and shown on Iraqi national television. But the Conventions also came into sharp focus once more as controversies like the Abu Ghraib prison scandal broke in the spring of 2004.

So it is hard to deny that the laws of war have played an important role in the conduct, but also–perhaps more important–the public perception of the war on terror since military action began in Afghanistan in October 2001. During the initial phase of the campaign the US military and its allies took care to demonstrate that while engaging in military activities, they were also feeding the Afghan population and going to great lengths to spare civilians. And it is clear that controversy and scandal relating to the laws of war had a great effect upon the conduct of the campaign and on the political leadership. When asked in May 2006 about what he most regretted about the 2003 Iraq War, in May 2006, Bush replied: "...I think the biggest mistake that's happened so far, at least from our country's involvement in Iraq is Abu Ghraib. We've been paying for that for a long period of time."[2]

The goal of this work is to tell the story, chronologically, of the engagement of the United States with the laws of war–its participation in drafting legislation, how it trains and disciplines its military, and how it ultimately implemented the laws of war on the battlefield. It will look at how US participation in these conflicts changed the way we look at the laws of war, through US failures and mistakes (in My Lai and Son Than) but also through what may be deemed US successes (such as the 1991 Gulf War).

Particular attention will be paid to the effect of ideology and its corresponding political imperatives in terms of the decisions the US has made with respect to the laws of war, and what happens when these ideological imperatives clash with the tenets of international law. The effect of ideological and political imperatives on implementation of the laws of war in the War on Terror will be examined to suggest reasons why the United States or, more accurately, the Bush administration chose to act in the manner it did and what the effects this will have on the ongoing military campaigns throughout the world. It is hoped that the book's largely historical approach will help show how policies have evolved over time and help explain why certain decisions were made by administrations and what the consequences of those decisions were. In other words, my assumption here is that we can better understand Abu Ghraib if we understand what came a decade or even a century before.

Prisoners of War (or prisoners in war?)

The laws of war cover a broad area and govern a wide variety of military activities. Traditionally, this includes targeting, protection of cultural property, and treatment of the sick and wounded, shipwrecked people, civilians in occupied territories, and prisoners of war. However, the law has increasingly expanded to cover blinding weapons, landmines and protection of the environment. Therefore, although the laws of war seem to be a small branch of international law as a whole, they cover a lot of ground.

For this reason, I have as chosen to focus on one particular aspect of the laws of war: issues relating to the treatment of prisoners of war, commonly known by the acronym POW. A case can be made for focusing on prisoners of war for a number of reasons, not least because the treatment of prisoners in the war on terror has been a major issue since the images of Guántanamo Bay were splashed across newspapers throughout the world. In this sense the issue of treatment of combatants or terrorists who themselves have little respect, and a lot of contempt, for the laws of war, and who refuse to abide by its rules, is seen as a very interesting, political and morally complex issue.

Yet perhaps it needs to be said that a lot of what is discussed in the book is also about the issues that surround POW status–significantly, whether or not one is recognized as a POW and what the consequences are if one is not. "Prisoner of War" is a legal status, but it does not cover all prisoners in an armed conflict. This dilemma was reflected in a title of a conference at the University of Oxford in December 2007 entitled "Prisoners in War", and the participants faced the problem that much that was under discussion involved those who were not given the conventional status. The way this is handled in the book is that the primary interest remains POWs, but to illustrate broader points, "prisoners in war" will also be discussed. Again, this is particularly relevant for those occasions (such as the war in the Philippines) where POW status was denied, and to make larger points about the way the laws of war were considered by the different parties.

This is not to say that other issues involving the laws of war are not important, or that decisions about what is and is not a legitimate target are irrelevant or boring. During the 1999 Kosovo War the issue of targeting was certainly a matter of highly contested debate. But during the heavy bombing phase of Operation Enduring Freedom or Operation Iraqi Freedom, there were few suggestions that the laws governing targeting were "obsolete", and the overall political impact of targeting in the Afghanistan and Iraq campaigns seems to be less than that of the recognition and treatment of POWs.

Issues concerning the environment and landmines are fairly new and do not have the same historical background for analysis. On the other hand, ever since there has been war, there have been victims of conflicts and moral doctrines as to how to treat one's enemy. Prisoners of war have featured prominently in almost every war that the United States has taken part in since its inception, and in this sense there is a history which can be examined, and analysed. The United States had to deal with POWs in its Revolutionary War, the War of 1812, the Mexican-American War, the Civil War and the wars against the First Nations–and this was all within the first 100 years of its founding.

Issues such as guerrilla warfare are given more consideration because this type of war was (and still is) considered to be outside the framework of the normal laws of war. In fact, it is frequently in guerrilla-style conflicts that the United States has experienced many, if not most of the problems affecting prisoners taken in conflict. Where guerrilla fighters were willing to launch night raids, attack civilian convoys or use tactics considered indiscriminate by humanitarian standards, it was likely that prisoners of war were not likely to fare well–if they were taken at all. Guerrilla-style warfare during the Seven Years War, the American Revolution, and the wars against the First Nations tribes, in the Philippines and up to Vietnam and Iraq frequently meant that captured enemies were not given any rights or were simply murdered. Clearly, this has relevance for prisoners of war in the sense that individuals were not given the opportunity to become POWs. In this sense, where the nature and effect of guerrilla warfare are discussed, it is normally to demonstrate larger points about the legal or moral framework in which prisoner of war issues were handled.[3]

Dealings with prisoners in the modern era continued as American military personnel were captured in the two world wars, and the issue of POWs became politicized in the Korea and Vietnam. And, of course, the treatment of prisoners of war has been one of the most prominent when it comes to the laws of war in the War on Terror. The recent debates over Guantánamo Bay, Abu Ghraib and the moral standing of al Qaida as an enemy suggest that these issues still challenge the United States, morally, politically and legally, today. Given this history and this blend of political, moral and legal concerns, the POW issue makes for an interesting case study in terms of the restraints on waging modern war. Still, it needs to be acknowledged that this did not happen in a vacuum, and other issues will be examined where it is felt that they had an impact on the laws of war as a whole which could affect the law relating to prisoners.

The laws of war as codified hypocrisy?

But before going any further, it will first be useful to determine just exactly what is meant by "the laws of war". For the purpose of this work, the laws of war will be considered to be the body of international law which governs military activities and defines the duties and responsibilities of participants and nonparticipants in conflict situations with the (usual) intention of preventing unnecessary suffering.

This clarification is important because the term "laws of war" is sometimes used to relate to several different areas of law that are all, confusingly, interrelated. This includes the law that governs when states may resort to conflict—sometimes known as *jus ad bellum*, or its less legal variation, just war theory. The law being discussed here has little to do with the reasons *why* states go to war and instead focuses on *how* states fight. This law is sometimes called the *jus in bello* (justice *in* war).

Unfortunately, the confusion does not necessarily stop there. The laws of war (*jus in bello*) are sometimes known as the "laws of armed conflict" or "international humanitarian law". The former definition attempts to get away from messy political discussions as to what exactly constitutes a "war", whereas the latter is more of a modern term which suggests the "humanitarian" sentiment supposedly behind the law.[4] The crucial thing here for readers to keep in mind is that no matter which label is used, they all refer to the same set of treaties and agreements which seek to place restrictions on the way states wage war, such as the Geneva Conventions and the Ottawa Landmines Treaty. The term "laws of war" has been used here because the events that this work is primarily concerned with are, in fact, wars as they have been traditionally understood—despite whatever names may have been attached to the conflicts by the media or politicians. Additionally, given the subject matter, there is a certain emotional or passionate response to the term and what we normally associate with it. "War" is definitely a word with baggage. However, for our purposes here, this is a useful baggage because of what war entails, what it has been able to achieve for the United States, and its commemoration in American memory.

Most of the sources of the laws of war date from the end of the nineteenth century through to the middle of the twentieth. However, many lawyers and theorists are eager to look back throughout history to the rules and norms which have traditionally guided and restricted the way wars were waged. Usually they point to ancient codes and medieval treaties to illustrate their point that the laws of war are really as old as war itself. Such a history suggests a sturdy foundation for the application of rules and the laws of war on the battlefield.

Yet anyone who reads of the savagery of the Napoleonic wars, colonial battles or the Russian front in the Second World War could probably be forgiven for thinking that this was not the case. Certainly it is true that the laws of war have their origins in chivalrous codes that are centuries old. But the historical record suggests that such codes were honoured more often in breach than in practice. How much of an impact could the laws of war really have had?

This work is interested in the engagement of the United States with the laws of war and therefore operates on the premise that the laws of war do matter. The question of whether or not the US takes the laws of war seriously (and the argument here is that, for the most part, the US military does) will be addressed in later chapters. However, before proceeding further, it is useful for the rest of the work to take seriously the question of whether the term "laws of war" is in fact an oxymoron.

In books on the laws of war it is not rare to find references to Cicero's dictum *inter arma enim silent leges* or "in war law is silent", and there has certainly been renewed use of the phrase since 9/11. The pessimistic tone of the saying suggests that matters of national interest or security will always triumph over well established rules and customs. The ideas of *"raison de guerre"*, *"raison d'Etat"* in earlier centuries and "military necessity" in times closer to our own have always been invoked by commanders and politicians justifying breaches of the laws of war. Although Napoleon is quoted as having said "The natural law...forbids us to multiply the evils of war indefinitely"[5] he was clearly quite content to have his soldiers raid towns and villages for food and supplies, leaving little left for the inhabitants to survive the winter.[6] Such policies, of course, were justified with reference to necessity. In the present, to answer charges of laws of war violations, many commentators and politicians in the United States have argued that the necessity of defeating al Qaida is much more important than any shallow humanitarian political obligations.[7]

To address the balance between ancient codes and their constant violation, a consideration of the role of law in war is needed. While one may point to the brutality and savagery commonplace in warfare, war always has had some kind of rules which guide its conduct. Without these rules, war cannot be distinguished from chaotic, purposeless murder, serving no goal or interest. As Michael Howard argues:

War... is not the condition of generalized and random violence pictured by Thomas Hobbes as the 'state of nature'. It is on the contrary a highly social activity–an activity indeed which demands from the groups which engage in it an unique intensity of society organization and control.[8]

Therefore, there is a link between war and discipline–states with unrestrained armies have often found that their goals cannot be achieved without enforcing discipline. Worse, such nations have been attacked by their own marauding troops. But beyond self-preservation, the rape and pillage of towns could often lead to disastrous consequences for the political and military objectives of an invading army. While such policies could create fear within a population to encourage docility, it could also turn a population against an army, making occupation or future advancement very difficult and costly. In this sense, restraint was not only humane, it was militarily advantageous.

In this way, claims that war is an ungovernable explosion of violence with no rule but kill or be killed are just as mistaken as the belief that law alone will ensure that civilians will never die in conflict zones. In short, the laws of war are a strange beast–frequently honoured in words, regularly broken in deeds. It is effective in so far as states want it to be–but to suggest that states do not have a choice in the matter is wrong. If war is a norm governed activity, then importance can be attached to those norms which do or should apply and the ways they are incorporated into military doctrine; and this in turn is worthy of academic scrutiny. Examining the development and implementation of the laws of war is the aim of this work–but through the lenses of the United States: its military, its politicians and its citizens.

The United States, politics and history

Anyone familiar with current events should not find it too difficult to understand why this work has chosen to focus on the United States. Because of its military engagement and status as a world power, the United States has had an effect on the development of (or at least the way we consider) the laws of war. It has participated in virtually every conference which aimed to modify or further develop the laws of war since the 1899 Hague Convention. Even where the United States has chosen not to sign on to various legal treaties for political or moral reasons, this has had an effect on the law. Although there are several of these treaties that ithas not signed, the United States has incorporated many of their principles into its own military doctrine. One only need look at the targeting provisions of Additional Protocol I to the 1949 Geneva Conventions and compare them with US practice to see that the US, for the most part, follows the rules laid out in the text. Furthermore, as it is the nation with a military that is the most heavily engaged throughout the world in terms of sheer scale and numbers, it is clear that US practice is going to have an effect on the interpretation of treaties and in the development of law whether or not the US is, itself, a signatory.

However, this discussion would undoubtedly be amiss if it did not mention the rather obvious fact that the US has probably been the nation most embroiled in controversy regarding the laws of war since 1945. Certainly it is not the only country to come under scrutiny in this regard. French military actions in Algeria shocked Western nations and Canada faced international shame when a scandal broke in 1994 over the torture and murder of Somali youths by its soldiers. Recently stories of UN peacekeepers (from several nations) sexually abusing women in conflict areas such as the Congo have also emerged.[9]

Yet whether it is because of the sheer scale of military operations the US has conducted since 1945, the nature of the conflicts in which it has chosen to participate, or its own moral understanding of itself as "a law abiding nation", there has been much domestic and international focus on the conduct of American and American-lead military operations. Clearly, US citizens expect that their soldiers will behave in a way that coincides with American values and principles. Part of the soul-searching which followed Vietnam (inside and outside the military) was a result of the realization that US soldiers could and did massacre civilians. That US soldiers could be induced to participate in such activities contrasted dramatically with public expectations. Additionally, because many of the conflicts that the US has participated in since 1945 have been controversial, American leaders and military commanders have gone to great lengths to ensure that more fuel is not added to the fire by laws of war violations, and this has sometimes produced strange results. For example, during the Kosovo campaign, the Clinton administration insisted on carefully going over and approving targeting lists, rejecting those which seemed likely to lead to civilian casualties.[10]

Therefore, it should not cause too much surprise that there is a lot of domestic and international scrutiny of US military operations in the ongoing "War on Terror". However, the public announcement that the laws of war would not technically apply to captured combatants in Afghanistan, and the outcry over Guantánamo Bay and Abu Ghraib, have thrown the US, and some of its more controversial policies regarding the laws of war, into the spotlight. This work seeks to examine these controversies, the arguments on both sides and the implication for the laws of war. Do the arguments and justifications make sense? And if so, on what grounds?

Politics and the laws of war

This brings us to the next question regarding this work—why "the politics of the laws of war" and not just the "laws of war"? The most immediate answer to this question is that the line of inquiry and arguments put forward are not legal *per se*. In fact, the book specifically aims to avoid legal debates over interpretation of treaty texts. Instead, it seeks to present an argument that is about law, but is not legal.

Since the War on Terror began, there have been many books and articles published on problems with the law, determining which law applies and the legal obligations of combatants.[11] Therefore, to present a legal work on these matters would be to follow a well trodden path. That the author of this work is not a lawyer would probably result in the presentation of an inaccurate, unoriginal argument.

However, it is an assumption of this work that the law cannot and should not be left to the lawyers alone. Rather, there is room for much non-legal scrutiny of how the law develops, is implemented and regarded by states, groups and individuals. Examining such attitudes does not require a law degree, but an understanding of politics and history. That law is often affected by politics and our ideological perceptions is a fact that a cold, ahistorical reading of a legal text cannot bring to light.

In this sense, the discussion here is "political" rather than "legal" because it is concerned with the activities and controversies relating to governing a particular area of international relations and how this interplays with domestic politics. It examines the way states exercise their power and the impact of laws that attempt to place restrictions on this in warfare. Moreover, the discussion in this book may be said to be political because it relates to a set of "political" beliefs regarding how states, individuals and the international community should interact with all of the above.

International lawyers and international law

Where lawyers have crossed over into the political realm, the results have been only somewhat satisfactory. Most international lawyers who have written on this area have written condemnatory books which present lists of violations of the laws of war and long tirades against the Bush and Blair administrations for their actions.[12] In these books there is little appreciation for the role of politics in law, especially international law. Instead, international law is treated as a sacred body of rules, any violation of which is presented as a betrayal of humanity as a whole. As Philippe Sands, a leading international lawyer who has written two damning critiques of the Bush administration's policies, writes, "The 'war on terrorism' has lead many lawyers astray"[13]—without ever explaining exactly what lawyers have led been astray from. Rather it is assumed that international law is good and international politics are bad. Michael Byers, an international law professor and commentator, concludes his book on war law arguing: "The immense power of the United States carries with it an awesome responsibility: to improve the world—for everyone. Obeying the requirements of war law is a necessary first step."[14]

The reader is therefore apparently to assume that law is the solution to our problems and unquestioning obedience to it is necessary for world peace and victory in the War on Terror. One cannot help being reminded of E.H. Carr's contention that among people interested in international affairs, there is "a strong inclination to treat law as something independent of, and ethically superior to, politics."[15]

Perhaps, one might argue, where politics leads to policies and practices of torture the ethical superiority of law is defensible. And this brings us to a second set of lawyers who are, perhaps, only too willing to dismiss international law as vague and without substance. These lawyers (who will be referred to as the "New Sovereigntists" in Chapter 4) argue that the only supreme law that binds a nation can be its own constitution; the only international law which matters is that which states have explicitly agreed to and ratified. Even then, they argue, states only too often ratify international treaties with absolutely no intention to do anything about their new international commitments, and this demonstrates the weakness and irrelevance of international law. As Jeremy Rabkin argues:

Without a sense that law follows from the national constitution and the past understandings of that constitution, "law" can be manipulated into anything a judge may like it to be and individual rights are as uncertain or as ephemeral as this [international] "law".[16]

Therefore, when it comes to the War on Terror, these lawyers argue that there cannot be any question of international law restricting US actions. The ultimate purpose of the state is to protect the inhabitants of its territory–even if this means violating the principles of international law.

To the former group of lawyers, international law is everything. To the New Sovereigntists, international law is very little indeed. With starting positions like these, both sides ultimately end up talking past each other and there is very little room for debate and reflection on the larger issue of the role of law in the War on Terror. It seems one is expected to believe that international law is an all or nothing phenomenon.

It is a central idea of this work that what has been lost in this debate is an examination of the role of politics in law and law in politics. The New Sovereigntists may argue that international law really does not matter, but this does not explain why the Bush administration worked hard to justify its policies legally in the War on Terror (as well as politically and morally). The international lawyers may argue that the actions of the Bush and Blair administrations worked to destroy the fabric of the international legal system–but this cannot account for the fact that the Geneva Conventions remain fairly intact and continue as the basis for our judgements of military actions in conflicts.

Perhaps, in setting out to look at the United States and the politics of the laws of war, it is interesting to consider Hersh Lauterpacht's suggestion that "If international law is, in some ways, at the vanishing point of law, the law of war is, perhaps even more conspicuously, at the vanishing point of international law."[17] The phrase is now virtually a cliché among those who write on the laws of war. But the question remains whether the same holds true for the politics of international law. In looking at the history of, and international debates over, conflicts engaged in and controversies relating to the laws of war, this work seeks to demonstrate that although the power of law may be questionable in war, the politics surrounding its implementation remains as important and interesting as always.

The book ahead

This book seeks to recognize that prisoners of war (or prisoners in war) seem to have been an issue of controversy in virtually all of the conflicts that the United States has fought. Throughout these conflicts the United States has had to grapple with the issues of how to implement the laws of war when faced with "unconventional" actors, or how to persuade an enemy that he should follow international guidelines. Where they have failed, the results have often been tragic—one only need to think of the American prisoners held by Japan in World War II or the prisoners held at Abu Ghraib.

Yet, as the book will illustrate, the treatment of prisoners of war in the conflicts that America has fought in has depended on a number of factors—not all of them obvious at the time. One of these is cultural perceptions; where there was recognition of a form of cultural equality, implementation of the laws of war could go very well, but where norms clashed, this does not seem to have happened. While not free of regrettable instances, the Mexican-American War, where a similar, if not identical, set of norms existed, was arguably much less bloody for prisoners than any of the conflicts fought against First Nations tribes where martial traditions differed substantially. Another major factor, as mentioned above, is the role of ideology—the framework through which nations carry out both domestic and international policies. The belief in "manifest destiny" and spreading the values of the American Revolution abroad had an impact on the way Americans looked at those who opposed them.

But it is not all "culture and carnage". The American legalistic culture ensures that international law is taken very seriously within the US government and its various apparatus, specifically as part of the "highest law of the land". To suggest that the story of the United States and the laws of war is nothing but a barbaric one would be as incorrect as suggesting that America has always held the moral high ground when it comes to prisoners of war. The United States takes the laws of war seriously, and this has prompted a moral crisis with regards to the challenges posed by the War on Terror. By going back and looking at America's wars, it is hoped that those who have been held at the mercy of their captors can tell us something about the way the United States, and the world, regard restraints on the waging of armed conflict.

The ordering of chapters is as follows: Part I gives a historical overview of America's relationship with the laws of war from its inception as a nation during the Seven Years War to the signing of the Geneva Conventions in 1949. Chapter One concentrates on the first wars that it fought which influenced the military traditions of the new republic–the Seven Years War, its wars of independence and the Mexican-American War–when little to no formal international law applied outside customary norms of warfare. Chapter Two will look at how the United States engaged with the first formal treaties relating to the use of force and how the wars it fought from the Civil War to the Korean War played a significant role in defining America's relationship with the laws of war and its own system of military justice. This section will argue that although the United States saw itself as an exceptional nation, in terms of the laws of war its approach was very European. This history demonstrates the origins of a "dualistic approach" in terms of the laws of war–the rules that applied to the Civil War and the rules that applied to the wars against First Nations people were very different. While the United States was engaged in a bloody counter-insurgency war in the Philippines it was, at the same time, working with other European nations to expand and codify international law and the laws of war at the 1899 Hague Conference. However, as the chapter will demonstrate, by the middle of the twentieth century it was clear that the United States was taking the laws of war seriously in terms of participating in their further expansion after the Second World War and in the development of the Uniform Code of Military Justice.

Part II will look at how modern wars have affected the relationship between the United States and the laws of war. Chapter 3 will outline the difficulties and disasters experienced by the United States in terms of the laws of war in Vietnam. However, the focus will be on the lessons US military lawyers drew from their experiences in that conflict and how they worked to change the US approach to the laws of war to make those laws a more "sellable" package to commanders and troops. This led to what may as well be called a "legal revolution" in terms of the American approach to the laws of war, which was apparent in the 1991 Gulf War–referred to by some as the most "legalistic" war in history.

Chapter 4 will begin to examine the relationship between the United States and the laws of war in the War on Terror, the focus of this work. It will seek to explain why, after a policy of strict adherence to the laws of war, the political leadership of the United States chose not to apply the Geneva Conventions to captured combatants in Afghanistan. In looking for answers, the chapter will look back to the experience of fighting in Kosovo–the difficulties of coalition politics when it comes to the laws of war, as well as legal battles with the International Criminal Tribunal for the Former Yugoslavia. Additionally, it will look at the rise of the "New Sovereigntist" critique of international law in the 1990s. Ultimately, the chapter will suggest that these factors, combined with the political imperative of winning the War on Terror and gaining intelligence, resulted in the Bush administration denying combatants formal recognition as prisoners of war. It will then assess the validity of the claims made in light of the threat posed by international terrorism.

In looking at the relationship between the United States and the laws of war in Iraq, Chapter 5 will look mainly at the scandal at the Abu Ghraib prison, but will also focus on other controversial issues such as the increasing participation of private military firms (PMFs) in military operations. In terms of the scandal at Abu Ghraib, the chapter will look at various explanations of why the events took place–whether individual soldiers gave in to sadistic tendencies in a chaotic environment with unclear rules, or whether the abuse at the prison emerged as a direct result of Bush administration policies. The chapter will look at the implications of generating uncertainty over the laws of war in implementing an overall comprehensive approach.

PART I

A WEAPON AND RESTRAINT

AMERICA AND RESTRAINTS ON CONFLICT IN THE AGE OF TOTAL WARS, 1750–1950

Since the founding of the Republic, adherence to the laws of war has been heavily supported by American lawyers and policy makers. It was expected of the American revolutionary and the soldier in the War of 1812; just means were seen as an important part of the justification key in maintaining popular support throughout these campaigns. The suffering of prisoners of war in British hands (and there was a lot of suffering) was held up as an example of British cruelties and the justness of the American cause. The need to protect its servicemen, and to maintain its "just cause" throughout the first two centuries of its existence, would lead the United States to pioneer some of the first legislation designed to care for prisoners of war.

Of course, in reality, eighteenth and nineteenth century warfare really never worked out so nicely. There were many violations of the normal customs of war during these conflicts, such as the use of guerrilla tactics and employing First Nations warriors[1] to strike deadly blows against the enemy.[2] In this way, it is not novel to suggest that America's adherence to the laws of war in the early republic was heavily qualified. One of America's foremost scholars on international law, Henry Wheaton, wrote in 1866:

Thus, if the progress of an enemy cannot be stopped nor our own frontier secured or if the approaches to a town intended to be attacked cannot be made with out laying waste the intermediate territory, the extreme case may justify a resort to measures not warranted by the ordinary purposes of war... The whole international code is founded upon reciprocity. The rules it prescribes are observed by one nation, in confidence that they will be so by others. Where, then, the established means of restraining his excesses, retaliation may justly be resorted to observance of the law which he has violated.[3]

This was, of course, the perfect justification for an unrestrained war against the First Nations of North America.

The next two chapters will provide a brief survey of America's relationship with the laws of war from 1750 through to the Korean War. It will be apparent that, as with most countries at this time, America's adherence to the laws of war was erratic. Indeed, even though they saw their nation as exceptional, the leaders of the Revolution deliberately set out to base their operations on European norms and conventions. Yet while this belief played a part in encouraging the newly formed United States to adhere to the traditional laws of war, the American imperative to expand its civilizing empire created a dualistic tendency in its application of this law. While the United States was crucial to the development of the laws of war–the Lieber Code and its influence on the early twentieth century treaties were key to the development of the laws of war–it would also use those same laws to justify the tactics it employed against non-Western peoples. Given the ferocious nature of many of these wars, the only thing which seems to be constant in the treatment given and received by Americans in these wars is inconsistency.

By the middle of the twentieth century, the US began to put into place a more coherent and doctrinal approach to the laws of war. This approach responded to the need of a growing military in a democracy, but also reflected its experience in fighting total wars. It was never a straight path, but the US would go from fighting unrestrained wars against its native populations to implementing a strong code of military justice and, for the most part, a decent respect for the laws of war.

1

CULTURE OR CARNAGE?

THE LAWS OF WAR IN THE FIRST WARS OF THE REPUBLIC, 1750–1860

As the newly formed American Army engaged in war against the British in the War of Independence, the first American Articles of War came into force on 30 June 1775 when they were adopted by the Second Continental Congress.[4] They were directly derived from the British Articles of War which themselves had been greatly influenced by an almost literal translation of Roman Law.[5] John S. Cooke notes that this led to a somewhat ironic result— the British Articles, with their medieval origins, rested on a particular relationship between leaders and the rank and file that was different from the egalitarian principles espoused by revolutionary Americans (particularly ironic since the class-based, hierarchical nature of the British Army had been one of the chief complaints of the enlisted Americans during the Seven Years War). Ideological inconsistency aside, Cooke notes that such a decision was not that surprising, given the urgent need to organize and govern the rebelling forces.[6] Additionally, despite Anglo-American rangers who had used guerrilla-style tactics during the Seven Years War, most of the training of American troops (many of whom went on to fight in the Revolutionary War) had been done firmly in British and European traditions.

Perhaps more importantly, it appears that the goals of the American and British systems were the same—to instill a command-dominated control to secure obedience. Courts-martial were not viewed as an independent mechanism for determining justice, but as a tool to serve the military. As Cooke notes, punishment, or the threat of it, was seen as the only way to motivate poor, uneducated and newly integrated men on the battlefield.[7] In the life and death struggle of conflict, not to mention the chaos of the battlefield, discipline was crucial for getting an objective accomplished. Writing just over a century later, General William T. Sherman (himself a lawyer) wrote:

Civilian lawyers are too apt to charge that Army discipline is tyranny. We know better. The discipline of the best armies has been paternal, just and impartial. Every general, and every commanding officer, knows that to obtain from his command the largest measure of force, and the best results he must possess the absolute confidence of his command by his firmness, his impartiality, his sense of justice and devotion to his country, not from fear. Yet in order to execute the orders of his superiors he must insist on the implicit obedience of his command. Without this quality, no army can fulfill its office, and every good citizen is as much interested in maintaining this quality in the army as any member of it.[8]

That there were few changes made to the Articles of War until the mid-twentieth century indicates that such a belief was firmly held by military and political leaders.[9] Flogging for offences was not abolished in the US Navy until 1850.

Given this emphasis on discipline (even overriding justice for the American soldier who found himself accused), extensive guidelines with regards to humanitarian restraint in warfare were not laid out in the Articles–though, in view of their European origins, it must be said that America was hardly alone in this. Still, the Articles remained the tool through which the customary laws of war were enforced.

Of course this did not always work in a time when many Americans felt that they were fighting a war for their very survival on the continent. Threatened as they were by the French to the north, the Spanish to the south and First Nations tribes in the interior, the willingness to apply restraints in wars deemed to be protecting the very existence of their young society was frequently tested and, occasionally, ignored all together. A desire to remove one's enemies, particularly those seen to come from a strange culture, meant that there was not always a strong aspiration to provide for enemy prisoners of war. However, even where there were cultural similarities, the ferocity of the first conflicts that Americans engaged in meant that there would always be some difficulties ensuring humanity in warfare–for the British, the rebelling colonists were just that, and not proper soldiers who deserved the honours of war.

This chapter will look at how Americans first engaged with the laws of war in the conflicts that helped to forge their nation. While American political leaders and commanders largely saw themselves fighting in the European tradition, the nature of colonial warfare in the quest for complete security in

North America meant that the Enlightenment principles which had been gradually developing more formal restraints on warfare were not applied. To fully understand why this was so, and the attitudes that Americans took with them into their Revolution, it is important to look back to the participation of the Anglo-Americans in the Seven Years War.

The Seven Years War

Even though it occurred in the eighteenth century, the Seven Years War (also known as the French and Indian War) had many of the aspects that would feature in the "total wars" of the twentieth century.[10] It was a war fought over many continents, including India, Europe, North America and the West Indies. The central actors frequently employed tactics which amounted to a form of unrestricted warfare. Key to this was a clash of cultures among the main protagonists. The First Nations tribes (particularly the Iroquois), through Europeans eyes, were seen as pitiless, torture-loving savages that made the killing and torment of prisoners a central activity of warfare. But the Europeans could easily give back as good as they got and quickly adopted methods such as scalping. They also categorically refused to give quarter to First Nations prisoners taken. According to some accounts, the conflict may have even involved germ warfare (in the form of disease infected blankets given to the First Nations peoples).[11]

Indeed, although historians of international law often point to the eighteenth century as the period which saw the use of reason, and rational and humane principles, applied to warfare, the frequently brutal and indiscriminate nature of the warfare in North America in the years 1755–62 suggests that this was not necessarily the case outside Europe. In reflecting on the conflict, John Shy recalls that the settlement of the European colonies coincided with the "frightfulness of the Thirty Years War" and that the development of European norms did not necessarily automatically appear in North America:

> From about 1650 to about 1750, when European states were moving toward forms of military organization, techniques of fighting, goals of foreign policy, and a generally accepted code of military and diplomatic behaviour that eliminated or mitigated the worst effects of warfare on society, the English colonists in North America found themselves re-enacting on a small scale the horrors of the Irish pacification and the Thirty Years War.[12]

Although European conventions would occasionally be applied by the French, English and Anglo-Americans, this would be done on an *ad hoc* basis, depending more on the personalities involved and the circumstances of battle rather than any systematic framework governing war fighting.

Therefore, our starting point needs to be understood not in terms of Enlightenment virtue, but rather as the impact of a modern form of medieval warfare. As the Seven Years War came to be seen as a struggle for survival by all parties, humanitarian standards frequently fell in the name of *raison d'Etat* and military necessity, but, importantly, also out of the very determined and unmitigated desire to see one's enemies eliminated from the New World for good. The French aimed to eliminate the Anglo-American hunters and settlers from the Ohio Valley, and the Anglo-Americans sought to remove the "Papist" threat posed by the Catholic Canadians. Armstrong Starkey writes that even in the Enlightenment era, soldiers might enjoy spilling the blood of their enemies: "Behind the courtly manners of the officers of the Old Regime, there were many who enjoyed war. Nighttime bayonet actions provided them with an opportunity to indulge themselves."[13]

Prisoners and hostages at the outbreak of hostilities

Given this environment, the treatment of prisoners of war depended very much on how and where one was captured, under what circumstances and by whom–something that would become a theme in the wars America engaged in during the eighteenth and nineteenth centuries. As Ian K. Steele notes, "the collision of Aboriginal, colonial, and imperial value systems was seldom displayed as clearly and fatefully as in the taking and treating of captives."[14] Before the actual outbreak of hostilities, tensions had been increasing between Anglo-American Virginians, French Canadians and the First Nations in the Allegheny borderlands. Competition for land and resources resulted in a cross-cultural flashpoint where the different groups in North America began to intersect. In the years running up to 1755, there had been a series of "hostage takings" in this area, although the actual status of the hostages taken was difficult to determine then and still is. While there was certainly an outbreak of skirmishes between the First Nations, Canadians and Virginians, there was no clear status of declared war. As a result, a captive taken in the various clashes had an ambiguous status as either criminal, hostage or prisoner of war–and frequently the results could be quite brutal.

Accounts about what became known as the "Jumonville incident" (the incident widely considered to have sparked the Seven Years War) differ, but what is clear is that in May 1754 a small band of soldiers lead by their then-British commander, George Washington, captured a French camp with the assistance of some First Nations warriors. Among the wounded after the attack was the commander of the camp, Josef Coulon de Villiers de Jumonville, who claimed to have been on a diplomatic mission to ask the English to withdraw from French territory. While there is no definitive account of what happened next, it is clear that the leader of the First Nations accompanying Washington set upon and killed Jumonville by striking his head and eventually washing his hands in his brains. The accompanying warriors interpreted the act as a signal and also began to set upon the wounded, killing them.

The French had the opportunity to retaliate at Fort Necessity where they dealt the Anglo-Americans (led again by George Washington) a defeat in July 1754. The two sides agreed to a very "European" capitulation agreement which allowed the defeated garrison to return to Virginia, taking all of their baggage except the artillery. The Virginians, under the "honours of war", could retreat without being taken prisoner, carrying small arms, and with their regimental flags flying. As Steele notes, "This was all *au courant* in western Europe."[15]

Of course, what he could not promise was the behaviour of the First Nation auxiliaries that accompanied the French. According to the terms of surrender, it had been promised that the French would "restrain as much as shall be in our Power, the Indians who are with us."[16] But as Steele notes, this did not include applying force against his allies to protect the surrendering force. While the First Nations were allied to the French, this did not mean they followed their customs when it came to the laws of war. After a day of fighting in the rain where one of their numbers had been killed and two wounded, the European surrender procedures seemed alien to the nearly one hundred First Nations warriors who had supported the French efforts.

The results were probably predictable, and in some ways inevitable. The warriors took or destroyed the English baggage and killed and scalped the wounded and others who were either drunk or asleep. The Virginians, having been promised safe passage, fled from the attacking First Nations warriors, leaving their belongings behind them. Ten Virginians were taken prisoner and given to the French, who promptly let them go to return to the rest of their fleeing soldiers. Resisting the imposition of European norms in warfare, the First Nations captured the Anglo-Americans who were stripped of what remained of their clothes and belongings, and three who resisted were killed and scalped. Six other Virginians were taken prisoner while trying to flee and eight Virginians had been killed after capitulation. To the Anglo-Americans, this was a clear violation of the law of nations.[17]

Culture clash: First Nations peoples

As is apparent from the above described situation, a recurring theme during the wars for North America at this time is the impact of the culture clash between the different groups fighting for control. In particular, the participation of First Nations peoples who had fought with and against white colonists since they had begun to arrive in North American *en masse* in the seventeenth century became very significant for the treatment of prisoners taken in these wars. The meeting of European and First Nations traditions of warfare was, of course, a meeting of two entirely different cultures, belief systems and codes of ethics, and this meeting did not go particularly smoothly. Aside from viewing the "irregular" tactics of the First Nations with disdain, Europeans were appalled at the practice of scalping and the "cannibalism-torture-human sacrifice complex" of the First Nations tribes of the northeast.[18] The First Nations, for their part, were shocked at the bloody nature of eighteenth-century conventional European warfare. For them, warriors' lives were not meant to be thrown away and the idea of standing in form in the face of a volley of fire made little sense. In addition, unlike the Europeans, the First Nations warriors did not rape women.[19] Mass casualties in warfare defeated the purpose of protecting and replenishing their communities.[20]

Because of this desire to prevent the loss of life, the First Nations usually engaged in a way of warfare that Europeans and Americans found cowardly. This included the use of ambushes and surprise attacks, the avoidance of frontal assaults, etc. Defensive tactics showed a similar emphasis on preventing the loss of life. If an enemy appeared too strong to resist, warriors and even entire villages would retreat. As Daniel Richter notes, "Houses and corn supplies thus might temporarily be lost, but unless the invaders achieved complete surprise, the lives and spiritual power of the people remained intact."[21]

Yet, in looking at the differences between the Europeans and First Nations tribes, it is important to note that when the two distinct styles did come into contact they adapted. Starkey notes that the striking differences sometimes mask the fact that there had also been a crucial exchange of ideas between the two cultures in the seventeenth century. First Nations peoples adapted to guns brought by Europeans and mastered them. When this was combined with their "skulking way of war", they became an incredibly deadly fighting force. For their part, some Europeans adopted First Nations technology such as light-weight canoes, snowshoes, and even clothing which was practical and, in the case of moccasins, quicker to dry than European shoes.[22] In addition, a number of white colonists and European regulars learned to fight in the forest and adapt to conditions in North America.

Still, the British and Anglo-Americans largely avoided using both the First Nations and their tactics.[23] Commanders found the First Nations difficult to subordinate, restrain and control owing to their warrior culture and the fact that they recognized themselves as allied and not dependent. While First Nations warriors were used to a certain extent throughout the war, when it came to alliance-making the British sought to neutralize rather than utilize.

Despite the efforts of the Europeans who tried to protect non-combatants and prisoners, the treatment of prisoners of war could be incredibly brutal. In some cases, the First Nations warriors felt justified in their actions against American captives—seeing them as direct revenge for attacks on their own homes and peaceful settlements or hunting grounds. Yet, as Starkey argues, although this represented a rising level of unrestrained warfare, whites taken prisoner by First Nations warriors probably had a better chance of survival and good treatment than did warriors seized by whites. As some historians point out, there is an absence of references to First Nations prisoners in the frontier wars.[24] While it was no doubt difficult to capture First Nations warriors who could easily run back to the forest, in all likelihood the Europeans and Americans may have chosen to dispose of their "savage" captives rather than to detain them.

Compared with the Europeans, the First Nations tribes had an entirely different code of ethics based upon their martial/warrior cultures. The First Nations tribes did not have or need laws of warfare that had their origins in drill and discipline. Rather, the First Nations warrior was regimented by his code of honour. But on top of this, Starkey argues that First Nations warfare was largely governed by a type of economy that sought to prevent unnecessary bloodshed: "Their warriors did not take unnecessary risks and were prepared to yield an apparent victory in the field if the cost in life was too high." In other words, the First Nations were willing to retreat in the face of hopeless odds. Combined with the fact that the First Nations did not accept European conventions on limiting warfare, this labelled them as savage and unrestrained.[25]

But this does not mean they were without an ethical code when it came to killing. Again, as Starkey argues:

The Indian approach to war seems to have been deeply ritualistic, seeking support from supernatural powers and purification for the unnatural act of killing. The treatment of prisoners was rooted in these customs... As members of warlike cultures which prized bravery above all things, Indians seem to have had little sympathy for those who surrendered. Anger and revenge certainly played a part in some of the most gruesome episodes, but many of the practices which Europeans found shocking seem to have had some ritualistic purpose...

The purpose of the most brutal episodes of torture and cannibalism is not always clear. In some cases torture was clearly revenge for a particular injury that the Indians suffered...

Scalps were a tangible token of a warrior's bravery. Indeed women's scalps represented a special sign of prowess by demonstrating that a warrior had raided deep into enemy territory.[26]

In addition, as mentioned above, prisoners were sometimes "adopted" into the families of First Nations tribes in order to replace dead loved ones. This was consistent with the practice of "mourning-war" that was found in many First Nations cultures–a war fought with the specific intention of capturing prisoners (the more important the better) as a means of restoring lost population, ensuring social continuity and dealing with death. The target population was usually a people traditionally defined as enemies.[27] After ceremonies which transformed prisoners into new human beings in the eyes of their captors, they would be welcomed and loved by all in the tribe.[28]

But by no means was adoption a guaranteed thing. Captives could be subject to abuse on the journey to a First Nations village and/or forced to run the gauntlet when they eventually arrived as a part of the introduction ritual.[29] The tribe could then decide what to do with the prisoner–adoption was an option, but so was holding the prisoner for ransom, making them a slave or killing the captive through a horrific torture ritual. Abler describes an all night process whereby a victim could be "caressed". This involved a victim being tied to a post, being burned with torches and red hot irons from the feet up, having portions of flesh cut off, being scalped and having their heart torn out. This seems to have been the practice of the Montagnais, Algonquin, Huron and Iroquois.[30] It is not surprising that the Europeans and Americans, viewing such customs through entirely different religious and cultural perspectives, did not understand, let alone appreciate the nuances of First Nations ethics.

There can be no question about whether racism played a role in the treatment, but more usually slaughter, of the First Nations peoples if they were captured by Europeans and Americans. Still, it is important to acknowledge that this was a racism that existed on both sides. Starkey makes an interesting point on this:

Often Indians did not recognize white enemies as fully human. Whites who attempted to impose "civilization" on "savage" peoples gave the latter something to fight about, whether or not land was at stake. Perhaps, if the two peoples had understood one another better, there would have been fewer innocent victims of the struggle for North America.[31]

In other words, what seems to have contributed to so much inhumanity when Americans fought the First Nations peoples was, to use a well known phrase, a failure to communicate. But beyond this, cultural practices often meant different aims in warfare. Whereas the Europeans sought to dominate a continent through set-piece battles, the First Nations fought for their own purposes–to ensure a steady supply of "gifts", to protect their hunting grounds and to prove themselves in battle and to take prisoners.

Roots of a tradition: the Anglo-Americans and British

Although the American colonists referred to the conflict as the "French and Indian War" after their opponents, this was actually a gross simplification of the dynamics of the global struggle which involved most of the major powers in Europe. Even within North America the war needs to be understood as more than just two sides fighting over territory–rather there were many parties to the conflict who fought for their own reasons and interests. Therefore, when it comes to the laws of war, part of the erratic way they were applied to the conflict very much reflects the different cultural norms and interests of these protagonists.

Although they were on the same "side", the American colonists and the British differed in their military outlook and customs. The class-based nature of the British Army bristled against American notions of merit and equality. Notably, the incredibly harsh system of discipline and the perceived arrogance of its officers rubbed up against the British view of the Americans as lazy and dangerously derelict in their willingness to defend the empire.

Yet, in looking at the life of the average British soldier, it is hard to see what, if anything, about serving with it would have been appealing to the Americans. As Stephen Brumwell observes, "Of all those ingredients that constitute the enduring image of the British Army in North America, none is more potent than the savage discipline under which the redcoats soldiered."[32] Similary Fred Anderson argues that there was little that would inspire the American colonists to emulate the Redcoat's way of being: "Service alongside the king's troops made nothing more obvious to the provincials than that a coercive disciplinary system was the engine that drove the British army, and that the blood of the common soldiers was its lubricant."[33]

The list of punishments that a British soldier could face is certainly chilling: execution, firing squad, flogging with the lash or cat-o'-nine tails, running the gauntlet (where an offending soldier was beaten by his comrades) and having to ride the wooden horse (where a soldier was forced to sit on a beam with heavy weights on his feet to weigh him down and increase the pain). Soldiers accused of cowardice were publicly humiliated in front of an entire regiment. There were also unofficial and arbitrary beatings from officers for offences (real and perceived). Such offences included mutiny, theft, striking a superior, ungentleman-like conduct, murder, rape and desertion. Insolence to an officer was a crime that carried a penalty of 500 lashes.[34]

Yet the British military commanders believed that such harsh measures were entirely necessary–and not without good reason. In such an harsh, unfriendly and dangerous environment, keeping order was quite simply a matter of life and death. Those that set a bad example or were considered to be disruptive while campaigning in the forests of North America needed to be dealt with so as to not inspire others, to avoid resentment building up among the troops. Many American colonists already harboured strong misgivings about having a standing army within their midst–discipline which prevented thefts, rapes and tensions with towns and villages was of the utmost importance.[35]

But it was a harsh regime of drill and discipline which also ensured that there was order on the battlefield. The regular way of eighteenth century warfare involved holding one's ground in the face of volleys, cannon fire and charging enemies until the very last minute when a commanding officer ordered troops to fire. For many, the courage or nerve necessary for this action required both the fear of the lash and the numbing of countless hours of practice so that a soldier could stand his ground in such incredibly unnatural circumstances. As Anderson argues: "No matter how horrifying their losses or how terrifying their situation, the regulars had been conditioned to stand their ground and fight; and fight they did, even if they did it in suicidally dysfunctional ways."[36]

It was through this order that the laws of war, as they were understood in the eighteenth century, could be followed; it prevented soldiers from fleeing, but it also ensured that they would follow commands which would prevent massacres and ensure relatively decent treatment for prisoners of war, even if this was not their primary aim.

The evidence is quite clear that the laws of war were frequently violated by both the French and the British during the conflict. However, there is no question that following, or, more correctly, being seen to follow the customs of warfare was very important to the British and Anglo-Americans. In British eyes good conduct on the battlefield, instilled through discipline, gave them the moral high ground against "Gallic perfidy". And when their opponents and their allies violated these rules it gave them an invaluable (if unfortunate) propaganda coup.[37]

As Brumwell argues, even after the French had been defeated in Canada, British commanders sought "a further, moral victory over his old rivals by documenting French complicity in what a later age would call 'war crimes'":

Real and imagined French contraventions of the laws of war allowed the Anglo-Americans to occupy the moral high ground throughout the journalistic wrangling that provided a printed refrain to the armed conflict; it was a commanding position they proved reluctant to relinquish during the remainder of the war. In coming years no opportunity was neglected to contrast Gallic cruelty with British humanity.[38]

In particular the English were very quick to criticize the French for their use of First Nations warriors as auxiliaries. Both sides in the conflict did make use of First Nations as auxiliaries, but as the English were far more numerous on the continent, and given the costs and inefficiencies involved in sending regular troops to the New World, the French depended more heavily on First Nations to back up their military efforts.[39] As Starkey notes, the First Nations alliances were the most important military asset possessed by the French Empire in North America who had used "intelligent leadership" to cultivate their relationship.[40]

As mentioned above, the First Nations did not see themselves as subordinate contractors, but as equals with their own ideas of how wars should be fought and how prisoners should be treated. While the French did not necessarily approve of the First Nations warriors' ways of warfare, they also did not go out of their way to control such behaviour. This may be explained in part by looking at the difference in the way the two European powers felt about exerting control or laws over the First Nations peoples. While the French, through a series of royal ordinances, edicts and official correspondence, sought to place and enforce a strict, if not severe, code of laws upon the First Nations in Canada, in practice this never came to fruition. Given the precarious nature of the French in North America, and their reliance on the First Nations, there had been, for the previous 100 years, little effort to implement or enforce the laws which had been handed down. Instead, those First Nations members accused of crimes (such as stealing or murder) were not prosecuted but were left alone or else faced their own system of justice through a trial by their own tribe.[41] On the other hand, the English, who established military dominance in the areas which they controlled in North America by 1637, began to implement the full spectrum of the law against First Nations by the late 1630s. Any First Nations tribe member charged with crimes against whites was brought to trial in English courts. This was part of the English push to "civilize" the First Nations through "moral" laws. By 1700, all First Nations living on reservations in Anglo-America were brought fully under English law and colonial authorities claimed jurisdiction over the outlying First Nations areas as well.[42]

Therefore, when it came to implementing the laws of war, it is unsurprising that the French did not take a very strict approach regarding implementing "civilized" war conventions on the First Nations. Such restraints were contrary to the First Nations' view of themselves in warfare and their purposes in fighting. As they were crucial allies, such an approach would have significantly gone against French interests. Even when the French wanted to exercise restraint in line with European conventions, this (as will be seen below) was usually not possible.

Additionally, it is worth pointing out Brumwell's observation that "for all their efforts to dominate the propaganda war by protesting France's use of tribal allies, British commanders had never hesitated to employ Indian warriors when they could recruit them." As the French Governor-General Vaudreuil wrote to General Wolfe on the matter, as far as he was concerned, both sides had always sought to attract the greatest number of First Nations warriors to their side and the cruelties that inevitably followed were viewed by French soldiers as the "fortunes of war".[43] Indeed, as Starkey notes, in the Seven Years War it seems rather that commanders who professed dismay at First Nations practices nevertheless eagerly sought their assistance.[44]

But it was true that not all French officials and commanders were satisfied with the use of First Nations warriors. The Marquis de Montcalm, commander of the French, whom Fred Anderson describes as a "soldier's soldier in the European mode", did not approve of the North American style of warfare and attempted to do everything he could to keep his operations in line with civilized standards as he knew them.[45] As a result, he believed that the war would be better fought by men who knew how to conduct themselves in a right and honourable way. Hence he sought to rely on regular forces rather than the colonial Canadians or First Nations as much as possible.[46] But for the prisoners who were captured at Fort William Henry, this disdain of both the First Nations and their tactics did not make much of a difference.

The massacre at Fort William Henry

The fall of Fort William Henry, the British outpost guarding the main approach to the Upper Hudson Valley, represented a significant military defeat for the British, but became much more infamous for the "massacre" which immediately followed. In terms of propaganda, it became a symbol of French duplicity and the barbarity of the First Nations peoples. For our purposes here, it may be the clearest example of what may happen when different norms of warfare and cultures collide.

Montcalm, who, as noted above, disliked using the First Nations warriors because of their "uncivilized" methods, was aware that he could not command them to follow his orders. Instead, Montcalm would have to try and use his influence to persuade his auxiliaries–who regarded themselves as equal partners–to do what he requested.[47] The signs, however, were not promising. Throughout the summer of that year there had been raiding parties which had captured British and Anglo-American soldiers who, as prisoners, frequently met gruesome fates in the hands of the First Nations. In one instance in late July there had been an ambush on a party from Fort William Henry (who themselves were on a mission to burn French sawmills and to take prisoners). Over 200 prisoners, or three quarters of the British party, were captured, drowned or speared by First Nations tribes. Most prisoners became slaves unless they were ransomed, but three of the prisoners were also killed and eaten.[48] The ambush was clearly a demonstration of French strength in the area, but also a grisly warning of what was to come. As Steele writes, "Although French commanders of the attacking army voiced forebodings of cannibalism and cruelty to prisoners, they indicated more helpless resignation than calculated cynicism."[49]

Originally, Montcalm intended to follow what he knew as the traditional, and civilized, manner of warfare when it came to taking the fort. As Anderson notes, the "second siege of Fort William Henry would be conducted in the European style."[50] The attack was formally opened by sending a messenger under a flag of truce. Montcalm warned the outnumbered British and Anglo-American force that it faced a formidable threat from French cannon, but also that he was uncertain whether he could restrain the First Nations Warriors when the Fort inevitably fell. Anderson records that the First Nations, who had their own cultural practices about the start of battle, hurled taunts at the Fort defenders and threatened, in broken French, that no quarter would be given.[51]

After several days of bombardment, and the notification that no reinforcements would be sent to relieve the besieged Fort, it was relinquished to the French on 9 August after formal terms of surrender were drafted. In honour of their valiant defence, Montcalm gave the British force the full honours of war. Therefore, rather than being designated as prisoners of war, the defending force was to be put on parole for eighteen months.[52] The British were also to be given safe passage to Fort Edward, and the right to retain personal items, small arms and their colours. According to the generous terms laid out by Montcalm, the severely sick and wounded would be cared for by the French and repatriated later. In return, Montcalm requested that all prisoners and captured civilians would be returned and that a British hostage would remain until their safe return had been achieved.[53] In this sense, the surrender of the Fort perfectly matched the eighteenth century customs of the day. There was only one problem: Montcalm did not consult the First Nations Warriors who had their own understandings and norms about what was to be done with the surrendering force.

The "massacre" started almost immediately after the surrender on 9 August. The First Nations warriors entered the fort to search for booty and, finding none, immediately set upon the approximately seventy sick and wounded in the hospital. On 10 August, as the British left the fort, the column was attacked by the First Nations warriors who had been waiting to collect what they felt was owed to them. The regulars who were protected by a French escort probably fared the best, but there were no protections for the provincials and civilians at the back, or straggling behind; many were immediately killed, seized, scalped or forced to hand over all of their possession as the First Nations Warriors went after the more prized soldiers beyond them.[54]

The killing, however, only went on for a few minutes. The First Nations wanted to take prisoners for the traditional reasons that it was proof of their bravery, central to their way of fighting, and so that they could collect a rich ransom later. Although there is probably no way they could have known it, those British and Anglo-Americans who did not resist stood a better chance of those who did; if a warrior could not take a prisoner, he needed at least some proof of his bravery in the second-best way–a scalp. Similarly, when the French did try to intervene to protect the British and Anglo-American force, many warriors chose to take a scalp rather than give up their prize.[55] Approximately 185 soldiers and camp followers were killed, 300–500 were captured by the First Nations and another 300–500 sought refuge with the French.[56]

Immediately, Montcalm attempted to retrieve the prisoners taken, but he did not have the military resources in which to intimidate the First Nations warriors.[57] However, Anderson argues that Montcalm had both humanitarian and practical concerns for doing so:

Montcalm desperately wanted to preserve the integrity of the capitulation proceedings, for as the officer who had guaranteed the safety of the surrendered garrison he would be personally dishonored by any violation of the surrender terms. Moreover, as he clearly understood, the British would be disinclined to behave generously toward any French garrison in the future...; and he could ill afford to antagonize an enemy so potentially powerful by the seeming to sanction uncivilized warfare.[58]

Some prisoners were recovered through complex negotiations and others were simply seized by the French on a mission to save the British and Anglo-Americans. Others were taken to First Nations villages where they were adopted, or to Montreal where they were held for ransom.

Yet, to the First Nations, what Montcalm had tried to do was unacceptable; he had tried to take away what they saw as rightfully belonging to them—prisoners and the spoils of war through which they could prove their bravery. The French had excluded the First Nations from the capitulation negotiations and only explained the terms after they had already been agreed. In the eyes of the First Nations they had fewer prisoners or scalps to display than their success warranted.[59] As the First Nations saw it, it was they who had fought bravely and more selflessly than the regular soldiers who had taken wages. In lieu of fighting for money, the reward that they had expected was the ability to plunder and take trophies and captives. Anderson writes: "When it became clear that the man whom they had called "Father" intended to do what no real father would and deprive them of the reward they had earned, most of the warriors decided merely to take what they had come for, and then to leave. And that was exactly what they did."[60]

Quite simply, Montcalm had been caught between two different and, in certain ways, diametrically opposed, ways of warfare, and knew that his personal honour would pay the price. He and the French were (not unreasonably) held responsible for the massacre by the British, but he also lost the trust of the First Nations warriors by trying to restrain them from their war practices.

Prisoners after 1757

Despite being a low point for the British and Anglo-Americans, the events at Fort William Henry also marked a crucial moment in the war which, for a number of reasons, would take on European characteristics for the next two years. This can be attributed to a number of different factors, including decisions made by the colonial powers as to the conduct of the campaign after 1757. In London, Pitt made the decision to attack French sources of wealth in North America via the British Navy. This, of course, implied conventional European warfare as British ships attacked France's Atlantic fleet and prevented merchant vessels from resupplying Canada with arms, provisions, and trade goods.[61]

Secondly, after Fort William Henry, the alliance between the First Nations and the French began to crumble. Montcalm, despite pressure from within his own camp, would never want to use the warriors again in warfare and relied mainly on regulars and Canadians.[62] Given the relative strength of the British in North America, this would severely hamper the French campaign, if not effectively ensure its defeat. However, as indicated above, the feeling amongst the First Nations was mutual; they had felt betrayed by Montcalm and would never again turn out in large numbers to support the French, even if they were wanted.[63] But Montcalm was right to be afraid of British retaliation based on reciprocity—for the next two years they were disinclined to offer the honours of war to any French force.[64] Major General Jeffrey Amherst cited the massacre in denying French troops the honours of war at the fall of Louisbourg and Montreal.[65]

Yet despite the increasing appearance of European norms after 1757, war was still very bloody and violent. Frustrated by his failure to crack the defences of Quebec City, Wolfe reduced his operations to something like a scorched earth policy that caused devastation to the lands surrounding the city; by the end of August 1759 Wolfe's "terrorism" had turned the countryside into "a smoldering wasteland": "A conservative contemporary estimate held that fourteen hundred farms had been destroyed. No one ever reckoned the numbers of rapes, scalpings, thefts and casual murders perpetrated during this month of bloody horror."[66]

While Wolfe professed humanitarianism towards women and children, he ordered cannon fire on Quebec City day and night, and did not stop ruthless rangers from indiscriminately killing those they could reach in the surrounding villages.[67] Still, when it came to prisoners, the results could still be surprisingly humane. In 1759, British officers were instructed to apply "the very latest European conventions concerning prisoners of war" to French prisoners taken at La Belle Famille—even though there were First Nations Warriors present who immediately joined in the fighting after they sensed the French were losing, and approximately 250 French soldiers were killed. Steele argues that this was not done in a fashion that went against European conventions: "Amerindians, colonials, and regulars, as well as military historians, all regarded the slaughter of fleeing enemies as an expected conclusion to a decisive battle; there were no accusations of 'massacre' at La Belle Famille."[68] Instead, British commanders reflected that their forces did not harm any of the French who had been taken prisoner. However, they were clearly only referring to their own soldiers and not the First Nations auxiliary supporting their efforts.[69]

Yet Steele argues that the British officers who captured the French prisoners of war had actually gone beyond European conventions. Other than the First Nations, the French force was composed of Canadian guerrilla forces using tactics that violated European norms, such as ambushing, capturing, torturing and killing civilians. Such behaviour on European soil would have instantly rendered a captured prisoner liable to a death sentence. Yet in this instance they had been offered prisoner of war status.[70] This allowed them protection from the First Nations warriors (although the French were threatened that the British did not know if they could restrain the warriors much longer if they did not agree to the capitulation terms quickly), to keep their personal belongings and a ceremonial military march to the British vessel that would take them to Albany.[71]

Battles with the First Nations, 1760–1765

The surrender of New France in 1760 did not end the conflict for the British and Anglo-Americans. Instead, a series of events lead to outbreaks of fighting with the First Nations tribes, in the "Cherokee War" (1760–61) and then in "Pontiac's Rebellion" (1763–65). This was due to anger with British policies which had allowed settlement into First Nations areas and had ended the "gift-giving" policies which had secured the alliance or at least neutrality of some of the First Nations tribes. In addition, there had also been a religious revival of sorts lead by a Delaware prophet named Neolin who helped to stir anti–European sentiment, as well as a form of First Nations pan-nationalism. This was taken up by the Ottawa Chief Pontiac who encouraged the First Nations Tribes to "drive off your lands those dogs clothed in red who will do you nothing but harm."[72]

Given the resentment of the First Nations and the impatience and loathing of many of the British and Anglo-Americans, it is not surprising that the resulting clashes were bloody. There does not seem to be any shortage of outrages against prisoners that one could describe. In the Cherokee War, warriors attacked along the borderlands and within a few months had killed or captured more than 100 settlers and traders. In the same month they began a successful siege at Fort Loudon that resulted in the Fort's surrender in August. The inhabitants gave up in exchange for safe passage, but when they set out they were soon attacked by 700 Cherokees and at least twenty-five people lost their lives. One of the prisoners was scalped and forced to dance until he died while others were stripped, beaten and sent into captivity. In return, Lieutenant Colonel James Grant was ordered by Field Marshall Jeffery Amherst to "chastise" the Cherokees and his forces burned all fifteen of the Cherokees' towns and destroyed their fields. "Any Indian [sic] man, woman or child luckless enough to be caught was summarily executed, by Grant's express order."[73] Upon hearing of Pontiac's Rebellion, Amherst ordered the "extirpation" of the First Nations, saying that no prisoners would be taken and that all First Nations that fell into British hands would be put to death.[74] As Anderson writes: "Bewilderment at the Indian's [sic] success in capturing forts and defeating redcoat detachments, delay in understanding what was going on, inability to restore order once the rebellion's scope became clear–all these factors now helped to promote a singular bloody-mindedness among the British commanders."[75]

Amherst had sanctioned the killing of First Nations people and those dressed like them before–easily rationalized as they themselves frequently killed their captives.[76] Therefore there were few if any restraints that he was willing to apply in warfare and virtually none applying to First Nations prisoners. Even as the sieges of 1763 died away, along with the First Nations' capacity to make war, Amherst had "a visceral need to put the Indians in their place."[77]

Yet, the result of the battles fought between the British/Anglo-Americans and the First Nations tribes also sowed the seeds for future conflict. Even as the Rebellion was raging, settlers continued to move westwards, which defeated all attempts at the British to maintain peaceful relations with the First Nations. The Anglo-American settlers resented the British attempts to impose regulations on their expansion but also resented the First Nations. In Pennsylvania in 1763 a group calling themselves the "Paxton Boys" murdered peaceful and defenceless First Nations villagers in their efforts to exterminate every member of the First Nations tribes in Pennsylvania. Anglo-American civilians, who had suffered the most casualties in the war in gruesome ways, would never be happy to accommodate the First Nations peoples, but would instead hope for their eventual elimination from the land that they were constantly encroaching on.

The beginning of the struggle for complete security

The Seven Years War was not the first Anglo-French battle in North America, and considering that the French gave a considerable amount of support to the

Americans in their Revolution, then it may not be considered the last either. Steele argues that the Seven Years War can be situated in a seventy–year battle (1689–1759) between European Powers for control of North America.[78] Of the conflicts that came before the Seven Years War (King Philip's War, 1675–76; King William's War, 1689–97; Queen Anne's War, 1702–13; and King George's War, 1740–48), many may actually be considered even more bloody than that which has already been described above. Starkey notes that King Philip's War was "the costliest American war in terms of relative population":

King Philip's War may also be considered a total war in the manner of its conduct. It was a war of attrition...Although the English and Indians initially employed different tactics, neither observed traditional European military conventions. Both sides waged war against the other's total population and without well defined military objectives, relied upon terror to overcome the enemy.[79]

There can be little doubt that the stories of the fate of prisoners taken by the First Nations, and the tactics that they used to wage warfare, solidified a prejudice against them in these wars that would carry through to the Seven Years War and beyond.

The discussion of the Seven Years War here has been lengthy but it serves to illustrate several points. The first is that the American way of warfare, including the way it considered and implemented the laws of war, was rooted in the Anglo-French battles for North America before the American Revolution. For the Americans, laws governing the treatment of prisoners were governed by a mixture of custom and the notion of honour–of both the prisoner who had surrendered and the officer who then had to guarantee the prisoner's safety.

However, attached to these customary ideas and notions of honour was an expectation that one's opponent was "civilized" and would behave in a certain manner. Both sides were expected to be playing from the same page in the rulebook–or at least share a very similar set of norms which guided ideas about behaviour in warfare. As the battles with the First Nations demonstrate, when those normative expectations were not met, the results could be incredibly deadly. The Europeans rarely, if ever, took First Nations warriors as prisoners because they did not fight in what was seen as an honourable manner. For their part, the First Nations did take many prisoners of war, but this was due to their martial culture and did not by any means necessarily guarantee the survival or good treatment of the captive. To say that the wars fought between the Anglo-Americans and the First Nations during these years left a bad impression on the white settlers would be an incredible understatement.

But the suspicion and hatred could go beyond the First Nations; Anglo-Americans had also learned to fear the French who were just as eager to see the Americans removed from the Allegheny borderlands and, to support their weaker numbers, were very willing to employ First Nations warriors against them. As John Shy notes, the dangers posed by these groups could be perceived in terms of anti–Catholicism (and at a time when religious antagonism was no longer a major factor in European diplomacy and warfare).[80] He writes that the Anglo-Americans felt "Strong but highly vulnerable, angered and frightened by repeated and ruthless attack, bewildered by the causes of war, disrupted by its effects, and powerless to prevent it" and this led them to concoct strong proposals against the enemies of their society: "Nothing would do, they wrote, but the complete elimination of French and Spanish power from North America; anything less... was worse than useless because it would create a false sense of security."[81]

He concludes that Americans began to believe that nothing less than a "complete solution" was required for American military security, and that the conflicts that arose in the eighteenth and nineteenth century would be seen in terms of putting the whole of American society in peril. In this way the concept of military security in the Seven Years War and the American wars of independence would be expressed in absolute rather than relative terms.[82] Similar attitudes would later be reflected in ideas like "manifest destiny" where resistance to the American domination of the continent would be seen as standing in the way of civilization, and it would lay the groundwork for future battles between not only the Americans and Europeans, but particularly between the Americans and the First Nations with whom, in 1765, there was still a lot of unfinished business. How these ideas translated into treatment of prisoners of war would very much depend on cultural perception, but also on the fierceness of fighting during these wars for complete security in North America.

The American Revolution

In the introduction to this chapter it was noted that the Americans' Continental Army adopted the British Articles of War at the outbreak of the Revolution for pragmatic reasons; it was a familiar code that could easily be adapted to suit Washington's purposes. Yet, it must be acknowledged that Washington's commitments to such norms went beyond pragmatism. He had spent years educating himself in the ways of European warfare and during the

Seven Years War he stressed strict discipline and formal training for his troops. In this sense it is only natural that he carried this tradition through to the American Revolution.

Additionally, as Higginbotham notes, Americans deemed it vital for their generals to conform to Revolutionary principles in their conduct of the war—principles which derived from their Protestant heritage as well as English radical Whig thought.[83] While such principles naturally included ideas about civil-military relations, it also meant that a "skulking" way of warfare would probably not fit into Washington's grand strategy. Where Washington did resort to partisan warfare, Wayne Lee notes that the revolutionary forces still did not resort to any kind of "Indian style war", but that even here the Americans were "firmly embedded in the European tradition of the *petite guerre*."[84]

Anyway there seems to be no doubt that although the guerrilla-style battles supported the war effort, the American Revolution would be won, and seen to be won through conventional battles such as Valley Forge and Yorktown. The Continental Army's "Europeanization" was also attributable to the military professionals who had come from France.[85] Interestingly, although the guerrilla fighting perfected by American commanders like Nathaniel Greene proved very effective against the British, it was not eagerly embraced by the Americans.[86] While the battles along the frontier were vicious and violent, they were marginal to the overall conflict. As Higginbotham argues, the Revolution was not primarily a guerrilla contest even though irregular warriors were occasionally used. Rather, both sides "fought largely within a military framework that had already become a living tradition."[87]

This emphasizes the fact that both the Americans and the British came from the same martial traditions and when it came to the laws of war, both sides were coming from a similar point of view, which may have had a limiting effect upon the violence of the conflict. Yet even the shared cultural background did not prevent savage outbursts of bloodshed throughout the duration of the war. As Starkey writes:

At the same time, both sides wanted to win the war and their interpretation of the rules were influenced by military priorities... While not as contemptuous of moral restraint as was say Clausewitz, both sides were prepared to do what was necessary to win. As always, military necessity remained the ultimate defense of extreme action in war.[88]

The laws of war could enable bloodshed as well as restrain it. For example, many believed that the laws of war did not apply to nighttime warfare and whatever violence happened to troops that surrendered then was not to be considered in the same way that fighting in the daytime was.[89] And of course, the laws of war were to be applied between two *legit* combatants. The British did not recognize their enemies as constituting a proper national force, but as a group of rag-tag rebels who did not deserve the protections traditionally afforded to prisoners of war.

These conflicting norms, Enlightenment attitudes and imperial and national resentment, form the background to the way prisoners of war were treated in the conflict. As in the Seven Years War, the only thing which seems truly generalizable seems to be difference; how a prisoner was treated after capture depended very much on where he had been caught, his rank, and which side he was fighting on.[90] Some British and Hessian officers were held in American towns where, on parole, they contracted themselves out as labourers and were frequently treated with kindness by the upper classes of the New England towns they were obliged to stay in.[91] On the other hand, captured American seamen were denied belligerent status and sent to Britain where thousands spent the remainder of the war living in harsh conditions on prison ships or in jail. Other American soldiers captured on the battlefields were sent to prisons in New York that had been hastily made out of warehouses and churches.[92] In this way, generalization becomes difficult; there seem to be as many experiences as there were prisoners.

The reason for this variation may be the nature of both wars. In looking at the overall adherence to the laws of war during the American Revolution, Best describes the impact of the confusing and confounding conflict:

It was a war of national liberation and a war between great European powers; it was 'conventional' in some respects ('regular'-looking armies fighting battles and performing sieges, war-ships maneuvering and exchanging broadsides), it was 'irregular' in others, involving 'native auxiliaries' in guerilla or partisan fighting on land, and privateering, its maritime equivalent, at sea; besides being international, it was also in many respects a civil war, and like all such it opened vistas attractive to many for the prosecution of vendettas and feuds. At one end of the moral scale, it boasted all of the niceties and refinements of contemporary European conventional warfare; at the other, it grimly displayed the tar-and-feathers, the scalping-knife, the fowling piece behind the hedge, and the torch in the hay barn.[93]

Flory argues that while the United States "apparently tried to live up to the rules of customary international law... the British usages appear to have vacillated between the practices observed in international law and the usages permissible in quelling domestic disturbances." Therefore, "it is probable that the treatment accorded Americans in British hands was less favorable than that given prisoners in Anglo-French wars prior to the Revolution."[94] Considering the above discussion of those conflicts, this is quite a claim to make. Yet Flory neglects the fact that treatment of prisoners depended very much on the way one was captured. In such a varied and diverse conflict, it should not be surprising that adherence to the laws of war and the good treatment of prisoners differed greatly. Despite the variations in treatment, the suffering of certain prisoners of war and the symbol of injustice they came to represent proved to be important in both the American Revolution and the War of 1812 for the people of the United States and its government.

Of course the variability of treatment also depended on whether or not each side actually bothered to take prisoners, which was not always the case. Enlightenment thinkers such as Vattel expected that officers would be able to control and restrain their men from harming prisoners; because they were bound by the chivalrous notion of honour, he did not suspect that they would actually encourage their men to commit atrocities, as did happen during the American Revolution.[95] On 20 September 1777 at Paoli, Pennsylvania 150 Americans were stabbed to death with bayonets with the apparent approval of British commanding officers. Exactly one year later, the British surrounded the village of Old Tappan, New Jersey and proceeded to bayonet the Americans who had been taken by surprise despite their pleas for mercy and quarter.[96] While some British expressed doubts and sadness over these British actions, others claimed that they were necessary and even well justified.[97]

Starkey argues that as the British realized that they could not kill or arrest all of the rebels nor occupy the entirety of North America, they increasingly turned to the idea that "one could strike terror into rebel hearts and attempt to prove that it was fruitless, even suicidal to resist the king's troops"; and when even this did not work, that "one might reasonably argue that all-out war was the only alternative."[98] Indeed, by 1779, the British commanders could only raise what British commanders described as a "pathetically small army" and had resorted to stealth attacks. For these operations, the British had turned to their light infantry troops that were "part cavalry, part infantry, ideally suited for that kind of warfare which was to become known as guerrilla... "[99] Hibbert notes that while many of the commanders of the light infantry were "honourable and chivalrous men", others, particularly the notorious Banastre Tarleton, commander of the irregulars called the British Legion, were not. Although he was arguably very successful in his chosen career, he seemed to have little inclination towards the laws of war or mercy. Throughout the battles that he waged in the south, Tarleton did not grant quarter to surrendering Americans. In South Carolina, the light infantry destroyed crops, farms, stole private property from civilians and attacked and raped women.

Against these forces, the Americans fought back with "a force of three thousand rough backwoodsmen, all armed with rifles which they used with uncommon skill".[100] They successfully fought back against the British in South Carolina at King's Mountain and, when they had the chance, applied "Tarleton's quarter"—which, of course, meant no quarter at all. Of the British who survived the affair, several were tried for treason and hanged after it was learned that there had been executions of American militiamen who had once served in the British army but now served in the Continental one.

Yet this action was in contravention of orders issued by Colonel William Campbell of the Virginia Militia to prevent the slaughtering of prisoners. Indeed, in keeping with the spirit of the Enlightenment values that the Revolution stood for, some American military leaders did their best to ensure that there could be a humane outcome for surrendering prisoners. After taking Stony Point in July 1779, the American forces spared 543 prisoners who had surrendered—which was a propaganda coup in a war that was essentially a battle for hearts and minds.[101] As Starkey notes, the British at the beginning of the war were inclined to believe that the American army comprised of barbaric villains who did not deserve respect or mercy. However: "Stony Point displayed American arms in a new light. Not only had the Americans proved their discipline and martial prowess, they had demonstrated a higher moral standard than their opponents."[102]

Similarly, Washington's order to treat Hessian prisoners of war taken at Trenton is often presented as an example of the enlightened attitudes of the Americans.[103] Yet the willingness of the Virginia Militia to readily give "Tarleton's quarter" suggests that the case was frequently otherwise; but Starkey's point is still worth noting.

The British were able to capture a large number of American prisoners early on in the American Revolution both on land and on sea, and the outcome of this was that the British had little incentive to exchange prisoners. They had even less moral inclination to do so. To the British government, the Americans were not a separate country but a colony in revolt. The official correspondence refers to them as "rebels" rather than "Americans" or even "enemies". In 1777 the "North Act" temporarily suspended *habeas corpus* for persons charged with high treason in the American colonies or on the high seas, or with acts of piracy.[104] Again, the differing experiences make it hard to generalize, but it can be argued that the result of this for captured prisoners was rather grim.

However, the treatment given to the Americans was not solely due to vindictiveness on the part of the British. Rather, several factors combined to make life generally miserable for those who found themselves in confinement. The first of these was a shortage of manpower in the British Navy. Taking note of the several thousand rebels in their hands, the British government sought to "encourage" as many of the prisoners to change sides as they could. There is no doubt that many of the prisoners were in bad shape and few had money or means to improve their lot through warm clothes or food supplements. Even if harsh treatment of the Americans was not a conscious policy on the part of the British (although several accounts argue it was very deliberate),[105] it is clear that little was done to alleviate their suffering.[106] As the prisoners languished in cold cells with inadequate food and clothing, British recruiters came to the prisons to encourage men to change sides with promises of payment, clothing and food. Not surprisingly, some of these prisoners readily accepted the offer, although it is hard to tell exactly how many.[107] By December 1776 the Continental Congress sought to stem the tide of prisoners enlisting with the British and, to reduce their mortality rate, appointed an agent to look into the conditions of the prisoners and look out for their interests.[108] In addition, Benjamin Franklin, who served as the US representative in France from 1777 to 1785, attempted to intervene on behalf of the prisoners, mostly US seamen, who were being held in Britain by providing cash and trying to arrange an exchange of prisoners between the two countries.

However, there were several problems with trying to bring about an exchange (sometimes referred to as a "cartel"). First, as already mentioned, during the period when the British held more prisoners than the United States, there was little incentive for them to have an exchange. An additional complication was a policy whereby American prisoners were treated differently according to where they were captured. Americans caught on land were, for practical purposes, considered prisoners of war and could potentially be exchanged. American seamen, on the other hand, were legally regarded as traitors and criminals and were therefore usually held abroad in Britain and did not have a similar right of exchange.[109] In some cases, American seamen were immediately impressed into service for the warship which had captured them.[110]

A second factor, noted above, relates to the refusal of Britain to recognize the United States as anything other than a rebelling colony. Although the problem clearly stemmed from the fact that the British did not want to confer legitimacy upon the American Revolution, the US Congress complicated matters for the prisoners by trying to link the issue of their release to *de facto* recognition of the United States as independent. As Knight argues, Congress was determined to make the British recognize the independence of America, and, to that end, was willing to stall negotiations on the exchange of prisoners: "Had Congress wanted a major exchange or prisoners, the issue [of independence] need not have been raised, agreement between commanders in chief might have been reached, and large exchanges could have been carried out without formal recognition."[111]

So, although there had clearly been outrage about the way American prisoners had been treated by the British, Congress was willing to hold up their exchange for the national interest. Despite their symbolism as victims of British injustice, the Americans were willing to use prisoners as political tools in their campaign for independence.

A third factor which relates to the national interest—but in a less idealistic way—was the realization by Congress that an exchange of prisoners would be a costly affair. The young nation, already financially strained in fighting the war, would soon be faced with a flood of petitions for back-pay, especially as many officers were already seriously in debt as they had to borrow money to survive while they were on parole.[112] In addition, the United States was obliged to pay for the board of the prisoners held by the British. Given the uneven numbers of prisoners held by each side, the Americans would find themselves in debt to the nation they were at war with.[113] Aside from the cost, such a proposition was clearly not appealing to Congress.

Improvement in treatment did eventually come for American prisoners as the war dragged on. Many accounts suggest that this was due to the Continental Army achieving its first military successes as well as being able to take large numbers of prisoners with the surrender of the British at Saratoga in 1777 and Yorktown in 1781.[114] With a larger number of hostages—many of important rank—the Americans were in a much better position to negotiate for the better treatment and release of their prisoners. Even George Washington took note of the connection between the defeat of the British at Saratoga and the almost instantly improved treatment for prisoners as far away as England.[115]

In addition, the formation of the Franco-American alliance in February 1778 had put new pressures on the British—and the prospect that new facilities were now available to detain British prisoners caught at sea.[116] Prelinger also notes that the entrance of the French into the war on the side of the Americans may have gained a greater diplomatic respectability, although American prisoners still needed to be officially pardoned by the King for their "treason" in order to qualify for their release.[117]

The direct link suggests that the British regarded their prisoners as tools rather than a responsibility. The American prisoners were a potential labour source and negotiating bargaining chip rather than unfortunate men owed sympathy and respect. But it is clear that the Americans felt very much the same way. John Paul Jones, who would become the first well-known naval hero of the American Revolution, deliberately set out to capture British sailors who would serve a similar purpose and could be used to ensure proper treatment of American prisoners and for their exchange. This idea was also supported by Benjamin Franklin who was frustrated with his inability to get the British to agree to a cartel.[118]

Finally, the Americans were able to better support their prisoners of war financially. In Europe, Benjamin Franklin was able to arrange a weekly cash allotment through voluntary British contributions and the American government. According to Prelinger, the increasing affluence of the prisoners was such that markets sprung up around the prison where local merchants sold their goods and the prisoners could sell products they had made (which were often wood carvings). This led the great British prison reformer John Howard (who himself had been a prisoner of war held by the French) to conclude that the American prisoners of war were better off at least than ordinary prisoners in British jails.[119]

A general exchange of prisoners did not take place until 1782 when the new Shelburne government agreed to a release. All of the complicating factors of the war, the differing approaches the British took to prisoners depending on where they had been caught, and the demands of Congress had come together to prevent a large-scale exchange prior to this point. Such policies suggest that both sides were inclined to sacrifice the welfare of their men rather than their interests or position. In fact, individual states in the new republic began to exercise their own authority to make exchanges–although these were mainly on a small scale–in an effort to get their prisoners back while the two governments argued with one another.[120]

The treatment of prisoners of war in the American Revolution has, in many ways, become part of the mythos of the Revolution itself. During the American Revolution and afterwards it was cited as proof of British injustice, and it would be invoked by lawyers nearly 150 years later as an example of abusive treatment.[121] Yet out of this experience, the United States signed its first agreements on the status and treatment of prisoners of war. The first of these was the 1783 Treaty of Paris which ended the American Revolutionary War; it stated in Article 7 that "All prisoners on both sides shall be set at liberty".

However, it was the 1785 Treaty of Amity and Commerce between the United States and Prussia that outlined the first major statement on the treatment of prisoners of war. The Treaty (subsequently updated and revived in 1799 and 1828) has more to do with trade and establishing relations, but stipulates in Article 24 that in case of war both sides will aim "to prevent the destruction of prisoners of war, by sending them into distant & inclement countries, or by crouding them into close & noxious places,..."[122] In addition, the Treaty went on to outline a fairly advanced state of rules for treatment of prisoners, stating that they must be placed in "wholesome situations", and that "that they shall not be confined in dungeons, prison-ships, nor prisons, nor be put into irons, nor bound, nor otherwise restrained in the use of their limbs". Additionally, prisoners were to be given the same rations as soldiers of equal rank on each side and entitled to visits from a commissary who would check on their welfare.

The experience of the American Revolution had clearly made an impact on the new Republic which wanted to ensure that its prisoners would be treated well in future conflicts. A less sophisticated provision was included in Article 16 of the 1786 Treaty with Morocco which stated that: "Prisoners are not to be made Slaves, but to be exchanged one for another, Captain for Captain, Officer for Officer and one private Man for another", and that each side would have to pay for any deficiencies in treatment.[123] Unfortunately for future American prisoners of war, the next major conflict was with Britain over the unfinished business of the Revolution.

The War of 1812

Given that the war of 1812 is sometimes known as the "second war of American independence", it is not surprising to see many similarities in the way the laws of war were adhered to and prisoners treated in both conflicts. In fact, prisoners played an important part in the lead up to the War of 1812 as thousands of American sailors were taken by the British and impressed into service. The British Navy, still desperate for men as it waged its wars with France, would board US ships and essentially "reclaim" any individual thought to have been born a British subject. The British, as a matter of policy, did not recognize "naturalized" citizenships given by the United States to its citizens, or any documents declaring the sailors as American.[124]

Also, much as in the Seven Years War and the American Revolution, there was a great difference in treatment of prisoners depending on when and where they were caught in the War of 1812. In North America, parole and exchange of prisoners widely prevailed, which meant that only a small proportion of prisoners were actually incarcerated by the enemy.[125] Under this system, paroled prisoners could actually return home upon giving their word not to participate in hostilities. A paroled prisoner was considered to have been released and was able to return to fighting once his exchange had been completed.

Such an approach was beneficial for both governments as the responsibility to care for servicemen was limited. Still, the system was not perfect. Perhaps the most obvious example of this occurred in November 1812 when Sir George Prevost gave orders to retain any of the thousand American prisoners taken at Queenston who appeared to have been British-born. Although nearly all of the prisoners were eventually sent to Boston on parole, twenty-three American soldiers of Irish birth were detained and sent to England to be tried for treason.[126] Vance describes the following sequence of events:

In May 1813,... Congress approved the close confinement of 23 British soldiers as hostages, and in October Prevost ordered the detention of 46 American soldiers in retaliation; he went on to decree that if any of the 23 Britons were executed, twice as many Americans would be put to death. A month later, American President James Madison responded by jailing a further 46 British officers as 'a pledge for the safety of those on whom the British Government seems disposed to wreak its vengeance.' Not to be outdone, Prevost announced that 46 more Americans would be confined, bringing the number of hostages on both sides to well over 200.[127]

Vance argues that although "the sequence of reprisals that followed is almost comical" and that "the exchange of indignant letters makes entertaining reading", the situation was a serious one as "the consequences for individual prisoners was dire."[128] In the United States, British and Canadian prisoners were crowded ten to a single cell and even handcuffed at times during their captivity. Some of the Americans held hostage in Quebec were found to be almost naked and suffering from a lack of food and water when eventually visited by their government's agent.[129] Each side threatened the other's hostages with death should its own soldiers be killed and the British went so far as to threaten unrestrained warfare against US cities, towns, villages and citizens.[130] Perhaps the most unfortunate aspect of this whole ordeal was that the British later revealed that none of the original twenty-three Irish prisoners was ever tried for treason—they had been imprisoned with the rest of the POWs. Essentially, the entire incident was unnecessary and occurred because both sides were willing to play a retaliatory game at the expense of the unfortunate prisoners.

At sea, US prisoners of war received very much the same treatment as during the American Revolution. In order to cope with the seemingly overwhelming power of the British Navy, Congress authorized large-scale privateering and some 100,000 men volunteered for the service.[131] As Fable argues that although the privateering was worthwhile—two thirds of the 2,000 British ships captured or destroyed during the War of 1812 fell to privateers—there was a severe cost to be paid. 300 of the 526 privateering voyages were fruitless or ended in surrender. Those seamen who survived engagements with the Royal Navy were sent to prison in Britain.[132] However, it should be noted that many of the American prisoners were men who had already been impressed by the British prior to the outbreak of formal hostilities. The Admiralty ordered that Americans should be allowed to choose imprisonment rather than continued service—although some British captains were apparently reluctant to release crew.[133] At first, many of these prisoners were housed in prison ships along the coast, but almost all eventually ended up at Dartmoor prison in Devon.[134]

Again, life for prisoners abroad was rough. This was partly due to corruption on the part of the contractors paid to provide food and services for the prisoners and the fact that the US agent appointed to look after the prisoner's interests was, by many accounts, useless and entirely negligent of his duties.[135] But again, British authorities apparently did not mind taking advantage of the poor conditions that the prisoners were in by frequently sending in recruiting agents to offer them the chance to serve in the British Navy. Indeed, Abell argues that in some ways the Americans were treated worse than the other nationalities at Dartmoor. For example, they were "denied many privileges and advantages allowed to Frenchmen of the lowest class; they were shut out from the usual markets, and had to buy through the French prisoners, at 25 per cent above market prices."[136] The Americans, however, seem to have been able to improve their lot over the course of their stay through money raised in subscriptions from the British public and an improved allowance from the US government, and through working for the prison authority as barbers, hospital orderlies, stablemen and lamplighters, or even through washing clothes and cooking food for other prisoners.[137] In addition, order was established through a primitive-democratic system whereby the different prison enclaves would elect a twelve–person committee that would look out for the interests of the prison population as a whole. This also included giving punishments to those prisoners who did not abide by the rules set out for everyone to follow.[138]

Nevertheless, prison was still prison and those who hoped for an exchange or early release were disappointed. Exchanges had been suspended in August

1813 when, as in the American War of Independence, the US ran short of British prisoners. Even when the war ended, many prisoners had to wait months until they were released as the US government and its agent in Britain were negligent in making arrangements to get prisoners home. Although the prisoners were technically free men after the 1815 Treaty of Ghent, the Americans continued to be detained and effectively treated as prisoners.[139]

Looking back at the first wars the new republic faced, it is hard to avoid the conclusion that prisoners of war were largely regarded, and used, as an instrument of policy. There are, of course, some notable exceptions–George Washington and Benjamin Franklin were clearly concerned about the fate of prisoners, although neither seemed greatly concerned at the prospect of threatening the safety of British prisoners or deliberately kidnapping British sailors to get their own men back. In Britain there were several subscriptions, often taken up by notable, noble and wealthy individuals, to alleviate the suffering of the enemy. Still, by and large, prisoners were hostages to games of diplomatic showmanship and their conditions were rather dire when neither their own government nor their hosts paid attention to their interests. Beyond this, the British seem to have gone beyond looking at the American prisoners on their soil as hostages to seeing them as a way to fill up gaps in the Royal Navy. The Americans, for all the suffering of their prisoners, were willing to drag out their detention so long as they could try and link the issue to recognition of the independence of the United States.

Conflict with the First Nations Peoples

The First Nations peoples did not play a significantly large role in the American War of Independence, for several reasons. Anderson notes that while Washington would never come to truly admire the First Nations, he recognized them as a formidable force that could, even in small numbers, make frontier life intolerable. Therefore he largely took a prudential approach during the American Revolution.[140] But this was also partly due to the fact that the First Nations desired to stay out of the conflict between England and its colonies, with one tribe explaining to the Americans, "We love you both–old England and new".[141] Still, the need to keep trading forced most First Nations peoples to eventually support one side in the conflict. Most of the First Nations supported England because the American colonists simply could not provide the same amount or quality of goods for trade. Those First Nations tribes that did join on the side of the United States were from small enclaves located among colonial settlements, but these were few in number compared to the approximately 13,000 First Nations warriors who would fight for the British.[142]

But what was also significant was the memory of the problems that had occurred with the participation of the First Nations populations in the conflicts fought by the British and Americans in the lead up to the Revolution. The memory of Fort William Henry and Pontiac's rebellion, which reinforced ideas and stereotypes of the merciless and godless native, meant that neither side in the Revolution would rely heavily on First Nations warriors. Eventually, the British sought to use the First Nations warriors along the frontier where the British military presence was sparse.[143] Yet doing so would again prove to be a mixed blessing. The First Nations tribes were plagued with serious problems such as smallpox and internal tribal divisions. Additionally, the use of First Nations warriors was in some ways a propaganda coup for the Americans, especially when it came to prisoners, who berated the British for unleashing "savages" against the white, Christian colonists.[144]

The real consequence of the War of Independence for the First Nations peoples was the ramifications of the Treaty of Paris in 1783 whereby the English ceded all territory east of the Mississippi River to the Americans. Setters, who had already been encroaching on the area, wasted little time in claiming the land they saw as theirs. This was emphasized by the view that by siding with the British, the First Nations peoples had also been defeated in the conflict and had lost the rights to their territory.[145]

Seeing the ferocity of their warriors, some in the new American republic recognized that crushing resistance at this stage would be futile. Hence the government sought to convert the First Nations peoples to "civilization" through education, religion, and teaching them to cultivate the land in order to give up their nomadic lifestyle. However, although Washington had pressed for a more "enlightened" policy towards the First Nations, states and individuals on the frontier were less inclined to follow the approach of their national leaders.[146] The First Nations peoples, coming from a martial/warrior tradition, were also reluctant to accept these policies. Resistance among the tribes emerged as prophets encouraged the First Nations peoples to get back to their cultural roots and protect their land.[147] This new spiritual movement and the relentless push westward by American settlers resulted in continual armed struggle between the Americans and First Nations peoples where, again, there was little mercy for captives on both sides. However, when First Nations tribal unity could not hold, and the British failed to support the resistance, the First

Nations were forced to recognize the land ceded under previous agreements through the Treaty of Greenville in 1795.

All of this forms the background to the War of 1812 where the First Nations played an important role in the fighting and in the conduct of the campaign. Although they had ceded land only ten years previous, another attempt to unite the First Nations tribes had emerged by 1805 under the leadership of Tecumseh and his brother known as the Prophet. The British, occupied with wars in the Old World, were very willing to encourage and support the First Nations tribes in the conflict, to spare their own troops and because they desired a First Nations buffer-zone between the United States and the British territories.

The British were not afraid of using the fearsome reputation that First Nations warriors had garnered for maltreatment of their prisoners to entice the Americans to surrender where they could[148]–even though it seems to be almost universally agreed that Tecumseh was a humane man who, despite adhering very much to his warrior culture roots, abided by a very modern set of norms regarding violence in warfare. He was largely responsible for restraining his men in battle and preventing harm to non-combatants and prisoners. The British, who wanted to avoid unrestricted slaughter, reckoned that they could therefore count on him to control the First Nations tribes and to ensure that their conduct adhered to something like the understood norms of warfare at the time. However, where Tecumseh was absent, tragedy frequently struck for Americans captured by First Nations and even British-led First Nations troops.

In one of the early battles of the conflict at Fort Dearborn, ninety-six retreating Americans were promised safe passage by the First Nations tribes. However, they were soon set upon by 500 First Nations Warriors and fifty-three Americans were killed and many more taken prisoner. After the 1813 Battle of Frenchtown, which soon became known as the River Raisin Massacre, 30–40 wounded American prisoners of war were murdered by the First Nations warriors whom the British had put in charge of their welfare. As one historian notes: "Tecumseh's discipline and concern for humane conduct were manifest only when he was personally present. When he was not, Indian warriors followed their own interests and customs."[149] However, as another points out, the "massacre" occurred "against the background of indiscriminate American scorched earth tactics in the Indian villages[150] Tit-for-tat massacres (if such a term can be used) are no way to evaluate, let alone excuse a conflict, but they do partially explain the actions of the angered First Nations warriors.

By the end of the war of 1812, the First Nations east of the Mississippi were a divided, broken force. To add to this, they were now regarded as vanquished in the eyes of the Americans—who, because of their decision to side with the British for a second time, felt little need to accommodate them on the continent. Still, the First Nations did not surrender quietly—they were the primary occupation of the US army until 1890.[151]

The newly emerging American way of warfare that came out of the struggle for independence demonstrated that the commanders and politicians of the young army were determined to stay within the European tradition so long as they were fighting European allies. This is not particularly surprising—it was the way that many of the Americans had been taught to fight and it was emblematic of a "civilized" state, in other words a good public relations move when trying to form a new country. However, although the British and the Americans had been fighting in the same tradition, the refusal of the British to recognize the legitimacy of the Americans' cause meant that their prisoners were recognized as traitors rather than prisoners of war. Americans too refused to recognize the legitimacy of the First Nations' status and they were frequently treated with little leniency in battle as a result. Soon the Americans would find themselves competing for space with another group as they sought to expand and secure their empire—the Mexicans to their South. Although this largely remained a conflict in the European tradition, there would still be difficulties for the implementation of the laws of war and prisoners of war ahead.

The Mexican-American War

The series of conflicts that occurred between Mexico, Texas and the United States between 1835 and 1848 differed from the American Revolution and the War of 1812 in several important ways where prisoners of war and adherence to the laws of war were concerned. Almost twenty-five years after the War of 1812, the United States armed forces, though still relatively new, were more established and more experienced. Improvements made in teaching and training at the United Stated Military Academy at West Point had provided the rapidly expanding nation with a capable, albeit still small army.[152] When it came to defending what they saw as American soil, the US was ready, willing and perhaps eager to use deadly military force to achieve its interests.

The Mexicans had inherited most of their military traditions from the Spanish, whom they had overthrown in their own separate and bloody eleven–year revolution. So the Mexican way of war was culturally similar to that of the Americans, and this would seem to have had an important impact on the fighting. Still, unlike the War of Independence and the War of 1812 when those involved noted how they fought "men who are so much like ourselves",[153] there is no doubt that perceived racial and religious differences did have an effect on the way the two sides regarded each other. As McCaffrey describes one encounter of US soldiers in Mexico:

To the Illinoisians, the people of San Antonio were just as unusual as the city's architecture. The soldiers were quick to form opinions of them, and those opinions, as was the case wherever American soldiers encountered Mexicans, was not very high. One man noted rather cynically, "The more *respectable* portion of them consists of *scape-gallows & black-legs* from the States."[154]

The scene seems set for violations of the laws of war, especially when dealing with prisoners. Yet, interestingly enough, by the standards of the day (which, admittedly, were pretty low) there seems to be a lack of atrocities committed by each side. Flory, writing just under a century later, argues:

During the Mexican War there appears to have been mutual satisfaction regarding the treatment of prisoners, for in 1847 the Commander-in-Chief of the American naval forces wrote, apparently with the knowledge of the President, to the Mexican Minister of Foreign Relations concerning the "kind and liberal treatment" granted American prisoners in Mexico, "which has been fully reciprocated by us towards those Mexicans who have fallen into our hands.[155]

With an inevitable few and tragic exceptions, this largely appears to be the case with regards to the War between the United States and Mexico.

This is not to say that prisoners of war were not an important issue in the overall conflict. In some ways, prisoners taken by the Mexicans in the Texas Revolution and "flare-ups" that followed before the war achieved somewhat mythic status during the Mexican-American War. In 1835, when Texas broke away from Mexico in a bid to become an independent state, the Mexican government refused to regard anyone who took up arms as anything other than a rebel who did not deserve any of the rights of a prisoner of war. At the famous battle of the Alamo, General Santa Anna ordered that no quarter be given.[156] Less famous, but more tragic was the incident at Goliad in March 1836 where 342 Texan prisoners who had surrendered on the understanding that they would be given quarter were executed *en masse* for their participation in the conflict. These incidents became infamous in the eyes of Texans and many sympathetic Americans and the slogans "Remember the Alamo!" and "Remember Goliad!" soon became the battle cries of the Texan Revolution.

In the stalemate that followed the Revolution in 1836, there were two more incidents involving prisoners where (mainly American born) Texans were taken prisoner by the Mexicans. These resulted from two ill-fated and ill-conceived incursions into Mexico by Texan forces. Despite General Santa Anna's defeat at San Jacinto in 1836,[157] the Mexicans were still reluctant to see Texas as an independent state. They continued to send raids into what they regarded as a rebel province. To protect their newly won independence, the Texans decided both to defend and to extend their territory. Unfortunately, the results were not what they had hoped for. The 1841 Sante Fe Expedition into Mexican territory resulted in the capture of over 300 Texan prisoners who were fortunately spared execution, but were marched to Mexico City where they were interned. A similar incident occurred in 1842 when a punitive expedition was abandoned as unsuccessful, but over 300 soldiers sought to continue their mission into Mexican territory regardless of an order to return home. This continued effort became known as the Mier Expedition with approximately 300 soldiers who were soon captured by the 3,000 Mexican troops that happened to be in the area.

Interestingly, General Ampudia, who was commanding the troops in the area, chose to treat the captured Texans as formal prisoners of war. As Haynes argues:

[E]ven if the Texans were not formally prisoner of war, General Ampudia chose to regard them as such. Indeed, [the men of the expedition] were treated as well as and probably better than they had reason to expect...They were soldiers of a country Mexico regarded as a rebel province, acting independently, wreaking havoc along the Río Grande with plunder as their only apparent motive. The punishment for insurgence and banditry was the same; Ampudia would have been well within his authority to execute them at once.[158]

Haynes goes on to argue that the Mexicans spared the Texans at Mier because, despite Mexican reservations, the country had been able to achieve a certain degree of legitimacy since 1836, having been recognized by Britain, France and the United States. Therefore, the prisoners deserved a certain level of respect and dignity–although whether they would have concluded this knowing that the Texans had been marking against the orders of their own government is up for debate.[159]

The troops were to be marched to Mexico City, but 181 soldiers escaped while en route at Matamoros. Unfortunately for the prisoners, 176 were recaptured and, upon hearing of the attempt to escape, the Mexican government ordered the death of all of the prisoners. The commander in charge,

General Francisco Mejía, refused this order and promptly resigned. By the time a new commander was appointed, diplomatic efforts by the Americans and British government led Santa Anna to decree that only one in ten would die, and seventeen prisoners were executed in March 1843.[160]

The remaining prisoners were marched to Mexico City where they stayed in prison until they were freed by Santa Anna in 1844. American diplomats worked hard to free the captured men of the Santa Fe and Mier Expeditions—something that is not too surprising, considering that many of the prisoners were American-born and that the United States was actively courting the Republic of Texas to join it. In 1842 the American Secretary of State, Daniel Webster, threatened "consequences of the most serious character... if Mexico treated American citizens captured with the Texan army as rebels, and refused to release them upon demand of the United States."[161] Additionally, Waddy Thompson, the American Minister to Mexico, argued for the release of the men. After Santa Anna announced that "only" one in ten prisoners would die, Thompson decried this new edict as tantamount to "cold-blooded and atrocious murder" and "a far greater act of cruelty than of the slaughter of the Alamo defenders or... the troops at the Goliad." He also added that the prisoners were not on parole and had every right to escape.[162] Although Santa Anna did point out that the troops were not American, Thompson argued: "They are human beings and prisoners of war, and it is the right and duty of all nations to see that Mexico does not violate the principles and usages of civilized war—more particularly it is the duty of the United Stated to maintain those laws and usages on this Continent."[163]

Santa Anna was clearly not moved by such pronouncements, as the execution proceeded as scheduled. Not deterred, Thompson continued his efforts to free the remaining Texans and continued to visit the prisoners. Using his personal connection with Santa Anna, he was able to persuade him to release the remaining prisoners in 1844. Although there were fears of a Mexican mob when the prisoners were released, Thompson records that the Mexican soldiers and civilians instead cheered the American soldiers and flocked to them with money, clothes and food:

I could not refrain from asking myself whether if the people of any other country had invaded ours and been made prisoners, they would under like circumstances have passed through such a crowd not only without insult, but with such demonstrations of kindness and sympathy. There were a few instances of atrocious barbarity practised upon these prisoners upon the frontiers of Mexico when they were first captured... But any treatment which the Texan prisoner received in Mexico was kind and humane in comparison with the treatment of American prisoners during our late war with England, at Dartmoor and elsewhere.[164]

Considering the tense situation between the United States, Texas and Mexico in 1844, when Thompson's book was published, this is rather high praise and respect for an enemy. And indeed, while the incidents outlined above are certainly unfortunate, the prisoners do seem to have been treated rather reasonably by an army whose only previous experience had been fighting an exceptionally bloody civil war against the Spanish, where it was frequently declared that no quarter was to be given to the soldiers of the rebellious colony.

The outbreak of formal hostilities, 1846–8

While it would be wrong to say the Mexican-American conflict was a war without violations of the laws of war or atrocities, as indicated above there does seem to be a general sense that both sides fought according to the rules and norms of "civilized" warfare as generally understood in the 1840s. This was, perhaps, especially important to the Americans who, despite describing the conflict as a war of self-defence and to bolster their security, were about to engage in a large land-grab to the Pacific Ocean at the expense of Mexico. The need to pacify an outraged Mexican public would clearly be on the minds of both politicians and military commanders. The Secretary of State James Buchanan "piously declared" on 14 May, "We go to War with Mexico solely for the purpose of conquering an honourable and just peace. Whilst we intent to prosecute the War with vigour, both by land and by sea, we shall bear the olive branch in one hand, and the sword in the other; and wherever she will accept the former, we shall sheath the latter."[165]

On 26 February 1846, General Zachary Taylor wrote to Washington:

I have [informed] some citizens of Matomoros... that the United States Government, in occupying the Rio Grande, has no motive of hostility toward Mexico, and that the army will, in no case, go beyond the river unless hostilities should be commenced by the Mexicans themselves; that the Mexicans living on this side, will not be disturbed in any way by the troops; that they will be protected in all their rights and usages; and, that everything which the army may need, will be purchased from them at fair prices.[166]

However, the military authorities, in particular General Winfield Scott who opened up a second front in the war in 1847, recognized that the 1806 Articles of War were not sufficient to cover the potential legal difficulties posed by an army which had suddenly been bloated with volunteers eager to take on the Mexicans. The authors of the 1806 Articles had never considered the idea that the United States would be fighting in foreign territory and therefore, for all practical purposes, the soldiers and civilians in Mexico had immunity for any crimes they committed. On 20 February 1847 he issued Order No. 20 which established the base upon which would become the basis for military government in the future.[167] The orders simply extended the jurisdiction of military courts to crimes that would be punishable in civil courts including rape, murder, assault, robbery, desecration of churches, disruption of religious services, and destruction of private property.[168] Order No. 20 applied to soldiers but also to Mexican and American civilians living in areas of US occupation. Carney argues that Scott had learned the lessons of the very bloody failed campaign of the French in Spain during the Napoleonic wars:

[Scott] was struck by the rancorous conduct of the French troops toward the Spanish population and the failure of harsh French occupational measures to quash the growing uprising there. As provocations multiplied on both sides, the fighting escalated out of control. The French responded by setting fire to entire villages, shooting civilians en masse, destroying churches, and even executing priests. The locals retaliated in kind... By the time an allied force under Arthur Wellesley, the Duke of Wellington, compelled the French to withdraw from Spain in 1813, Napoleon's force had seen some 300,000 men killed and wounded, compared with Napoleon's preoccupation estimate of approximately 12,000 casualties. In fact, Scott saw Wellesley's stress on strict discipline—insisting his soldiers respect personal property and meet the basic needs of Spanish civilians—as the proper model for operating in a potentially hostile land.[169]

General Scott therefore issued Order No. 20 with the lessons of history very much in mind.[170]

American soldiers who committed offences against Mexican civilians or who violated military regulations received punishment that could be very severe. Flogging was still in use and corporal punishment was still very frequent. Soldiers might have to march for several hours at a time while carrying a heavy weight, be confined in dark holes in the ground for several days without proper nourishment, or even be placed in stocks.[171] Punishments were meted out at courts-martial–regimental or garrison courts-martial for lesser, non-capital offences and general courts-martial for the most severe punishments. At the regimental/garrison courts-martial, officers were rarely lawyers but apparently did their best to stick to the spirit of the laws as they saw it.[172] Still, very few crimes carried automatic sentencing at this point, and this allowed the courts a great deal of leeway in giving out punishments. McCaffrey notes that because of this leeway, soldiers frequently received different punishments for the same crime.[173]

Additionally, having a system of justice in occupied Mexico did not necessarily mean that justice was guaranteed. McCaffrey suggests that just as the soldiers committing crimes against Mexican civilians would not have done the same thing to white Americans, racism may have influenced the outcome of how army officials dealt with cases. In one incident in February 1847, American soldiers from Arkansas had picked on and pushed the local Mexican civilians too far and they retaliated by killing one of them. The Americans came back with two companies in search of the killers. They came upon a group of Mexicans who were trying to get away, apparently from an anticipated battle between Santa Anna and the Americans. One of the Mexicans had personal property from the killed American soldier and the order was given to open fire on the civilians. The Mexicans were pursued to a cave where the killing continued. By the time General Wool sent troops to investigate, 20–30 Mexicans had been slain. In the subsequent inquiry, it was impossible to positively identify which individuals participated in the action—the only punishment inflicted on the suspected individuals was to miss out on the coming battle.[174]

Several factors contributed to soldiers violating the laws of war and the military regulations while US forces were in Mexico. The first of these was the rapid expansion of the army at the outbreak of the war. The US regular army was small and, for a large-scale invasion of Mexico, needed to be supplemented by a large numbers of volunteers. These volunteers were given brief training and would not have been familiar with the customs of land warfare as the regulars in the army were. In all likelihood, many joined up out of a sense of adventure, attracted by the idea of relaxing in the "the halls of Montezuma" or, no doubt, plundering the odd Mexican village. Concerns about civilized warfare were probably not foremost in the minds of many volunteers.

Taylor and the other army officers frequently blamed most of the legal problems of the army on the volunteers, noting that they had not been subjected to the harsh and demanding discipline required of the regular troops.[175] McCaffrey notes that from the army records it does appear that the volunteers committed more acts of violence than the regulars against Mexican civilians.[176] Yet, as Carney notes, Taylor was also at fault given his lax approach to discipline with his volunteers. While the regulars under his command seem to have largely had reasonable relations with the locals, the problems started when the volunteers arrived:

As thefts, assaults, rapes, murders, and other crimes perpetrated by the volunteers mounted and Taylor failed to discipline his men, ordinary Mexican citizens began to have serious reservations about the American invasion. Taylor's lackadaisical approach to discipline produced an effect utterly unanticipated by the Polk administration, many of whose members, particularly pro-expansionists such as Secretary of the Treasury Robert J. Walker, believed that Mexicans would welcome the Americans as liberators. Instead, public opinion turned against the Americans and began to create a climate for guerrilla bands to form in the area.[177]

Mexicans from all classes took part in the guerrilla attacks which suddenly began to plague the US army in the occupied parts of northern Mexico. This became a serious distraction to the Americans who then came down hard upon the insurgents. Essentially, the US forces under Taylor had played a part in bringing about these activities by neglecting military discipline and punishment of those who had been harassing the Mexicans. The guerrilla campaigns were addressed through increasing patrols but also by Order No. 20 which allowed for the trial of Mexican civilians caught engaging in guerilla activities.

Still, as regards prisoners of war, the record seems rather decent by contemporary standards. Part of the reason for this may have been the sweeping success the Americans had in fighting the conflict. The Mexican army was poor, badly trained and lacking in discipline. When the Mexicans stood their ground they tended to fight valiantly and could be very deadly. However, the army and civilian militia raised to defend Mexico from the invading Americans suffered from a chronic shortage of weapons, ammunition and clothing, to the point where many corps organized through the country "lacked the equipment needed to reach a state of respectability."[178] The resulting series of military victories meant that the US army was faced with an overwhelming number of prisoners who came with an expensive price tag when it came to feeding and looking after them. The result was that over 10,000 prisoners of war were unilaterally released by US troops because they placed such a heavy burden upon supplies.[179] Still, the results were not always humane. General Winfield Scott became alarmed by the number of paroled prisoners who re-entered combat against their oath. In accordance with the laws of war at the time, he announced that he intended to hang every combatant who was retaken after violating his parole of honour.[180]

The Battalion of Saint Patrick

One of the strangest incidents involving prisoners, indeed a controversial one, to come out of the Mexican-American War involved a battalion of former American soldiers who had, for one reason or another, joined the Mexicans during the course of military operations. This battalion was composed of approximately 265 men and led by a deserter, Bennet Riley. Accounts differ as to how this group of soldiers got its name, but they became known as the Battalion of Saint Patrick or the *San Patricios*, apparently to reflect and/or reinforce the fact that the battalion was made up mainly of Irish Catholics (although the names of the men indicate that many were in fact of English, Scottish and German heritage).[181] The Mexicans had made efforts to entice the Americans to desert and priests and propagandists frequently appealed to Catholic soldiers to join their brothers in the faith to fight for Mexico. In addition, they were promised $10 and 20 acres of land[182] However, many of the San Patricios had probably fallen into enemy hands while drunk and had got lost in the bush where they soon found themselves captured and impressed into service. Others claimed that they were set upon by the Mexicans while they were trying to desert and had got lost.[183]

The San Patricios saw action in several of the conflict's major battles, but the men of the battalion were either captured or killed at Churubusco. Knowing that capture by the Americans would result in dire consequences if they surrendered, the San Patricios did everything they could to avoid it—including preventing the Mexicans from raising a white flag three times.[184] After being overwhelmed by US forces, sixty-five men were taken prisoner, the rest presumably perishing in the fight.

The prisoners were divided into two groups and put on trial. Many claimed that they had been severely mistreated as prisoners of the Mexicans and had joined the fight only when faced with starvation and relentless abuse.[185] Still, there was little mercy for the San Patricios: all of the first twenty-nine men tried by court-martial were convicted and sentenced to hang. General Scott commuted the sentences of seven to fifty lashes, and branding with the letter "D" on their cheek. According to McCornack, Scott reprieved these men because they had deserted before the actual declaration of war took place; this was, he argues, a literal interpretation of the Articles of War. Two men were pardoned outright for being legitimately captured and forced into the San Patricios where they refused to fight.[186] A second group of thirty-six were all sentenced and hanged except for two men who were remitted and four others whose sentences were commuted to lashings and brandings.[187]

It is not surprising that Scott did not intend to treat the San Patricios as prisoners of war. In sending the men to be tried as traitors and having the bulk of them executed, there is no doubt that Scott was trying to send a very clear warning to the men of the US forces. Certainly, the move may be seen as harsh today, and was seen so in fact in Scott's time, when Mexican newspapers used the incident as a way of demonstrating alleged American brutality and a group of "citizens of the United States and foreigners of different nations in the City of Mexico" appealed for the release of the men.[188] Still, given customary notions at the time, as well as the emphasis on discipline, Scott would not have had a lot of trouble justifying his behaviour under the laws of war of the day. Indeed, the Americans themselves did not have too many qualms about enticing men who fell into their hands into their service.[189] Scott, however, would have probably done so knowing that the men they recruited would have been despised by the Mexican people and charged with treason had they been captured.

Culture or carnage?

This war was hardly free of violence and violations of the laws of war, but given the problems that had occurred between the white American settlers and the First Nations, why were there not more problems when the United States battled the Mexicans who were, without any doubt, seen as a different race of people? As already discussed, many Americans looked down on the Mexicans. Even the American Minister Waddy Thompson, who seems to have had a certain amount of respect for the Mexicans, described their religious practices as "revolting in its disgusting mummeries and impostures, which degrade the Christian religion into an absurd, ridiculous, and venal superstition."[190]

There are a couple of reasons why this may be the case. In the Mexican War, the Americans (although they publicly claimed otherwise) were the aggressor nation. It is true that the Mexicans had been posing a threat to Texas, but whether this justified a full-scale invasion combined with the largest land-grab in US history was still somewhat questionable. In this way, the United States needed its troops to behave well in the field to ensure that the population, already angry about the American invasion, did not take up arms against it. Again, as already suggested, where violations against civilians took place, guerrilla warfare took root and caused US troops many problems. Government and army officials knew that assuring the Mexican population that they would be treated well would certainly make the job of occupation much easier. This was especially the case for Scott who knew that preventing violations meant that there was a need for discipline and to keep service men busy—many of the violations of the war occurred when Taylor did not keep his men occupied and they found ways of entertaining themselves at the expense of Mexican civilians.

Another reason for a relatively low number of violations may be that in a war where the United States secured overwhelming and quick victories, there was little resentment built up against the Mexican army. In this way, revenge attacks against Mexican prisoners would have been reduced and overall resentment towards enemies would have been lower than in previous or future conflicts.

But perhaps the most important factor here is the fact that the Mexicans, having inherited the Spanish military tradition (which, admittedly, was not always compassionate), would have been fighting with a recognized version of warfare. The uniformed army may have been poor but, for the most part, it fought according to European custom. The practices employed were also extended to prisoners who, in the majority of cases, seem to have been treated reasonably under the circumstances. Where the Mexicans offered treatment according to the laws and customs of war, the Americans seem to have reciprocated.

In other words, it does not seem unreasonable to suggest that application of the laws of war, for the Americans, depended more on culture than race. If you fought along "civilized" lines then you received similar treatment. However, to achieve this, enemies needed to fight according to the European way of warfare: set-battles of soldiers who had been drilled and disciplined. Obviously, the First Nations were never going to fight this way and were therefore never going to be given the same rights as captured Mexicans in the war.

Conclusion

Throughout the first wars that the new republic faced, prisoners of war often became a symbol of injustice and suffering. The treatment that American soldiers received at the hands of the British, and the idea that the French and then the British King had unleashed "savages" who perpetrated atrocities, would help to justify war in the eyes of many.

However, the symbolic status of the prisoner as a helpless victim did not stop the Americans from using prisoners as political tools when it suited them. The first American administrations were clearly willing to link the issue of prisoners to recognition, which put their own men in jeopardy. Additionally, for all of their complaints about injustice, they were clearly willing to retaliate in kind. As with the other European powers, the idea that prisoners were ultimately hostages seems to have guided policy. This was not necessarily inhumane—just a manifestation of the golden rule.

Yet, taking hostages only worked in a system where both sides were playing by the same rules—or at least had a shared understanding of what they were. In the case of the United States, their understanding of the "rules" was clearly based upon an inherited tradition from Europe. It is true that there had been some exchanges and modifications made to accommodate the vast forests of the New World. But the early American armed forces, by and large, remained a "continental" army–trained, drilled and disciplined according to the European way of warfare. It was a tradition totally foreign to the First Nations tribes.

In this sense, application of the laws of war may be best understood as a problem of culture rather than race. This would certainly help to explain why the laws of war were, for the most part, applied to the Mexican army but not to Mexican guerrillas and not to the First Nations. As mentioned above, issues of race and racism clearly had a role to play in terms of dehumanizing the enemy. This was the case on both sides of the wars between the white Americans and battles with the First Nations. But where cultural similarities existed on the battlefield, restraint became possible. For all of the harshness of the American wars of independence, the fighting between the white Americans and British was never as savage (though it was certainly bloody) as it was between the Americans and First Nations, where denying quarter seems to have been the order of the day.

Again, perhaps this is where ideology plays a role in helping to understand how the laws of war were applied and how prisoners of war were treated. If, as Shy suggests, the Americans began to look for a "complete solution" to the problem of their security by eventually coming to dominate the continent which they resided, then it is probable that they also applied restraints in warfare through this notion as well. In wanting to control, if not eliminate the French, Spanish and First Nations peoples, humanity in warfare was probably not the first priority. Yet, as the Mexican-American War demonstrates, it did not always have to come down to carnage, particularly where culture seems to have intervened. In this way, there was clearly a strong interplay between ideological imperatives from wars for complete security and cultural factors that helped govern the implementation (or not) of the laws of war, including the treatment of prisoners.

This would become a continuing trend in American policy on applying the laws of war. However, that is not to stay that this relationship remained constant: once the US had established its dominance over North America, the need to ensure security would eventually give way to a desire to spread American values abroad. Additionally, even as the laws of war became codified and settled international norms, their application would be inconsistent up to and during the First World War. How the United States, with notions of manifest destiny, continuing wars with the First Nations and an emerging empire, handled the development of the laws of war in the nineteenth century is the topic of the next chapter.

2

'MANIFEST' HUMANITARIANS

THE UNITED STATES, INTERNATIONAL LAW
AND MODERN WARFARE, 1860–1950

During the historical period covered in the last chapter, the rules of warfare might best be characterized as an unwritten code of conduct followed between the "civilized" nations of Europe. While there were experts and authorities like Grotius, Vattel and Suarez, international law as applied to force sprang from natural law and was therefore subject to interpretation, and did not have much force. This would change in the second half of the nineteenth century. As the methods and means of warfare grew more powerful and more bloody, a humanitarian movement began which sought to place formal restraints on the waging of war in a treaties. Such agreements, it was hoped, would remove some of the unnecessary suffering of the victims of war.

Though this chapter will examine how the United States was, for various reasons, a reluctant player in these negotiations, the US would go on to play a large role in the development and codification of the laws of war. But the story here is not always a pleasant one. Humanitarian developments were achieved during the war which was the most costly in terms of lives in US history—and one where prisoners again greatly suffered. And even then, the laws of war did not always serve humanitarian ends. They could be deliberately invoked as justification for harsh treatment and occasionally deadly force.

The American Civil War

The American Civil War which lasted for just over four years, from April 1861 to May 1865, can be considered in many ways the first mechanized total war.

It was the first conflict where there was widespread use of railways, telegraphs, ironclad ships and even aerial observation from balloons. In addition, new developments in the weapons of war ensured that there was a very high cost in terms of bloodshed; the war would take more than 600,000 lives.

It is not surprising, then, that prisoners of war were again a feature of the conflict. As one historian notes: "During and after the [Civil] war the prisoner from Johnson's Island to Andersonville played much the same part that the Belgian atrocities played in the [First] World War. In each case the stories fed the fires of hate and inspired war-crazed peoples with savage impulses."[1]

While many of the contemporary accounts were "embellished" by former prisoners who sought to demonize their opponents, there can be no doubt that prisoners again suffered in the Civil War. There are several reasons for this. The first (resembling some of the difficulties between the British and Americans during the American Revolution) stemmed from a concern of the Lincoln administration that an exchange of prisoners would implicitly recognize the Confederacy.[2] While there was a prisoner exchange in 1862, both sides soon put a stop to cartels, particularly once the sensitive issue of exchanging black prisoners of war emerged. As David Williams notes, at the beginning of the war prisoners were typically exchanged or paroled as soon as they could be processed, usually within days or weeks, and there were few military prisons to speak of. After the Union army began to enlist black troops in 1863, the Confederate government refused to recognize them as legitimate combatants. By order of the Jefferson Davis administration:

...black soldiers were to be treated as rebellious chattel, subject to enslavement. Their white officers were to be viewed as leaders of slave insurrection and subject to execution. Neither blacks nor whites serving in any regiment of the United States Coloured Troops, as such units were designated, would be exchanged or paroled by the Confederacy.[3]

The end result was that Lincoln halted the practice of exchange and parole altogether. As a result, prisons on both sides soon began to fill. Given that some prison officials mistakenly anticipated that the exchanges would be resumed, there were no attempts to modify the prisons either to handle larger numbers or to make life for the now long-term inmates more comfortable. In some cases, particularly in the South, the hastily constructed prisons (which were often converted warehouses) began to be overpopulated and rapidly became full of vermin. At Libby prison, Union soldiers were largely confined in small spaces and there was no place for them to exercise.[4]

It did not help that the prisoner exchange had been discredited by the Secretary of War, Edwin Stanton, who believed that Union soldiers, tired of army life, were deliberately trying to be captured so as to take advantage of being paroled, which would prevent them from being forced to stay in the army. In order to drive home the point that life in a Confederate prison was not a vacation, the War Department undertook a propaganda campaign that the South was committing inhumane crimes against the prisoners of war. Aside from scaring its own soldiers, the campaign had the added advantage of demonizing the South in the eyes of Northern civilians.[5]

Union prisoners also suffered from the eventual economic collapse of the South, which resulted in a complete breakdown of the transport and distribution system. Although one historian argues that "Reason could hardly demand that a nation accord better treatment to captive enemies than to the fighting forces",[6] the consequences for the Union soldiers were dire. Susie King Taylor, a black Savannah resident, described the city's prison stockade as "an awful place. The Union soldiers were in it, worse than pigs, without any shelter from sun or storm."[7] Perhaps the most famous case of problems involving prisoners during the Civil War is also the most tragic. During the war more than 45,000 Union soldiers were confined at the Confederate Prison at Andersonville, Georgia. Of these, almost 13,000 died from disease, poor sanitation, malnutrition, overcrowding, or exposure to the elements. Pictures of the survivors very clearly resemble those of the survivors of modern concentration camps. In other Southern prisons there was a chronic shortage of food, and wood for fires by 1863. Confederate soldiers similarly suffered at the Elmira prison in New York which had a death rate of 24 per cent–double the average rate for Confederate prisoners.[8]

Other than these miseries, there were the common problems that American prisons and prisoners had experienced since the Revolution. Aside from the politics of recognition involved in cartels, both sides were willing to use the prisoners as tools and hostages. In November 1863, the Union stopped the delivery of relief packages for Confederate prisoners of war, to protest against alleged abuse against its soldiers in the South. In December, the Confederacy retaliated by cutting off the shipment of food and clothing by the US government.[9] In addition, in a war that placed considerable pressure on manpower, it is unlikely that either side in the conflict put its best soldiers on prison duty. Although one historian notes that the "second rate" officers made real efforts to obtain supplies for their prisoners, these efforts were largely lost in the "inefficiency of the prison system of the South."[10]

The result of these unfortunate circumstances was a miserable life for prisoners. Withholding rations became a common means of prisoner control.

Prisoners themselves frequently became targets of retaliation. After hearing allegations of starvation in Southern prisons, William Hoffman, the Union General Commissary of Prisoners (and himself a prisoner of war who had been exchanged in 1862), reduced prison rations for Confederate prisoners even more. Prisoners, out of desperation, resorted to eating the pets of their guards or, more frequently, rats. The mortality rate for prisoners of war in Union and Confederate prisons was 12 and 15.5 per cent respectively.[11]

Humanitarian innovations of the Civil War

Yet the demands of such a large scale war also resulted in two innovations that were to have a major impact on an emerging spirit of humanitarianism that was beginning to take shape in Europe and the United States. The first of these was the formation of the United States Sanitary Commission. The Commission took its name and some of its inspiration from the British Sanitary Commission which had been established during the Crimean War a few years earlier. It comprised civilian volunteers who, besides supporting the Union war effort, worked to alleviate the sufferings of wounded soldiers on both sides of the conflict and to distribute supplies to prisoners of war.

The Civil War also brought about one of the founding documents of the laws of war, which was used for the next fifty years by the American armed forces and served as the inspiration of several major treaties. It was during this time that the American government realized that it needed an explicit code for its soldiers to follow with regard to the laws of war. At the outset of the conflict, it became apparent that most of the professional officers in the US armed forces were going to be on the Confederate side.[12] This was a serious problem in a system that largely relied on custom to prevent atrocities in warfare. The generally less experienced men in charge of the Union's forces would need some kind of instruction as to how to conduct themselves in battle and engage with hostile populations. To meet this need, the Union looked to Europe–or at least to a European–for advice. Francis Lieber, an old Prussian soldier, was a professor at Columbia University in 1861 when he gave a series of lectures on the laws of war. This he subsequently published as a sixteen–page paper "of concise, sensible notes about the treatment of guerrilla forces, spies, brigands and 'bushwhackers.'"[13] When one of Lieber's audience, General H.W. Halleck, became the General-in-Chief of the Union's armies, he ordered five thousand copies of Lieber's paper and invited him to propose amendments to the few existing army regulations.[14] As a result *General Orders 100: Instructions for the Government of Armies in the United States in the Field* was published in the spring of 1863 (six months before the meeting of the Geneva Society for Public Welfare which would go on to establish the International Committee of the Red Cross), and became known as the "Lieber Code".

The code covered military discipline and an explanation of the laws of war and their status between two opposing armed forces. It strictly adhered to the view that tactics in warfare were not unrestricted by the law of nations or natural law. It was a set of guidelines for soldiers on the battlefield and offered some innovations. One of Lieber's main contributions was to provide what was then the clearest definition of who a prisoner of war was and what his rights were according to customary international law. According to Article 49:

A prisoner of war is a public enemy armed or attached to the hostile army for active aid, who has fallen into the hands of the captor, either fighting or wounded, on the field or in the hospital, by individual surrender or by capitulation.

All soldiers, of whatever species of arms; all men who belong to the rising en masse of the hostile country; all those who are attached to the army for its efficiency and promote directly the object of the war, except such as are hereinafter provided for; all disabled men or officers on the field or elsewhere, if captured; all enemies who have thrown away their arms and ask for quarter, are prisoners of war, and as such exposed to the inconveniences as well as entitled to the privileges of a prisoner of war.[15]

According to Best, so far as POWs are concerned, Lieber's language indicates both a keen awareness that among the law's classical purposes was the prevention of things being done in war which might hinder the return to peace, and an awareness that popular passions were actually pressing for the execution of such drastic and severe war measures as were sure to do that.[16] Additionally, Best argues that this definition was important because it clarified the fact that prisoners of war were not to be considered criminals. Instead, Lieber made it clear that POWs were to be considered a distinct category of war's sufferers or victims and thus deserving of protection like the wounded.[17]

Ultimately, despite this impressive step, Lieber's rules were more like guiding principles than binding rules. Because reciprocity was necessary for the rules to apply, the Confederate forces technically did not qualify. Still, the Lieber Code did have some impact in the field on the behaviour of government troops. And significantly, Lieber's overall contribution would become very influential in the US and Europe, as well as in the future treaties on the laws of war that were negotiated in the later half of the nineteenth century.

But this Northern Code did little to stop the maltreatment of Union soldiers, particularly black soldiers in the South. At the "Massacre of Fort Pillow",

Confederate soldiers denied quarter to black soldiers. Additionally, wounded black soldiers were often shot rather than treated. One Confederate officer, who argued that such behaviour was "shameful", recorded in the aftermath of one battle near Jacksonville, Florida: "Negroes, and plenty of them, who I had seen lying all over the field wounded, and as far as I could see, many of them moving around from place to place, now... all were dead. If a negro had a shot in the shin another was sure to be in the head."[18]

Williams argues that ultimately, the take-no-prisoners policy worked more against the Confederates than for them. Enraged at the stories and rumours of poor treatment and slaughter, black soldiers treated surrendered Confederate soldiers in the same way. Williams explains this, arguing: "...few of their comrades faulted black soldiers for giving no quarter to men that they believed would give them none. The general rule was killed or be killed. Even for those blacks who survived initial captivity, life as a prisoner of war was always brutal and often brief."[19]

Indeed, black prisoners of war could expect poor (if any) medical cares and food, and frequent encounters with the lash. Blacks held in Confederate prisons died at a rate of 35 per cent, more than twice the average for white captives.

Finally, these humanitarian developments did not necessarily translate into either domestic or international commitments. In the domestic sphere, Lincoln took drastic steps to expand presidential powers in order to save the Union, including suspending the writ of *habeas corpus* and imprisoning thousands of individuals who were deemed Southern sympathizers, saboteurs, spies and agitators. Lincoln ignored an order from the Chief Justice of the Supreme Court to release a prisoner who was deemed to be detained illegally, and many civilians were tried in military commissions. Lincoln's approach to security in a national crisis would be invoked as precedent to justify a similar expansion of powers by the Franklin Delano Roosevelt and George W. Bush administrations.[20]

There were also limitations to exactly how far the guidance provided in the Orders went. The Lieber Code was an attempt to provide an explanation of what the laws of war were in terms of natural law which, of course, implied a universal application for civilized nations. However, the United States did not feel it necessary to go beyond this statement in the form of international treaties. Although there were often American representatives present at the many humanitarian conferences that met throughout Europe in the second half of the nineteenth century, the United States did not sign or accede to any of the resulting treaties until 1882. The agreements it did not sign included everything from the Treaty of Paris in 1856 through to the Brussels Declaration of 1874, although it should be pointed out that the United States was often not the only great power holding back. Nevertheless, it seems strange that the nation which had established the Lieber Code, the most modern statement of the laws of war at that time, should fail to sign and ratify much less demanding humanitarian agreements.

Several reasons, however, can be suggested for this. The first of these is simply national interest. The 1856 Declaration of Paris sought to protect private property of belligerents in times of war on neutral ships and to outlaw piracy. The United States withheld its consent to the Declaration because it wanted a complete exemption of private property at sea. Additionally, unlike the European powers, the United States was without a strong navy and, in case a major war was to break out, wanted to continue to rely on piracy as an instrument of warfare.

When it came to the 1864 Geneva Convention, the United States sent two representatives, George Fogg, who was the US Minister at Berne, and Charles Bowles, a representative of the US Sanitary Commission. Although Fogg requested instructions from Washington as to what to do about the treaty, he never received any directions and the Convention was never signed by the US. Although the United States received several letters inviting it to do so over the next fifteen years, in most cases it did not even bother sending a reply. However, in this second case, it seems reasonable that the US government, embroiled in the Civil War, was not in any position to make international guarantees. In addition, the familiar problem of recognition soon reared its head; there was some concern that the representatives assembled in Geneva would recognize the legitimacy of the Confederacy. One of the few directions that Fogg did receive from Secretary of State William Seward was that if a Confederate representative was received at the Conference, the United States would at once withdraw.[21]

Finally, in the case of the 1868 St Petersburg Declaration which outlawed munitions under 400 grams, and the Brussels Declaration of 1874 which attempted to codify many of the customs already in the Lieber Code into international law, the US argued that its policy of manifest destiny did not allow it to get involved in making treaties with the European countries and that such treaties would violate American neutrality.[22]

These policies are consistent with an isolationist stance—invoking the national interest and avoiding alliances. Yet they only tell one part of the story. Although the United States did not sign the Treaty of Paris in 1856, it agreed to abide by the principles of the Treaty at the outbreak of the Civil War in 1861 for the duration of the conflict.[23] And although the United States refused to participate in the Brussels Conference in 1874, even Baron Jomini, president of the Conference, noted to a US official that "the project was by no means so severe as the regulations prepared by Professor Lieber, and put into force by the United States during the recent rebellion."[24] In other words, the protection offered combatants under the Lieber Code was just as strong, if not stronger than, anything the Europeans proposed. Suspicions of the Europeans also remained. The persistent violations of the 1864 Geneva Convention during the Franco-Prussian War may also have suggested that the some of the parties to the treaties were not exactly negotiating in good faith. There also remained some suspicion that the Russian Tsar had an ulterior motive for calling the conference–that it would help support the *status quo* in Europe.[25] That the Brussels Declaration was never ratified may have confirmed some of these speculations. However, this left the United States in the position where it still had some of the strongest regulations regarding the laws of war until the Hague Conventions of 1899.

It would take domestic pressure from the current and former members of the US Sanitary Commission, including the famous humanitarian (and heroine of the Civil War) Clara Barton, and a change of government to eventually bring about ratification of the 1864 Geneva Conventions in 1882, and along with it the establishment of the American Red Cross. Additionally, the ratification opened the way for the United States to fully participate in future humanitarian conferences–in time for the major conference that would be held at The Hague.

The Hague Peace Conference of 1899 was a major gathering of the world's powers of the time. Called together by Tsar Nicholas II, the Conference had three goals: to establish a world court for the peaceful settlement of disputes, to produce an arms reduction treaty and to codify the customary laws of war. For its part, the United States took the Conference very seriously and sought to play an important part in its proceedings. The Secretary of State, John Hay, had instructed the Hague delegates that "any practical propositions" based upon ideas to protect those *hors de combat* should receive "earnest support". Indeed, in his instructions he expressed the hope that "The proposed Conference promised to offer an opportunity thus far unequaled in the history of the world for initiating a series of negotiations that may lead to important practical results."[26] Despite its prior reservations, the United States did not have many objections to the idea of ameliorating the suffering of the victims of war.

Andrew D. White, head of the American delegation to the Hague Conference, recorded in his diary the events and the occasionally stressful negotiating process.[27] Interestingly, according to his and most accounts, the prospect of codifying the laws of war does not seem to have captured the imagination of the participants or the throngs of groups and individuals who sought to influence the Conference. Instead most of the hope lay in the idea of ending wars for good through the establishment of a mandatory international court for the peaceful settlement of disputes—this was certainly one of White's main goals. White recalls that the American delegation spent a lot of time trying to achieve the international court, and convincing a very sceptical German delegation of the need to agree to the final documents of the Conference. The correspondence between White and the German Chancellor von Bülow is an interesting mix of religious-inspired humanitarianism and *Realpolitik*.[28]

Despite the lack of enthusiasm, the agreement pertaining to the laws of war at the Conference was arguably the most successful project undertaken by the representatives present. The Hague Rules successfully codified the principles of the Lieber Code and two of the documents which had taken inspiration from it: the failed Brussels Declaration of 1874 and the Oxford Manual of 1880, which had been prepared by the Institut de Droit International but not formally adopted by any nation.

Therefore, although the United States refrained from humanitarian treaties until late in the nineteenth century, it was clear throughout this period that Europe and the United States continued to speak the same humanitarian language even when it was codified only by European powers. In fact, despite European attempts to codify the laws of war between 1864 and 1880, the US, with its Lieber Code, continued to have some of the strongest laws of war legislation in the world despite its refusal to sign formal treaties.

However, despite the ever increasing humanitarian movement and conferences which took place in the late nineteenth century, this period also some incredibly bloody conflicts throughout the world as the European powers fought "savages" in the "uncivilized" lands of Africa, Asia and, of course, North America. The rules between European nations had been carefully crafted, but there was no doubt that such rules did not apply to those who did not fight in customary European fashion. Therefore, although the United States had some of the strongest rules on the conduct of warfare of any "civilized" nations, they were largely not applied to most of the conflicts it fought. And, as the next section of this chapter will demonstrate, even when the rules were considered to apply, the results were not always entirely humane.

Wars with the First Nations and Manifest Destiny

Although the First Nations peoples were deemed to have "lost" the War of 1812, this did not mean they were willing to take their "defeat" lying down. The American army continued to battle First Nations warriors in skirmishes, as in the Black Hawk War of 1832 which, like so many of the skirmishes involving First Nations peoples, led to villages on both sides being burned and civilians and prisoners tortured and killed.

The battles continued through the Civil War period, when the United States simultaneously fought the Sioux in Minnesota and the Confederate armies in the South. In comparing the treatment received by both groups, it is first interesting to note that neither group opposing the government of the United States was treated as legal combatants. As mentioned above, the South was not entitled to the full protection of the laws of war (as defined in the Lieber Code) because the Confederate forces did not adhere to it. On the other hand, as in earlier wars, the First Nations were considered savages who did not have the opportunity to be a part of the shared international law of civilized nations. In 1818, Secretary of State (and future president) John Quincy Adams cited Vattel:

When at war... with a ferocious nation, which observes no rules and grants no quarter, they may be chastised in the persons of those of them who may be taken; they are of the number of the guilty and by this rigor the attempt may be made to bring them to a sense of the laws of humanity... if he has to contend with an inhuman enemy, often guilty of such excesses, he may take the lives of some of his prisoners, and treat them as his own people have been treated.[29]

And there is little reason to think that this had changed by 1860. Throughout this period, the First Nations would find themselves considered hostile, rounded up and placed into reservations or killed should they resist the US government—which they inevitably did. While it would be incorrect to suggest that prisoner of war camps housing the Southern prisoners were luxurious, Confederate soldiers were treated far more fairly and with much more dignity than the warriors of the First Nations ever were.

Given that Adams invokes an international lawyer to support his argument, it is clear that the United States was not alone in the treatment of its "savages". Rather, at time such treatment of the "uncivilized" was consistent with the military practices of the European powers who fought formal restrained wars against one another but used very harsh tactics in their colonial wars.[30] Yet, America's situation still remained unique in some respects. In the words of Peter Maguire:

It became increasingly difficult to justify an expansive, essentially imperialistic foreign policy within the framework of an egalitarian political ideology.... More than the obvious gap between words and deeds, from the beginning there was a tension between America's much-vaunted ethical and legal principles and its practical policy interests as an emerging world power.[31]

In other words, America by the beginning of the twentieth century simultaneously championed rights, law and the rule of law—and denied these protections where affording them would have clashed with the national interest. This, Maguire calls "strategic legalism": "the use of laws or legal arguments to further policy objectives, irrespective of facts or laws."[32]

Maguire goes so far as to describe the American interpretation of international law at this time as "cynical". Whether one agrees or not with this description, it is certainly possible to point to a dualist trend in American thought on international law. First there was America, the idealist who championed rights, and second there was the expanding empire, first over North America and then overseas. This tension only grew as America increasingly developed international interests abroad, for example in China and Japan.

What is key here is that these policies, and America's understanding of international law, including the laws of war, were increasingly seen through the prism of "manifest destiny". Although it was the same manifest destiny which had delayed the United States from signing on to humanitarian treaties, there was more to the concept than staying out of European affairs when it came to international law. The messianic overtones which accompanied the founding of the republic argued that America was to be the "shining city on a hill" and represent all that was good and possible for civilization. However, as the United States grew increasingly expansionist, those groups that opposed its influence were increasingly seen as standing in the way of civilization. Civilization, in return, was no longer obliged to provide protections to those who were standing in the way of progress.

These sentiments can be seen in American engagements from the Revolutionary War up to the First World War. Although one often reads about the strength of the isolationist movement in the United States at this time, America fought wars with Britain, Spain, Mexico, China and the Filipino insurgents (just to name the most prominent). Yet, while the wars with the European powers were relatively restrained and adhered to the laws of war as they were known, those who were not European, and were seen as rejecting the civilizing influence of the United States, were treated as savages and outlaws, and America's power would come down on them hard.

Although many of the founding fathers of the American republic considered the First Nations to be barbarians, there were others, such as Thomas
Jefferson and Henry Knox, who wanted to demonstrate the purity of America's institutions and the moral worth of the republic's enterprise in policies
towards the First Nations. They therefore placed much emphasis on reasoning
and negotiation with the tribes with the eventual goal of converting them to
"civilization" as Americans.[33] This republican idealism can be seen in policies
that provided the First Nations tribes with gardening implements in the hope
that they would turn from their nomadic ways and cultivate the land like the
American settlers.

However, not everyone subscribed to these "enlightened" views: the western settlers had no problem with clearing out rather than converting the First
Nations. Apart from the fact that their uncivilized ways were seen as making
them unworthy to inhabit the land, many First Nations tribes had twice sided
with the British, as discussed in the previous chapter. Therefore, as "losers" in
the conflict, the First Nations forfeited their rights and land claims in the new
republic. The culture of suspicion and hatred of the First Nations peoples, no
doubt continually inspired by the memories of their participation in the
Anglo-French wars prior to the Revolution, had been perpetuated and added
to the sense that they did deserve any rights to American territory.

Ultimately, as the perception grew that there was a need for more land,
these divergent positions were united. The view that the First Nations had no
rights to soil that they refused to cultivate was ever more being accepted. In
this regard, war with the First Nations tribes was increasingly seen as a just
war.[34] The outcome of the fighting between 1775 and 1815 was that the West
was now considered open for American settlement and the First Nations'
claims were delegitimized even further.[35] By 1850s, in the face of the California Gold Rush and a general push westward, the land promised to the First
Nations, the so-called Permanent Indian Frontier, was abandoned and an all-
out war over settlements began.

Much of the fighting took place right before, during and after the Civil
War. As the regular army was distracted by the conflict, the forces fighting
the First Nations were mostly made up of citizen-soldier volunteer armies.
Many of the confrontations were sparked when civilian-settlers provoked the
increasingly frustrated and volatile First Nations tribes. As one historian
describes it, "In a sense, the Army was left with the dirty work by others. It
was called in at the last moment, usually, to clean up a mess made by civilians."[36]
Still, this did not mean that the tactics of the army were restrained. Soldiers

were known for sparking confrontations with the First Nations during tense moments.

The First Nations, of course, had not been reacting to the encroaching Americans peacefully. They continued to wage their deadly way of warfare which fell outside of European conventions, in daring raids against American settlements. Therefore, "because the customary laws of war forbade guerrilla warfare, the taking of hostages, and the massacre of civilians, the early colonists and the US government never recognized the legitimacy of the American Indian resistance."[37] So, when First Nations warriors were captured in the fighting that occurred throughout the nineteenth century, they were not charged with violations of the customary laws of war, because the US did not consider them lawful combatants. To grant them such a status would have been to recognize a right to wage war.[38]

Thus the skirmishes with the First Nations tribes quickly became a part of a larger war of extermination on both sides. First Nations leaders, tired of the lies and false promises of Washington, would attack the encroaching settlements without mercy–attacking soldier, civilian, woman and child alike. The American forces responded in kind–attacking anyone and everyone within range of their bullets. Soldiers would boast of not taking prisoners–and those who were taken were often subject to torture and abuse. Scalping and desecration of the dead, which was not uncommon in the War of 1812, continued to be rampant on both sides.

America's 'small wars' and the laws of war

Given its preoccupation with western expansion, the Civil War and recovery from that war–not to mention an inherent distrust of all things European–the nineteenth century is often characterized as a period of isolationist tendencies for the United States. This does explain why the United States was reluctant to sign and ratify treaties–even those with a humanitarian purpose–during most of the century. However, as Max Boot argues, the label "isolationist" is misleading. In his book *The Savage Wars of Peace*, he provides an account of just some of the many expeditions abroad undertaken by privateers, sailors and marines. He concludes that far from being isolationist, "American foreign policy in the nineteenth century can best be described as unilateralist, meaning that America acted without benefit of formal allies to defend its interests."[39] In fact, the United States had been fighting abroad since 1804, when it fought the Barbary Pirates. And although the primary campaigns of manifest destiny were waged within the boundaries of the United States, American ships continued to explore and seek out markets and ports overseas in South America, the Caribbean and the South Pacific.

Throughout these journeys, Americans would encounter the local inhabitants of these places whose customs, like those of the First Nations peoples, were foreign and strange. Eventually, owing to either a perceived slight, a conflict of interest or a misunderstanding, many of these conflicts would turn violent and blood would be shed. On such occasions, where the small bands of Americans found themselves surrounded by hostile locals who did not have European conventions of warfare in mind, the laws of war were probably not the foremost consideration. Boot describes a pattern in these meetings between nineteenth century Americans and their frequently unfriendly hosts:

Yankees arrive with the best of intentions, but soon find themselves sucked into the vortex of war. During the nineteenth century this pattern would repeat itself from the Falklands to Formosa, from Sumatra to Samoa, from China to Chile. After killing some natives, the Americans seldom stayed long;...

The U.S. strategy, if that is the right word for such a haphazard enterprise, might best be characterized as "butcher and bolt"–a bit of slang popular in Britain's Indian Army to describe punitive expeditions against troublemaking tribes, expeditions designed not to occupy territory but to "learn 'em a lesson".[40]

These skirmishes were undeclared wars where neither belligerent (for the majority of the nineteenth century) would be a party to any sort of international convention. Because there was no way to rapidly communicate back with Washington, any campaign would be fought according to the whims of the commander–which would, of course, therefore govern how enemies and civilians should be treated. Given the circumstances under which these conflicts were fought, there is little wonder that the Lieber Code was rarely, if ever, applied.

The Americans, naturally, had superior firepower on their side. But the often deadly guerrilla-style tactics employed by local resistance to the US presence created difficult and frustrating environments for those sailors or marines abroad. Perhaps the best example of how this could go wrong was one of the bigger "small wars" fought by the United States, in the Philippines.

War in the Philippines

As the process of settling the West neared completion by the end of the nineteenth century, America found itself in a war with Spain which started over Cuba but resulted in the destruction of the Spanish Empire and the US in control of Cuba, Guam, Puerto Rico and the Philippines. The war was not only one of the first serious military engagements that the American republic had fought overseas, it also was the first time America had colonies within its possession.

The actual war with Spain was over very quickly on all fronts, although the war in the Philippines was more or less a sideshow to the one in Cuba;[41] the American fleet had destroyed the Spanish fleet and with the help of the local independence movements, Spanish soldiers were quickly routed. The laws of war were, for the most part, respected and followed by the Americans and the Spanish. In fact, both sides agreed to abide by articles 6 and 15 of the 1868 Additional Articles relating to the Condition of the Wounded in War, which allowed each side to collect the shipwrecked and wounded at sea after a military engagement.[42] The war between the Spanish and the native Filipinos who were fighting for independence, however, was brutal. In skirmishes before the US intervention, the Filipino leader Emilio Aguinaldo y Famy oversaw the massacre by the rebel forces of fleeing Spanish soldiers.[43] If the Americans were paying any attention, it was an ominous sign of things to come.

Almost immediately after the Spanish capitulated and the Americans took over there were difficulties with the native Filipinos who, somewhat naïvely, expected the Americans to help them throw off the Spanish yoke and then leave them to form their own independent government. The United States had different plans in mind for the islands, for two reasons. The first was the concern that the collapse of the Spanish in the Philippines would result in a vacuum in Asia that would be filled by the Germans, Russians or Japanese.[44] Second, although President McKinley had been reluctant to engage in war with the Spanish, there were others who believed that now was the time for America to bring its enlightened message and civilization to the rest of the world. The future Senator Albert Jeremiah Beveridge told an enthusiastic audience in 1898: "We are a conquering race... American law, American order, American civilization and the American flag will plant themselves on shores hitherto bloody and benighted, but by those agencies of God henceforth to be made beautiful and bright."[45]

The US saw itself as a different colonizer–differing from its European counterparts because it would apply an "enlightened" colonialism on its new subject-citizens. It would build schools, hospitals and roads and help the Filipinos to develop their own society based on American principles. However, in return, the US expected unquestioning loyalty and compliance. "Their welfare is our welfare," said McKinley, "but neither their aspirations nor ours can be realized until our authority is acknowledged and unquestioned."[46] The Americans would not take lightly the rejection of their attempts to bring the benefits of civilization.

Therefore, when war broke out on 4 February 1899, the legitimacy of the resisting Filipinos was not acknowledged. The subsequent conflict was termed "the Philippine Insurrection". As one historian writes:

...the euphemism contrived to convey the impression that they were subduing a rebellion against [the American] lawful authority. For the same reason, they later referred to their Filipino enemies as insurgents and rebels, and in some instances...bandits. But to the Filipino nationalists, America had embarked on a war of conquest against an independence movement that had formed a government no less legitimate than the young republic founded by the American revolutionaries a century earlier.[47]

The tense situation that followed had serious results for the ensuing conflict. After some disastrous fighting where the Filipinos had tried to take on the Americans in conventional style fighting, they switched to guerrilla style tactics by the end of 1899. Aguinaldo's new strategy was intended to protract the war until either the US Army broke down from disease and exhaustion or the American public demanded a withdrawal.[48] Therefore, they employed traps such as sharpened bamboo stakes in concealed pits and spears and arrows triggered by sudden trip wires. Americans taken prisoner could expect brutal treatment–there were several reports of American POWs found dead castrated with their genitals in their mouths, or eaten alive by ants.[49] Additionally, the Americans were frustrated by the fact that the Filipino militia operated as part-time guerrillas who would otherwise continue their normal civilian lives when not out in the field, thus rendering it difficult to tell friend from foe.[50] This resulted in the Americans burning down villages in attempts to wipe out the insurgents.

Part of the problem, as Boot points out, was that for all of their fighting the First Nations peoples, the Americans had still not learned to cope with guerrilla-style tactics:

Even though its chief occupation throughout much of the nineteenth century was fighting Indians [sic], the army never bothered to develop a doctrine of anti–guerilla warfare because the generals always viewed the Indian Wars as a temporary diversion from their "real" job–preparing to fight a conventional army.[51]

In trying to come up with a solution, the Americans came down on these new tactics hard. US Chief Administrator (and future president) William Howard Taft described the Filipino resistance as "a conspiracy of murder and assassination" and proposed that the enemy troops be executed or exiled as they were captured.[52] Arthur MacArthur, the US Commander in the Philippines, declared in December 1900 that guerrillas would be considered war rebels and traitors and would be punished accordingly. Captives unaffiliated with a "regularly organized force" were not to be classified as soldiers and were to be denied the rights of prisoners of war. This, argued MacArthur, was part of the laws of war as defined by the Lieber Code. Unfortunately, this had the effect of delegitimizing virtually all of the Filipino participants, whatever their status.[53] Military commissions tried and executed captured guerrillas and army provost courts operating in areas subjected to martial law were given a free hand to try and punish suspects without evidence.[54]

There are many incidents which could illustrate the brutality of the Philippine insurgency, but one particularly sad example will be sufficient for our purposes here. In September 1902, the Filipino forces used deception in carrying out a vicious attack against a US Army detachment at Balangiga, resulting in the death and mutilation of forty-eight of the seventy-four soldiers stationed there. In planning his retaliation for the attack and out of a sense of frustration at the continuing insurgency, Brigadier General Jacob H. Smith ordered his officers to turn the island of Samar into a "howling wilderness" and to shoot any males over the age of ten. "I want no prisoners. I wish you to kill and burn. The more you kill and burn, the better you will please me."[55] The men under his command carried out his orders perfectly. Smith would later face court-martial for his actions despite the fact that no clear laws governing the use of force were in place. Interestingly, or perhaps tellingly, Smith was not tried for murder, but for "conduct to the prejudice of good order and discipline." As one commentator describes it, Smith "was tried for making a verbal gaffe".[56] Smith was found guilty of the charge but the punishment for his actions was only admonition–a verbal scolding. This caused many to denounce the sentence as far too lenient. To ease the outcry, President Roosevelt, upon the advice of Secretary of War Elihu Root, compulsorily retired Smith.

Dualistic tendencies?

At this point it may be useful to reflect on some trends that seem to be emerging. Perhaps the most significant of these is the question of whether a hypocritical distinction was being made by the United States concerning prisoners of war. Considering the Southern violations against Union prisoners and the attitude of the Union government towards the legitimacy of the South's cause, why were the Confederate soldiers treated humanely and the First Nations treated far worse? As one historian writes:

However, given the Confederates' early battlefield successes, the Union had no choice but to grant them *de facto* recognition by largely observing the laws of war on the battlefield. Even though the United States considered the Confederates rebels, they were not 'others' who stood outside the circle and so not considered barbaric. This distinction was reserved for racial and cultural others who flouted the military customs of the West. The Confederates were both white and American.[57]

There was a similar situation in 1899 as the Americans fought a savage war in the Philippines and, at the same time, were sitting down on the other side of the world laying out the laws of war with other "civilized" nations at The Hague. By the beginning of the twentieth century, although the Americans continued to claim that their republic differed from European nations in terms of its policies and in its attempts to spread civilization, it very well matched the Europeans in its treatment of non-Western peoples. The Lieber Code, which in turn had greatly influenced subsequent international treaties, was based on European thinking on the laws of war. The different treatment handed out to captured First Nations warriors and Confederate soldiers (even though both had violated the Lieber principles) was not at all inconsistent in American eyes.

Actually, the effect of the Lieber Code went even further than that: it was on several occasions specifically invoked by the Americans to justify their actions. MacArthur invoked it to severely punish civilians thought to be aiding the guerrillas and to distinguish between regular organized forces and "war rebels".[58] Major Littleton Waller, brought before a military court in Manila in March 1902 for war crimes, had planned to defend himself using the Lieber Code which authorized reprisals and described them as "the sternest feature of war".[59] Major General Smith, who had ordered the attack on Samar, made a similar argument and claimed that his actions were totally justified under the Lieber Code.[60] Specifically, he invoked Article 24 which states:

The almost universal rule in remote times was, and continues to be with barbarous armies, that the private individual of the hostile country is destined to suffer every privation of liberty and protection and every disruption of family ties. Protection was, and still is with uncivilized people, the exception.

The laws of war themselves were therefore invoked to excuse brutal conduct. As one historian explains, the main purpose of MacArthur's invoking of the Lieber Code in the Philippines "...was to educate Filipinos on their violations of the laws of war and the punishments that awaited transgressors. As a statement of policy, it provided little guidance and there was much debate and confusion over what punitive measures were sanctioned."[61]

Therefore, the major contribution of MacArthur's proclamation that invoked the Lieber Code was to "provide official sanction for some of the more stringent policies either advocated or already applied in the field."[62] So while one writer may argue that "it was ironic that the new international humanitarian laws came at a time when America's Indian wars were entering their most brutal phase,"[63] it is perhaps less so when put in the context of the way America sought to legitimize these policies of dealing with the First Nations and the Filipinos. Tough political justifications and questions of "dirty hands" could be avoid by invoking a Code that was more or less seen as neutral and customary by Western powers.

Walter Russell Mead offers one further explanation as to why this was the case in his examination of the "traditions" of American foreign policy.[64] He uses four schools of thought named after Thomas Jefferson, Alexander Hamilton, Woodrow Wilson and Andrew Jackson to explain approaches to American foreign policy. Jeffersonianism, Hamiltonianism and Wilsonianism represent emphasis on maintaining a democratic system, the protection of commerce, and the promotion of moral principle respectively. In terms of international law and the rule of war, Jacksonianism differs from these three traditions in its emphasis on populist values and military power. As Mead describes it: "Jacksonianism is less an intellectual or political movement than it is an expression of the social, cultural and religious values of a large portion of the American public."[65] Therefore:

Jacksonians are more likely to tax political leaders with a failure to employ vigorous measures than to worry about the niceties of international law. Of all the major currents in American society, Jacksonians have the least regard for international law and international practice. In general Jacksonians prefer the rule of custom to the written law, and that is as true in the international sphere as it is in personal relations at home. Jacksonians believe that there is an honour code in international life... and those who live by the code will be treated under it. But those who violate the code, who commit terrorist acts against innocent civilians in peacetime, for example, forfeit its protection and deserve no more consideration than rats.[66]

Mead argues that while the Jacksonian notion of national honour prohibits America from carrying out some military activities, it also often spurs America on to some of its bloodiest battles. The notion of honour also carries onto the battlefield. Jacksonians, according to Mead, recognize two kinds of enemy and two kinds of fighting. Honourable enemies fight in a clean fight and are entitled to be opposed in the same way; dishonourable enemies fight dirty wars and in that case rules do not apply.[67] This then helps to explain the dualistic tendencies–why Civil War soldiers, seen as honourable fighters, were treated well and the First Nations warriors often were not:

In Jacksonian terms, Indian war tactics comprised a dishonourable, unscrupulous, and cowardly form of combat. Anger at such tactics led Jacksonians to abandon the restraints imposed by their own war codes, and the ugly conflicts along the frontier spiraled into a series of genocidal conflicts in which each side felt the other was violating every standard of humane conduct.[68]

Therefore, a Jacksonian point of view ("whose influence in American history has been, and remains, enormous"[69]) does acknowledge a set of international laws governing conflict–but prefers to think about such "laws" as customary rules. These rules apply as long as both sides in the conflict agree to abide by them. However, where these rules have been violated, there is little mercy for perpetrators. Since foreign foes have forced America into war, whatever casualties the other side suffers are self-evidently the fault of their own leaders rather than of the United States. Therefore Jacksonian opinion takes a broad view of the permissible targets in war and views targeting civilian morale as legitimate.[70]

Mead's argument is a persuasive one and helps to explain the dualistic tendency in American foreign policy towards the laws of war. Interestingly, he points out that all sides believe that there are norms governing conflict, but suggests that the influential Jacksonians are willing to "take the gloves off" should those rules be violated or should the need arise.

However, such influence can only be said to go so far. By 1900, the terrible fighting and harsh policies in the Philippines would provoke outrage among many Americans. East Coast papers would occasionally speak out against the mass execution of First Nations prisoners and there was much outrage at the actions of American troops at Samar. The headline of the *New York Journal* on 8 April 1902 read "KILL ALL: MAJOR WALLER ORDERED TO MASSACRE THE FILIPINOS" and the media vilified the perpetrators of the action.[71] While it is true that outrage over the actions against the First Nations peoples was more muted, the public anger over policies in the Philippines had a significant impact on that war. In fact, after 1902, the war dramatically lost popularity in the United States and became more a source of embarrassment than anything else. The brutality of the conflict (on both sides) greatly tarnished the perception of the just cause the Americans claimed. While they could approve of the civilizing missions abroad, especially when contextualized as combating threats to the republic, Americans were becoming less inclined to tolerate massacres and collective punishments in order to obtain their goals.

And, in fact, another encounter with the British over prisoners of war could only make this stance look duplicitous. On 16 October 1900, at the same time as difficulties in the Philippines were beginning, Secretary of State John Hay directed the American Ambassador to Britain to investigate the conditions of twenty-two prisoners, captured during the Boer War, who claimed American citizenship. The American consul in South Africa was denied visitation rights, and there was great concern over the fact that the men were shipped to Ceylon for detention. In his letter Hay wrote:

The principles of public law which exclude all rigor or severity in the treatment of prisoners of war beyond what may be needful to their safety imply their nonsubjection to avoidable danger from any cause. These admitted principles have found conventional expression in treaties, as in article 24 of the treaties of 1785 and 1799 between the United States and Prussia, and the enlightened practice therein specified to be followed with respect to the custody of prisoners of war is believe to represent the general view of modern nations, as it certainly does the sentiment of humanity and the law of nature which its claims rest.[72]

Such "enlightened practice" was clearly conditional.

America and the laws of war 1900–1952

The eighteenth and nineteenth centuries provided the framework for how the US would cope with total war at the beginning of the twentieth. As we have seen, the results of the previous 130 years had been somewhat mixed and the new republic's ideological foundations had played a complicated role in this. Americans wanted to demonstrate that they were different from other nations, yet relied on the European laws of war (and implemented them–or not–accordingly). The impetus to continue with its civilizing mission also played a role in promoting a dualistic tendency regarding implementation of the laws of war. Clearly, the US record was not perfect–but then again, the same could be said for most, if not all nations. Britain, Germany, Belgium and France were certainly not known for compassion in warfare. Perhaps the only thing exceptional about America in this regard was that it saw itself as an exception–albeit one that followed the traditional laws of nations.

While the dualistic tendencies would continue into the twentieth century, US policy towards the laws of war, including its own system of military justice, was becoming increasingly standardized into a more cohesive doctrine. In 1882 it had begun to formally participate in drafting humanitarian treaties and ratifying them. In 1901 and 1903 the United States responded favourably to an invitation by the Swiss government to update the 1864 Geneva Conventions, but this time it was the European powers that were reluctant to attend.[73] Although the United States, along with several other European powers, suggested that achieving the goals outlined by the ICRC could be achieved at the Second Hague Peace Conference of 1907 and that the two conferences should be combined, the Geneva Conference went ahead separately, culminating in the 1906 Geneva Convention which sought to tighten up and make more specific the language of the 1864 Geneva Convention, as well as adding protections for sick and wounded falling into the hands of an enemy. The US also participated in the Second Hague Conference which resulted in the 1907 Hague Convention, but for the most part there was not much progress made and the Conference was widely seen as failure at the time. The two Conventions differ only slightly from each other and of the states that had ratified the 1899 treaty, seventeen did not sign on to the 1907 Convention.

Interestingly, Elihu Root, now Secretary of State, gave a warning in the instructions to the American delegates at the 1907 Conference: "...the object of the conference is agreement, and not compulsion... If such conferences are to be made occasions for trying to force nations into positions which they consider against their interests, the powers can not be expected to send representatives to them."[74]

Root added, "The immediate results of such a conference must always be limited to a small part of the field which the more sanguine have hoped to see covered... Each conference will inevitably make further progress and, by successive steps, results may be accomplished which have formerly appeared impossible." His comments are interesting in that they seem somewhat defensive. They suggest a continual need for the United States to stand up for itself against the great powers of Europe in terms of treaty making. However, they also suggest a sentiment somewhere between a moderate scepticism and a cautious-progressive outlook with regard to the evolution of international law. Root was remaining sceptical of what international agreements could achieve, and yet believed that progress would occur as long as the parties involved could agree to a small step-by-step approach. Root, a lawyer from New York, had been Secretary for War from 1899 to 1904 and was Secretary of State from 1905 to 1909 before he eventually entered the Senate. As one of his biographers notes, this instruction was part of his "long-range" view that believed failures were necessary in the carrying out of any human endeavour, including international law.[75] However, Root and President Roosevelt did believe that the United States had a stake in world peace. Despite the caution in his Instructions, the Hague Conferences represented the way forward for Root: periodic gatherings of nations which would hammer out agreements on small points.[76] For the most part, this is how the United States would proceed towards international law, including the laws of war, until 1918.

The First World War

Even though the US had signed and ratified humanitarian agreements before the war, it could sometimes take a peculiar view as to the laws of war and how they applied to a conflict. Fulfilling an obligation of the 1899 Hague Convention that "The High Contracting Parties shall issue instructions to their armed land forces, which shall be in conformity with the 'Regulations respecting the laws and customs of war on land' annexed to the present Convention" (and perhaps sensing that tensions were brewing on the European continent), the United Stated drafted its first law of war manual, published in 1914.[77] However, after entering World War I in 1917 (and reissuing a revised draft of the 1914 manual), the United States took the position that neither the Hague Rules nor the Geneva Conventions applied to it. In a telegram to the US Minister in Switzerland, Pleasant A. Stovall, Secretary of State Robert Lansing wrote that "The Government of the United States... does not consider the provisions of the Geneva convention of 1906, or of the Hague Convention No. X of the 1907, as binding on the United States in the present war."[78] This was also confirmed in a telegram to Stovall from Acting Secretary of State Frank L. Polk which stated: "... that the United States does not regard the Hague conventions as applicable in the present war..."[79]

The ICRC, which had been working to monitor POWs in the conflict, wrote to express its "astonishment" that the United States government had taken such a position:

... we cannot well understand how today America says that the convention is not binding upon her.

At present, there are only such states as Liberia and Costa Rica among the belligerents who have not signed the convention, and certainly they play an insignificant part in the present war. Therefore we cannot help thinking that America's action is a dangerous precedent.[80]

The letter from the ICRC went on to warn the United States that if this was the position of its government, it would "prevent us from doing anything in favor of her prisoners" as action was always carried out under the Geneva and Hague Conventions. However, the United States continued to stand by this decision, arguing in a telegram that: "...this government does not consider the Geneva convention binding in present war on account provisions of article 24 thereof, and because all belligerents not signatory to convention. Similar interpretation has been constantly given to Hague conventions since beginning of war in 1914."[81]

The shock of the ICRC is somewhat understandable, considering that this seems to be an incredibly literalist approach to the Geneva and Hague treaties. According to this understanding the 1907 Hague Convention, which had never been ratified by Serbia, could not apply. This meant the 1899 Rules were in effect, but this too was no longer the case after Liberia entered the conflict on 4 August 1917.

Yet this does not mean that the United States considered the conflict to be lawless or without regulation. Complaints made by the United States about the treatment of prisoners of war by Germany and its allies frequently invoked the laws of war. Besides diplomatic wrangling over payment for the work of prisoners and attempts to arrange an exchange of medical personnel, the major concerns for the United States regarding American prisoners were that some were allegedly being forced to work in mines and held in poor conditions with insufficient food and that they suffered frequent beatings from prison guards. Regarding these allegations the US demanded:

that the German Government immediately take such steps as will effectively guarantee to American prisoners in its hand, both in letter and in spirit, that humane treatment which by all the principles of international law and usage is to be expected from the Government of a civilized state and its officials;... [82]

This seemingly contradictory policy seems to make more sense given that rather than invoking formal humanitarian treaties, the United States threatened flat-out retaliation against German prisoners of war in its hands.[83] As already discussed, threatening retaliation was not always an advisable policy as it could worsen the treatment of America's own prisoners. But as far as attempting to improve the treatment of its captured servicemen was concerned, the United States followed two other policies. First, rather than invoking the Geneva or Hague treaties, the American government took the position that its treaties with Prussia signed between 1799 and 1828 covered the law which applied to the conflict; this ensured a basic level of treatment for prisoners and a legal starting point.[84] Yet, given the statements demanding humane treatment in accordance with the principles of the laws of war, it is clear that the United States was invoking customary international law. As one scholar notes of the principles of the 1899 Hague Rules in their relation to the First World War: "It would seem then that these requirements were precisely the terms which any civilized and self-respecting nation would impose upon itself in the treatment of its prisoners without the obligation of any treaty stipulation."[85]

However, while there may have been a universally accepted view of what "humane treatment" was in 1899, 1906 and 1907, the Americans decided, probably given the unprecedented nature of the war and some of the terrible reports that had been coming out of prisons on the continent, that setting out the treatment to be given to prisoners in the greatest of detail was in their interest.[86] In June 1918, the United States proposed that a conference on prisoners of war be held between itself and Germany–originally for the purpose of repatriating invalid prisoners, but this was quickly expanded to the overall treatment and exchange of all prisoners on both sides. The conference began on 25 September 1918 and a document with 184 articles and several annexes was eventually laid out in incredible detail. Where the vague "humane treatment" had been the governing principle, this was replaced by regulations that went so far as to indicate how high off the floor a prisoner's bed had to be in centimetres. Yet the agreement, signed on 11 November 1918–Armistice Day–clearly would not have been much use to prisoners on either side; it was immediately superseded in effect by the terms of the ceasefire.

Again this seems rather puzzling. If the United States was so concerned about the treatment of prisoners of war, why did it not use the international treaties that virtually every other party to the conflict had signed? Even if it wished to maintain the argument that the humanitarian treaties did not apply, why did it not seek to at least use the Hague Rules as a declaration of state practice? This can only seem more peculiar considering the incredibly long and detailed agreement regarding the treatment of prisoners that it eventually developed with Germany, which was clearly the most progressive treaty on prisoners in existence at the time. But if there was a rush or a concern for the welfare of prisoners, why did the US wait until the end of the war to come to an agreement?

One international lawyer offers a possible solution to this dilemma:

The Hague conferences did not repeal the existing body of war law and substitute a new code in its place. They confined their efforts to defining and stating in precise rules the established usages and the best practice of the past. To maintain, therefore, that the essential parts of the Hague Conventions were not binding because the Conventions were never formally ratified by all the powers in accordance with the procedure specified, is to hold that the larger body of well-established and universally accepted rules of war is without obligatory force. The provisions of the Hague Conventions which are merely declaratory of the existing law and practice were therefore no less binding that that other large portion of international law which the Hague conferences did not attempt to define and embody in the conventions which they adopted.[87]

It might seem to be cheating, but such a position would allow the United States to claim the benefits of the laws of war while maintaining a strict literalist stance on humanitarian treaties. But aside from the finer points of international law, there may be some *Realpolitik* involved here as well. It is interesting to consider whether the United States could really have taken such a position if it had not been on the side that was obviously winning the war. Regardless, the treaty between the United States and Germany regarding the treatment of prisoners of war is interesting–even if only as a statement of policy as to what the "modern" standard treatment of prisoners of war should be.[88]

Given the incredible scale of the war, the numbers of prisoners on both sides and the suffering that many encountered, it became clear to humanitarian agencies such as the International Committee of the Red Cross that a further convention on prisoners' rights was needed. Still, in terms of international law, the immediate post-war period was more concerned with attempts to outlaw war altogether rather than to mitigate its effects.[89] In 1925 the United States again responded favourably to an invitation from the Swiss government to participate in a conference for furthering protection of prisoners of war. To prepare for the conference, a study was drafted and there was extensive correspondence between the Departments of State, War and the Navy to formulate the American position on the matter.[90] The Conference met during July 1929 and succeeded in updating 1906 Convention and developing a separate convention relative to the treatment of prisoners of war. Significantly, unlike previous humanitarian treaties which were effective only if ratified by all of the belligerents (through a *si omnes* clause), the Conventions reached in 1929 were effective for all of the states which ratified it.[91]

The Second World War

It is, perhaps, one of those ironies of history that just as the strongest regulations for the protection of prisoners of war had been established, a world war that would see incredible amounts of suffering for prisoners was set to begin. All of the major players of the Second World War, with the notable exception of the Soviet Union, had signed (but not necessarily ratified) the 1929 Geneva Conventions. However, prisoners captured by the Japanese or those along the Eastern Front would receive none of the protections laid down in the treaty text.

There was no question that the United States believed the 1929 Geneva Conventions were applicable to the conflict. In fact, in 1941, American diplomats in Russia spent a considerable amount of time trying to convince the Soviets that it would be in their interests to adhere to the Convention. In August 1941, the Soviet Union informed the United States that it would observe the 1907 Hague Rules, the 1925 Gas Protocol and the 1929 Geneva Conventions, but that they would only be applied to Germany on a basis of reciprocity–a basis that clearly was not coming.[92] The United States was interested in helping the War Prisoners' Aid Committee of the YMCA get assistance to German POWs in the Soviet Union and to give the American Red Cross freedom of observation. Additionally, there was some concern that if the Germans did not treat Soviet prisoners according to the Geneva Conventions, then suffering might be made worse for all prisoners captured by the Axis powers, regardless of nationality.[93] When it was clear that the Soviet Union would not be adhering to the Convention because of the way Germany had treated its soldiers, the US also tried to encourage the two sides to reach a formal understanding or agreement regarding the treatment of prisoners, but this too was rejected. After five months of trying, the American diplomats in the Soviet Union gave up on this endeavour.

By this time, however, the United States had entered the war after the Japanese attack on Pearl Harbor. On 18 December 1941, Secretary of State Cordell Hull informed the Swiss government that the United States would apply the provisions of the Geneva Conventions to the conflict. Hull also requested that the Swiss government find out if the Japanese government would reciprocate even though it had only signed those Conventions and had not ratified them. The Japanese did not immediately reply. On 13 January 1942, Hull outlined the steps that the United States was taking with regard to meeting its requirements under the Geneva Conventions and requested a reply, via the Swiss government, as to whether the Axis powers were carrying out similar measures. Again Hull requested a response from the Japanese government as to its intentions regarding the humanitarian treaties.[94]

Eventually the Japanese responded that they would apply the Geneva Convention on condition of reciprocity, but it soon became clear that this would not be the case. American concern for its prisoners grew in 1942 as the Japanese only allowed ICRC officials to visit prisons and detention camps on Japanese soil and in Shanghai where there were few Americans being held. By

September the United States issued complaints that it had not received any news or names of the American prisoners that had been taken in the Philippines. The situation only seemed to worsen as time went on. In October, Japanese radio broadcast that the Imperial Government would execute American airmen for war crimes. As concern grew, Hull wrote a lengthy telegram to the Japanese government complaining of the "instances of gross mistreatment suffered by American civilians and prisoners of war in the power of the Japanese Government in violation... of the Geneva Prisoners of War Convention of 1929..."[95]

Indeed, the situation on the ground for American prisoners (in fact, prisoners of all nationalities) in Japanese hands was incredibly poor. A Japanese military ethos which looked upon those who had surrendered as without honour or dignity was not a good basis upon which to apply the laws of war. Prisoners were forced to work hard for long hours and given insufficient amounts of food upon which to survive. In perhaps one of the most infamous episodes of the war involving American prisoners, the "Bataan Death March", thousands of American prisoners, already exhausted from battle, were forced to march for three days with no food or medical treatment. Those who could not keep up were left to die on the side of the road or were murdered by their Japanese captors. Survivors would spend the rest of the war in terrible conditions in prison camps in the Philippines and Japan. By the end of the war 41.6 per cent of the American prisoners had died in prisoner of war camps in the Pacific theatre.[96]

In Europe, the story is better–as far as being a prisoner of war can possibly be. The US, Germany and Italy were able to come to an agreement on prisoners of war soon after the American entry into the war. Earlier fears that bad treatment given to Soviet POWs would be reflected onto prisoners of other nationalities did not appear to be borne out. Still, there were definitely cases of brutality. On 17 December 1944, during the Battle of the Bulge, a Waffen-SS battlegroup encountered a lightly-armed American force outside of the Belgian town of Malmédy. Outgunned, the Americans surrendered. Details at this point have never been entirely clear, but after their capture, 100 of the American prisoners were brought to a field and fired upon by the Germans, who killed approximately seventy-two. The incident, which became known as the "Malmédy Massacre", was the single greatest war crime carried out against Americans by the Germans during the war.[97]

The Americans shipped many of its prisoners to camps which had been set up in the United States. Over the course of the conflict, this amounted to

425,000 prisoners of war from Germany, Italy and Japan. There are some questions as to whether or not the Americans were actually prepared to deal with such a large number of prisoners (although there were always going to be some problems when handling such a sudden influx).[98] There was also a problem with hardcore Nazis influencing the less ideological prisoners and taking political control;[99] many Japanese prisoners had to be placed on a suicide watch after facing the dishonour of being captured alive;[100] and some of the prisoners refused to work for the Americans.[101] However, it would be hard to deny that prisoners of war in the United States were treated comparatively well when compared with Western prisoners held abroad.

One special case followed the capture of eight Nazi saboteurs on the east coast of the United States in early June 1942. The Nazis had been sent to cripple US production and target railway stations as well as Jewish-owned department stores. Upon their capture, President Roosevelt insisted upon a military trial where, in the words of Jack Goldsmith, "ordinary procedural niceties would not stand in the way, justice would be swift and the death sentence imposed."[102] Although the regular civilian courts were operating normally, military commissions were deemed both the expedient and the appropriate choice. The trial began on 8 July 1942 in total secrecy in a room in the Justice Department. However, three weeks into the trial the Supreme Court announced that it would convene a special session to entertain the *habeas corpus* petitions of the accused which challenged the legality of their military commissions.[103]

Although the Supreme Court's interference was not welcomed by the Roosevelt administration, the Court upheld the military commissions for the saboteurs, stating:

By universal agreement and practice, the law of war draws a distinction between the armed forces and the peaceful populations of belligerent nations and also between those who are lawful and unlawful combatants. Lawful combatants are subject to capture and detention as prisoners of war by opposing military forces. Unlawful combatants are likewise subject to capture and detention, but in addition they are subject to trial and punishment by military tribunals for acts which render their belligerency unlawful. The spy who secretly and without uniform passes the military lines of a belligerent in time of war, seeking to gather military information and communicate it to the enemy, or an enemy combatant who without uniform comes secretly through the lines for the purpose of waging war by destruction of life or property, are familiar examples of belligerents who are generally deemed not to be entitled to the status of prisoners of war, but to be offenders against the law of war subject to trial and punishment by military tribunals.[104]

Three days after the Supreme Court issued this judgement, the "secretless and juryless" military court pronounced the Nazis guilty. Less than a week later six of the eight were executed by electrocution and the other two had their sentences commuted by Roosevelt.[105]

Of all of the Germans held on US territory, the treatment of the eight saboteurs was exceptional–reflecting the extraordinary circumstances of their capture. Rather than being taken on some battlefield in France, these individuals had intended to do direct harm to the American homeland; a harsh response was seen as necessary and desirable. Although they represented only a fraction of the number of detained individuals on US territory during the war, the accused in *Ex parte Quirin* set an important precedent in terms of the treatment of prisoners which would be frequently invoked by the Bush administration to justify its plans to try suspects accused of being involved in terrorist activities against the United States and its troops.

There has been much speculation as to whether Roosevelt's actions were legal at the time and whether they can be construed as legal now.[106] But legal or not, it seems clear that Roosevelt was determined to put the saboteurs on trial and have them executed as quickly as possible. With the support of several major newspapers, including the *New York Times*, the *Washington Post* and *The Nation*, as well as public opinion (by some estimates 10–1 in favour of the death penalty), Roosevelt does not seem to have had much difficulty in getting his way on the matter.[107]

Another irregularity, if not discrepancy regarding prisoners held in the United States becomes apparent when they are examined by nationality. Of the 425,000 prisoners, only 5,424 were Japanese. There are several probable reasons for this. First, the War Department made the decision to turn the majority of its captives from the Pacific theatre (with the exception of those prisoners deemed to be important for military intelligence, or captured close to the United States) over to its war allies, particularly Australia.[108] Under this arrangement, the United States assumed a proportionate share of the cost of their maintenance and remained responsible for their final disposition at the end of the war.[109]

Yet there were other factors at hand. First was the fact that, unlike the Germans and Italians who were familiar with the Geneva Convention, many of the Japanese had been conditioned to die rather than surrender.[110] As mentioned above, some of the Japanese prisoners tried to commit suicide while in US hands rather than live with the disgrace of captivity. Even the government refused to acknowledge the fact that a soldier of the Imperial Army would surrender. In a letter, Japanese Foreign Minister, Shugemitsu Mamoru explained that "As you know, our Army maintains the position that Japanese prisoners of war do not exist."[111]

However, it was clear that the Americans did not and probably did not want to take many Japanese prisoners. As Krammer argues:

Major battles in the Pacific theatre often accounted for no more than a dozen Japanese captives, as against thousands of enemy killed. During the Burma campaign, for example, Commonwealth and American forces captured only 152 enemy prisoners (most of whom were badly wounded or unconscious) while killing 17,166!...

The war was nearly over before significantly large numbers of Japanese soldiers, usually malnourished and disillusioned, surrendered to Commonwealth and American forces.[112]

As atrocity stories began to pour in during the war, and the knowledge that the Japanese had no intention of adhering to the 1929 Geneva Convention spread, strict adherence to the Geneva Conventions had clearly lost some appeal to Washington and perhaps to the common soldier. As Krammer points out, the Americans certainly "bent" some of the articles of the Geneva Convention when it came to interrogation and "encouraging" the prisoners to work. However, the Americans had done so with the knowledge that "the treatment of American prisoners in Japanese hands could not have been made much worse by violations of the Geneva Accords".[113]

However, it cannot be denied that there were probably what we would now consider war crimes committed by American soldiers serving in the Pacific theatre. Yet, probably the truth of this needs to be qualified with the fact that, unlike the Japanese, this was never an official policy of the American government. As Mackenzie argues:

"In Japan", [General of the Imperial Army Hideki] Tojo explained, "we have our own ideology concerning prisoners-of-war, which should naturally make their treatment more or less different from that in Europe and America." Hence POWs were to be placed under "strict discipline" and made to work as hard as possible. In effect Tojo was stating that the philosophical basis of the Geneva Convention did not apply.[114]

At no point did the United States government argue that the Geneva Convention, or the norms underpinning it, did not apply or that prisoners were dishonourable and deserved to suffer. There can be little doubt that Americans probably committed crimes against the Japanese, that there was a duty to investigate these crimes and that a failure to do so would be a failure of responsibility under the Conventions. But at no time was it the official policy that its soldiers should commit deliberate war crimes.

Overall, during the Second World War the suffering of prisoners added to the growing belief among American officials that there needed to be a postwar system of justice. In other words, that the Allies should put not only the leaders of the Axis powers on trial, but also those who had committed battlefield war crimes. This impetus only increased as the sheer horror of the Japanese treatment of prisoners of war and the Holocaust became known. Supported by the International Commission for Penal Reconstruction and Development, and the United Nations War Crimes Commission, the Allies announced that German and Japanese soldiers would be prosecuted for obeying improper orders and would not be allowed the defence of superior orders.[115]

Prisoners of war at the end of WWII and repatriation

There were other challenges for the Americans after the end of the war: the millions of POWs stranded in the countries in which they had been held. For the Allies (particularly the US but also the UK), the issue of repatriation posed two problems—mostly stemming from the fact that both countries were exhausted from the war and wanted to deal with this humanitarian issue as quickly as possible. In the first instance, 400,000 German POWs held by the Americans were handed over to the French *en masse* in the summer of 1945. The Germans, who were kept in POW camps and then sent to work throughout France in post-war reconstruction projects, fared far worse than they had under the Americans. Thousands died from what one critic of the policy called "the politics of vengeance": POWs were poorly treated, forced to work long hours and, not infrequently, forced to clear minefields.[116]

On the other hand, there were those who did not want to go back. Throughout the Second World War, besides taking millions of Soviet POWs, the Nazis had deported millions of Russian slave labourers to Germany and throughout their occupied territory. Repatriation accords were concluded at Yalta in February 1945 and an agreement in Halle in May 1945 formalized this policy. Therefore, the US and the UK adopted a policy whereby all claimants to Soviet nationality were to be released to the Soviet government irrespective of their wishes. Once repatriated to the Soviet Union, most of the Russian prisoners vanished in the Gulag system.[117]

The problem lay with the legislation as it was written. Article 65 of the Hague Convention specified that repatriation would take place "with the least possible delay" after the end of hostilities, even in the absence of a formal treaty.[118] There was no provisions made for prisoners who wanted to claim asylum from their home country—if anything, their journey home had been made quicker by the legislation.[119]

However, there were other reasons why the Western nations (especially the US) were willing to trade the reluctant Soviets home: blackmail. In December 1944, after several POW camps had been liberated by the Russians, Foreign Affairs Commissar Vyacheslav Molotov refused the US access to its POWs and went so far as to accuse it of mistreating Soviet prisoners.[120] There have been several reasons given for this policy. First, the US Ambassador to the Soviet Union, Averell Harriman, speculated that the Soviets had implemented this policy to keep Western observers out of Poland until the pro-Soviet Lublin regime was established.[121] Second, it has been suggested that the Soviets may also have been embarrassed over the presence among their POWs liberated in the West of thousands captured in German uniform.[122]

Repeated demands for access to the American POWs were met with continued refusals, assurances that the Americans were being treated well, and recurring charges that the Americans were the ones who were really abusing the Soviet prisoners. Given the fact that the Russians were still holding thousands of American POWs, the Americans were understandably nervous about returning the only bargaining chips they had to ensure they got their soldiers back; however, as both sides gradually came round after some diplomatic wrangling, the exchange process was speeded up.

For what it is worth, as Cathal J. Nolan points out, the decision to repatriate the Soviet prisoners was not as clear-cut as it seems to us now in hindsight. Aside from the confounding factors of blackmail listed above, the Soviet Union had been an ally in the war and some of the Soviets caught in German uniforms had actually inflicted casualties on Allied soldiers, while others willingly collaborated with the Nazis.[123] Still, for those caught up in this process, the result was tragic. In one camp in Austria, 134 Russians committed suicide in June, after which the British authorities forced the remaining 30,000 onto the train to Moscow.[124] It was only in mid-1947 that Secretary of State George C. Marshall decided that not even those who had collaborated with Nazi Germany should be repatriated to Soviet bloc countries against their will, declaring that forced repatriation went against the American tradition of granting political asylum.[125]

The Geneva Conventions of 1949

Despite these difficulties, at the end of the war the Americans were willing to help codify and draft a new version of the Geneva Convention in 1949, which would greatly expand and codify the laws of war and extend it to cover civilians in occupied territory. Best notes that, despite the increasing hostility between the US and the Soviet Union, the Americans took a relatively relaxed approach to Soviet participation in the conference.[126]

However, this does not mean the Diplomatic Conference was free of controversy–or hostility between the new superpowers. As Best argues, "From the moment that Soviet participation became known ...an infusion of politics was to be expected."[127] The first of these issues was indiscriminate bombings. To the clauses protecting civilians, the Soviet delegation proposed banning "all other means of exterminating the civilian population" causing "extensive destruction of the [civilian] property."[128] It was clear that the Soviets were aiming to ban the atomic bomb. This put the Western delegations in the unfortunate position of having to vote down the Soviet proposal and looking as if they were somehow supporting indiscriminate bombing. Although they looked for a better way out of the situation, the Soviet proposal was voted down on 6 July 1949.

Prisoners of war were another hotly contested issue during the course of the Diplomatic Conference. The point in dispute was the text that would eventually form Article 85 of the Third Geneva Convention. The 1929 Convention dealing with prisoners of war contained no provision concerning the punishment of crimes committed by POWs prior to their capture. Those provisions which did deal with offences and punishment only referred to acts committed during captivity.[129] With an increase in the number of special tribunals for War Crimes, the ICRC became increasingly concerned that POWs would be tried under special *ad hoc* legislation rather than by tribunals based on international legal principles. Therefore, it was proposed that POWs should continue to receive all of the benefits of the Convention until their guilt was definitively proven. The suggestion, however, received only limited support–the Anglo-Saxon powers were particularly hostile. This was especially the case as the Allies, especially the United States, had spent considerable effort on prosecuting Axis military officials for war crimes, including crimes committed against prisoners of war.

Perhaps because of the chilling of the Cold War and the increased likelihood that Western soldiers would soon be fighting against communist nations, the Anglo-Saxon nations had changed their mind on the issue by 1949 and now agreed with the ICRC position. In fact, they even went further, arguing that POWs should continue to enjoy those benefits of the Convention even after they had been judged. Article 85 was therefore submitted to read: "Prisoners of war prosecuted under the laws of the Detaining Power for acts committed prior to capture shall retain, even if convicted, the benefits of the present Convention."

The objection now came from the Soviet Union which argued for the original proposal–that POWs were only protected under the convention until *after* they had been convicted. The Soviet delegation argued that there was no reason why prisoners of war convicted of such crimes should not be treated in the same way as persons serving sentence for a criminal offence in the territory of the detaining power.[130]

Best points out that it was the Soviets who had consistency on their side. Beyond that, "they could also plausibly claim to represent the general opinion of mankind. That POWs accused of perhaps terrible crimes should enjoy the benefits of the Convention through the period of arrest and trial, was not unreasonable, and the USSR was not proposing anything else; but that such lavish benefits should continue after conviction was incredible."[131]

The Article was voted on and passed as written above. The Soviet Union, maintaining its position, insisted upon a reservation to the Article:

The Union of Soviet Socialist Republics does not consider itself bound by the obligation, which follows from Article 85, to extend the application of the Convention to prisoners of war who have been convicted under the law of the Detaining Power, in accordance with the principles of the Nuremberg trial, for war crimes and crimes against humanity, it being understood that persons convicted of such crimes must be subject to the conditions obtaining in the country in question for those who undergo their punishment.[132]

The other Socialist-bloc countries expressed similar reservations upon their ratification as well.[133]

Aside from the (fairly successful) attempt at putting the West in a no-win situation regarding a prohibition on the use of atomic weapons, the political role of the 1949 Geneva Conventions was rather mild. For the most part, the Conventions and the humanitarian goals behind them were supported within the US government. However, the impact of the Conventions, including the Soviet Bloc's reservation to Article 85, would play a major role in the fate of POWs throughout the Cold War. This was especially so as international wars became less frequent and the wars of decolonization–conflicts with a very ambiguous status–became the norm rather than the exception.

The Uniform Code of Military Justice

The Articles of War–the American legislation used to try soldiers for military infractions and war crimes–had come under significant pressure for reform by the late 1940s. First, the experiences of millions of civilians of the rather uneven and often harsh system of military justice led to calls for reform.

Nearly one in eight American men and women served in the armed forces during World War II, and with over two million courts-martial many of those had been exposed to this system and were not pleased with what they experienced. As Cooke notes:

The system appeared harsh and arbitrary, with too few protections for the individual and too much power for the commander. To Americans who were drafted or who enlisted to defend their own freedoms and protect those of others around the world, this was unacceptable and complaints and criticisms became widespread.[134]

There had been a similar push for change after World War I and during the 1920s, but such attempts had not succeeded.[135] However, there were several other several important reasons for reform by this point, including new developments in international law. As Solis notes, the Allied position rejecting the defence of obedience to superior orders by those charged with war crimes at the post-war International Military Tribunals mandated a re-evaluation of the US' policy of allowing its own soldiers to employ such a strategy as an automatic and complete defence.[136] Additionally, with the threat of communism spreading, it was becoming clear that the size of the peacetime armed forces would be unprecedented.[137] A larger army would not tolerate such an uneven and, arguably, unfair system of justice.

A major push came from the first Secretary of Defense, James F. Forrestal, who took office in September 1947. The War Department had been abolished, which had the effect of bringing all of the service branches under the newly formed Department of Defense.[138] Forrestal wanted to have one system of military justice applicable to all of the services.[139] On 1 June 1951 the new Uniform Code of Military Justice (UCMJ) came into force along with a new *Manual for Courts-Martial* which further outlines and expands upon the military law in the UCMJ. The UCMJ is federal law and sought to make the courts-martial system more fair. However, under Article 18, the UCMJ also incorporates war crimes into military law and meets America's obligations under the 1949 Geneva Conventions.[140]

Although the full implications of the new UCMJ were still unknown when it was passed into law in June 1950, it had not been anticipated that it would take effect during the height of the Korean War.[141]

Korea

During the Korean War, America (and its allies in the United Nations Command) confronted an enemy who employed Western military tactics and technology but not the laws of war. The result for prisoners of war caught by the North Koreans was disastrous as Cold War politics came to dominate the way they were treated. Wounds were left untreated and prisoners were given an insufficient diet, especially in the first year of the war. POW camps were left unmarked and several were accidentally attacked by the UN Command forces. This made the implications of Soviet reservations to Article 85 very clear. It was also a foreshadowing of the unfortunate events to come. This would not be the last time that the Americans would face problems with ensuring reciprocal respect for the laws of war in a conflict in the twentieth century, especially as the number of wars of national self-liberation was on the increase, including that in Vietnam.

For now, the implication of the Korean War was that the American approach to the laws of war began to emphasize heavily the rights of American soldiers who were captured. Concern over the twenty-one Americans who chose to stay in North Korea after having spent years there as POWs (most of whom had collaborated with their captors) prompted President Dwight Eisenhower to establish the Military Code of Conduct.[142] The Code was applicable to all soldiers and geared towards providing them with a standard of behaviour expected of them, especially if they were captured. Many Americans were shocked at the idea that Americans would betray their country while in Communist captivity, and allegations that their troops had surrendered too easily did not sit well with the American government or its people. In some ways the text of the Code reads as a way to maintain the honour of the armed forces and/or the individual soldier if he is captured. However, the Code of Conduct reflected another American realization/assumption about future conflicts; that soldiers were not likely to be treated according the standards of the Geneva Convention. Principles like "I will evade answering further questions to the utmost of my ability" seem to assume that American POWs would be pressed to answer questions with tactics that went above and beyond those practices allowed by the laws of war.[143]

Conclusion

Many have written on the tendency of the United States to see itself as an exceptional nation from its very founding. Yet during this period its approach to the laws of war, the republic remained very European, keeping with the traditions that had been established by the British before the Revolution. This resulted in what Peter Maguire calls a "dualistic tendency" in the American implementation of the laws of war. At the same time as the US applied the laws of war to the Confederate Army (albeit not in a strictly legal sense), it did not do the same for the First Nations. The US could go to The Hague and play a major role in strengthening the laws of war while at the same time engaging in fairly brutal tactics and torture in the Philippines.

Despite what we would see as the two-facedness of these policies today, it somehow seems incorrect to suggest that they were deliberately hypocritical in the full meaning of the word. American policies were based on the European or "civilized" understandings of the time. It seemed perfectly sensible to apply the laws of war to rebel Confederate forces and not the natives who shared neither the same legal or military traditions as the white American settlers did; in other words, cultural recognition was key. So in a sense, the policies were two-faced–operating on different legal pages, with two separate lists of means, weapons and restraint permitted. Those who stood in the way of the ideological imperatives created by manifest destiny, civilization and progress would not be considered a legitimate combatant or an object of sympathy in the eyes of many Americans. The conflicts could then take upon a brutal character on both sides.

Yet, as we can see by the end of this chapter, there had been significant changes in the American armed forces by the time of the Korean War. These changes had been prompted by growth in the military, the development of international tribunals which began to regard violations of the laws of war as punishable crimes on the global stage, and the creation of the 1949 Geneva Conventions. The new Uniform Code of Military Justice, which came into effect during the Korean conflict, embodied many of these changes. Despite the tactics of an opposing side, increased protection was increasingly provided for America's enemies by the rules of engagement that American soldiers lived and died by–especially when compared to the wars that had been fought just fifty years before.

Still, as the next twenty-five years would show, these rules were based on a way of warfare that was rapidly disappearing and being replaced by guerrilla tactics. The latter was a mode of warfare that would prove to be especially frustrating for American troops and very confusing under their rules of engagement and the laws of war. In this way, the "dualistic tendencies" of the American approach had, for the most part, ended, but a difficult period involving violations of and frustrations with the laws of war was just beginning. This is the subject of the next chapter.

PART II

THERE AND BACK AGAIN?

THE UNITED STATES AND THE LAWS
OF WAR FROM VIETNAM TO ABU GHRAIB

When it comes to the laws of war, a picture not only speaks a thousand words, but it may also spark a thousand debates. Thinking about the laws of war and Vietnam, one may automatically think of the photograph of a naked, burned nine year old girl screaming as she flees a napalm attack on her village, or the pictures of the victims of My Lai. Just over three decades later, a similar link may be made between the war in Iraq and photos showing the abuse and humiliation of prisoners in the care of US forces at Abu Ghraib. In both cases, the photos were seen as evidence that the United States was committing war crimes while engaged in missions to either protect or promote democracy abroad. They provided propaganda to those who opposed the war and, to some, irrefutable evidence that the United States military operated outside the boundaries of the laws of war. Indeed, pictures from Vietnam and Abu Ghraib seem to suggest that some things never change; that the US military did not learn the lessons of Vietnam, that despite its talk of fighting for freedom, the US was committing and always would commit war crimes, bombing civilians and abusing its prisoners.

But in this sense, pictures may not tell the whole story. After Vietnam, lawyers in the US military, who had experienced first-hand the difficulties of implementing laws in an unconventional conflict, set to work changing the way the United States implemented the laws of war in its training and decision making. The effect was to create a "legal revolution": training in the laws of war was made more practical and lawyers, over the next fifteen years, fought their way into the "war room". The results speak for themselves: although war can never be said to totally free from accidents and violations, the 1991 Gulf Conflict was carried out in such a manner as to perhaps be considered the most legal in history. In terms of implementing the laws of war in a conflict that involved tens of thousands of prisoners, the United States had come a long way from Vietnam.

So how did the situation go from the heights of legality to the tragic debacle at Abu Ghraib?

The next three chapters will attempt to describe the rise and arguable fall—despite the apparent efforts of lawyers within the military—of America's relationship with the laws of war. Although rigorous procedures and training had been put in place, 9/11 created an environment where arguments challenging the legal power and morality of international law became prominent and were adopted into policy. In the face of new threats from the War on Terror, it was argued that the United States could not and should not be bound by a vague and unaccountable international law. Rejecting calls to apply the Geneva Conventions to prisoners, the United States was effectively arguing that in a new framework of warfare, old rules could not apply.

But just how should democracies respond when they are faced with a War on Terror, when it comes to balancing liberty, a commitment to international treaties and security? Are states entirely wrong when they seek to alter the balance between these ideas? The next chapters will show how arguments emerging from this debate played a role in establishing and justifying Guantánamo Bay's Camp Delta. But it will also suggest that the answers that were given by the Bush administration to these questions helped to undermine overall standards of restraints which lead to the torture and abuse at Abu Ghraib.

3

LEGAL REVOLUTION

AMERICA AND THE LAWS OF WAR AFTER VIETNAM

Introduction

Having signed and ratified the 1949 Geneva Conventions, updated its Law of War Manual in 1956[1] and developed the Uniform Code of Military Justice (UCMJ), the United States looked well placed for its future military engagements in terms of the law of war. In Korea the US had demonstrated that it took the issue seriously and, on balance, the US commitment to the law of war looked fairly certain to remain stable for the immediate future.

Of course, what did not remain stable was the nature of conflicts in the Cold War. In many ways, Korea was to be the last "classic" war the United States would fight for nearly forty years. Replacing this paradigm of state-to-state warfare were Third World insurgencies, involving non-traditional, non-Western tactics and guerrilla warfare. This emerging pattern of warfare did not fit well with the conception of war implicit in the Geneva Conventions or in the mindset of Americans as to how the law of war could be applied to conflicts.

As is well known, the result was disaster. Writing of his experience interviewing the mother of a Vietnam War veteran who was accused of committing war crimes at My Lai, Seymour M. Hersh wrote: "She told me that when he came home, 'He looked like he had just been whipped...' And then she said with a look I wish those who send young men and women off to war could see, 'I gave them a good boy and they made him a murderer.'"[2]

Hersh broke the My Lai massacre story on 14 November 1969 in newspapers across America. The story prompted widespread domestic and international condemnation and gave powerful ammunition to the anti–war movement. Combined with the new and powerful media images being broadcast in American homes each night of villagers fleeing napalm attacks or prisoners being executed, the Vietnam War, for many people, became and remains synonymous with American war crimes and brutality.

Yet the Vietnam War did not occur in a legal vacuum. There were lawyers on the ground, rules of engagement were drafted and disseminated, superior orders which demanded respect for the laws of war were issued. The question after the war was then "how did this happen?" and, perhaps more crucially for the US military, how to ensure "never again"? The tragedies at My Lai and Son Thang, as well as the experience of military lawyers in Vietnam, would prompt a major rethink in the way the US military regarded the laws of war, and how it implemented them.

By the 1991 Gulf War, what could reasonably be described as a military legal revolution had taken place within the Department of Defense. "Activist lawyers" lobbying for reform brought about revised rules, strengthened training and developed the concept of "operational law" as a powerful tool that the US could use in war and peace time. At the close of the First Gulf War an article in the *American Bar Association Journal* described the conflict as "a lawyer's war",[3] and one judge advocate who served as a legal adviser to General H. Norman Schwarzkopf's described it as "the most legalist war [the United States] ever fought."[4]

This chapter will follow the path from the confusion, mistakes and crimes of Vietnam to the legal sophistication of First Gulf War. In doing so, it will look at what went wrong in Vietnam and how the disasters there prompted change in the US military's attitude to, and implementation of, the laws of war.

Vietnam

There can be little doubt that its experience in South-East Asia from the early 1960s until 1973 left a major impression, if not a painful scar, upon the United States and its military. The conflict influenced a generation of soldiers who, having served their country in this controversial war, sought to overcome the legacy of that conflict. This group of soldiers includes the military lawyers who saw significant room for improvement not only in the role of the military lawyer, but in the way the whole defence establishment thought about the laws of war and methods of training the military in them.

In terms of thinking about the conflict's relationship with the laws of war, the Vietnam record is often automatically linked to the massacres at My Lai (and the less well-known Son Thang[5]), images of terrified villagers fleeing attacks by US forces, and the speeches of anti–war organizations such as Veterans Against the War describing alleged US war crimes in Vietnam. Certainly this is one side of the story. But there was also a great deal of concern among lawyers and the defence establishment that the US should adhere to the laws of war to the very best of its ability. Often, this was the result of individual initiatives in a difficult environment. The first section of this chapter will look at America's relationship with the laws of war after Vietnam, but particularly the conflict's role in planting seeds for reform that would come in the mid-1970s and through to the mid-1980s.

Challenges–jurisdiction

One of the first challenges that the US faced was related to the problem of jurisdiction. Although it is a basic tenet of international law that the courts of a country have jurisdiction to try all cases arising out of wrongful acts committed in that country, the US wished to retain the greatest possible measure of jurisdiction over its own forces in Vietnam.[6] While normally, in peace time, matters of jurisdiction are sorted through a Status of Forces Agreement (SOFA), in the case of Vietnam the Agreement for Mutual Defense Assistance in Indochina (commonly referred to as the Pentalateral Agreement) solved the issue for the US forces. The Agreement, signed on 23 December 1950 by the United States, France, Cambodia, Laos and Vietnam, governed the legal status, rights and obligations of American personnel in Vietnam. All American forces entering Indochina were to be considered members of the US diplomatic mission. As the former military lawyer and historian Gary Solis notes, "Few Marine riflemen in Vietnam knew that in terms of legal jurisdiction they were considered to be diplomatic mission clerks."[7] The agreement was brief (less than six pages long) and its terms were broad and generous. It provided a minimal but adequate framework and the generality of its provisions allowed for a flexibility that would leave many legal questions to be solved on a case-by-cases basis but also happened to meet the many legal complications that were to arise.[8] George Prugh, who served as the Staff Judge Advocate from 1964 to 1966, argues: "It is unlikely that the diplomats who signed the Pentalateral Agreement in 1950 ever imagined that its simple provisions would govern the legal status and activities of almost 600,000 Americans in Vietnam."[9] However, he adds that the South Vietnamese had good reasons for maintaining this broad document, all of which were pragmatic. Distracted by protracted military crises and political turbulence, the government did not desire to enter into a long and detailed negotiation with the US on the matter.[10] In this way Vietnam had neither criminal nor civil jurisdiction over American personnel–prosecution for crimes, including war crimes, was exercised exclusively under the Uniform Code of Military Justice.

There was, however, one complicating issue—how was misconduct by US civilians connected with the war effort, who by the late 1960s numbered over 6,000, to be dealt with? Such misconduct fell into three categories: disorderly conduct, abuse of military privileges, and black market activities and currency manipulation.[11] In April 1966 the Military Assistance Command Vietnam (MACV) Staff Judge Advocate prepared a study on the problem. It was determined that the ambassador could issue police regulations for all US citizens in Vietnam, or punishments could be meted out through administrative measures (such as the withdrawal of military privileges and the loss of employment).[12] Yet the seriousness of crimes being committed by US civilians soon made criminal prosecutions more appropriate–but the question then became, by whom? The problem was never adequately solved. While employment could be terminated, prosecution had to be carried out either by Vietnamese civilian authorities (who were either unable or unwilling to prosecute Americans) or by the US military under the UCMJ–whose authority over civilians in Vietnam was tenuous at best.[13] While Staff Judge Advocate Prugh recommended that the most effective remedy would be trial in a Vietnamese court, the MACV eventually decided upon a policy to try civilians, when absolutely necessary, through courts-martial.[14]

Yet, this policy proved to be ineffective–a total of four US civilians were tried by military courts-martial during the Vietnam War. When one of those convicted under the UCMJ appealed against his conviction to the US Court of Military Appeals, the highest court in the military system, it ruled on 30 April 1970 that the military had no jurisdiction over civilians in Vietnam. In the Court's opinion, Article 2(10) of the UCMJ was applicable only in time of a declared war.[15] Thus, the question of whether, as a matter of policy, the military should try civilians in Vietnam was rendered moot–the services no longer had jurisdiction over civilians in Vietnam and no further cases were tried.[16]

As mentioned above, most crimes committed by civilians were related to black market activities rather than violation of the laws of war. Still, the point mentioned here is important as this was one of the first instances where the military found itself having to deal with the problem of jurisdiction over civilian contractors. The failure to solve the problem in Vietnam or afterwards would have repercussions for the military as it would face the same problem in many of its future conflicts, especially as the number of civilian contractors and private military firms would exponentially increase by the year 2000–and alleged wrongdoing would begin to include violations of the laws of war.[17]

Challenges–classifying Vietnam under international law

The Gulf of Tonkin Resolution in 1964 by the US Congress resulted in an increased US presence in Vietnam by 1965. While the conflict had assumed an international character by this point, in terms of the issue of jurisdiction under the laws of war, classifying the conflict as a war was problematic. Quite simply, under international law and the laws of war, Vietnam was a conflict with an identity crisis. This became readily apparent when the conflict was broken down into separate components. While the conflict between North and South Vietnam and the conflict between North Vietnam and the US were clearly interstate conflicts as envisioned by the 1949 Geneva Conventions, the conflicts between South Vietnam and the National Liberation Front (NLF) and the US and the NLF were not. The former could be considered a civil war of international character, with the second being an international–but not interstate–conflict. The issue was complicated as the South did not necessarily want to recognize that it was engaged in an international or interstate war with the North.

The issue may seem to be one of semantics–perhaps not least to the American soldier who faced the reality of a guerrilla-warfare struggle for survival in the jungle against the Vietcong–but it was important. Prugh accurately summed up the problem:

The battlefield was nowhere and everywhere, with no identifiable front lines, and no safe rear areas. Fighting occurred over the length and breadth of South Vietnam, on the seas, into Laos and Cambodia, and in the air over North Vietnam. It involved combatants and civilians from a dozen different nations. Politically, militarily, and in terms of international law, the Vietnam conflict posed problems of deep complexity. The inherent difficulty of attempting to apply traditional principles of international law to such a legally confusing conflict is well illustrated by the issue of prisoners of war.[18]

In short, a determination of the type of conflict that was being waged was crucial for determining how the law of war applied, and especially what was to be done with prisoners caught in military operations and how US forces should conduct operations against combatants in the field.

Yet the very nature of the conflict rendered carrying out operations in accordance with the laws of war exceptionally difficult. The problem related to the fact that the laws of war had traditionally presumed two kinds of warfare: interstate warfare and civil war. Yet, it was clear that since the end of the Second World War internationalized civil wars were rapidly becoming the more common form of warfare, and the US now found itself engaged in one such conflict where it was confronted by a guerrilla force that did not adhere to the laws of war.[19]

In order to ensure that operations were conducted in a controlled manner, a determination of the status of the conflict would have to be made by the MACV. Eventually the official position adopted by the US, stated by 1965, was that the hostilities constituted an armed international conflict, that North Vietnam was a belligerent, that the Viet Cong were agents of the government of North Vietnam, and that the Geneva Conventions applied in full.[20] Therefore, on 6 March 1966 Directive 381–11 was enacted which provided POW treatment to any Viet Cong taken in combat.[21] To deal with situations where uncertainty still remained, a separate directive, MACV Directive 20–5 (1968), established procedures for convening tribunals consistent with Article 5 of the Third Geneva Convention in order to determine the status of any captured combatant.[22] As South Vietnam was severely lacking in the proper facilities to deal with an influx of POWs, a POW programme was established which called for the construction of five POW camps, administration and management of the camps, labour and educational programmes, and managing visits from the ICRC.

There were several reasons why this decision was made. One was that Prugh and his staff believed that such a move might be good for public relations in at least three ways: first, Prugh writes that it was part of the campaign to win over the "hearts and minds" of those who had been taken prisoner;[23] second, such a move might help to ease domestic and international criticism of the conduct of the war;[24] finally, there was the hope that if the US provided good treatment for POWs, North Vietnam and the NLF would reciprocate towards the prisoners that they had taken. The Viet Cong were very harsh in their treatment of their captives. South Vietnamese soldiers were executed as a matter of routine and although US personnel were initially spared, several were killed in retribution for the execution of Viet Cong agents in South Vietnam.

In the absence of a statement whereby the Viet Cong acknowledged that they were bound by international law and/or the Geneva Conventions, the

US sought to ensure better treatment for its captured personnel. After the reciprocal killings had taken place against US captives, it was concluded by Prugh and his staff that the Viet Cong might also reciprocate with better treatment for American POWs if they could convince the South Vietnamese to provide better treatment for Viet Cong POWs. The South Vietnamese often killed guerrillas outright as they were seen as "Communist rebel combat captives" who deserved summary treatment as illegitimate insurgents.[25] It had been the position of the South Vietnamese that the Viet Cong were not POWs as South Vietnam was engaged in a civil conflict and not an international armed conflict.[26]

An effort was made to convince Colonel Nguyen Monh Bich, the Director of Military Justice, that it was in South Vietnam's best interest to improve conditions for enemy POWs, and the US was ultimately successful in its efforts to persuade the South Vietnamese (at least officially).[27] Sadly, however, the North Vietnamese were not moved to improve treatment for the "war criminals" that they had captured. Prisoners taken by the NLF or the North Vietnamese, for the remainder of the war, would exist on starvation diets of rice and water, and suffer beatings and torture in filthy prisons.[28]

Implementing the law of war

In accounts of the military lawyers who went to Vietnam—often written by the lawyers themselves—it is clear that Vietnam presented huge challenges to their "traditional" role. Many accounts describe the first lawyers as arriving with little more than a *Manual for Courts-Martial*, a JAG Manual and a yellow legal pad.[29] As lawyers began to arrive in the early 1960s, their mission was unclear and overseas communication was difficult, creating a situation where judge advocates were pretty much on their own.[30]

Traditional duties of judge advocates basically involved providing legal services to the command and ordinary soldiers. This included assisting with wills and power of attorney, tax assistance, advice on domestic relations, civil suits, and the filing of claims for damaged property. Yet, as the war escalated, it was felt that there was room for expansion in terms of their contribution to the overall mission. Three areas were identified that went beyond the traditional judge advocate role. The first (as seen from above) concerned the status and treatment of captured enemy personnel. The second was to develop an official policy on the reporting and investigation of war crimes. Originally Directive 20–4, *Inspection and Investigations of War Crimes*, only dealt with the investigation of war crimes committed against US forces, but by mid-1965, MACV judge advocates were advising, assisting and reviewing all war crimes investigations in Vietnam, including those committed by US forces. A third area, of less concern for our purposes here, involved the control of South Vietnamese resources and material and preventing them from getting into enemy hands.[31] In order to encourage adherence to the laws of war, military lawyers also promoted programmes to help increase respect for the rule of law in South Vietnam and to help bring along improvements to its system of military justice.[32]

By 1966, in order to deal with the new challenges emerging out of the escalation of the war, the MACV transferred some responsibilities for the judge advocates (such as claims adjudication) elsewhere and the legal office had a "slimmed-down" organizational structure which involved a Civil Law and Military Affairs Division, a Criminal and International Law Division and an Advisory Division.[33] In terms of war crimes, criminal and disciplinary matters, the Criminal and International Law Division gave out advice on the Geneva Conventions, handled investigations and developed policies in these areas.

Soldiers first received their training in the laws of war and the Geneva Conventions during basic training.[34] Ideally, further training was incorporated with other subjects and principles during field training and commanders were instructed to continually incorporate the Geneva Conventions into their training programmes.[35] Further actions taken to promote teaching on the law of war included the development of instructional films and, in October 1965, the issuing of 3x5 yellow cards to both American and Vietnamese forces outlining the basic requirements of the Geneva Conventions on the treatment of prisoners of war. The card, entitled "The Enemy in Your Hands", included Vietnamese translations and reminded military personnel that they were to adhere to the Geneva Conventions and not to humiliate or degrade their prisoner or refuse him/her medical treatment if needed.[36] The basic principles of this training were repeated in a MACV bulletin issued in October 1966 which emphasized that the Geneva Conventions applied to the conflict despite the absence of a formal declaration of war. Additionally, it was emphasized that the United States was applying not only the letter of the law but also the spirit of the Geneva Conventions, which were designed to protect the individual who could no longer protect himself.[37]

War crimes

Clearly, there was a lot of effort put into implementing and enforcing the laws of war in Vietnam by the MACV and its judge advocates. However, these steps taken, while positive, and in many ways transformative of the role that military lawyers played, were simply not enough. As mentioned in the introduction of this section, Vietnam is often linked with war crimes in the popular media and imagination. Part of this linkage may actually have something to do with the politics of the war and the campaigns of the anti–war movement. While there had been war crimes committed in previous wars, never before had American citizens been so aware of what was actually going on overseas. The rapid development of media communications enabled television networks to air unedited footage of the US military campaigns into American living rooms. War crimes could easily be edited out of newsreel footage in the Second World War, but television brought the gory reality of war home to a shocked viewing public.

However, it is clearly the case that awful crimes were committed by US forces in a deliberate matter despite the efforts put forward by MACV. Some military leaders voiced their concern for the treatment of POWs as reports of abuse meted out by US soldiers came in. In September 1965, the Commanding General, Fleet Marine Force, Pacific, Lieutenant General Victor H. Krulak, contacted Major General Walt, saying:

I am anxious that all of our people are made fully aware of their obligations, under the Geneva Convention, as to the treatment of Prisoners. This point acquires particular importance now that the flow of replacements will bring you a large group of new and uninitiated people each month.[38]

He made a similar point only two months later to Walt: "Ensure that every officer in the chain of command knows the rules, the reasons for the rules and the penalties for their violation, and then accept no compromise at all."[39]

But the problem was not going away. Prugh states that between 1965 and 1975 there were 241 cases in which Americans were alleged to have committed war crimes, of which 160 were found to be unsubstantiated on various grounds. thirty-six war crimes incidents resulted in trials by courts-martial on charges including premeditated murder, rape, assault with intent to commit murder or rape, involuntary manslaughter, negligent homicide, and the mutilation of enemy dead.[40] Sixteen trials involving thirty men resulted in not guilty verdicts or cases being dismissed after arraignment, while twenty cases involving thirty-one soldiers resulted in conviction.[41] Yet these numbers do not tell the whole story. The infamous case of My Lai, not included in Prugh's accounting, illustrates this point.[42] Fourteen officers were charged with covering up information related to the massacre, but most charges were eventually dropped; twenty-six men were charged with taking part in the massacre, but only Lieutenant William Calley was convicted.[43] Additionally, there were at least several cases on the record of the mistreatment and torture of prisoners to extract information. In some cases American personnel were present at, or participated in, the abuse of prisoners by South Vietnamese personnel, and in others they were directly responsible for acts of torture themselves.[44]

Given the fact that American soldiers had been given training, and that there seemed to be a genuine concern for implementing the laws of war at senior levels, why were these war crimes taking place? At some level it probably came down to the very nature of the conflict that was being fought. As Parks notes, "For the first time in a half-century, U.S. military forces in Vietnam were confronted with guerrillas who failed to comply with the traditional requirements for classification as a prisoner of war."[45] Fighting in the jungles in Vietnam against combatants who were farmers by day and guerrillas by night was an exceptionally frustrating and dangerous experience for soldiers on the front lines. Being confronted with booby traps and ambushes rather than traditional forces was a confusing experience. As Guenter Lewy argues:

> In trying to understand why [war crimes] took place, one must again remember the overall Vietnam environment–the frustrations from fighting an often unseen enemy, the resentments created by casualties from booby traps frequently set by villagers, the decline in discipline during the years of disengagement. None of these factors justify the atrocities, but they help provide explanations for them.[46]

Yet there were clearly more factors than difficult circumstances at work here. The demoralization and breakdown in military discipline that occurred in the US military worldwide, but especially in Vietnam, was a key factor. Theft, insubordination, black market activities and drugs were rampant in the US forces in Vietnam (according to Prugh during 1970 there were 11,058 arrests of which 1,146 involved hard narcotics such as heroin).[47] "Fragging"– the murder of officers by their own men–became a serious problem, reflecting this sense of malaise as well as serious racial tension between black and white troops. In this environment, enforcing basic military discipline was a major challenge, let alone enforcing the laws of war.

One of the factors aggravating this problem was "Project 100,000" implemented by the Secretary of Defense, Robert McNamara. The "Project" required the armed services to accept men who had previously been rejected– mostly because they had failed to meet intelligence standards. All of the services were forced to lower drastically their standards to accept an additional 100,000 men into their ranks. Solis argues that the influx of lower standard recruits had an immediate negative effect on discipline and remained a significant problem for commanders and military lawyers until the enlisted "Project 100,000" recruits were phased out of the armed services in the mid-1970s.[48] As Parks notes, the average marine or soldier involved in a serious incident or charge had less than ten years of formal education, was socially disadvantaged and had below average intelligence.[49] A lower quality of recruit also had an effect on leadership. Lewy argues that weak leadership was the "the most important single element, present in almost all incidents".[50] Ineffective leadership, he argues, leads to weak discipline. Additionally, it also meant "inadequate planning of operations and loosely issued orders."[51] The Rules of Engagement (ROE) handed out to forces in the field were not consistently observed or implemented.

Finally, prosecuting these crimes seems to have been exceptionally difficult in Vietnam. Aside from a lack of resources, the situation was one of constant turnover of military personnel. Often witnesses had been sent back to the US before they were called to testify. Additionally, in cases involving Vietnamese there were many difficulties with locating witnesses and arranging translation. Moreover, the US military justice system was a very foreign and intimidating prospect for Vietnamese villagers. Witnesses might have to travel for hours or days from their villages to a court-martial where they would face individuals accused of committing crimes, possibly against themselves. For this reason trials could indeed be a frustrating endeavour for prosecutors–trying to instill a modicum of order in what was a very chaotic conflict.[52]

Peers Report

Many of these problems were revealed in the aftermath of My Lai. As the tragedy became public, the Chief of Staff of the Army began formal investigation into how the incident occurred, and its findings were published in the *Report of the Department of the Army Review of the Preliminary Investigations into the My Lai Incident* (otherwise known as the "Peers Report" after the general ordered to investigate the incident, General William R. Peers). As well as providing a very critical account of what occurred, the Report provided a list of findings and recommendations to be implemented.

Crucially, the Peers Report looked at the issue of training. The Report made it clear that part of the problem stemmed from the fact that the soldiers in the brigade taking part in the My Lai incident were inadequately trained in "their responsibilities regarding obedience to orders received from their superiors which they considered palpably illegal", "their responsibilities concerning the procedures for the reporting of war crimes", and "the provisions of the

Geneva Conventions, the handling and treatment of prisoners of war, and the treatment and safeguarding of noncombatants".[53]

Certainly this was a grim verdict on the military's efforts to promote the law of war in Vietnam. Yet it was also clear that the criticism reflected some underlying problems that were going to have to be taken seriously if the military wanted to prevent another My Lai. It was acknowledged by high-level MACV officials that laws of war instruction provided by the judge advocates had tended to be abstract and academic, rather than concrete and practical.[54] Beyond this, despite efforts to emphasize duties towards enemy POWs, training in the law of war had tended to placed more emphasis on the rights of an American soldier when captured than on his or her obligations towards others, or on compliance with the law of war.[55] As Parks notes, the nature of the counterinsurgency operations in Vietnam required increased training on the protection of civilians–but the attempts to provide such training were not always effective or consistent:

The effort was uneven and often personally driven. If a commander believed in the law of war, and in the importance of a disciplined military force, law of war training was emphasized, as was the investigation and prosecution of incidents when they occurred...Without positive command enforcement, and adequate realistic training, a law of war program is not likely to succeed.

Where law of war training occurred in Vietnam, it occasionally left much to be desired.[56]

Where commanders believed in the laws of war, it would usually be enforced and followed. Where leadership was weak, or belief in and desire to enforce the law were lacking, it was not. Troops would not necessarily follow the law on their own, without guidance or leadership. Rather than a comprehensive or a systematic approach, the implementation of the laws therefore depended very much on the personalities on the ground. Poor leadership, weak discipline and inadequate training in a hostile and frustrating environment clearly created a recipe for disaster.

Still, Prugh argues in the introduction to his book on military law in Vietnam that the legacy of My Lai "beclouds the record" of the many well led and legally conducted military operations.[57] This is not a surprising claim coming from someone who dedicated most of his career to improving the law of war, and who personally worked very hard in Vietnam to improve legal services there. While Prugh's claim has its basis in fact, it was also clear that there was a need for change in the way the US taught and implemented the law of war. In Vietnam there had been many mistakes made in terms of training and implementing the law. Changes were to come in the post-Vietnam period.

America and the laws of war after Vietnam

The Vietnam years demonstrated that there was an immediate need for change in the way that the US taught and implemented the laws of war in its armed forces. Guenter Lewy writes that although the ROE were republished every six months to ensure maximum visibility to all US personnel, the distribution of the rules to the lower levels was often inadequate.[58] Only the Air Force made a systematic effort to test the actual knowledge of the ROE among its personnel. In other services familiarity with the ROE was inconsistent or lacking entirely.[59] Many officers had therefore relied on "common sense" rather than training.

The shock of My Lai and the apparent sense of crisis regarding discipline in the armed forces prompted some immediate changes. Effort was put into improving the training of military personnel in the field. The improved training revealed flagrant disregard of the ROE in some units, thus indicating what kinds of corrective action could and should have been taken years earlier.[60] The military was trying to make up for years of lost time. As Lewy notes:

An inspection of US Army Vietnam in May-June 1969 noted that about 50 per cent of all personnel had not received their required annual training in the Geneva and Hague Conventions. At that time, the pressure for body count and the free use of heavy weapons in populated areas probably made this kind of instruction rather academic and irrelevant.[61]

By May 1970, the amount of time required for training in the laws of war was increased. In the revamped training there was greater emphasis placed on dealing with illegal orders and the responsibility to disobey them. In terms of leadership, there was also a new section on command responsibility. However, as Lewy argues:

All these reforms probably came too late to have much of an impact on the final years of the American combat in Vietnam. The failure to implement and enforce proper training in the humanitarian conventions of the law of war until a major incident like My Lai revealed the inadequate training prevailing until then must be considered the responsibility of MACV and of the military and civilian chiefs of the military services.[62]

While the US military had made efforts to increase training time and to revise the rules to make them clearer and stronger, the underlying causes of disaster in Vietnam outlined above would require more measures than this to prevent another My Lai.

In certain ways, some of the problems in Vietnam solved themselves–or were solved institutionally–outside the system of military justice and regardless of concern for the laws of war. With the end of the "draft" in 1973 (as well as "Project 100,000"), those who did not wish to be enlisted in military service, or for that matter those who would not have regularly qualified, finished their time in the military and were discharged. Teaching the laws of war to an all-volunteer force that could meet certain standards of intelligence would, in many ways, be a much simpler task for US military lawyers than that they had encountered in Vietnam.

In terms of improving implementation of the laws of war, one of the first steps taken in this direction was the 1974 Department of Defense (DoD) Directive 5100.77.[63] This was the DoD's first overall law of war directive which set out the specific duties and responsibilities for law of war training for military personnel and the reporting of suspected violations of the law of war by US personnel. As Parks describes it, the Directive contained four key points:

It assigned responsibilities within the Department of Defense for law of war implementation. It assigned primary responsibility for training and compliance to each unit commander. It required reporting of war crimes for timely and proper investigation and appropriate disposition. Finally it established a training requirement, mandating training for each member of the military 'commensurate with his duties and responsibilities.'[64]

The Directive was implemented in the Army in 1975, the Navy in 1976 and the Air Force in 1976 with the expectation that each service would meet the standard established by the DoD. Military lawyers were also assigned the task of providing specific law of war training programmes for the services, as well as providing reference and training materials.[65]

'Activist' lawyers and 'operational law': 1975–1989[66]

In the face of incontrovertible evidence that the US military had serious problems regarding the laws of war, several immediate steps were taken to improve compliance and implementation by the Department of Defense. Yet, bringing about change was not that simple, and by the late 1970s still did not go very far in changing the culture of military operations—at least in a legal sense. As Borch argues, successful implementation of a Law of War Program would require that military lawyers would be able to communicate directly with commanders and their staff principals throughout the operational planning process, identifying issues of both a legal and a non-legal nature.[67]

While the changes that had been made went beyond the purely cosmetic, there was still a lot more that could be done at the command level to ensure that the mistakes of Vietnam would not repeat themselves. Again, as Borch notes:

Institutionally, the [JAG] Corps failed to view its years in Vietnam as a basis for engaging in any substantial modification of the way in which it had traditionally practiced military law. With the exception of an extensive effort to incorporate Vietnam lessons learned into both the Law of War training materials prepared and provided by the Judge Advocate General's School, little was done to capture the unique aspects of the Corp's Vietnam experience.[68]

It was not that the judge advocates were entirely unaware of the potential for change. By the early 1980s, JAGs had become involved in the detailed review of operational plans, pursuant to DoD Directive 5100.77, for nine years and "were far more aware of the potential for encountering legal issues impacting on the conduct of an operation."[69] Yet, as Parks notes, lawyers serving as law of war instructors in the late 1970s found themselves "confronted with hostile clients. Lawyers and the law of war were blamed for restrictions placed upon the use of military force during Vietnam."[70]

Change would come about on two fronts—the creation of a new way of looking at the implementation of the laws of war in military operations, called "operational law", and the emergence of "activist lawyers" to implement it.[71] The former of these two factors came about as an attempt to rethink and reintroduce the law of war as it related to military operations. In the late 1970s, the term "law affecting military operations" was developed to indicate that there were a myriad facets of the law that affected both wartime and peacetime operations. The concept brought together all of the areas that, as the name indicates, affected military operations in war and peace. While the basis of operational law remains the laws of war, it also includes US domestic law, such as laws and directives relating to security assistance, foreign military sales, intelligence oversight, contracts for goods and services overseas, foreign claims, and authority to negotiate agreements on behalf of the United States.[72] This also included aspects of public international law, such as base rights agreements, status of forces agreements, and questions of sovereignty.

Therefore, rather than presenting the law as a set of restrictions, emphasis was placed on the use of this law as a planning tool that not only dictated responsibilities but also set out the legal rights of the military.[73] Additionally, the use of the phrase (quickly shortened to "operational law" or OPLAW[74]) temporarily reduced to a minimum the use of the term "law of war", which had pejorative connotation in the aftermath of Vietnam.[75] In this way, military lawyers tried to present operational law as a positive tool rather than a set of bureaucratic restrictions.[76]

However, implementation of operational law required lawyers to be in the war room, and this required that the rapport between lawyers and commanders would have to be improved. While it would be wrong to suggest that all doors were shut to military lawyers, it was clear that they would have to present a case to offer their services. Military lawyers needed to convince their commanders that they would be helpful to the conduct of military operations, and not meddlesome. In other words, it was imperative for lawyers to overcome their Vietnam-stereotype whether it was deserved or not. This, in turn, required getting the military lawyer and his or her commander talking to improve understanding.

"Activist lawyers" therefore emerged in the Department of Defense to make the case for their presence in the war room. As Borch notes, the increase in individual initiative had its roots in the fact that the unconventional nature of the war in Vietnam required non-traditional thinking, and this realization was brought back by many lawyers who went to Vietnam. Additionally, by the late 1970s there were more lawyers in the military than ever before—and these were better educated.[77] Individual lawyers would approach individual commanders to convince them that military lawyers could provide a "package of total legal services" from the planning stages through to withdrawal. As Parks describes it, "The idea was to make the client aware of the many politico-legal facets of the lawyers work, in peace and war" while also educating the lawyer on the work of his superiors.[78] This was done through a series of symposiums, the first of which took place at the Judge Advocates General's School at Charlottesville, Virginia in 1982—and was found to be sufficiently useful to ensure that it has been held annually ever since. Additionally, military lawyers worked to get security clearance to perform their job in the war room as operations were actually carried out.[79]

American military operations in the 1980s

Grenada: Operation Urgent Fury

By the time of the 1983 intervention into Grenada in Operation Urgent Fury, there had been substantial improvements in the way that military lawyers conceived and sought to implement the laws of war in US military operations. However, there were still some problems; operational law, in its infancy, had not been completely implemented and integrated into military planning procedures. While by this point commanders had certainly warmed to the idea of military lawyers in the war room, their role in preparing for missions was limited at best. A few military lawyers had little knowledge of Urgent Fury until a few days before it began. The first judge advocate on the ground in Grenada had little more than twelve hours' notice of his deployment.[80] Additionally, the Army still only expected lawyers to focus on specific issues such as those related to the status and treatment of prisoners of war and detainees.[81]

Therefore, when it came to prisoners of war, there were several problems caused by a lack of planning, including legal planning, for the mission. Most of these stemmed from the fact that the military command had not expected to assume control over so many persons so quickly. After the first forces in the region had set up a camp for prisoners of war and other detainees at Point Salines, it was soon full with approximately 1,200–1,300 persons. Food and water were in short supply, and there was no electricity or sanitary facilities. While American forces had initially looked after the civilians, this job was soon handed over to forces from other Caribbean nations (Barbados and Jamaica) which had no experience in administering such camps. Security was lax and no attempt to organize or classify the prisoners was made.[82]

Among the prisoners taken there were more than 600 Cuban citizens who had taken part in the fighting, but many also claimed that they were merely construction workers and/or diplomats. Sorting out their status and exactly who was what was not straightforward. The fact that no declaration of war had ever been made by the United States with regard to Operation Urgent Fury, and that there was no acknowledgement from either the United States or Cuba that they were at war, complicated matters further.

Despite the tight media controls put in place, there started to be some public concern for the welfare of prisoners after the publication of an Associated Press photograph showing two captured soldiers with their arms bound behind their backs.[83] Amnesty International expressed its concern in a telegram to the US mission chief in Grenada about the conditions of the camp, citing reports that inmates were held up to three days in wooden crates, fully exposed to the heat of the sun with no facilities for water or personal hygiene. There were also some questions as to whether uncooperative prisoners were abused.[84]

Several steps were taken to remedy the situation. First, the troops from Caribbean nations who did not have POW-training were replaced with troops from the US 82nd Airborne Division and later military police. Within a week of arriving in the camp, approximately seventy Cubans were put to work constructing improved detention facilities in which they could stay until they were sent home. These included a concrete building with bathrooms and a shower. The ICRC sent representatives to check on the status and treatment of the prisoners as well as helping to facilitate the repatriation process.

The easiest solution for dealing with problems posed by POWs was to release them as quickly as possible, as soon as it was safe to do so. Still, as mentioned above, the over 600 Cubans in US custody posed several problems in this regard. The issue of classification was resolved when US commanders made the decision to consider all detainees (whether civilians or soldiers) as being entitled to prisoners of war rights under the Geneva Conventions "until a more informed determination of their status could be accomplished."[85] This decision was made on the basis that although no formal state of war had been declared, a state of hostilities was in existence and the Geneva Conventions were in effect. It also ensured that, formally, all prisoners were entitled to a high standard of rights.

The next question was how to get the Cubans home. Spain and Colombia volunteered to act as intermediaries between Cuba and the United States, but arrangements were made to send prisoners home through Barbados. There was also some concern as to whether the Cuban leader Fidel Castro would accept wounded prisoners (two of whom had been sent to US hospitals in Puerto Rico) and the bodies of those who had died in the fighting. Castro had previously refused to allow the bodies of Cubans killed in combat abroad to be shipped home.[86] Arrangements, however, made under the auspices of the ICRC and the first group of Cuban detainees was repatriated by 5 November.[87]

As Operation Urgent Fury wound down, one outstanding issue was the detention of the leaders (approximately forty in total) of the Marxist-inspired coup which had brought about the American invasion. After the prisoners of war had been released and the POW camp was closed down by mid-November, these individuals were handed over to the Grenadian authorities for trial and held at Richmond Hill Prison at St. George's. Here too there were some concerns. The *New York Times* claimed that two of the overthrown leaders, General Hudson Austin and Bernard Coard, were photographed handcuffed and blindfolded and that a US psychological operations unit had made posters of their "humiliation" to plaster around the country.[88] The ICRC continued to monitor the situation of the detainees at the new facility and, according to one report, expressed concern to the authorities that the inmates did not have adequate exercise and that there was an excessive heavily armed military presence.[89] Finally, throughout the country there were also concerns raised as to whether American military policemen had been conducting warrantless searches, detaining suspected troublemakers on flimsy grounds.[90] Army lawyers, however, had set out "strict limits on the authority of foreign military personnel to apprehend, detain, search and interrogate Grenadians" by 15 November as US and Commonwealth soldiers continued to man roadblocks throughout the island.[91]

Although Operation Urgent Fury was short (major operations lasted for just over a week), it indicated that there was still room for improvement regarding the role of military lawyers and operational law.[92] Military commanders reached the decision that judge advocates must be included in the planning of contingency operations from the beginning. The lack of notice given to military lawyers hindered preparation for potential legal problems, especially as giving correct and complete legal advice depends on having a full understanding of the nature and purpose of the deployment.[93] Additionally, it was clear that military lawyers would have to be prepared to solve or advise on quasi–legal issues and unanticipated legal matters. As Marc Warren argues, the task for lawyers was to facilitate operations, and this called for versatility as well as the ability to serve as an "honest broker" or "sounding board" in matters other than those involving law and other regulations.[94] For example, Army lawyers in Grenada were involved in setting up of a graves registration system.[95] As Borch argues, "Both the nature and the tempo of the deployment to Grenada presented novel legal challenges for the twelve or so judge advocates who served there from 25 October to 15 December."[96]

In this way, Borch sees Grenada as more of a "wake-up call" than Vietnam was for the Judge Advocates Corps in that, unlike Vietnam, Grenada led to an "institutional recognition" that military lawyers had a greater role to play: "[The] experiences of judge advocates in Grenada resulted in the Judge Advocate General's Corps' formal acknowledgement, as an institution, that judge advocates must be trained and resourced to provide timely advice on a broad range of legal issues associated with the conduct of military operations."[97]

By 1986 there was a renewed effort to impress the importance of operational law in the war room. This was facilitated by the Goldwater-Nichols Act of 1986 which, among other things, dramatically increased the authority and responsibility of legal advisers.[98]

Panama: Operation Just Cause

By the time that Operation Just Cause began in Panama in 1989, the scale of the transformation was readily apparent. First, unlike what happened with Operation Urgent Fury, Army lawyers began planning almost a year and a half in advance of the deployment of US troops. In this way the ROE could be tailored to the operation and to ensure that they strictly adhered to the laws of war.[99] Additionally, by the time the Operation Just Cause was underway, the revised ROE were fully in place. To military lawyers, Operation Just Cause demonstrated that the Department of Defense was taking the laws of war seriously, and this enabled them to implement a comprehensive operational law programme. Eckhardt argues that the changes signified that "the profession of arms reclaimed the rules of its own profession. The law of war came out of the library and off lawyers' desks and once again became the province of the practical profession of arms."[100]

In the eyes of the military lawyers, there was little choice in the matter. When interviewed, the Staff Judge Advocate for the US Southern Command, John Wallace, added: "All of the traditional rules were for the classic war, but the more likely conflicts in the future are these dirty little brush wars we keep tripping into... When you take those rules and translate them to Panama, they don't work very well."[101]

Therefore, prisoner of war issues in Panama seemed to be somewhat less chaotic than in Operation Urgent Fury. Of course the proximity of several large military bases (which also allowed for a steady troop build-up prior to the invasion) facilitated the establishment of detention facilities for those captured during the invasion. These facilities soon became very necessary; within a few days of the invasion, over 4,000 persons had either been captured or surrendered. A collection camp for detainees was built by US Army engineers at Empire Range, approximately 20 miles outside Panama City. For the United States, it was the largest prisoner of war camp set up since the Vietnam War.

One of the first tasks for the military was to quickly sort through the individuals who had been taken. In carrying out its invasion, the US military had "a pretty wide swath" when it came to taking prisoners.[102] As with Urgent Fury, captured persons were considered to be "detainees" rather than prisoners of war, but all individuals were given full Geneva rights until it could be determined that they did not deserve such privileges. According to several reports on the matter, the reason for this was that Operation Just Cause was not an act of "war" in the view of the United States but a "hostility", and that the term POW had "pejorative connotations".[103]

Those prisoners who had ambiguous status were given "Article 5 tribunals" (referring to Article 5 of the Third Geneva Convention) where a three-person tribunal was established to determine the status of detainees where there was any doubt. This included the many criminals and looters who had been taken with Panamanian soldiers (the Panama Defense Forces or PDF) and Noriega's "Dignity Battalions" (a more fanatical paramilitary group established by the dictator). Additionally, the tribunals screened for those individuals who were known to have tortured or been involved in drug trafficking. By the beginning of January, it was determined that all but approximately 100 detainees merited continued detention and approximately 4,000 were handed over to the Panamanian government. The remaining 100 were subject to further screening and some were brought to the US to stand trial.[104]

Operations were also scrutinized by several international organizations. Just over a week after the invasion, the ICRC was making daily visits to the detainee camp. Additionally, human rights organizations such as Americas Watch, the Panamanian Committee for Human Rights and the Washington Office on Latin America monitored the treatment given to the detainees (as well as investigating the levels of civilian casualties and other legal aspects of the mission).

But the most famous "prisoner of war" was the now-deposed leader of Panama, Manuel Noriega. After the Americans invaded, Noriega fled to the Vatican Nuncio's residence seeking sanctuary. After a standoff, Noriega surrendered to US forces on 3 January and he was taken to the United States to face trial in Miami. On 26 January, a letter from Noriega to President Bush was read in court where the former leader claimed that he was a prisoner of war because he had surrendered in wake of the US invasion. He therefore demanded full rights under the Geneva Conventions, including the right to wear his military uniform in court. On 2 February, the Justice Department announced that Noriega and one of his associates would be given POW rights but that this in no way changed any of the charges against them as the Conventions allowed prisoners to be tried for crimes.[105]

Criticism of the invasion in terms of the laws of war came from several sources. In terms of the treatment of prisoners of war, there does not seem to have been as much controversy as in other areas. In one controversial incident, a US soldier, 1st Sergeant Roberto E. Bryan, was charged with unpremeditated murder after he emptied his M16 rifle into an injured Panamanian being dragged towards some medics. The shooting followed a situation where a grenade had gone off as US soldiers were arresting several Panamanians suspected of hiding weapons and soldiers had opened fire, killing all of the suspects. Bryan argued that it appeared that the injured Panamanian, who was still alive, had moved his arm as if to reach for a weapon. But accounts differed and he was ultimately sent to a court-martial. A five-day trial ensued where it was alleged that Bryan's actions were little more than "a summary execution". However, the trial took place on 31 August 1990, at the outbreak of the Gulf Crisis where troops were facing immediate deployment to Iraq. According to Borch, although there were good grounds for prosecution, a conviction was unlikely as "no one was anxious to second-guess a decision made by a senior noncommissioned officer in the head of battle". Bryan was acquitted after two hours of deliberation.[106]

Criticism from NGOs tended to focus on civilian casualties and whether or not the US armed forces had "failed in their duty under the Geneva conventions to minimize harm to the civilian population."[107] Americas Watch focused most of its criticism on the failure of the United States to protect civilians who had been caught up on the battlefield, and said the effort to count the dead was inadequate. With regard to prisoners of war, America Watch also alleged that prisoners of war were not immediately repatriated upon the cessation of hostilities and that due process was not followed when individuals were captured. Some of the criticism for this rested with the newly installed Panamanian government to which the US had turned over nearly 4,000 POWs by the beginning of January.

America and the laws of war on the international stage

The mistakes made in Vietnam and the pressures of operations in the 1980s prompted the US military to reform itself and the way it implemented the laws of war. As we have seen, these changes were largely brought about by domestic developments (such as the notion of operational law) and even individual "activist" lawyers pushing for reform. Yet, internationally, these developments did not occur in a vacuum. In order to generate a fuller picture of what is going on, it is necessary to take a look at international developments with regard to the laws of war and the US reaction to them. It was going to be a bumpy road ahead.

Law and politics: the Geneva Diplomatic Conference 1974–77

By the end of the Vietnam War, it was becoming very clear that the 1949 Geneva Conventions, if not falling out of date, were not well designed to deal with the increasing numbers of wars of national self-liberation occurring across the globe.[108] Naturally, this did not escape the notice of humanitarians who grew concerned over the lack of law governing conflicts that fell between the civil war and interstate war categories. In such cases, invoking Common

Article 3 of the Conventions could ensure a bare minimum of regulation in the conflict, yet this was far removed from the protections of the full Conventions properly carried out.[109] Convincing governments or rebels to adhere to even these basic standards was more often than not an impossible task. The truth of the matter was that the states gathered in 1949 did not truly take wars of national liberation into consideration or believe in the possibility that a liberation movement could become a contracting party to the Conventions or be bound by them.[110] However, conflicts like Vietnam had demonstrated the deadly danger of this gap in the laws of war.

The issue had been raised by the ICRC at the 1957 International Red Cross Conference in New Delhi but had met an adverse reaction from the major powers. Yet, clearly the US was beginning to warm to the idea when it sought support to apply the Geneva Conventions to the war in Vietnam at the Vienna International Red Cross Conference in 1965. However, debates and conferences at the UN and UN institutions in the 1960s were a major force behind the movement to update the laws of war. The matter was brought up at the 1968 Tehran Human Rights Conference and in various UN bodies and reports between 1968 and 1972.[111] However, while the United Nations may have served as "a focal point" for pushing forward this humanitarian agenda, by 1972 the ICRC reasserted its role in terms of managing the debate on and development of the laws of war.[112] This came after a period when the ICRC had concentrated much of its efforts in the 1950s on issues relating to weapons of mass destruction, without much success. Suter argues that by the mid-1960s, "the Red Cross movement had no clear idea of how–if at all–the law of armed conflicts should be developed", and the organization had some difficulty adjusting to the developments which were taking place at the UN.[113] He therefore speculates that the ICRC remained cautious at best out of concern that the global political climate would not be conducive to generating the necessary international cooperation required to update the laws of war. The organization's recent failures on nuclear weapons/weapons of mass destruction did not provide much incentive for the organization either:

...the ICRC knew how troublesome such a revision [to the laws of war] could be, whichever organization did it, and so did not want itself or the UN to be hastily rushed into such a major undertaking. Indeed, the ICRC, later, reluctantly taking on this work, tried to follow a policy of avoiding too extensive a revision of the law of armed conflicts.[114]

Still, a resolution was passed at the 1969 International Red Cross Conference in Istanbul to support an ICRC mandate to convene a diplomatic conference which would move forward efforts to further codify the laws applicable in armed conflicts. Therefore, although it had been unenthusiastic, the ICRC reestablished itself in a leadership role on updating the laws of war. To prepare for a major diplomatic conference, several consultations were held and the ICRC recommended an extensive draft protocol "that was in effect a miniature Convention."[115]

The Geneva Diplomatic Conference and the 1977 Additional Protocols

What eventually emerged out of the Diplomatic Conference on the Reaffirmation and Development of International Humanitarian Law Applicable in Armed Conflicts were two Additional Protocols to the 1949 Geneva Conventions. The first was the Protocol Relating to the Protection of Victims of International Armed Conflicts (Protocol I) and second the Protocol Relating to the Protection of Victims of Non-International Armed Conflicts (Protocol II). But while the Diplomatic Conference, which was to meet for four negotiating periods over four years, did succeed in expanding the laws of war, the end result was so controversial that many states would not ratify until decades after it was signed, or, in the case of the US, would refuse to ratify it altogether.

How did this happen? Western nations, including the US, went along with the idea of further developing the laws of war, while the Socialist states and the Non-Aligned Movement saw the Convention as an opportunity to make political stands (particularly against the US and the West), to score points in the international arena and, in some cases, to secure recognition for particular political struggles and objectives throughout the world. Additionally, there were several national liberation movements invited to ensure "broad representation".[116] There had already been controversy and a heated political battle in the United Nations regarding national liberation movements and the laws of war prior to the Diplomatic Conference. However, few diplomats predicted just how contentious events would become. Christopher Greenwood argues that it was "probably naïve" of the ICRC and the Swiss Government not to anticipate a "hijacking" of their agenda.[117] However, Suter, present for some of the proceedings from 1974 to 1977, argues that this lack of foresight was universal among Western countries, including the United States:

... no delegate predicted that the conference was going to be a rough event. Everyone misread the signs. The Western governments... believed that somehow the Third World and Eastern European governments would not take to Geneva the views they were espousing in New York in 1973. Meanwhile, these latter governments believed that the minority Western government would recognize that they were no longer able to dictates what the law of armed conflicts ought to be and so would go along with the majority view expressed in New York.[118]

Predictions aside, the presence of the national-liberation movements guaranteed that Cold War politics and the politics of the Non-Aligned Movement would play a major role in shaping the Diplomatic Conference.[119] The ensuing controversy resulted in several contentious provisions in Protocol I. Perhaps the most familiar of these was the success of the Third World and Socialist countries in having the first session of the Conference elevate three categories of wars of self-determination to the status of international armed conflicts: "peoples fighting colonial domination and alien occupation and against racist regimes in the exercise of their right of self-determination". Such a stipulation would assure that forces fighting in these conflicts had the status of POWs should they be captured. Not only did this guarantee a certain standard of treatment, it also afforded a respectable international status which was valuable in wars for "hearts and minds". This provision, which eventually fell under Article 1 Paragraph 4, was opposed by the United States and other Western states but was passed by a vote of seventy in favour, twenty-one against and thirteen abstaining. Perhaps because of the sheer force of numbers presented by the alliance of Third World and Socialist states on the issue, or the desire to achieve at least some form of agreement, Western opposition to the provision gradually diminished during the Conference. When it was finally voted upon in the final draft of 1977, a general agreement emerged and it was passed eighty-seven in favour, one against with eleven abstentions.[120]

The purpose of Protocol II was much narrower than that of Protocol I as it sought to apply humanitarian standards to internal conflicts not covered by Protocol I. Yet it is clear that the issues covered in Protocol II were subject to the same Cold War/political pressures and controversies that affected Protocol I. Important here is the scope of Protocol II itself. An ambitious plan to adopt an extensive, detailed set of rules for governing internal conflict which are not liberation wars as defined in Protocol I was rejected owing to the intervention of Third World representatives. Some states, such as India, indicated concern that any such plan would "be tantamount to interference with the sovereign rights and duties of states", and other Third World states were quick to agree.[121] From this viewpoint, wars against imperialism and racism could be placed under the rules laid out in the Geneva Conventions, but any regulation of internal conflicts, including regulation of treatment of prisoners taken inside national territories, would infringe rights of sovereignty and self-determination.[122] Those who revolted against their own regime were to be considered criminals and as traitors who did not deserve the rights and protections afforded POWs.

A dispute as to where the Protocol should go emerged among the negotiating countries. It is possible to divide the different positions into four groups: nations that wanted a unified law for all armed conflicts (mostly Scandinavian counties led by Norway), those countries wanting a separate yet strong Protocol for internal wars (Western and Eastern European states), "realists" who wanted a shorter/minimal set of laws that would realistically be followed in internal conflicts (the Canadian delegation submitted a "simplified" Protocol in 1975), and those states that opposed any laws for internal conflicts but "nevertheless participated intensively in the detailed discussions in order to prevent a possible consensus" (Third World and Latin American countries).[123]

The United States for its part—perhaps reflecting some of the difficulties experienced in Vietnam—was a supporter of Additional Protocol II. (That the Protocol would only apply to internal wars which were unlikely to happen on US soil may have also encouraged US support.) While perhaps not as enthusiastic as the Scandinavian states, the United States was committed to strengthening the law in this area. However, opposition and intransigence from the Third World meant that the final draft of Protocol II resulted in a compromise which dramatically pared down the provisions that had been originally laid out. This effort was led by Pakistan in an effort to save the Protocol, but ultimately the new draft "completely or practically eliminated certain parts" of the original draft such as the sections on the means and methods of combat, relief and execution of the Protocol.[124] However, the Western states, realizing that it was better to have "half an egg instead of only an empty shell", went along with the Pakistani initiative.[125]

Looking back at the Diplomatic Conference, Forsythe argues:

Because of the nature of its origins, [the Diplomatic Conference and the Additional Protocols] was to be concerned as much with *realpoltik* as with war victims. The ICRC might see IHL as a means to regularize improved humanitarian protection for victims of war, but states might very well see IHL as another policy instrument to advance their primary policy concerns—concerns that might not prioritize the well-being of victims.[126]

Indeed, the politics of the Diplomatic Conference meant that a "quasi-consensus procedure" was used on many provisions that involved the use of compromise and bargains. To the head of the US delegation, George Aldrich, this was an advantage–the United States would have not got the results that it did without such a procedure.[127] However, the results of the Conference, the content of the Protocols and the method used to achieve them were soon under heavy scrutiny in the United States.

The American rejection of the 1977 Additional Protocols

Any narrative of the rejection of Additional Protocol I in the United States must begin by acknowledging that a new domestic factor was in play by 1980: the election of Ronald Reagan as President of the United States. The new administration immediately made it clear that it was taking a hard line stance to combat Communism, which did not blend well with the new protections for those engaged in wars of national liberation in the Additional Protocols.

The US delegation to the 1974–77 Diplomatic Conference had felt that the legislation represented progress in terms of the laws of war. George Aldrich argued in a series of articles that the Protocols represented a "new life for the laws of war"[128] and "a major accomplishment for international law and for human rights".[129] One of the main arguments Aldrich put forward for ratification was improved protection for prisoners of war. Aldrich had actually worked on the problem of treatment of American POWs in Vietnam for the State Department during that conflict and felt that he, as well as America, had a vested interest in strengthening guarantees for captured personnel.[130] Additional Protocol I, Article 5 stipulated that each side of the conflict must designate and accept a protection power that would ensure that prisoners of war were not being abused, and Aldrich argued that this provision would have been very valuable in Vietnam.[131] Additionally, Aldrich argued that the Protocols drafted a single, non-discriminatory set of rules which were applicable to all combatants.[132] Exceptions to the rules, which Communist forces had argued in the past, were made as narrow as possible and provided presumptions and procedures to prevent abuse of the exceptions.

Yet some would later argue that the US delegation suffered from the fact that the actual negotiation of the Protocols was left in the hands of international lawyers, "not all of whom were entirely conversant with either the law of war" or Pentagon priorities.[133] Although the military was certainly involved in helping to develop guidance, the participation of military lawyers in crucial negotiations was minimal. Military lawyers, commanders and Department of Defense personnel came together to review the 1977 Protocols in December of that year. In this way, for the first time, the documents were reviewed by those who would live or die by the rules set forth in the Protocols. The review process looked at the provisions, whether or not they were acceptable and if not, why not, and whether or not things could be fixed.[134]

In this way, the review process marked a drastic change in how the DoD looked at the laws of war and considered their effects on the military, and how they would be implemented. Yet, the legal review–whatever its verdict was going to be–was going to be overruled by the new ideological considerations of the Reagan administration. While Aldrich certainly believed that the Protocols marked progress for the laws of war and was concurrent with the US position, the White House made it clear that it disagreed.

In particular Douglas Feith, the Deputy Assistant Secretary of Defense Negotiations Policy from 1984–86, had deep concerns regarding US ratification and spoke out critically against it while he was in that position. In particular, he spoke out against the politicized negotiations process, provisions that would shield "terrorists" and render protection to their illegal tactics.[135] Feith, who is often associated with the neoconservative wing of the Republican Party, was clearly going to have ideological opposition to the Additional Protocols whether they were found workable or not.[136]

In 1987 it was announced by President Reagan that while the US would sign and ratify Protocol II, Protocol I was fundamentally flawed and would not be sent to the Senate. In an address to the Senate, Reagan argued:

[Protocol I] would give special status to "wars of national liberation," an ill-defined concept expressed in vague, subjective, politicized terminology. Another provision would grant combatant status to irregular forces even if they do not satisfy the traditional requirements to distinguish themselves from the civilian population and otherwise comply with the laws of war. This would endanger civilians among whom terrorists and other irregulars attempt to conceal themselves. These problems are so fundamental in character that they cannot be remedied through reservations, and I therefore have decided not to submit the Protocol to the Senate in any form...

It is unfortunate that Protocol I must be rejected. We would have preferred to ratify such a convention, which as I said contains certain sound elements. But we cannot allow other nations of the world, however numerous, to impose upon us and our allies and friends an unacceptable and thoroughly distasteful price for joining a convention drawn to advance the laws of war. In fact, we must not, and need not, give recognition and protection to terrorist groups as a price for progress in humanitarian law.[137]

Thus, while the US committed itself to accepting those parts of Protocol I that are considered customary, it refused to sign Protocol I and is not likely to do so in the near future.[138] While Protocol II was transmitted to the Senate for ratification, to date the US Senate has taken no action on the treaty.

The most legal war in history: the US and the 1990–91 Gulf Crisis

Certainly the rejection of Additional Protocol I, especially in such strict ideological terms, was controversial for the United States internationally and for those lawyers at home who wished to see the US as a model global citizen. Still, going into the First Gulf War, the US military clearly had a vastly different approach and attitude to the laws of war than it had had in Vietnam–with or without ratification of the Protocols. This new approach represented the culmination of the efforts of "activist lawyers" in the Department of Defense who realized that a better appreciation of the law did not only mean complex restrictions–law-guided policy could help operations to run smoother. The result, as has been described at the beginning of this chapter, was what turned out to be the most legalistic war fought in the history of the United States.

Yet, the US still faced difficulties regarding Protocol I. At the outset of the conflict, there had been the very real threat of "legal-interoperability".[139] The Allies in the Gulf all subscribed to different laws of war treaties, including Protocol I, and each had its own separate reservations and interpretations. In some ways this was, of course, somewhat of a moot point as Iraq had not signed or ratified the Protocols and they were therefore not binding on any of the parties. Still, even in its refusal to adhere to the Additional Protocols, the US had declared on several occasions that it would adhere to those provisions of the Additional Protocols that were considered customary.[140] There was good reason to do so. As Christopher Greenwood argues: "The nature of the hostilities, which involved, for example, the heaviest aerial bombardments since the Second World War, meant that many of the provisions of Protocol 1 were potentially of great importance."[141]

Prisoners of war in the Gulf

In terms of war crimes or violation of the laws of war, most of the debate was over the targeting policy employed by the United States. In particular, the bombing of the Amiriya bunker was the subject of much controversy.[142] However, as in most of the wars in which the United States engaged in the twentieth century, POWs were again a major issue.

The legacy of the way Americans had suffered in Vietnamese prisoner of war camps continued to linger over troops participating in Operation Desert Shield/Desert Storm, and Saddam Hussein's brutal record treatment of Iranian prisoners of war taken during the Iran-Iraq War of the 1980s seemed to suggest that any soldier unlucky enough to fall into Iraqi hands was in for a rough ride. These concerns were only heightened when approximately forty-seven Coalition forces members were captured and taken prisoner during the course of the campaign in Iraq. By most accounts, the treatment received by Allied prisoners did not even come close to the standards outlined in the Geneva Conventions—although the experiences of different prisoners varied. On the one hand, some prisoners were beaten, tortured or dealt some other kind of physical abuse. Additionally, the Iraqi government threatened to use the prisoners as human shields against the coalition bombing and also refused to allow the ICRC to visit. Air Force Major Jeffrey Tice was subjected to electric shocks as his captors tried to coerce him into making a video to air on television, and Major Rhonda Cornum was sexually assaulted while being transported to a prison.

However, several Americans taken indicated that they had also received reasonable treatment. Some Air Force pilots who were injured when they either crash landed or parachuted to the ground were given rudimentary medical care. Others reported that Iraqi soldiers shared their food upon capture.[143] In this way, treatment afforded to captured personnel taken by the Iraqis appears to have been due to the kindness of the individuals involved rather than a coherent policy of the Iraqi government.

For the Coalition, captured personnel became both a rallying point and symbol of the brutality of Saddam's regime. Already outraged at the prospect of having their soldiers used as human shields to protect certain targets, Coalition countries were outraged when British and American POWs appeared on television appearing beaten and bruised and muttering statements condemning "aggression" against the Iraqi people. It was therefore unsurprising that one of the requirements for the Iraqi surrender was an immediate release of all prisoners of war and hostages taken. Along with a map outlining where mines had been laid in Kuwait, the release of prisoners was one of the top priorities for Coalition troops. Britain insisted on linking a ceasefire to the releasing of prisoners of war. The United States argued that there would be no prisoner "exchanges" (where one US prisoner was released for a certain fixed number of Iraqi POWs) but that Iraq needed to release all Coalition personnel immediately.[144] Iraq complied and all prisoners of war were released by 6 March 1991.

The major prisoner of war issue for the Coalition after hostilities was what to do with the approximately 80,000 Iraqi POWs in their hands (and there seemed to be little, if any, dispute that they were prisoners of war). Even before hostilities began, the issue posed significant challenges for Coalition forces which had prepared for thousands of surrendering Iraqis. With over 500,000 Iraqi troops fielded—most of whom were presumed to be poorly trained and motivated conscripts–it was hoped that thousands could be convinced to give up in the hope that it would shorten the conflict and lessen the cost of battle.[145] Several large POW camps were constructed by the Coalition and a psychological-warfare programme encouraging Iraqis to defect and/or surrender was devised. Arabic-language radio broadcasts and 14 million leaflets dropped on occupied Kuwait promised those who surrendered good treatment, food and "Arab hospitality".[146] With nearly 1,000 soldiers having surrendered by the beginning of February, before the ground invasion began, it was already becoming clear that the Iraqis in Kuwait, under attack from a constant aerial bombardment, were suffering from deprivation, eroding morale and dread at the prospect of facing Coalition forces.[147]

Yet, once the ground invasion began on 24 February, the sheer number of Iraqis who surrendered, and the speed at which they did so, posed difficulties. As long columns of ragged Iraqis waving white flags marched towards US troops, bombing had to be conducted in such a way as to provide a lull from time to time, to enable the Iraqi forces to come forward and surrender.[148] In terms of logistics, POWs had to be issued with gas masks and evacuated from the battlefield.[149] As violence and civil strife continued within Iraq a few weeks after the end of formal hostilities, more and more Iraqi soldiers surrendered to escape the uncertainty within their own country. By April, the Army troops from the First Armored Division near Basra had taken 3,000 POWs–1,000 more than they had during actual ground hostilities.[150]

Finally, as with previous conflicts, the Gulf War again brought about problems of repatriation. Large numbers of prisoners of war resisted being sent back to Iraq out of fear that they would be punished for surrendering. Many countries in the Coalition, including the US and the UK, having had negative experiences in the Second World War and Korea, agreed that no prisoner should be forcibly repatriated. The main problem was where to send the POWs who did not wish to return to Iraq–a problem largely resolved when King Fahd of Saudi Arabia offered to take in 50,000 Iraqi refugees and prisoners of war including army deserters.[151]

A Success Story?

Can we regard the 1991 Gulf War as a success story in terms of the law of war? The numbers alone tell part of the story. By one estimate, the ratio of American legal advisers sent to the Gulf Region in comparison to the other allies was 70:1.[152] Yet these numbers are ultimately meaningless unless there are actions to suggest that the level of legal influence was substantial. However, to demonstrate this, it is possible to look at the judgments and statements of officials, journalists and NGOs in reflection on the conflict. Colin Powell, then Chairman of the Joint Chiefs of Staff, indicated in an interview for the American Bar Association Journal that "Decisions were impacted by legal considerations at every level... Lawyers proved invaluable in the decision making process."[153]

Steven Keeva adds in the article:

Lawyers were everywhere during the Gulf War. They worked out of the headquarters of Central Command... and they slept in the sand alongside troops in the field. They negotiated host-nations agreements and advised commanders on the legal implications of targeting decisions and weapons use...[154]

Additionally, given the genuinely unprecedented legal oversight of the operations, Human Rights Watch and Greenpeace concluded that the US generally "behaved in accordance with provisions of the Geneva Protocol".[155]

Of course these efforts did not and could not prevent any law of war violations from taking place; mishaps are bound to happen in war, as are controversial actions.[156] Expecting an entirely accident free-conflict or bloodless war is unrealistic. However, the American military's policy of following the law of war clearly lead to a smoother operation than might otherwise have occurred. The treatment of prisoners of war in the 1991 Gulf War seems to demonstrate this point. By promising and providing Iraqi POWs good treatment, the Coalition sought to make its job easier by having its enemy surrender rather than fight it out. Warren argues that the purpose of a law of war adviser "is to lawfully facilitate mission accomplishment, thereby enhancing the versatility of already capable units to meet diverse mission requirements.[157] If we evaluate the implementation of the law of war on these grounds, it is then possible to agree with the assertion that law played a significant role in the 1991 Gulf War.

America and the laws of war in the twentieth century

To look back at the course of the twentieth century, comparing the US in the Philippines at the beginning with the US in the First Gulf War at the end, we can see a clear difference in the way the US considered, enacted and taught the laws of war. It is worth examining why this is the case. As we have seen, there are several reasons one can point to that seem to have played a role in what as well might be called the "legal revolution" in the American military. The first goes back to an idea that even Clausewitz recognized in *On War*: "Any unnecessary expenditure of time, every unnecessary detour, is a waste of strength and thus abhorrent to strategic thought... Thus theory demands the shortest roads to the goal."[158]

The concept that Clausewitz is referring to is the idea of the "economy of force". Simply put, it is the idea that armies should attempt to achieve their goals as fast, efficiently and effectively as possible. While this may sound like an invitation to trample on the laws of war in the name of "efficiency" (and on numerous occasions throughout history it has been invoked to do just that), in fact the notion of economy of force has had quite the opposite effect. For example, in so far as precision guided missiles (PGMs) have replaced carpet bombing as a means of warfare, this may be considered an illustration of the economy of force. New possibilities for discrimination thus become possible when you have a bomb that can find its target within a one metre radius, as opposed to the relative indiscriminate damage caused by traditional "dumb" bombs that required far more firepower to ensure that a target was hit.

But the idea has wider implications and this point was driven home by the massacres in Vietnam: that major violations of the laws of war are quite costly in terms of resources, manpower and reputation. The US missions in Mai Lai and Son Thang were not just brutal in their attacks–they were quite useless. Aside from the sufferings of those who were there, it cost the Americans in terms of resources, but also heavily in terms of international reputation. Going out of one's way to commit atrocities is a direct violation of the principle of "economy of force", and over the course of the twentieth century this became increasingly recognized by Western armies throughout the world, including the United States. If the good will of civilians and prisoners of war will help you achieve your goal easier and faster, then you have every incentive to treat them well. As argued in Chapter One, this was the lesson realized by General Winfield Scott in the Mexican-American War who, having read about the disastrous campaign of the French in Spain, tried to implement policies that ensured respect for the civilian population. Similarly today, international support, which is crucial for military endeavours, is damaged by violations of the laws of war. Military commanders have every incentive to ensure that such violations do not happen. History demonstrates that troops out of control are indicative of an inefficient force, and therefore commanders have every reason to ensure that their troops stay in line. As the US Department of Defence report on the First Gulf War argued: "...no Iraqi action leading to or resulting in a violation of the law of war gained Iraq any military advantage. This 'negative gain from negative actions' in essence reinforces the validity of the law of war."[159]

Thus, the US military redrafted and rewrote its rules of engagement (ROE) and drafted its operational law to combine policy with tactics, methods and means and the laws of war.

Another crucial factor was the improvements made in the teaching of the laws of war. As Parks argues, "it is likely that some see the [laws of war] training as 'checking the box'".[160] The difficulty, as he describes it, is the common notion that American military personnel are automatically going to do the right thing in the field. "It is sometimes difficult for our soldiers to see the necessity for repeated law of war training, because they do not believe this to be an American problem."[161] Yet, My Lai and Son Thang showed that this was clearly not the case—and demonstrated that if training was not revamped, revised and made mandatory, then mistakes would happen again. The new approach which sought to increase the amount of training, to rely on a simplicity of principles to keep rules straightforward, and to take a positive approach which emphasized rights as well as responsibility helped to make this the case.

In short, by the 1990s, law seemed to be fully integrated into US military operations. As the decade progressed, the focus turned to those areas where circumstances and the law were not so clear-cut. Increasingly the United States found itself involved in situations like Somalia and Haiti where the roles of combatants, civilians and criminals were blurred. Engaging in such dangerous environments proved to be a legal nightmare. Thus, a lot of the effort regarding the law of war within the US military in the 1990s looked at how the law applied to "operations other than war". Increasingly, the law of war was applied to issues such as police training, and rules of engagement were drafted to fit peacekeeping and peace enforcement operations (which typically emphasized self-defence and restraint).[162] In Panama, Somalia and Haiti, the decision was made to treat captured persons—termed "detainees"—according to the provisions of the Geneva Convention, although persons captured may not have qualified or may often have fallen between categories. Each detainee was visited by a "detainee judge advocate" within seventy-two hours of detention and, through an interpreter, told the reasons for detainment and given an opportunity to communicate with his or her captors.[163]

Although such operations would often prove frustrating, if not deadly, to US troops, the US military continued to say that it would under all circumstances abide by the law of war. While serving as the Commanding General of the First Marine Expeditionary Force, Lieutenant General Anthony C. Zinni argued: "Operational law is going to become as significant to the commander as maneuver, as fire support, and as logistics. It will be a principal battlefield activity... Operational law and international law are the future."[164]

Conclusion

On 4 May 2000, the US Ambassador at Large for War Crimes Issues, David J. Scheffer, addressed the US Army First Corps at Fort Lewis in Washington on US adherence to the laws of war:

> The US military leads the world in the art of integrating legal advice into the process of planning and executing operations.... The Army leadership is committed to reinforcing legal principles in the real world of military practice because the laws of armed conflict do not simply exist as some ethereal smoke in the ozone. They are not some ethereal smoke in the ozone. They are not some rigid code of unrealistic regulation imposed upon you by a disinterested chain of command.... [Violations of the laws of war] are the acts of criminals and the law recognizes that brand of conduct as criminal even in the context of conflict.[165]

The sentiments expressed in this statement reflect the attitude of the United States by the end of the twentieth century towards the laws of war, but as discussed in the last two chapters, in many ways it also rings true with the sentiments expressed at the beginning. The US, in its idealism and belief in the rule of law, had committed itself to improving the laws of war. Yet, where ideology and interest conflicted with the desire to fight wars humanely, the US, like the European countries, would find legal reasons why the law did not and could not apply. Such decisions were not *Realpolitik*, but were based on standards of Western civilization and normative assumptions as to who qualified for rights under the laws of war and under what circumstances.

This had changed by 1945, but especially so with the drafting of the 1949 Geneva Conventions and creation of the UCMJ. Increasingly it was harder to justify denial of rights to prisoners and punitive targeting policies. However, if this was the case, why does Vietnam remain powerfully linked to the idea of American war crimes?

As this chapter has tried to argue, there were several important factors involved. First there was the nature of the conflict which, conceptually, did not lend itself very well to the idea of international law or the laws of war. However, there were problems in the US military regarding discipline and weak leadership, which created the space for violations of the laws of war to take place. Orders were not properly handed down, the rules of engagement were ignored, training was lacking, frustration and agitation were allowed to flourish and weak leadership only served to aggravate these problems.

While the military walked away from Vietnam in a mood to forget rather than implement any lessons learned, "activist lawyers" and the concept of "operational law" began the process of reform in terms of how the laws of war were implemented in the American armed forces. Talking to commanders and advocating the usefulness of the law as a tool rather than as a restraint gradually led to a process where law took on a greater importance than ever before. By the time of the 1991 Gulf War, the law seemed to have become a major consideration in military operations. It is possible to regard some of these activist lawyers as the largely unsung champions of the laws of war in terms of US military policy. While certainly the Department of Defense was going to have to change the way it implemented the law regardless, "activist lawyers" in the 1970s and 1980s played a major role in bringing about a "legal revolution" by speaking with commanders and making the case for the laws of war.

The other lesson to be drawn from the Vietnam and post-Vietnam experience is that implementation of the laws of war requires constant effort and diligence on behalf of not only lawyers, but also commanders in operational centres and on the ground. Where war crimes occur, it is virtually always possible to point to a lack of vigilance, discipline or willingness to implement the law. My Lai and Son Thang demonstrated that regardless of the respect for the laws of war in one's own country, in the fog of war a nation cannot assume that its soldiers will always do the right thing. Improved training in the laws of war and a belief in its effectiveness by commanders played a major role in the improvements seen in the military operations of the 1991 Gulf War compared with Vietnam.

By the end of the Gulf War, it seemed to many that the future lay with "operations other than war"–peacekeeping, peace-enforcement operations as well as the delivery of aid. Throughout the operations of the 1990s (including the difficult missions in Somalia) the US maintained the position, policy and procedures regarding the laws of war that had been in place during the 1991 conflict. The post-Vietnam "operational law" regime looked to remain in place for some time. Yet, the attacks of 9/11 and the ensuing War on Terror posed a massive challenge to the policies that had been put in place–and many began to question whether they should have been put there to begin with. This will be the focus of the next section of the book.

4

JUST CAUSE AND JUST MEANS?

LINKING THE PURPOSE AND TACTICS OF WAR AFTER 9/11

Introduction

In terms of the laws of war, the US began the 1990s with what has been called the most legalistic war in history. Many acclaimed the First Gulf War as an indication of what could be accomplished with a proper military ethos, implementation of the laws of war, precision guided weaponry and a coalition of like-minded states–a relatively humane war with relatively minimal loss of civilian life during combat operations.[1]

The reaction to 9/11 would seem to mark a reversal in this regard. Within five months of the start of the "War on Terror" and Operation Enduring Freedom in Afghanistan, pictures of prisoners, blindfolded and chained, appeared, prompting worldwide allegations of US torture and serious violations of the laws of war. Why, within a ten-year period, was the US openly refuting what many considered some of the key principles of the laws of war? Where many had once praised the United States for its efforts to institutionalize laws of war training in its military doctrine and its careful implementation when it came to targeting issues, now its actions received almost universal condemnation from friend and foe alike.

The explanation of this apparent about-face is complex–and the issues involved not as black and white as many international lawyers and commentators often argue. In looking for the explanation, this chapter will briefly look at the issues facing the laws of war in the 1990s and the response of the United States, including its reaction to Kosovo's "war by committee". It will also look at the impact of what has been called the "New Sovereigntist Critique" of international law in America. In doing so, the chapter will examine the reasons why, as events unfolded, the United States ultimately downplayed the significance of the laws of war, specifically the Geneva Conventions, in the War on Terror. Rooted in an increasing suspicion of the direction of international law, frustration with formally organized coalition warfare, and, crucially, a belief that the rules of the game had changed after 9/11, the United States argued that its right to self-defence trumped its international "obligations" and that the War on Terror would be fought on its own terms.

America and international law in the 1990s

It is the purpose of this section to demonstrate that the decisions made regarding the laws of war in the War on Terror did not come from out of the blue. Rather, they partially reflect an increasing frustration with and suspicion of international law, including the laws of war, in the 1990s. In particular it will look at the creation of the International Criminal Court, and at the implications of NATO's Kosovo campaign in the spring of 1999.

The 'new' human rights agenda and the ICC

As is now well known, the end of the Cold War brought about in many countries a new faith in international institutions, not only for maintaining or even establishing peace, but also for the protection of human rights. This could be seen with the establishment by the UN General Assembly of the Office of the High Commissioner for Human Rights (OHCHR) in 1993. As Julie A. Mertus argues, "Decades of human rights standard-setting had at last given way to a new age of human rights implementation and enforcement.... When the Cold War ended, anything seemed possible."[2] Hundreds, if not thousands of NGOs claiming some interest in human rights emerged in the 1990s and many states, such as South Africa and Chile, began to confront human rights violations that occurred during their dark Cold War years.

At the same time, the end of the Cold War resulted in a surge of internal and intra-national state conflicts now outside superpower control and usually involving some kind of ethnic hatred. The failure of the international community, if not Western countries, to respond appropriately to these crises resulted in a bloody, protracted war in the former Yugoslavia and genocide in Rwanda. To address some of the wrongs committed during these conflicts, criminal tribunals, the International Criminal Tribunal for the Former Yugoslavia (ICTY) and the International Criminal Tribunal for Rwanda (ICTR), were set up under international auspices to try those accused of war crimes and/or crimes against humanity. These efforts lent force to the movement already pushing for a permanent international criminal court. In 1989, Trinidad and Tobago persuaded the UN General Assembly to instruct the International Law Commission to prepare a draft statute which was to be submitted back to the UN General Assembly by 1994. After the text of the Statute was finalized by a three-year Preparation Committee, the ICC Statute was adopted by the 1998 Rome Diplomatic Conference, and came into force on 1 July 2002.

While many heralded the agreement as the hallmark of a new era in the protection of human rights and prosecution of war criminals, the ICC was greeted with suspicion in the United States. Some of the specific reasons for this caution will be dealt with below. For now it is sufficient to say that US leaders and military officials were concerned about over-enthusiastic, independent prosecutors who would not be accountable to any national or international authority. They also had a concern that the Court would be used more as a political tool to wield against the US than as a harbinger of justice.

Additionally, it was becoming clear that there were many who did not agree with the direction that human rights were taking in the 1990s—in so far as they related to warfare. Human rights advocates argued that international human rights law should be applied in conflict situations. Although the laws of war and international human rights law have developed separately, there are many who would argue that they are increasingly intertwined. As Cassese argues:

...the human rights doctrine has operated as a potent leaven, contributing to shift the world community from a reciprocity-based bundle of legal relations, geared to the 'private' pursuit of self-interest, and ultimately blind to collective needs, to a community hinging on a core of fundamental values, strengthened by the emergence of community obligations and community rights and the gradual shaping of the public interest.[3]

Therefore, "humanitarian law has become less geared to military necessity and increasingly impregnated with human rights values."[4]

There was and (continues to be) a great deal of apprehension about this situation.[5] As the laws of war and human rights law are brought together, there is a concern that this convergence extends and overcomplicates the law further than what states are willing to tolerate. In disseminating information about the laws of war to ordinary soldiers, any blurring of the laws by adding human rights considerations may only serve to complicate matters. Militaries seek to ensure that the law is kept as simple as it possibly can be, so that, to the highest degree possible, it is obvious to soldiers which law is applicable and when. A blending of the two legal regimes may complicate matters, and to insist upon it on the battlefield will only serve to make decision making more complicated for military commanders.

In addition, such an understanding downplayed the role of reciprocity which had traditionally played an important role in enforcing the laws of war. For example, good treatment of prisoners on one side could be ensured by providing good treatment for prisoners on the other. Throughout the twentieth century, the idea that any state wanting to maintain the moral high ground in conflict had to abide by the laws governing conflict regardless of the actions of the other side gained ground in conflicts like the Korean and Vietnamese Wars.[6] However, blending of human rights and humanitarian law in the 1990s posed a vision of the laws of war which completely eliminated any role for reciprocity and therefore suggested a very different basis for the laws of war. For some, there was a concern that this approach could be viewed as eliminating a potentially crucial bargaining chip when it came to ensuring that an enemy abided by the law of armed conflict.

Still, by the end of the 1990s, some states, and many NGOs, were increasingly willing to subject military actions, especially those by Western armies, to international human rights tribunals such as the European Court of Human Rights (ECHR) and international courts such as the International Court of Justice (ICJ) and the ICTY. This was certainly the case during the Kosovo conflict—to which we will now turn our attention.

The impact of Kosovo I–targeting[7]

With the goal of stopping Milošević's forces from massacring Albanian civilians in Kosovo, NATO began an eleven-week bombing campaign against (what was then) the Federal Republic of Yugoslavia, which lasted from 24 March to 11 June 1999. As the alliance did not have any formal approval from the UN Security Council (owing to the inevitability of a veto by Russia, if not by China), the issue was politically divisive and, according to many international lawyers, legally dubious. Although the campaign took seventy-seven days, it is generally accepted that NATO's intervention did indeed stop Milošević—leading to a period of relative stability in Kosovo, if not a perfect peace.

Still, despite this outcome, the NATO campaign left a bitter taste in the mouths of many within the Atlantic Alliance, including the United States.

Two issues in particular–the impact of coalition warfare, and the laws of war and the ICTY's actions during and after the campaign–are noteworthy here. First, the impact of coalition warfare, what was later referred to as "war by committee" by General Wesley Clark and other American military officials, certainly seems to have tested American patience.[8] NATO, an alliance that relies on consensus when it makes decisions, needed to be unanimous in its agreement when selecting targets. Therefore, each target was subject to up to nineteen different interpretations of the laws of war. This in particular became an issue over "dual-use" targets, objects which may have both civilian and military uses, in the later and intensified part of the campaign.[9] The Americans, who have traditionally taken a much wider view of what constitutes a legitimate target, frequently disputed with nations, such as France, which adhered to a much stricter interpretation of the applicable targeting law.[10] According to Lieutenant General Michael Short, the NATO Air Commander during the campaign, planes were often sent up in the air on a mission, only to have that mission recalled at the last moment when one nation indicated that it could not support the targeting of a particular object.[11] As one of the commanders in the campaign, he argued:

Unfortunately, because NATO was an alliance of 19 nations, you get the lowest common denominator. All those folks have to agree on something... Targeting was not mine to decide. Targeting decisions were made in the White House, at Number Ten Downing Street, and in Paris, Rome and Berlin... We did our best to target those things that we thought would have the effect of bringing Milosevic to the table. Instead, because those targets were not picked by professional soldiers and professional sailors and professional airmen, we bombed targets that were quite frankly inappropriate for bringing Milosevic to the table. I would say to you that in terms of targeting this was a victory by happenstance more than victory by design.[12]

It was argued that an overly strict interpretation of the applicable law dragged out the campaign by hindering its effectiveness. Ivo H. Daalder and Michael E. O'Hanlon argued that it was not until the NATO Commanders were able to persuade the political leadership to authorize a much wider range of targets in Belgrade and elsewhere in late May that the campaign became truly effective. By early June, Serbia was reeling as its electrical grids were severely damaged and water distribution was adversely affected in all major cities.[13]

Many NATO officials, and certain members of the Clinton administration, have argued that the United States would have conducted a much more vigorous bombing campaign from the outset of the war if only the other NATO members had allowed it to do so. However, as Daalder and O'Hanlon argue, while France did exercise some restraining power on NATO planners, particularly after the first couple of weeks of the war, the net effect was generally to push back the bombing of some specific targets by, at most, a few days. Additionally, France was not the only country to scrutinize the target sets in detail–it is apparent that the Joint Chiefs of Staff had to request permission on a daily basis from the White House to strike certain targets.[14]

Still, it is clear that the impression that the Americans were left with after Allied Force was that their allies' overly strict interpretation of the laws of war prevented them from conducting an effective campaign in the first stages of the war. Again, as Short has argued:

[The United States] wants to fight as part of the coalition. We want to be with our allies... However, as a professional soldier, I would tell you I prefer to be a member of a coalition of the willing as we had in the Gulf War.

In 1991 if you chose to throw in your forces with us... you were welcome, but you came under our terms. We explained to you how we were going to make war and that if you did not like that explanation, or if you could not sign up for those terms, then you did not need to be part of our coalition. However, in 1999 it was NATO, not a coalition of the willing. All nations had to agree, and so we ended up with the lowest common denominator. This is how it was that a nation that was providing less than 10% of the total effort could say to the most powerful nation on the face of the earth "you cannot bomb that target."

The United States of America lost its leverage on the first night. On the first night of the war we lost any leverage we had, and we ended up being leveraged.[15]

General Wesley Clark, who recounts the war in his memoir, *Waging Modern War*, seems to agree conditionally: "As for NATO, political approval from each member nation has been necessary before any military plans can be developed, and the general political resistance in the West to signal readiness to use force means that the Alliance's military planning will almost inevitably be too slow."[16] He adds:

In the American channel there were constant temptations to ignore Allied reservations and attack the targets we wanted to strike. It was always the Americans who pushed for the escalation to new, more sensitive targets... and always some of the Allies who expressed doubts and reservations. For a US administration anxious to finish the operation and avoid the problems of a ground intervention, these Allied reservations were, no doubt, exasperating.

But though there was discussion in U.S. channels about striking unilaterally, we never did. We always maintained that no single target or set of targets was more important than NATO cohesion. This was the most crucial decision of the campaign, and one of its most important lessons, for it preserved Allied unity and gave to each member of

NATO an unavoidable responsibility for the outcome. This made it a true Allied operation–a pattern for the future.[17]

Clark may have felt this way, but the comments of Short above make it clear that not everyone was eager to make this a model for future warfare.

The impact of Kosovo II–The ICTY's Report to the Prosecutor

But if the US government felt uncomfortable with the outcome and the implications of Kosovo, in its eyes the ICTY was about to add insult to injury. On 14 May 1999, while hostilities were still ongoing over Kosovo, the ICTY Prosecutor, Carla Del Ponte, established a committee to investigate possible war crimes committed by NATO in its conduct of Operation Allied Force. The news was not taken well within NATO or the United States. As Adam Roberts remarks:

In 1999 the United States, having been campaigning diplomatically against the projected International Criminal Court for the previous six months on the grounds that the actions of US forces should not be the subject to a foreign prosecutor and tribunal, chose to wage war in the one part of the world where ongoing war was subject to such a tribunal.[18]

Although the ICTY eventually recommended that "neither an in-depth investigation related to the bombing campaign as a whole nor investigations related to specific incidents are justified" (owing either to insufficient evidence or to the fact that the law in a particular area remained too unclear),[19] there was a sense of outrage among many in the United States. As the Americans saw it, it was they who put their money and soldiers on the line during a conflict to stop genocide; any attempt to prosecute NATO officials was politically and unjustly motivated. Judith A. Miller, who served as General Counsel for the US Department of Defense during Operation Allied Force, argued that while she was gratified that the Report to the Prosecutor warranted that there should be no further investigation, the manner in which the committee reached its conclusions was "deeply disturbing":

To have twenty-twenty hindsight scrutiny, done at leisure, of decisions and determinations made in the fog of war... based on allegations by those who do not hold Western nations in very high regard, is a chilling and frightening prospect. I fear that the reservations of the United States with respect to the International Criminal Court are well-founded, based on the aftermath of the Kosovo Conflict.[20]

David B. Rivkin and Lee A. Casey gave a similar note of caution:

Significantly, while no prosecutions against NATO officials are currently planned, even the relatively tame Yugoslav tribunal did not give the alliance a clean bill of health. Future outcomes in the permanent ICC, a court that will be less dependent upon U.S. and NATO largesse than is the Yugoslav tribunal, may be very different.[21]

The significance of the ICTY's actions was also not lost on the American Congress. The controversial, yet influential American Senator, Jesse Helms, while he was Chair of the Foreign Relations Committee, argued:

Most recently, we learned that the chief prosecutor of the Yugoslav war crimes tribunal... conducted an eleven month investigation of alleged NATO war crimes during the Kosovo campaign... the very fact that she entertained the idea brings to light all that is wrong with the UN's conception of global justice, which proposes a system in which independent prosecutors and judges, answering to no state or institution, wield unfettered power to sit in judgement of the foreign policy decisions of Western democracies.[22]

The ICTY's actions reinforced the suspicions emerging within the US towards the ICC but also towards the idea of international normative standards and international law. It was, after all, at this time that John Bolton argued that "while treaties may be politically or even morally binding, they are not legally obligatory. They are just not 'law' as we apprehend the term."[23]

American Exceptionalism and the 'New Sovereigntists'

That the United States often sees itself as a "shining city upon a hill" is nothing new in its history. From the founding of the republic, Americans have often viewed their country as a good and great nation, divinely inspired to lead the world by example at home or activism abroad to promote individual freedom.[24] Hence the US has often viewed itself, its Constitution and Bill of Rights as exceptional among nations. So, to the American Exceptionalists, US law was not to be trumped by any international law to the contrary.[25]

While American Exceptionalism was very prominent during the Reagan administration, its impact on thinking about international law began to be strongly felt in the 1990s. Many of those who were to become key figures in the administration of George W. Bush began to question the legitimacy, sources and even existence of international law. They were united in their critique of an "unaccountable" and "vague" international human rights agenda or any attempt, as they saw it, to limit the US Constitution.

In an article in *Foreign Affairs*, Peter J. Spiro referred to the application of American Exceptionalist thinking to international agreements as a "New Sovereigntist" vision of international law and proceeded to critique it.[26] In making his argument, Spiro outlines three New Sovereigntist lines of attack. The first is that the content of the emerging international legal order is vague and illegitimately intrusive on domestic affairs. The second condemns the international law making process as unaccountable and its results as unenforceable. Finally, New Sovereigntists argue that the US can opt out of any international legal regime as a matter of power, legal right and constitutional duty.[27]

Given the name "New Sovereigntists", it should come as no surprise that the key to these arguments is the idea of sovereignty which, according to this line of reasoning, protects the American Constitution that embodies the rights and way of life chosen by Americans for themselves. Striking out against those who argue that sovereignty is constructed or "organized hypocrisy" (that sovereignty does not really exist but happens to remain an organizing feature of the international system),[28] New Sovereigntists lay out a moral defence of sovereignty as a doctrine underlying the social contract which determines how a particular people will let themselves be governed.[29] As Jeremy Rabkin argues, "Sovereignty is at the heart of all [social] compromises, because it supplies the idea of a political authority which can accommodate differences...and yet still demand (and sustain) ultimate political allegiance."[30] In other words, rights are best protected from within a sovereign community rather than by fuzzy international standards which international bureaucrats may wish to impose from above. Thus, any surrendering of sovereignty to international regimes or international courts is a threat to the American people. Naturally this poses problems for the application of international law.

New Sovereigntists are reluctant to admit even that international law is "law". In their book, *The Limits of International Law*, Jack L. Goldsmith and Eric A. Posner conclude:

International law is a real phenomenon, but international law scholars exaggerate its power and significance... [T]he best explanation for when and why states comply with law is not that states have internalized law, or have a habit of complying with it, or are drawn by its moral pull, but simply that states act out of self-interest....

More often, international legal rhetoric is used to mask or rationalize behaviour driven by self-interested factors that have nothing to do with international law.[31]

In a controversial article, Robert Bork argued in 1989: "There can be no authentic rule of law among nations until nations have a common political morality or are under a common sovereignty."[32] In 2000, John Bolton, who had worked in the Reagan and George H.W. Bush administrations, argued, "there is no reason to consider treaties as 'legally' binding internationally, and certainly not as law in themselves... There is no legal mechanism—no coherent structure—that exists today on a global level to enforce compliance with treaties, a fact that international law advocates flatly ignore."[33] Since, in addition, there are no agreed upon sources for international law, it follows that treaties are mere "promises" and international law is reduced to a political obligation for states to follow if it is in accordance with their national interest.

Thus, as the 1990s came to a close, there was a serious, significant and relatively powerful critique of international law that was attracting notice by sympathizers and detractors alike. Significantly, as already pointed out, many of these individuals would later assume influential positions within the George W. Bush administration, where their arguments were applied to the standing issues of the day.

However, it is also important to note that neither American Exceptionalism nor concerns about sovereignty can be seen as only reflecting the views of neoconservatives or those in the Republican Party. Although Clinton did sign the ICC Statute on 31 December 2000, in doing so he described it as having "significant flaws". He also reaffirmed that the US had substantial concerns about the way the Court and the independent prosecutor would operate and whether the Court would respect domestic judicial processes.[34] In this sense, it is important to remember that the controversies that emerged during the George W. Bush administration reflected a wider debate rather than just one falling strictly along partisan lines.[35]

Reconsidering the relationship between ends and means in the laws of war

There is one more argument along these lines that merits attention. At a conference in early August 2001 entitled "Legal and Ethical Lessons of NATO's Kosovo Campaign" (the proceedings of which were later published into a book of the same name)[36] Professor Ruth Wedgwood, who was appointed by Secretary of Defense Donald Rumsfeld, to the Defense Policy Board, argued for a change of thinking about the laws of war after Kosovo:

It is commonly believed that the tactics of war must be judged independently of the purpose of a war... But this asserted independence of the two regimes may be no more than a fiction...Whether one's framework is utilitarian or pure principle, it is possible to admit that the merits of a war make a difference in our tolerance for methods of war fighting. This teleological view can be incorporated, albeit awkwardly, in the metric for "military advantage" in judging proportionality, for surely we do not value military objectives for their own sake. But it may be better to be forthright, even at the cost of questioning homilies... Democratic leaders and publics may believe that there is an important link between the legitimate purpose of a war and its allowable tactics—at least within the limits of basic humanity and the protection of civilian lives.[37]

In short, although she acknowledges that the "divorce of purpose and tactics is designed to allow agreement on humanitarian limits even when there is no consensus on the merits of the underlying dispute,"[38] Wedgwood is basically making the argument that noble ends justify almost any means.[39] This line of thinking is certainly a challenge to the laws of war as they have been written for at least the past 100 years. Concerned that such thinking may result in a bloodbath of self-righteousness, proponents of the laws of war have argued that guilt, motives and moral standing should not influence the application of the relevant laws of war as such views are inherently political. Yet using World War II as an example, Wedgwood argues, "Defeating Nazism, for example, required measures that are now seen as harsh and even punitive. Even where their legality is conceded under the earlier standards of air war, it is commonly taught in American military curricula that their repetition would now be illegal."[40] However, because the Allies had been fighting "radical evil represented by Nazism–an ideology posing the ultimate threat to human welfare", we can still see these actions as justified, if not legal.[41] Therefore, according to Wedgwood, a quiet linkage between *jus ad bellum* and the *jus in bello* often exists politically, if not explicitly legally.

The outcome of these arguments was a substantial and influential critique of international law within the United States by the late 1990s. This can be seen through a number of developments: critiques questioning the validity of international human rights "norms" and international institutions that seek to hold states (and individuals) accountable for their actions beyond domestic authority; anger over the difficulties encountered in the Kosovo campaign as related to the pro-international criminal justice movement and allied warfare; and the emergence of a challenge to the traditional dichotomy between *jus ad bellum* and *jus in bello*. These arguments all contributed to a strong scepticism among many academics and policy makers towards international law, including the laws of war. As Wade Mansell argues, "there is a great deal of evidence which suggests that a reconsideration of international law and the use of force has been under way in the United States at least since the end of the Cold War."[42]

It is important to point out that this was not necessarily a universal attitude within the US government.[43] Despite the difficulties encountered in the military operations of the 1990s, many still considered the laws of war as alive and well and very relevant to modern warfare. As James E. Baker, who served as the Special Assistant to the President and Legal Adviser to the National Security Council during the Kosovo campaign, argued:

...the law of armed conflict is hard law. It is US criminal law. Increasingly, it will also serve as an international measure by which the United States is judged. The law of armed conflict addresses the noblest objective of the law–the protection of innocent life. And the United States should be second to none in compliance, as was the case with Kosovo.[44]

Still, it was clear that by the time the Bush administration came into power in January 2001, there existed a certain amount of criticism and scepticism towards the idea of international law.

However, this criticism did not comprise one united approach. Military figures like Short were expressing frustration at what they saw as an overbearing international law and overbearing international lawyers who had little idea of what it was like to make decisions in the heat of battle. On the other hand, the New Sovereigntists, for cultural reasons, objected to the idea that the American Constitution could be constrained by a vague and undemocratic international law. There is a significant difference here in that the former group of military commanders and government officials were speaking out of a concern regarding what limits can be placed on the exercise of power; they did not object outright to the idea of international law or restraint on the use of force. For these individuals, international law, though occasionally inconvenient, had become an important part of military operations. The New Sovereigntist argument must therefore be viewed as an entirely different animal owing to its emphasis on the Constitution and ideas about a social contract. On the basis of certain cultural ideas relating to American Exceptionalism, adhering to international law over state interest was ultimately seen as the betrayal of one's own people.

Out of these two criticisms of international law–one with concerns about power and the other about culture–the latter would become significant in the War on Terror. The political fallout from 9/11 mixed well with arguments which placed national interest over international law and justified such actions within a cultural context. When the obligation to adhere to international law and the need for security seemed to collide, the arguments of the New Sovereigntists (many of whom had now found themselves in a role as advisors to the George W. Bush administration) seemed very relevant.

'Unlawful combatants' and 'quaint' conventions[45]

The purpose of this section is not to provide a detailed history or description of Guantánamo Bay. Rather, it is to argue that doubts about international law and the New Sovereigntist critique played an important role in determining the Bush administration's post-9/11 policies regarding the laws of war. The Geneva Conventions, typically not a mainstream media issue, were thrust into the spotlight on 11 January 2002 when the Secretary of Defense, Donald Rumsfeld, announced that the detainees in Afghanistan "will be handled not as prisoners of wars, because they're not, but as unlawful combatants. The–as I understand it, technically unlawful combatants do not have any rights under the Geneva Convention."[46] But what was the background to this decision and how was it defended?

Defending the detainee policy

Already, this chapter has tried to suggest that by 9/11 there existed a significant moral, political and legal critique of international law. Many of those who subscribed to these views (particularly Bolton and Yoo) would come to hold posts in the Bush administration, and, perhaps unsurprisingly, began to apply their arguments to the administration's policies, including policies towards the detainees in the War on Terror.[47] These policies were defended on the basis of a complex mix of moral, political and legal opinions regarding international law and presidential (executive) power. An examination of the legal logic will be presented in this next section of the chapter. In order to fully flesh out the complexity of the arguments, a look at some of the background moral and political concerns will also be noted, which will provide a better understanding of the legal reasoning employed by administration officials.

Any analysis of these policies should begin with the fact that immediately after the attacks of 11 September the Bush administration argued that it was fighting a new kind of enemy. In an interview with reporters on 17 September, Bush remarked:

I know that this is a different type of enemy than we're used to. It's an enemy that likes to hide and burrow in, and their network is extensive. There are no rules. It's barbaric behavior...

But we're going to smoke them out. And we're adjusting our thinking to the new type of enemy. These are terrorists who have no borders...

It's going to require a new thought process. And I'm proud to report our military, led by the Secretary of Defense, understands that; understands it's a new type of war, it's going to take a long time to win this war.[48]

In this way the Bush administration maintained that the War on Terror needed to be considered as a conflict unlike any other in history in terms of scope, the participants involved and the very nature of the fighting which is being undertaken world wide. For this reason, it was argued that the President required powers that enabled the executive to protect the United States from attack and use force against those threatening the safety of the nation and its citizens. These powers are in fact authorized by "the text, plan and history of the Constitution, its interpretation by both past Administration and the courts, the longstanding practice of the executive branch, and the express affirmation of the President's constitutional authorities by Congress".[49] This authority, which gave the President strengthened powers in a time of national emergency, also allows the President to override international law and state practice where necessary and for the safety of the United States and its armed forces. Additionally, the administration argued that presidential powers to wage the war on terror were recognized by Congress in the Authorization for Use of Military Force of 18 September 2001, which indicated that "the President has authority under the Constitution to take action to deter and prevent acts of international terrorism against the United States". The President was sanctioned:

to use all necessary and appropriate force against those nations, organizations, or persons he determines planned, authorized, committed, or aided the terrorist attacks that occurred on 11 September, 2001, or harbored such organizations or persons, in order to prevent any future acts of international terrorism against the United States by such nations, organizations or persons.[50]

Under this authorization, the President determined that the Taliban and al-Qaida constituted the organizations that carried out the attacks of 11 September. What emerged in the following months was a new model for treating prisoners of war captured in the War on Terror. Below is a rough outline of the features that comprised this new paradigm.

Military commissions

Consistent with the powers authorized by the Constitution and Congress, the President issued an executive order which set up military commissions to try enemy combatants captured either within or outside the territory of the United States on 13 November 2001. The use of military commissions, it was argued, is "firmly based in international law, [the US] Constitution, the Uniform Code of Military Justice..., our nation's history, and international practice."[51] This includes the use of commissions to try eight Nazi saboteurs during World War II (1942 *ex parte Quirin*) and some 500 war criminals at the cessation of that conflict.[52] Additionally, such commissions and other military tribunals are expressly recognized by Congress through Article 21 of the UCMJ as a legitimate means to try violation of the laws of war. Article 36 of the UCMJ authorizes the President's authority to prescribe pretrial, trial and post-trial procedures for military commissions, and this includes rules about the conduct of the hearing and access to evidence.[53]

Prisoner of war status

Aside from the tribunals, the Bush administration also made determinations as to the status of captured fighters in the War on Terror. Lawyers, mostly from the Department of Justice, were tasked with determining the applicability of domestic and international law, including the Geneva Conventions, to enemy combatants. In a memo dated 9 January 2002, it was argued by John Yoo, then Deputy Assistant Attorney General, and Robert J. Delahunty, Special Counsel, that "neither the federal War Crimes Act nor the Geneva Conventions would apply to the detention conditions in Guantanamo Bay, Cuba, or to trial by military commission of al Qaeda or Taliban prisoners."[54] In particular, the Geneva Convention and Common Article 3 did not apply because the Geneva Conventions never anticipated that there could be an insurgency movement that was not a nation state, it did not anticipate a conflict such as the Global War on Terror, and it was not clear that Congress would support an interpretation of Common Article 3 that supported its application in a war on terrorism. The same memo went on to conclude that "customary international law has no binding legal effect on either the President or on the military because it is not federal law, as recognized by the Constitution."[55] Similar findings were put forward in a memo by Jay S. Bybee on 22 January 2002.[56] Adding to these legal findings, the then White House General Counsel, Alberto Gonzales, argued that because the war on terrorism was essentially a new kind of war, the laws of war was rendered mostly irrelevant: "In my judgment, this new paradigm renders obsolete Geneva's strict limitations on questioning of enemy prisoners and renders quaint some of its provisions..."[57]

On 7 February 2002, President Bush accepted the conclusions of the Justice Department. The President "determined that the Geneva Convention applies to the Taliban detainees, but not to the al-Qaida detainees."[58] A final breakdown of the Bush administration's legal argument was presented in a press release:

- The United States is treating and will continue to treat all of the individuals detained at Guantánamo humanely and, to the extent appropriate and consistent with military necessity, in a matter consistent with the principles of the Geneva Convention.

153

- The President has determined that the Geneva Convention applies to the Taliban detainees, but not to the al-Qaida detainees. al-Qaida is not a foreign terrorist group. As such its members are not entitled to POW status.
- Although the US never recognized the Taliban as the legitimate Afghan government, Afghanistan is party to the Convention, and the President has determined that the Taliban are covered by the Convention. Under the terms of the Geneva Convention, however, the Taliban do not qualify as POWs as they do not meet the criteria spelled out in Article 4 of the Third Geneva Convention.[59]
- Therefore neither the Taliban nor al-Qaida detainees are entitled to POW status.[60]

Interrogation

So far we have seen that new policies regarding POW status and military tribunals rested on a powerful argument that the President was authorized to do whatever it took to protect the nation's security in a national emergency. These arguments, essentially asserted that the President needed strong powers to protect the nation, its citizens and their rights under the Constitution, went together well with the ideas of the New Sovereigntists. In this "new paradigm" of warfare, the President was morally, politically and legally obliged to violate international law if necessary in order to punish those who carried out the attacks of 11 September and to prevent future attacks.[61] This, naturally, included obtaining as much information as possible from those captured in the War on Terror and suspects at home.

The idea that the United States now found itself in this "new paradigm" was also used as a basis for the arguments regarding the interrogation of captured enemy combatants. On 26 February 2002 Bybee concluded that information derived from military interrogations may be admissible in court, even without *Miranda* warnings.[62] Also, a reading of the Torture Convention by Bybee argued that the text only prohibited "the most extreme acts" as criminal penalties only applied to "torture" and not "cruel, inhuman, or degrading treatment or punishment".[63] In a letter to Gonzales, Yoo maintained that because the President had determined al-Qaida members were not POWs under the Geneva Conventions (and because he had the power to do this), they could not be entitled to any protections of any of the Geneva Conventions. Therefore actions carried out during the interrogations of al-Qaida members or suspects could not constitute a war crime under Article 8 of the ICC Rome Statute.[64] In October 2002 a series of memos were issued considering acceptable counter resistance techniques in interrogations. As well as the seventeen methods listed in *Field Manual 34–52* ("The US Army Field Manual on Interrogation"), sixteen additional techniques were authorized by Secretary of Defense Donald Rumsfeld after a legal review.[65]

In summary, the legal argument rested on the assumption that the United States had entered a "new paradigm" of warfare and a national emergency requiring strengthened presidential powers which, according to this view, were authorized by Congress and the Constitution of the United States. This authority allowed the President to override international law and state practice where necessary and for the safety of the United States and its armed forces. In this way, the laws of war and other international legislation (such as the Torture Convention) could either be overridden or reinterpreted in light of the imperatives of the Global War on Terror.[66] By the spring of 2009 it had become very clear just how far this legal advice took the Bush administration in its actions against some of those captured in the War on Terror. In April 2009 the *New York Times* reported that two suspects, Abu Zubaydah and Khalid Shaikh Mohammed, were waterboarded 266 times (at least 83 and 183 times respectively).[67] The news report, which was based on a 2005 Justice Department memo, indicated that the waterboarding had been carried out by the CIA who believed it had been given legal authorization to do so—but that the agents had also constantly worried that they had crossed a legal line.

Internal debate

As is now fairly well known, not everyone in the US government was pleased with the outcomes of the legal review provided by (mostly) Department of Justice lawyers. From late 2001–3 a debate emerged among the Justice, State and Defense Departments as to what exactly America's obligations under international law entailed and whether or not the laws of war could and should apply. The Bush administration wanted to obtain as much information from detainees as possible and had asked its lawyers to investigate the applicable international law. What was perhaps peculiar about this arrangement, and came as surprise to many within the government, was *who* the administration had turned to for advice. Rather than turning to the experts within the Department of Defense or State, who had officials that were thoroughly familiar with the laws of war, state practice and US practice and had actually engaged in the process of negotiating the treaties to which the US was a party, the administration seems to have asked the Department of Justice to provide most of the advice. For example, while John Yoo had proficiency in the area of international law, he had little to no laws of war training or expertise, and many felt that he had got some of his legal interpretations of the applicable treaties very wrong.[68]

It was not until late 2001 and early 2002 that officials in the Departments of State and Justice became aware of the legal opinions which had been rendered and were about to be put into practice. The legal adviser to the State Department, William Howard Taft IV, and Secretary of State Colin Powell both spoke out within the administration against the policies that were being put in place.[69] Colin Powell, who was advising in his role the Secretary of State but also as a former General, argued that the administration's position jeopardized the safety of captured US personnel and undermined previous policy: "It will reverse over a century of U.S. policy and practice in supporting the Geneva conventions (sic) and undermine the protection of the law of war for our troops, both in this specific conflict and in general."[70] But these views appear to have been largely ignored in favour of the arguments being put forward by the Department of Justice.

Given this history, and as argued above, it is reasonable to assert that the critiques of international law put forward by the New Sovereigntists became very influential after 9/11. The Bush administration (and, it should be remembered, the Clinton administration) had already demonstrated a willingness to "take on" the international community over Kosovo and the International Criminal Court, in favour of cultural arguments which emphasized sovereignty and the supremacy of the Constitution.[71] It is not surprising that the administration was willing to do the same with humanitarian norms in conflict, especially after 9/11. When pictures of detainees being transported to and living in Guantánamo emerged in early 2002, public shock and outrage over the 9/11 attacks lent support to the administration's arguments that the security needs and the right of self-defence gave the US the right to deny the full protection of the Geneva Conventions to the prisoners. Besides, it was argued, the methods employed by the Taliban and al-Qaida, their failure to live up to what the laws of war required, and their obvious contempt for Western/international human rights norms, meant that they did not deserve such protection, either legally or morally.[72]

Yet, despite its downplaying of international law, the arguments that the US administration has rested on are legal arguments to some degree. It is clear that the Bush administration sought out a legal solution to carry out its desired security policy and relied on moral arguments to support this solution. While the Bush administration frequently referred to its enemies in the War on Terror as "evil", its arguments have continued to rely on the legal argument that those held in Guantánamo do not meet the conditions for being covered by the Geneva Conventions.

Perhaps this should not be surprising. This work has already suggested that there is a dualistic tendency regarding the implementation of the laws of war to conflicts: while policy and political concerns have often pushed for the downplaying of international law where there is a significant cost associated with full implementation, US administrations have still usually attempted to present legal arguments to back up their policies. Therefore, considering that the US had been very important in drafting many of the laws of war conventions, and that such conventions were considered "hard law" by many of the international lawyers in the Pentagon, a legal solution to the issue is more politically and morally palpable than a straight denial of the Geneva Conventions. Still, if it is not surprising, it is certainly ironic that the US had spent much time and effort making the exact opposite case with regards to its prisoners in Vietnam.

However, this must be qualified in some respects. The Bush administration had (and the many former officials, particularly Cheney, continue to have) a very particular view of what role the laws of war were to play in the new paradigm, and believed that the president had clear authority to override or redefine the law as appropriate. Lawyers were required to find legal justifications for the "new paradigm" of warfare and to assert the president's authority to fight the war on terror as he saw fit. The legal threshold for torture was to be lessened to accommodate harsher interrogation techniques while, at the same time, administration officials could claim that the US was not torturing detainees. Lawyers not willing to accommodate these administration policies within the framework of international and domestic law soon found themselves in a different career. They included Jack Goldsmith, Assistant Attorney General, Office of Legal Counsel, and Daniel Levin, who took his place but soon joined the National Security Council.[73] Patrick Philbin, Goldsmith's deputy, apparently had his promotion blocked by Dick Cheney for disagreeing with certain policies towards prisoners (and for opposing the NSA eavesdropping programme).[74]

International lawyers and the legal response

It is fairly clear that the "international legal community"–made up of mostly Western lawyers and NGOs–was not on best terms with the Bush administration even before 9/11. Despite a considerable amount of international support for the US after the attacks, international lawyers soon found themselves troubled by the measures that the US was taking to fight the war on terror.[75] Domestically, the Uniting and Strengthening America by Providing Appropriate Tools Required to Intercept and Obstruct Terrorism Act 2001 (more commonly known as the USA PATRIOT Act) gave new powers to the federal government to detain and monitor individuals suspected of being involved with terrorism, which was a matter of concern for some civil and human rights lawyers. Yet, our main concern here is the reaction to the announcement that detainees would not be provided with the full protections of the laws of war, specifically the Geneva Conventions and customary aspects of the Additional Protocols, which the US had previously indicated that it would adhere to.[76]

There have been many legal arguments made against the Bush administration's argument that the detainees do not qualify for, and therefore do not deserve the protections of the Geneva Conventions. Since the outbreak of hostilities, there have been several studies published by international lawyers arguing for the full application of the law to the military activities involved in the War on Terror and criticizing the Bush administration's policies. For the sake of brevity, they can be summed up as follows:

1) No one is "outside" the protection of the Geneva Convention. If an individual is not protected under the Third Convention Relevant to the Treatment of Prisoners of War, they are automatically considered civilians under the Fourth Geneva Convention Relative to the Protection of Civilian Persons in Time of War. Therefore there is no legal black hole into which the US can put the detainees.

2) It is customary law that belligerents do not need to meet the requirement of wearing a uniform or having a fixed, distinctive mark—they need only to carry their arms openly. In addition, all prisoners are protected under the customary principles codified in Article 75 of Additional Protocol I to the 1949 Geneva Conventions ("Fundamental Guarantees"), which includes prohibitions on the use of violence towards prisoners and torture as well as provisions on fair trial.[77]

3) If the administration wanted to argue that the detainees do not qualify for POW status, then it must do so in a tribunal operating in accordance with internationally recognized legal principles and procedures.

4) The administration considered all of the detainees as a group, and not as individuals. This also violated the presumption of innocence.

5) The Bush administration's actions undermined its own military manuals and procedures which indicate that all prisoners are immediately assumed

to be prisoners of war and that they must be treated in line with the laws of war. For example, the Army's *Field Manual 27–10*, "The Law of Land Warfare" deals with the treatment of prisoners of war as well as the military's *Operational Law Handbook*.

Lawyers also point out that there is precedent for the US treating as POWs insurgents or those who do not strictly meet the requirements of that status. Duffy, for example argues that there was such a precedent in Vietnam with regard to the Viet Cong and the North Vietnamese forces.[78]

The summary of the legal arguments here has been brief–for several reasons. First, there have already been a number of detailed books written about why the legal arguments made by the Bush administration are incorrect. While there is always room for debate and discussion, it would be difficult to add substance to what has already been written. Second, the intention of the argument and analysis being made here is to be more political than legal. This relates to the third point, that the main problem with the arguments made by international lawyers is that they are, in fact, mostly legal. While this should not be a shocking revelation concerning lawyers, it does render their argument somewhat ineffective against an American administration which essentially downplayed the importance of international law (albeit partly through legal arguments about constitutional powers). If the argument being made is essentially that "international law as it has operated in the past does not apply and cannot be applied to a war on terror", counterarguments emphasizing the bits and pieces of customary law seem somewhat lacking in strength, if not substance.

The case against the 'New Sovereigntists'

But if legal arguments are insufficient, can anything effectively challenge the "New Sovereigntists" or those who argue in favour of "enhanced interrogation techniques"? Naturally, the answer is yes–but the best answers may lie outside the law and with political and moral arguments which can be (and have been) raised against the cultural arguments being put forward.

The Constitution

The first and one of the most powerful arguments challenging the New Sovereigntist position is that their arguments are based on a particular reading of the US Constitution and its history. As Peter Spiro argues:

These arguments are grounded in highly formalistic readings of the Constitution and selective interpretations of its history... [T]he New Sovereigntists forget that the Constitution–hardly blind to the national interest–has always adapted itself success-fully to new exigencies of the international system. Such values as federalism, the separation of powers, and individual rights are not so brittle that they will shatter at the intersection with globalization.

Indeed, the Constitution will have to adapt to global requirements sooner or later, for the New Sovereigntist premise of American impermeability is flawed.[79]

Spiro raises an important point–to suggest that the Constitution cannot adapt, and that individual rights are so weak as to crumble when faced with globalization, seems to be a flawed argument. Relying on Jacksonian thinking for problems that are occurring well over a century later may be emotionally appealing in its harkening back to the historical roots of the foundations of the Republic, but at the same time it seems to be completely out of touch with modern considerations.

Origins of the laws of war

New Sovereigntists argue that the laws of war and the norms that it embodies are standards which have been set by undemocratic international bodies that are accountable to no one–or international judges that do not have America's best interest in mind. As Rabkin argues, "We cannot delegate our own deci-sions about national defense to prosecutors in The Hague or moral monitors in Geneva any more than we would give final word on these matters to the spiritual admonitions of the Pope in Rome."[80]

Some have argued against this point, stating that the Geneva Conventions and other laws of war treaties are international "objectively verifiable stand-ards" that all parties are bound to meet in warfare.[81] One can only presume that "objective" in this case means politically neutral. Given the fact that the law has typically been drafted and decided after wars, largely influenced by its victors who are in turn also looking towards the next war, this does not quite fit. A better argument, ironically, stems from one of Rabkin's own points–that the dispute over the Geneva Convention "is a dispute about treaty law–but law with a history."[82]

Unlike international human rights law (for which the New Sovereigntists seem to save a special variety of loathing),[83] the laws of war have been carefully acknowledged, negotiated and (mostly) accepted by states via diplomatic conferences where they were able to consult with their own military profes-sionals and protect their national interests. Where international human rights law remains vague and full of generalities, the laws of war are generally more specific and can be broken down relatively easily to be incorporated into military doctrine and taught to soldiers during training and in the field. This does not turn the law into "objective standards" but certainly into a stronger form of law that states have explicitly agreed to through treaties. As the New Sovereigntists themselves argue, it does create political obligation. However, this seems to imply to the New Sovereigntists that the "political obligation" can be easily denied and downplayed without too much political consequence; given the relative strength of the US in the international system in comparison to its allies and enemies, it is contended that states will have to come back and conform to the US no matter what they wish. As Rabkin argues:

As the strongest and richest country in the world, the United States can afford to safeguard its sovereignty... we have every reason to expect that other nations, eager for access to American markets and eager for other cooperative arrangements with the United States will often adapt themselves to American preferences.[84]

However, is a dismissal of political obligation really so easy? If it was, it is doubtful that so many words would have to be written justifying the Bush administration's policies, or that this justification would have continued to rely on a legal basis. Even the New Sovereigntists, in arguing that the laws of war do not fully apply to the War on Terror, often point to legal reasons why this is so, aside from constitutional limitations. Jeremy Rabkin argues that the Geneva Conventions are treaties and "a treaty, as *The Federalist* (No. 64) explained in 1788, 'is only another name for a bargain.'"[85] In other words, the Geneva Conventions do not apply because terrorists have not lived up to their side of the bargain. Therefore, what Rabkin's argument ultimately comes down to on this point is a different interpretation of the law from that of lawyers supporting the laws of war–not saying that the law itself is entirely irrelevant.

The value of the laws of war

It is clear that the US military and Pentagon lawyers value the laws of war, if only from the comments made prior to 9/11. Although there were many who experienced difficulties and frustration with the way the law seemed to be expanding and applied in the 1990s, military leaders tended to (mostly) feel the same way. There will always be concerns as to whether law interferes with the exercise of military power or whether the armed forces will be able to do their job. Yet, since Vietnam, law of war training has essentially become entwined with US military doctrine. Lawyers have become integral to the conduct of military operations. Although he was critical of the overall conduct of the campaign in Kosovo, Short argued:

My lawyer most of the time was a lieutenant colonel. It is very difficult for him to come in and say to a three star 'you are out of bounds, sir you are about to break the law.' But [military lawyers] have got to be able to do that. [They] have got to know [their] business inside and out and [they] have got to think like an operator.[86]

A fairly robust commitment to the laws of war within US military culture is apparent in other ways. Within the Pentagon there exists the Department of Defense Law of War Working Group, and the US military has the highest number of judge advocates in the world–the Marine Corps, the smallest of the US armed services, has more active duty judge advocates than the UK, Canada, Australia and New Zealand combined.[87] The Army has established a Centre for Law and Military Operations (CLAMO) at the Judge Advocate General's School which publishes "lessons learned" reports including rules of engagement and laws of war training information. While respect may at times be grudging, it is clear that the laws of war are taken seriously by most Pentagon military lawyers and officials. It is clear that much effort has gone into ensuring that the applicable law has been incorporated into the everyday training of US soldiers.

Why this is the case is also understandable. Aside from the ideal of protecting innocent life–something that is inherent in Western human rights culture–it is widely acknowledged that soldiers who play by the rules in all respects of their training and in terms of operational doctrine are the ones who best accomplish their mission. Unruly and ill-disciplined troops are not only more likely to commit war crimes, they are also most likely not to effectively complete their missions.[88] This claim–of the consistency between following the laws of war and military effectiveness–is backed up by the Department of Defense's report to Congress on the Gulf War discussed in the previous chapter, where it was noted that "no Iraqi action leading to or resulting in a violation of the law of war gained Iraq any military advantage."[89] Considering this attitude towards that which helps to ensure military effectiveness, it is unsurprising that Pentagon officials draw a link between war making, policy and law. These three factors are inherently intertwined to create a lethal yet effective fighting force that follows Clausewitz's teaching on the economy of force.

If military lawyers and Pentagon officials can see this importance, then why are those who argue in favour of "enhanced interrogation techniques" so casual about dismissing these links? In arguing that it is America's right to take whatever steps are necessary to defend itself, are these arguments actually undermining some of the key components that the Pentagon has regarded for years as essentially required for fighting effective wars? Perhaps this is why several accounts reported dissatisfaction within the Pentagon and the Department of State about the way the Bush administration handled the Guantánamo issue—and its attitude towards the laws of war.[90] As we have already seen above, Colin Powell argued that such policies did not just contravene international law, but also undermined US state practice for over a century and put the lives of American soldiers at risk.

Therefore, some of the New Sovereigntists and those who argue in favour of using "enhanced interrogation techniques" can be accused of ignoring the views of many American military lawyers when they suggest that the US is above, or can choose to ignore, the laws of war.[91] Considering that those who were making these arguments in the Departments of Justice or Defense were political appointees (few had any military experience or any specialty in the laws of war), ignoring the link between effective fighting, policy and law seems to be a serious omission in their arguments.

As many officers and soldiers have come to realize and value the links between effective fighting and adhering to the laws of war, it is clear that many of these individuals believe that they have an interest in preserving the law in US military training and working to ensure its implementation in war. After all, it is apparent that soldiers would probably know best that the laws of war are written in the blood of war's victims, and that they themselves have a significant interest in ensuring that they are not thrown away.[92]

Nature of the threat

But what about arguments that the US is now in a new paradigm of conflict? It is clear from the statements made by many former Bush administration officials during and after their time in office that they and much of the US public believe they hve been engaged in a new kind of war. Besides the quotes listed above, six weeks after 9/11 Vice President Dick Cheney argued: "We cannot deal with terror. It will not end in a treaty. There will be no peaceful coexistence, no negotiations, no summit, no joint communiqué with the terrorists. The struggle can only end with their complete and permanent destruction..."[93]

In other words, in fighting the War on Terror, the Bush administration saw itself as confronting a dangerous, nihilist peril that seeks to destroy the liberties and freedoms of the West. In this sense, al-Qaida has become an enemy of all humanity and civilization, an enemy that cannot be negotiated with, only exterminated because of the nature of the threat it poses.

Thus it seems logical that when a nation is fighting a war against this kind of ultimate threat to the Western way of life, the requirement of restraint becomes questionable at best. To what extent should a nation restrain itself when it is clear that its opponent clearly rejects the idea of humanitarian limitations? This point is reinforced when one considers the fact that it is actually al-Qaida and the Taliban who brought the war on themselves in a horrific and bloody manner on 9/11. Rumsfeld hinted at this line of thinking when he addressed the nature of the challenge that the US was facing:

We did not start the war... The Taliban, an illegitimate, unelected group of terrorists, started it when they invited the al Qaeda into Afghanistan and turned their country into a base from which those terrorists could strike out and kill our citizens.

So let there be no doubt; responsibility for every single casualty in this war, be they innocent Afghans or innocent Americans, rests at the feet of Taliban and al Qaeda.[94]

To Rumsfeld, where violations of the laws of war may have occurred, the US is excused, if not justified, because it is confronting a major threat to itself. The fault ultimately lies with the terrorists for making the war necessary and the laws of war should not constrain the US in doing what it needs to do to ensure its safety.

After leaving office, and speaking on national television, Cheney, who said "watching a coordinated, devastating attack on our country from an underground bunker at the White House can affect how you view your responsibilities", indicated that the Bush administration acted to protect the security of the United States through tough measures including ones that liberals might find distasteful. Specifically, Cheney defended the Terrorist Surveillance Program (a "Top Secret" programme designed to intercept messages between al-Qaida operatives) and the "enhanced interrogation program" put in place by the administration as vital and necessary for making sure that a "9/11 with nuclear weapons" did not happen again:

In top secret meetings about enhanced interrogations, I made my own beliefs clear. I was and remain a strong proponent of our enhanced interrogation program. The interrogations were used on hardened terrorists after other efforts failed. They were legal, essential, justified, successful, and the right thing to do. The intelligence officers who questioned the terrorists can be proud of their work and proud of the results, because they prevented the violent death of thousands, if not hundreds of thousands, of innocent people.[95]

Right or righteous, true or false, in reality these arguments are nothing new. One need only think of the clichés such as that the Constitution or Bill of Rights should not be allowed to become "suicide pacts" to be reminded that we have faced similar questions before.[96] Yet the controversies regarding humanitarian restraint and civil liberties in the War on Terror seem to have placed a new urgency on old debates. Does the severe and extreme maliciousness of a threat justify a response that violates customary and/or legal norms? Does the fact that the terrorists brought war on themselves mean that they deserve to suffer whatever harm befalls them in the ensuing conflict?

What unites these two questions is that consideration of the nature of the threat is key when considering the restrictions we want to place upon our response to the terrorists. We have already seen an argument for an answer to the first question emerge from Ruth Wedgwood before 9/11. She argues that Nazism was a threat so severe that it necessitated violation of the rules of war in order to confront that evil. At the time of her comments, she was arguing about the war in Kosovo; stopping the genocide on the ground in Serbia must surely legitimate a looser interpretation of targeting restrictions or even a bending of the laws of war to achieve this greater good.[97] In other words, to Wedgwood, *jus ad bellum* in both of these cases should (and politically did) alter the way *jus in bello* was considered.

As argued earlier, this line of argument challenges thinking about the laws of war as they have existed for the last 100 years. Yet the division between just war and just conduct in war has existed for centuries with the increased recognition that no state had a monopoly on true religion or justice. This partition between the two branches of the law has been regarded by virtually every laws of war scholar as instrumental in preserving humanity and restraint through the insistence that no cause could ever undermine the need for restraint in warfare. Whether this argument is made on the basis of custom, honour or treaty, it is a cornerstone of the modern law of war. But can it still hold in an era of nihilistic terrorism? And if it does not, does this mean that the terrorists are liable to suffer whatever consequences that the US can impose on them for engaging in activities which clearly violated international treaty and customary law—as well as virtually every norm of civilized conduct?

Part of the problem, it must be acknowledged, is that the questions here address not only international law, but also fundamental issues of how democracies and the leaderships of those democracies make decisions in times of crises. In the US context, this has involved key issues about executive power and what the president may or may not decide or do in the face of a national emergency. In this way, the issues at stake involving international law must be brought down to a domestic level. But this does not make the debate any easier.

Finding a lesser evil

The legal, but more importantly the political and moral debates over Guantánamo highlight the problems that democracies face when they are confronted with emergencies: a balance between liberty and security. The argument that Guantánamo Bay may represent an affront to international law, human rights or democratic values is a strong one. However, what has been argued here is that the Bush administration has based its case on necessity, security and honour—and no matter how much one may disagree with its line of reasoning, it is not an entirely incomprehensible argument. Not bestowing protection to those who not only refuse to play by the rules but distain the very existence of the rules in the first place is not morally unintelligible. And allowing international law or constitutions to become the very instruments by which democracies expire (or become suicide pacts) will not ultimately serve the cause of human rights or freedoms.

Perhaps it needs to be recognized that arguments limited to domestic and international law may only be able to take us so far in this dispute. Although law has certainly played a major role in the debate over security and liberty, in complex emergencies it may only take us to an unsatisfactory quandary as to what is legal and what is illegal, not what is right or not what is necessary. In the eyes of the Bush administration the political and moral imperatives of 9/11 took the dispute beyond a mere legal debate. But the same can probably be said for commentators, academics and individuals living in democracies. The events of 9/11 and the ensuing War on Terror challenge commonly accepted notions as to how far a nation may act to protect itself from harm and threats that pose a significant risk to the life of its citizens. Answering the difficult questions which result may demonstrate the true limits of international law.

"What lesser evils may a society commit when it believes it faces the greater evil of its own destruction?"[98] This is the question that Michael Ignatieff tries to answer in his book *The Lesser Evil: Political Ethics in an Age of Terror*. In trying to answer the question he sets out, Ignatieff takes an approach that seeks to combine legal, political and ethical theory by looking at the lessons learned in emergencies in the UK, Canada, Italy, Germany, Spain, Israel and

Sri Lanka.[99] In this way, Ignatieff provides an alternative approach for thinking about the role of law (including international law) when states are faced with acute threats that demand immediate action.

The crux of this problem, argues Ignatieff, is that for liberal democratic societies confronted with terrorism, "what works is not always right. What is right doesn't always work."[100] Necessity may require us to take actions in defence of democracy which will stray from democracy's own foundational commitments to dignity. Therefore, liberal democratic societies must act on the principle of the "lesser evil". Ignatieff does not provide an exact definition of the "lesser evil", but what is implied is the idea that in confronting terrorism, choices must be made on laws and rights–to what degree they should be allowed to bend without breaking. That when societies are faced with a real threat or "evil", stopping this may require methods that reply to the threat in kind.[101]

Importantly, this differs from opportunistic selectivity–a "cafeteria-style" approach to international law where governments pick and choose to follow international law and norms where they can and when it suits their strategies. Rather, Ignatieff's arguments imply the need for a greater deal of democratic oversight and, ultimately, democratic accountability when tough decisions need to be made in an emergency.

Yet, Ignatieff is cautious enough to specify several caveats in his opinion that "human beings can justify anything as a lesser evil as long as they only have to justify it to themselves."[102] After all, there is a clear difference between claiming that emergency measures need to be put in place and having to justify such measures via democratic institutions. First, he says, the argument that violence can be a lesser evil has real meaning only for liberal democratic societies as they are guided by a constitutional commitment to minimize the use of force, violence and dubious means.[103]

The second qualification is somewhat more defensive and relates to Ignatieff's larger argument–that qualifying evil would seem to excuse it. He notes that it is essential to a "lesser evil" position that one can justify a resort to it politically without ever denying that it is evil. The lesser evil is only justifiable because any other measure or means would be insufficient or unavailable.[104] The crucial factor is having the appropriate institutions that can guide debate and judgments that we have to make in extreme circumstances. As Ignatieff argues, democracy is designed to cope with tragic choice, and it does so by understanding that if anyone can justify anything, people are less likely to be able to carry out some evil action if they are forced to do so in adversarial proceedings before their fellow citizens.[105]

Ignatieff's approach is geared towards answering the age-old question of liberty and security, or how can rights be best preserved when democracies face emergencies. In this way it is a useful approach for assessing at the arguments for security measures post-9/11 and for Guantánamo. However (perhaps unsurprisingly given the political and moral nature of the discussion) harsh evaluations of Ignatieff's argument are not in short supply. Much of this often passionate criticism stems from the idea that Ignatieff is using a model that is too legal or legalistic and places too much emphasis on, if not faith in, democratic oversight. Ignatieff's arguments, caveats and explanations ultimately sound more like rationalization than restraint.[106]

One of the most vocal critics has been Conor Gearty, who goes so far as to describe Ignatieff as "Rumsfeldian" and a "hand-wringing, apologetic apologist". In a scathing critique, Gearty argues:

...if we change our rules to allow us to respond in an evil way, or our operatives stray over the boundary into evil behaviour without our explicit authorisation, it is really not so bad (fine even?) because all that is happening is that evil is being met with (lesser/theoretically accountable) evil...

Our evil is better (because less bad) than theirs. If Abu Ghraib was wrong, then that wrongness consisted not in stepping across the line into evil behaviour but rather allowing a 'necessary evil' (as framed by the squeamish intellectuals) to stray into 'unnecessary evil' (as practiced by the not-so-squeamish Rumsfeldians).[107]

From this point of view, the problem with Ignatieff's lesser evil argument is that even officially sanctioning or justifying emergency measures in democratic institutions does not make them right or just. It is to conflate morality and legality and/or process; or, to use one of Gearty's examples, it is "like reacting to a series of police killings with proposals to reform the law on homicide so as to sanction officially approved pre-trial executions."[108]

Does Ignatieff's argument, which emphasizes the virtue of democratic oversight, lead down paths where Ignatieff would no doubt be uncomfortable? Arguably, the most interesting "lesser evil" case study to come out of the War on Terror is the issue of torture and its use on detainees. It is this case study which may demonstrate the major difficulty for the lesser evil argument outlined above—that legality is often conflated with morality and the idea that democratic oversight, due process and legalities can morally excuse an activity. After all, the Bush administration constantly maintained that it did not commit torture. However, this argument has been heavily dependent on a redefinition of what, exactly, constitutes torture. Essentially, the argument being put forward was that the United States did not torture and therefore whatever interrogation policies were followed were, by definition, not torture. It amounts to a very strange and very flawed logic.

In fairness to Ignatieff, he recognizes this point–that certain activities are simply beyond what a democracy can do, no matter how much justification, legal or otherwise, is put forward:

> The problem with torture is not just that it gets out of control, not just that it becomes lawless. It inflicts irremediable harm on both the torturer and the prisoner. It violates basic commitments to human dignity, and this is the core value that a war on terror, waged by a democratic state, should not sacrifice, even under threat of imminent attack.[109]

Ignatieff has been fairly adamant on an absolute ban on torture, although he admits that certain coercive measures (such as sleep deprivation) would likely meet the standards of the lesser evil approach.[110] Yet there remain two problems with Ignatieff's line of thinking if we are to apply it to the problems encountered in this chapter. First, if we are truly fighting what he calls "apocalyptic" or "nihilistic" terrorists who will stop at nothing to carry out their goals, at what point can we say something is *not* justified?[111] If the enemies of liberal democratic societies plan to fight us using every means they can, at what point do we say that the means to protect ourselves are no longer appropriate? Labelling someone, or a group, apocalyptic is to imply their irrationality, and this characterization would seem to create a slippery slope which would justify any and all means to combat them. Second, Ignatieff argues that if states act on threats, these threats must be real in order to be justified.[112] Yet he does not seem to acknowledge that threats are to a large extent constructs–*subjective*, not *objective* calculations. What happens when a state acts in a way that it feels is consistent with the lesser evil, only to find out that the threat it has acted upon does not exist? Does this mean it has now become the greater evil? Does intention matter when evaluating the lesser evil? Or only outcome? If serious doubts have emerged over the usefulness of the information gathered from the detainees at Guantánamo, at what point has the greater/lesser evil distinction been crossed?

Coping with choice?

Yet in some ways these criticisms seem to be somewhat off the mark with regard to what Ignatieff is arguing. As mentioned above, he outlines in his first chapter that he is writing on the premise that "Democracy is designed to cope with tragic choice".[113] He notes that his argument does not imply that politicians in democracy do not commit evil, but that "Only liberal democracies have a guilty conscience about punishment."[114] Lesser evil thinking suggests that a greater tragedy would be to pretend that there is no choice at all: that there are no circumstances in which rights may be violated; that there is no other way to combat terrorism. Both of these positions deny the possibility of choice and constitute an "easy-out" for leaders and citizens who are faced with tough decisions. But the reality of the War on Terror is that there are choices which must be made if democracies are to successfully balance liberty and security. In his book describing the activities of the American intelligence community after 9/11, Ron Suskind describes how the age-old dilemma of walking a fine line between "right" and "wrong" was opened for reappraisal in the days following 9/11:

The "dark side" is a complex, shape-shifting term—its meaning altered by tone and inflection. When Cheney spoke about it on national television a few days after the attacks, he had given it a note of resignation—*this is what we must do, where we must live, like it or not...*

There is, however, always a choice in such matters, in the actions that ultimately define character. The character of an individual or nation.[115]

And, as Ignatieff describes his intentions: "The book is designed to make people think about hard choices—like interrogation, assassination and pre-emptive war—and to show how democratic societies can make these choices without sacrificing key liberties and key constitutional restraints."[116]

In this way, what lesser evil thinking implies is that the measures taken to preserve the security of liberal-democracies in times of emergency need to be justified. But this justification cannot come about via claims that "there is no other way". Rather, such measures need to be explained and defended through democratic institutions, such as courts, and limited through sunset clauses. Claims that Guantánamo Bay was morally acceptable were only valid in so far as the Bush administration could prove it was necessary—not by claims that there was no other choice in the matter.

Yet this is where Ignatieff's caution that societies may justify anything so long as they can justify it to themselves comes into play. The premise of the lesser evil argument is that democratic governments are willing to go to their national legislatures—and this is exactly what the Bush administration refused to do. When it comes to the War on Terror, particularly on detainee issues, the administration constantly asserted that the Constitution provides the president with authority to do whatever it takes to win a War on Terror. Lawyers within the Bush administration, such as David Addington, argued that presidential power, in the War on Terror, does not need Congressional approval–that there is no need for democratic oversight at all.

Putting 'lesser evil' to the test

Arguably, this is one of the areas where the Bush administration failed the lesser evil test. In arguing for new powers after 9/11 the administration did all it could to restrain the powers of Congress and challenge the powers of the Supreme Court, so as to maintain its policies. While it should not be too shocking that a political body tried to assert power in a time of crisis, it is possible to argue that the Bush administration took this practice to a new level. Some cite Lincoln's example of suspending *habeas corpus* during the Civil War as a measure to protect national security. Or they remind us that military commissions have been used through out US history to prosecute individuals in the "chaotic and irregular circumstances of armed conflict".[117] However, as Arthur Schlesinger argues, Lincoln never claimed an inherent right to do what he did. In this way, the Bush White House has seized on historical aberrations and turned them into a doctrine of presidential power.[118]

A similar argument has recently been presented by Jack Goldsmith in his book, *The Terror Presidency*.[119] In it, Goldsmith recounts the decisions made by the Bush administration regarding the detainees in the War on Terror and critiques the logic put forward to justify its policies. While Goldsmith does not disagree with the idea that nations facing emergencies may have to reconsider their commitments to human rights and/or international law (although he did, apparently, argue that the Fourth Geneva Convention on the treatment of civilians applied to terrorists in Iraq, even if they were al-Qaida members), he suggests the way this was done by the administration was wrong. He argues that the decisions made, particularly those regarding the torture of detainees, were bad policy, driven by an ideological view that asserted presidential power over not only America's international legal commitments, but also domestic institutions like Congress. According to Goldsmith, the administration was driven by a belief that any consultation with democratic institutions would give away the President's power which was necessary in a time of crisis. When he argued against this, Goldsmith was warned that he might be leaving the nation more vulnerable to terrorist strikes.

Goldsmith, however, disagrees with this assessment. He argues that the administration would have been better off–politically and legally–if it had gone to Congress with its plans. He also looks at the example of Abraham Lincoln's suspending of *habeas corpus* during the US Civil War and some of

Franklin Roosevelt's policies which gave him sweeping powers in World War II. In both cases, despite the controversial nature of their policies, the presidents worked with Congress to ensure legal and political support, and to give some kind of democratic oversight to what was being undertaken. Goldsmith suggests that this history demonstrates that working with democratic institutions like Congress may actually help the executive fight the War on Terror, rather than hindering it.

However, this is where the Bush administration has got it wrong. As Goldsmith explains: "The Bush administration has operated on an entirely different concept of power that relies on minimal deliberation, unilateral action and legalistic defense. This approach largely eschews politics: the need to explain, to justify, to convince, to get people on board, to compromise."

It is an approach that seems to closely mirror's Ignatieff's lesser evil approach, although both men are coming from very different political views. Goldsmith believes, writing about the Bush presidency, that bringing Congress into the moral, political and legal questions surrounding prisoners of war/detainees in the War on Terror would have strengthened the president's case. Instead, the president's policies were in a state of confusion given recent court decisions and a Congress that was increasingly more suspicious of the executive's assertions for power. This, Goldsmith suggests, could have been avoided:

If the administration had simply followed the Geneva requirement to hold an informal "competent tribunal" or had gone to Congress for support on its detention program in the summer of 2004, it probably would have avoided the more burdensome procedural and judicial requirements that became practically necessary under the pressure of subsequent judicial review.

Despite this argument, Goldsmith is not compromising his "New Sovereigntist" credentials here. Even for the most vocal of New Sovereigntists, there is still a role for international law—albeit within the framework of a domestic constitution. What, perhaps, is less common among the New Sovereigntists is the idea that international law may actually help provide a form of democratic legitimacy in the larger fight. Goldsmith, hardly an ICRC advocate, seems to be acknowledging that this may be the case.

Yet given this history, it is not hard to understand why cynics might remain sceptical of a lesser evil approach—and for good reasons. Democratic institutions are not always known for their willingness or ability to stand up to executive power. The Republican controlled Congress (until 2007) was relatively silent on the issue of law—the 2005 Detainee Treatment Act perhaps being a significant, albeit rather late, attempt by Congress to limit the administration's policies towards detainees. However, the Act actually had the effect of denying the Guantánamo detainees the right of *habeas corpus* (or, in their context, the right to challenge their detention).[120] In addition, the Act did not apply to suspects in the custody of the CIA, and while it forbade "cruel, inhumane and degrading treatment", the Act did not define what activities constitute such treatment.

Yet even here the Bush administration sought to limit the impact of the weak oversight and legislation through "signing statements"–that is, declarations upon presidential signature of legislation reserving the right to re-interpret or ignore portions of the law. For example, on a bill that sought to prohibit federal funding to programmes that collected intelligence in a manner that violated the Fourth Amendment, a signing statement was added upon signature which stated that the Commander-in-Chief had the right to collect intelligence in any way he deemed necessary.[121] A similar signing statement was made on the Detainee Treatment Act.

It is possible, then, to remain sceptical about the ability or willingness of domestic and international institutions, including international law, to protect rights and freedoms. So far there have been many court cases and challenges to these policies–perhaps the truest test of the lesser evil argument.[122] A look at one of these cases reveals the balancing of liberty and security through process.

Hamdan v. Rumsfeld

On 29 June 2006 the Supreme Court rendered judgment on the Bush administration's policies in *Hamdan v Rumsfeld*.[123] The case involved the legal situation of Salim Ahmed Hamdan, a Yemeni citizen and the former driver for Osama bin Laden, who was captured in Afghanistan. Hamdan was charged with "conspiracy to commit terrorism" and was to be tried by a military commission. The government had argued that Hamdan was not a prisoner of war, that the Geneva Conventions could not apply to him (or any enemy combatant who was not a POW) and that the President had the authority, given by Congress, to establish military commissions to try these enemy combatants in the war on terror. These assertions, of course, matched the political determinations and legal arguments presented to the public regarding the treatment of detainees captured in the War on Terror.

However, the arguments presented by the Bush administration were dealt a serious blow in the Court's ruling which declared that military commissions are not expressly authorized by any congressional act. While Congress had sanctioned the use of military commissions to try offenders and offences against the laws of war, "conspiracy" is not a breach of the laws of war and therefore a suspect could not be tried for such an act by a military commission. Neither the Authorization for the Use of Military Force (AUMF) or the Detainee Treatment Act (DTA) can be read to provide specific overriding authorization for the military commission to try Hamdan.

Together, the UCMJ, the AUMF, and the DTA at most acknowledge a general Presidential authority to convene military commissions in circumstances where justified under the Constitution and laws including the law of war. Absent a more specific congressional authorization, this Court's task is...to decide whether Hamdan's military commission is so justified...

The military commission at issue lacks the power to proceed because its structure and procedures violate both the UCMJ and the four Geneva Conventions signed in 1949.[124]

Additionally, the Court added that the "procedures adopted to try Hamdan also violate the Geneva Conventions." The Geneva Conventions were found to be applicable US law that the President's authority could not overturn without express direction/instruction from Congress. Finally, it was determined that Common Article 3 applied to Hamdan as the Court found that it was intended to provide protection to individuals regardless of the characterization of the conflict. The argument that the Conventions did not apply because al-Qaida was a non-state actor and therefore not a party to the Geneva Conventions was not valid.

This ruling essentially undermined many of the Bush administration's arguments—that the AUMF and Constitution granted the President sweeping powers to deal with a national emergency, and that the Geneva Conventions did not and should not apply to a War on Terror. Naturally, the Bush administration was not pleased with this turn of events. The Acting Assistant Attorney General, Steven G. Bradbury, indicated to the Senate Committee on the Judiciary that he found many aspects of the Court's judgments "problematic", although he indicated that the Bush administration would abide by the ruling.[125] Daniel J. Dell'Orto, the Defense Department's Deputy General Counsel, testified to the same Senate Committee that the military tribunals remained the best way to try enemy combatants for war crimes:

While tradition and common sense...provide strong support for alternative adjudication processes for terrorists and other unlawful enemy combatants, military necessity is perhaps the strongest reason of all. It is simply not feasible in times of war to gather evidence in a manner that meets strict criminal procedural requirements.[126]

Dell'Orto also expressed his wish that Congress and the President would work quickly to resolve the matter.

The ruling in *Hamdan* immediately forced the Bush administration to make some changes in its detainee policy. On 7 July 2006, a two-page memo was issued by Gordon England, the Deputy Defense Secretary, which indicated that the US military would abide by Common Article 3 of the Geneva Conventions.[127] This marked a significant adjustment to the administration's strict stance that the Conventions did not apply to the War on Terror. Additionally, President Bush acknowledged, for the first time, that the CIA was operating "black sites", but ordered all detained persons to be held at Guantánamo Bay. The effect of this announcement, however, proved to be somewhat less revolutionary for several reasons. Common Article 3 provides a bare minimum standard of humane treatment and is far less demanding than the full Conventions. It has always been the Bush administration's stance that they are treating detainees "humanely" and that all policies towards suspects in Guantánamo meet this requirement. Therefore, it is questionable whether there were changes in the way detainees were treated.

Perhaps even more dubious have been the constant denials that the administration carried out torture. It is clear that the administration simply did not consider several very harsh interrogation methods used against detainees (such as waterboarding) to be torture. Arguably, even worse, while the Justice Department declared torture "abhorrent" in December 2004, in 2005 Alberto Gonzales–having just been appointed Attorney General–issued a new secret opinion on detainee treatment which essentially amounted to "an expansive endorsement of the harshest interrogation techniques ever used by the Central Intelligence Agency".[128] Despite several attempts by Congress to prevent such practices as well as several Supreme Court decisions suggesting that the Geneva Conventions applied to the detainees, Gonzales' secret legal opinion seems to have remained in effect. The practice of waterboarding and other such techniques were briefly suspended after the decision in Hamdan. However, after a month-long debate within the administration, Bush signed a new executive order which authorized "enhanced" interrogation techniques.[129] The details of this order remain secret but were reviewed by the Office of Legal Counsel, and the administration remained adamant that such practices did not constitute torture. Yet torture was now considered to be those acts which "shock the conscience"–a rather vague standard at best.

The Bush administration also took legislative steps to restore its ability to wage the War on Terror in the ways of its choosing. It began to press Congress to support its policies regarding the military commissions. For example, the *New York Times* reported in July 2006 that after the *Hamdan* decision, legislation was being drafted by the Bush administration that set out new rules on bringing terror detainees to trial. The legislation would allow hearsay evidence to be introduced "unless it was deemed 'unreliable' and would permit defendants to be excluded from their own trials if necessary to protect national security, according to a copy of the proposal."[130]

Gonzales indicated that the administration's proposal for changes to the military commissions would permit hearsay to be used as evidence–not permitted under the UCMJ–along with several other controversial changes. These were presented in the Military Commissions Act 2006 which was passed by both houses and signed into law by President Bush in October 2006. Among other powers, the Act gives the President final authority to interpret the Geneva Conventions (and Common Article 3), provides immunity for government officials from prosecution, and extinguishes claims for a writ of *habeas corpus*. The Act also allowed for evidence gained under torture to be used against defendants. Unsurprisingly, the Act was a massive disappointment for human rights activists who hoped that *Hamdan* had marked a turning point.

Yet, it was soon clear that not everything had been going according to the administration's plans. Within a few months there were only three cases brought to trial under the Military Commission system. In one case, the detainee (the Australian David Hicks) pleaded guilty and was subsequently repatriated. The two other cases were dismissed in June 2007 when the judges in both cases found that the military tribunals had been created to deal with those detainees who had been designated "unlawful" enemy combatants, not "enemy combatants".[131]

Certainly, it was a technicality, but it was enough to throw the military commission system into confusion. This was certainly not helped by the Supreme Court decision in *Boumediene v Bush* in June 2008 which ruled that the detainees held in Guantánamo as "enemy combatants" had the right to challenge the lawfulness of their detention in a court of law.[132] Effectively, the decision declared the portion of the Military Commissions Act which stripped the detainees of their rights to *habeas corpus* as unconstitutional. The administration was then immediately confronted with a number of *habeas* cases which again disrupted the system–and the legal branches of the DoD which had to deal with them.

Throughout 2008 the administration seemed to be on the defensive as detainees began to increasingly win the right to challenge their detention and, in some cases, the right to release, in District and Federal courts.[133] The administration did eventually secure the conviction of Hamdan (discussed above) for "providing material support for terrorism", but he was sentenced to time already served and was sent to Yemen in November of that year to reserve. Meanwhile, the military commissions continued to be a source of criticism for the United States inherited by the Obama administration, they are a source of political tension in Congress. By the Spring of 2010, attempts to bring several trials to New York City were under heavy attack by Republicans.

What is to be made of all this? At the very least, the Court ruling in *Hamdan* recognized that the Bush administration went too far in asserting powers in the post-9/11 environment. Specifically, the Court indicated that the administration needed to get permission from Congress and operate within the limits of the law—even when it came to matters of national security. Additionally, in *Hamdan* and *Boumediene*, the Court recognized that even in a "new paradigm", there were still domestic and international standards and obligations which applied to the conduct of hostilities despite the assertions of the administration. Finally, the Court recognized the role of international law that the US Congress has acknowledged as binding. In this way, the Courts recognized that there are limits regarding the treatment of detainees regardless of the characterization of the conflict.

Yet, in the push and pull between liberty and security (or just stubborn determination), the Bush administration tried to swing the balance back to its preferred policies through the sweeping powers and policies of the Military Commission Act. The Supreme Court continued to sidestep making decisions on procedural grounds rather than deciding cases. This in and of itself does not speak well for the lesser evil approach which places so much emphasis on domestic institutions. Additionally, many political figures outside the administration seemed quite willing to tolerate, even expand presidential powers to fight the War on Terror. One candidate for the 2008 Republican nomination argued that he would "double" Guantánamo and several did not have any difficulty with the Bush administration's policies on interrogation techniques.[134]

Vindicating the lesser evil?

For all the criticism directed at the Bush administration, it is important to remember that the American detention policies went through substantial changes between 2002 and 2008. After all, it was Bush, not Obama who began the process of trying to shut Guantánamo Bay down—even if it seems to have been out of a realization that Guantánamo was an inconvenience rather than ideological commitment to limits on what the US could do in the name of its own security. For better or worse, policy regarding detainees during this period went through a substantial evolution partly due to a response to domestic and international criticism. However, perhaps a more important factor in this evolution was the changes forced by democratic institutions, especially the Supreme Court decisions, as well as legislation brought forward—even if the process has been slow or not quite straightforward.

In this sense there may be some merit to the lesser evil argument. Domestic and democratic institutions seem to have had an effect on Bush administration policies where international pressure did not. Policies which restricted the rights of detainees, justified under arguments about a "new paradigm", were challenged in courts and legislatures. The overall effect proved to be mixed. The courts seemed to be willing to assert authority, but Congress was arguably very lax in its monitoring of or input into detainee policies—a criticism that still applies after the Democrats took over in 2007. But the changes that came out of democratic institutions at least had some effect in forcing the administration's hand to act or respond to these developments.

Enter Obama

However, there can be little doubt that the most public changes (even if only in terms of rhetoric) have come with the new Obama administration. Obama, who frequently criticized the Bush administration's detainee policies on the campaign trail, immediately set about resolving the Guantánamo issue upon taking office. One of his first acts as president in January 2009 was to order the closing of the detention centre at Guantánamo Bay within a year. As well as doing so, he immediately froze the military commissions while they underwent a review. These acts were well received internationally and were deemed to be a sign that the new administration was committed to doing things differently when it came to the War on Terror.

Yet, by the middle of 2009 the results of the new approach were mixed. This partially reflected Obama's desire to act pragmatically and the limits of Congressional cooperation—but also the very difficult complexities of Guantánamo itself. The immediate effect of freezing the military commissions was to once again throw the status of detainees into question. Although not opposed by the lawyers for the defendants, it once again delayed any final resolution to their status. In May 2009 Obama's request for $80 million to fund the closure of the detention facilities was turned down by Congress, which demanded to see a clearer plan of action as well as having serious concerns over whether the administration would bring terror suspects to the US mainland for trial. In the same month, Obama infuriated some of his supporters on the political left when he announced that his administration would revive military commissions. Although only twenty of the inmates would be tried by such a system, the policy was decried by the American Civil Liberties Union and Amnesty International.[135] Additionally, although it is clear that the administration will continue to be working towards the closing of Guantánamo, this did not happen within the one-year deadline that Obama had been aiming for.

Some have raised the question whether or not anything has actually changed regarding detainee policies with the new administration. In an article in *The New Republic*, Jack Goldsmith argued: "The new administration has copied most of the Bush program, has expanded some of it, and has narrowed only a bit. Almost all of the Obama changes have been at the level of packaging, argumentation, symbol, and rhetoric."[136]

It is true that the results of the first few months of the administration suggest that there may be more in common with the Bush administration when it comes to detainee issues than what the average Obama supporter might be inclined to believe. That the administration has been arguing that Afghan detainees at Bagram Airbase do not have *habeas corpus* rights seems to be very much in line with the positions taken by Dick Cheney.[137] Also there can be little doubt that the failure to close down Guantanamo within the one year deadline set by Obama was met with disappointment.

However, there are important differences, particularly when it comes to the trial of suspects, which should be acknowledged. The administration has broken down the detainees into five categories–those deemed to have broken US law, to be tried in US federal courts (provided that there is sufficient evidence); those deemed to have broken the laws of war, who will be tried by reformed military commissions; those who have been ordered released by the courts, who will be released to their own countries; those who may be released to countries other than their home countries, so long as it is deemed safe to do so and a suitable country is willing to take them; and those who are deemed to be a continual danger, who will remain in detention and for whom a new legal system will be developed. With regard to the military commission system, the Obama administration has indicated it believes the system was flawed and will be reformed. Some of the changes that will be made are a ban on the use of evidence obtained through cruel, inhumane or degrading treatment, stricter rules on hearsay evidence, and allowing defendants to choose their own lawyers.

Certainly, the system is not a perfect one–particularly for those committed to international law and/or civil liberties. However, there are more changes here than what Goldsmith acknowledges in his article. Certainly, giving the defendant more rights and prohibiting the use of evidence gained by torture bring the military commission system more in line with international standards, including the Geneva Convention requirement for a "regularly constituted court affording all the judicial guarantees which are recognized as indispensable by civilized peoples". Whether or not some individuals deemed dangerous will remain for ever behind bars because they are deemed to represent a continued and serious danger to the security of the United States is still uncertain, but it is quite possible. The push and pull of liberty and values versus security and necessity seems set to continue, even with a president who seems ideologically committed to bringing America back in line with Geneva traditions.

Conclusion

The problems encountered when societies need to balance liberty and security are nothing new. The need to fight an effective campaign that also reflects the core humanitarian agreements of the last 100 years is a somewhat more recent problem–but was hardly a new issue by the time the War on Terror began in 2001. Yet the horrific attacks of 9/11 and America's Guantánamo policy have caused these questions to reemerge in an urgent manner.

In some ways, the questions come down to legal interpretation. But the underlying political and moral arguments which form the backdrop to the legal debate seem to hold the key to understanding why the Bush administration chose the path it took, and the justification for its policies. The arguments of the New Sovereigntists are moral and political arguments, defending the idea that political communities should not be accountable to any form of international law, especially when it comes to their self-defence. The idea that actions to protect the life of a political community should be subject to an unaccountable prosecutor is, in this view, irresponsible if not immoral. Yet humanitarians are correct to point out that such an attitude leaves the road open to unrestricted slaughter. The US has signed treaties on the laws of war because it participated in their negotiation, and signed them because it was seen as being in its interest. In the last thirty years, it has put a remarkable amount of effort into ensuring that laws of war principles are included in training and targeting. That it should turn its back on such a tradition has come as a deep shock to many.

This chapter has put forth the argument that the origins of the Guantánamo controversy began with the rise of the New Sovereigntist critique in the 1990s, as well as the frustrations encountered with the Kosovo campaign in 1999 in terms of the requirements of coalition warfare under NATO and the actions of the ICTY. The sudden and brutal realization of the nature of the threat that America (if not the West) was now facing after 9/11 suggested to many that the War on Terror was going to require a new type of fighting, and that the nature of the threat called for a new evaluation of the international law applicable to warfare. Such arguments also emphasized the need for presidential powers–able to override domestic or international legislation–which, in the eyes of the Bush administration, were necessary to protect the United States.

This chapter has also tried to show that arguments criticizing US policy coming from the international legal community have (unsurprisingly) relied heavily upon legal analysis, and have been mostly very severe in their critique of the interpretation of the law that America has presented. The difficulty with these counter-arguments is that they ignore and thus fail to deal with the political and moral arguments being put forward by the New Sovereigntists and the Bush administration. To argue that violations of international law are occurring to an administration that has essentially downplayed the relevance of international law is probably going to be ineffective. Instead, it has been domestic courts which have brought about the most (albeit gradual) change and political arguments that continue to hold sway. At the very least, on an academic level, arguments that take the New Sovereigntist position seriously need to be presented.

One such argument, briefly touched on here, is that the Bush administration and, perhaps, certain New Sovereigntists tend to downplay the links between law, policy and effective fighting. If effective fighting depends on policy, and policy to a great extent depends on law, including the laws of war, then is not the argument that the Geneva Conventions do not matter dangerous for US effectiveness? This question will be addressed in the next chapter.

5

FAILURE OF AN ETHOS?

OPERATION IRAQI FREEDOM, AMERICA AND ABU GHRAIB

Introduction

If the 1991 Gulf War indicated how effective the laws of war could be in modern warfare, the 2003 Iraq War might be considered to demonstrate the opposite. In terms of the "war" aspect of Operation Iraqi Freedom, the fighting may be said to have been relatively uncontroversial in terms of the laws of war, and was certainly over with very quickly.[1] Beginning on 19 March 2003 and lasting for twenty-seven days, Operation Iraqi Freedom was conducted with remarkable speed and in a relatively humane manner.[2] By 15 April, Coalition forces were in control of all major Iraqi cities and the Baathist leadership had disintegrated. On 1 May 2003 President Bush declared a formal end to major combat operations.[3]

Yet it was precisely when the fighting ended and the occupation phase of Operation Iraqi Freedom began that the trouble seems to have started. The Coalition's presence in Iraq has been plagued by a violent and bloody insurgency, described in July 2003 as "a classical guerrilla-type campaign" by the then Commander of the United States Central Command (CENTCOM), General John Abizaid.[4] It is typically assumed that the insurgency is led by a core group of fighters and supported by a larger pool of active and passive supporters sympathetic to the cause, predominantly drawn from the Sunni Muslim population.

In terms of the law of war, this proved to be a frustrating situation. With the onset of looting and violence immediately following the invasion, as well as the emerging insurgency, the law which properly governed the military operations in Iraq was unclear. Did the situation remain an international armed conflict, or was it a case of an internal armed conflict, or a mixture of the two? Further, there was the legal issue of occupation to sort out in terms of policies and obligations on the ground.[5] As Adam Roberts argues, there is no dispute about the fact that between April 2003 and 28 June 2004 there was a foreign military occupation in Iraq.[6] However, after the transition to the Iraqi Interim Government on the latter date and the election of a government, the situation grew more confusing. While the Iraqis have increasingly taken charge of their own country, the continued presence of Coalition troops, ongoing hostilities, and the instability of the new Iraqi government suggest that the law governing occupation (albeit a changing occupation), and the law of war, remain important issues in post-war Iraq. In fact, in terms of law, the Iraq conflict appears to have been the most problematic for the US since Vietnam. And these issues only became more complicated when, in 2004, pictures of abuse committed by US troops at Abu Ghraib prison were splashed across the pages of newspapers around the world.

The last chapter examined how the case for a rebalancing of the need for security and obligations to international law was put forward by the Bush administration after 9/11, but also how a sceptical sentiment towards international law had been growing in certain legal circles and came to influence the administration's response. Yet when such a rebalancing was implemented, there appear to have been several crucial errors made by the Bush administration, including failures of oversight, failures to consider the roles of new actors in the ongoing conflict, and failure to establish whether the "new rules" were robust enough to withstand the pressures of an emerging insurgency. This chapter will look at the implications of Operation Iraqi Freedom for America's relationship with prisoners and the laws of war through the prism of the Abu Ghraib controversy. The argument will proceed on the basis that the abuse which took place at the prison highlights several issues for this relationship, including the Bush administration's policies regarding the laws of war, private military firms and military training. In doing so it will look at whether American policies regarding the laws of war and its military doctrine, which are designed to enforce an "ethos", are adequate for the ethical challenges posed by the War on Terror.

What went wrong at Abu Ghraib?

Background

Even before the pictures of detainees being sexually humiliated, terrified and physically abused were made public in the spring of 2004, it had become apparent to many in Iraq and Washington that something was not quite right about the prison arrangement. The prison itself, which had been one of Saddam Hussein's most notorious, was reopened as the Baghdad Central Correctional Facility by the Coalition Provisional Authority in August 2003, after it was increasingly becoming apparent that the conflict was transforming itself from a traditional war into an insurgency.

Originally, the intention was to house only criminals, but as more and more insurgents and "security detainees" were captured throughout the autumn of 2003, these individuals were kept in the same centres. According to several military reports on conditions at Abu Ghraib, the flood of incoming detainees overwhelmed the staff. This was compounded by the fact that relatively few individuals were being released. Significantly, while this initial peak of detainees were being collected, many of the military police and interrogators coming from the US Reserves had reached the mandatory two-year limit on their mobilization time and were being sent home. According to one report, this resulted in a situation where "the ranks of soldiers having custody of detainees in Iraq fell to about half strength."[7]

By virtually all accounts, conditions at Abu Ghraib were exceptionally poor for both detainees and military personnel alike. Part of the problem seems to have stemmed from the fact that the Bush administration had failed to properly anticipate post-war conditions. This includes the failure to commit enough troops necessary to ensure order in post-war Iraq, the failure to anticipate a resistance that had been coordinating its efforts months before the initial invasion, and, finally, an ideologically led belief that Coalition troops would be welcomed as liberators. Ultimately, few had anticipated the resistance that American troops would encounter, and those who did had been shoved aside in the lead-up to the invasion.[8]

As a result, there was inadequate preparation for the establishment of prisons or a prison system, and the conditions at Abu Ghraib were appalling for soldier and prisoner alike. Janis Karpinski, the commanding general in charge of rebuilding the civilian prison system, described Abu Ghraib "as the worst MP assignment possible".[9] A psychological assessment of the conditions at Abu Ghraib, included as a part of one of the reports on the prison scandal, concluded, "all present at Abu Ghraib were truly in personal danger. Daily

185

mortar attacks from without and sporadic prisoner riots from within led to several deaths and numerous injuries of both Soldiers and detainees alike."[10] As conditions worsened, prisoners began to attempt to escape from the prison and several succeeded. By November 2003, there were riots in protest against living conditions. This lead to the shooting of twelve detainees on 24 November, with three fatalities. By the end of December 2003 there were at least four more shooting incidents and numerous escapes.

Although military staff at Abu Ghraib requested more personnel to help with the situation, this was denied by superiors in Combined Joint Task Force–7 (CJTF-7),[11] the Combined Forces Land Component Command (CFLCC) and US Central Command (CENTCOM). Still, as conditions deteriorated, it was becoming rapidly apparent that the situation at Abu Ghraib needed a great deal of improvement. Assistance was requested from the Provost Marshal General of the Army, Major General Donald Ryder, who was tasked with providing suggestions and recommendations for reform. Yet, as the Schlesinger Report indicates, "There seemed to be some misunderstanding of the... intent, however, since MG Ryder viewed his visit primarily as an assessment of how to transfer the detention program to the Iraqi prison system."[12] In other words, Ryder, who assessed the operations at Abu Ghraib from 11 October to 6 November, seems to have failed to pick up on the major abuses of prisoners that were taking place by this point.

Indeed, according to the dates of the pictures of prisoners being abused in Abu Ghraib, most of the abuses occurred between October and December 2003. On 13 January 2004, Specialist Joseph Darby alerted his superiors to the abuse taking place and turned in a CD-ROM of incriminating pictures, taken from the laptop of one of the perpetrators. This immediately spurred an investigation into the abuse that was summarized in the March 2004 Taguba Report. Although the military did announce that an investigation was taking place at a press conference in January 2004, the nature of the abuses which took place or public awareness of them did not truly turn into outrage until the photographs were made available to the public at the end of April 2004.

Source(s) of the abuse?

Once leaked, photos of the abuse that had taken place at Abu Ghraib were splashed around the world on the cover of magazines and newspapers and transmitted on the internet. The images they presented were nothing short of appalling; prisoners were shown naked, terrified by dogs, forced into human pyramids and with women's undergarments on their head. It was clear evidence that prisoners at Abu Ghraib were being physically assaulted, psychologically tormented and sexually abused in an utter disregard for the laws of war.

International and domestic reaction to the photos was (rightly) severe. As one might expect, since their publication, there has been no shortage of explanations as to how such actions–clearly in breach of international law, military codes of conduct and criminal law–could have occurred. How could trained soldiers of a Western democracy treat individuals, detainees or not, in such a manner?

In terms of the theories, commentaries and criticisms which have emerged, it is possible to argue that there are two generalizable categories. The first group of theories are those which have often come out of US military investigations and reports themselves. These arguments tend to suggest that the source of the abuse at Abu Ghraib lay with low-ranking individuals and their direct superiors. In addition, they tend to argue that conditions, doctrinal training that did not match actual conditions, and failures to supply adequate equipment, but more problematically troops, to the prison played a significant role in leading to the ultimate deterioration of order inside Abu Ghraib.

The second typically comes from journalists and human rights advocates who argue that Abu Ghraib was the direct result of America's failure to adhere to international law–that the abuse which occurred is undeniably linked to US policies in Afghanistan and Guantánamo Bay's Camp Delta. One argument of this group is that the ultimate responsibility for Abu Ghraib lies at the highest levels of the George W. Bush administration.

What divides these two groups is where responsibility ultimately lies and whether the root causes of the abuse were in fact systemic. A brief look at these two groups of arguments will be useful here in order to determine implications for the American military and its relationship with the laws of war.

Arguments for 'condition specific' roots of the abuse

There have been several reports on the Abu Ghraib prison events conducted by the US Department of Defense–some of which have already been mentioned.[13] For the purpose of this section the reports examined include the March 2004 "Article 15–6 Investigation of the 800th Military Police Brigade" (the Taguba Report), the July 2004 "Department of the Army, The Inspector General–Detainee Operations Inspection" (the Mikolashek Report), the August 2004 "Final Report of the Independent Panel to Review DoD Detention Operations" (the Schlesinger Report) and the August 2004 "Investigation of Intelligence Activities at Abu Ghraib/Investigation o the Abu Ghraib Prison and 205th Military Intelligence Brigade, LTG Anthony R Jones/Investigation of the Abu Ghraib Detention Facility and 205th Military Intelligence Brigade, MG George R. Fay" (the Fay-Jones Report).[14]

Although these reports were commissioned at different times, by different people with similar yet differing purposes, they all seem to suggest similar conclusions about what went wrong at Abu Ghraib. First, all comment on the poor conditions at Abu Ghraib, not only for detainees, but also for the military staff working there. The reports make it clear that the prison was often under attack by insurgents and the staff were left to manage a mixed population of prisoners (who included both men and women, criminals, insurgents, enemy prisoners of war, "security detainees") who were very hostile to their captors. Poor quality food for prisoners and military personnel, a lack of resources (such as secure radios for communication or an internet connection and even, according to some reports, clothes) and a serious overcrowding of prisoners combined with a shortage of personnel (which in turn led to shortcomings in leadership oversight) to make an incredibly stressful environment. The Taguba Report included an annex dealing with a psychological assessment which argued, "Given this atmosphere of danger, promiscuity, and negativity, the worst human qualities and behaviours came to the fore and a perverse dominance came to prevail, especially at Abu Ghraib."[15]

Part of the problem, according to the above reports, included the fact that the training received by the individuals at Abu Ghraib was insufficient or inadequate. Detention training was only given to some of the soldiers. While the 800th Brigade–the brigade which most of those charged with war crimes came from–had planned for a major detention exercise during the summer of 2002, this was cancelled following the activation of many Reservist troops after 11 September. The Schlesinger report also claimed that training in managing detention facilities at mobilization sites failed to prepare units for conducting detention operations:

Leaders of inspected reserve units stated in interviews that they did not receive a clear mission statement prior to mobilization and were not notified of their mission until after deploying. Personnel interviewed described being placed immediately in stressful situations in a detention facility with thousands of non-compliant detainees and not being trained to handle them. Units arriving in theatre were given just a few days to conduct a handover from the outgoing units. Once deployed, these newly arrived units had difficulty gaining access to the necessary documentation on tactics, techniques, and procedures to train their personnel on the... essential attacks of their new mission. A prime example is that relevant Army manuals and publications were available only online, but personnel did not have access to computers or the internet.[16]

The Taguba report draws similar conclusions, especially as regards the laws of war:

I also find that very little instruction or training was provided to MP personnel on the applicable rules of the Geneva Convention relative to the Treatment of Prisoners of War, [and applicable Field Manuals]. Moreover, I find that few, if any, copies of the Geneva Conventions were ever made available to MP personnel or detainees.[17]

Additionally, as the Mikolashek Report notes, because most personnel were not trained in detention operations, they were unaware of the requirements of Army doctrine or policies and procedures that address the responsibilities for confinement, security, preventative medicine and interrogation.[18]

Related to this, all of the reports conclude that military doctrine was also insufficient or inadequate for the situation that the personnel on the ground at Abu Ghraib found themselves in. As the Taguba report notes, the 800th MP Brigade was originally designed to conduct standard prisoner of war operations in Kuwait and that the doctrine used to train military personnel was based on templates predicated on a compliant, self-disciplining prison population rather than criminals or high-risk security detainees.[19] The Mikolashek report also noted that:

Doctrine does not address the unique characteristics of [Operation Iraqi Freedom] and [Operation Enduring Freedom], specifically operations in non-linear battlespaces and large numbers of detainees whose status is not readily identifiable as combatants, criminals or innocents.... Detainee doctrine does not address operations in a non-linear battlespace.[20]

In other words, the doctrine that the military was dealing with had its origins and thinking firmly rooted in the Cold War and in a European-battlespace mentality, with compliant prisoners of war who would be quickly and relatively easily evacuated from the battlefield.

Yet although conditions were bad in Abu Ghraib, they did not have to lead to what several of the reports describe as "purposeless sadism".[21] Clearly other brigades and soldiers faced moral dilemmas or shortfalls in doctrine while carrying out operations in Operation Iraqi Freedom or Operation Enduring Freedom, but without this leading to the levels of abuse seen at Abu Ghraib. This is where the reports tend to place blame on low-ranking individuals who actually committed the abuse and, for the most part, their direct superiors. As the Mikolashek Report claims, the occurrences of abuses at Abu Ghraib are "aberrations" and atypical of the military:

The abuses that have occurred... are not representative of policy, doctrine or soldier training. These abuses were unauthorized actions taken by a few individuals, coupled with the failure of a few leaders to provide adequate monitoring, supervision, and leadership over those soldiers.[22]

And later on the Report declares that "In those instances where detainee abuse occurred, individuals failed to adhere to basic standards of discipline, training or Army values..."[23]

Yet it is also interesting that two of the reports include psychological assessments of the situation of Abu Ghraib and of those who committed the abuse. The Schlesinger Report explicitly cites several studies dealing with obedience to authority and with prison environments, in trying to explain what went wrong in Abu Ghraib.[24] Taguba found that psychological factors played a major role in the abuse, including cultural differences, the poor quality of life and the real presence of mortal danger over an extended time period.[25] The report also notes that "There was a complex interplay of many psychological factors and command insufficiencies."[26] The Mikolashek Report gives several reasons why detainee abuse may occur despite efforts to eliminate it, including "the psychological process that increases the likelihood of abusive behaviour where one person has complete control over another".[27]

Arguably, by placing blame on psychological factors, the responsibility for the abuse can be placed more on individuals rather than on policy. Part of the criticism emerging from this line of argument is resounding criticism of the immediate leadership of the Abu Ghraib abusers for failing to observe and take note of the deteriorating material and psychological conditions at the prison. Taguba is extremely harsh in his criticism of the military leadership involved in the abuse at Abu Ghraib. This includes Brigadier General Janis Karpinski, Commander, 800th MP Brigade who, the Report alleges, did a poor job in allocating resources and ensuring that there were appropriate standard operating procedures for dealing with detainees at detention facilities in Iraq. Additionally the Report notes that Karpinski failed to take appropriate action regarding ineffective staff and that numerous reported accountability lapses were not corrected.[28] The Schlesinger Report goes so far as to argue that Lieutenant General Ricardo Sanchez, commander of CJTF-7, "should have taken stronger action in November when he realized the extent of the leadership problems at Abu Ghraib" and that both he and Walter Wojdakowski, his Deputy General Commander, failed to ensure proper staff oversight of detention and interrogation operations.[29]

The leadership point is an interesting one. Certainly the failures to punish those who were carrying out the abuse and to rectify the serious failings at

Abu Ghraib seem to have led to a culture of permissiveness that allowed the abuse to continue. Yet this is one of the areas where the reports tend to differ. The Taguba Report concentrates most of its blame on the leadership of Karpinski and her immediate subordinates who failed to adequately monitor what was going on in Abu Ghraib. This may be a result of the fact that the report was researched and written before the photographs of the abuse were in the public domain and there was less pressure to look at leadership further towards the top or bottom of the command chain. The Mikolashek Report tends to place increased responsibility on the individuals who actually carried out the acts, several times stating that there were no "systemic" causes for the abuse.[30] The Schlesinger Report makes specific arguments about higher levels of leadership, including Secretary of Defense Donald Rumsfeld, perhaps making it more controversial. Rumsfeld, it is claimed, should have better utilized the legal opinions of the Judge Advocates and General Counsel regarding detainee policies so as to have ensured a more consistent practice.[31]

This is perhaps indicative of the fact that there is still much uncertainty as to where the responsibility for the abuse should go. However, as mentioned above, there is another group of theories holding that the events at Abu Ghraib were the direct result of the George W. Bush administration's policies–and that the real responsibility lies at a much higher level.

Systemic causes of the abuse

Since the discovery of the abuse at Abu Ghraib, there have been many editorials and books written that tend to blame systemic factors and deliberate actions by the Bush administration. These arguments tend to come from journalists, lawyers and academics who argue that it is possible to directly trace the actions of the prison guards at Abu Ghraib to the confused legal and material situation on the ground created by high-ranking military officials and even members of the Bush cabinet.[32] Although each argument comes with its own agenda[33] and understanding of the circumstances depending on the time it was written, it is possible to put forward a summary of points that are being made.

The first point relates to the discussion in the last chapter of the alleged distain for international law held by the Bush administration and its supporters. Philippe Sands argues that "Disdain for global rules underpins the whole enterprise",[34] and David Rose writes of the way the administration was "isolationist and disinclined to fetter its autonomy through treaties and international law". Therefore, in the wake of 9/11, Bush's decision that the War on Terror would be fought "according to new rules of his own administration's devising" was really a "reflex" response.[35] This disdain led to the downplaying of international humanitarian and human rights law and has encouraged policies which, when carried out against detainees, amounted to torture.

This, it is argued, was arranged by a group of "political appointee" lawyers who, rather than serving the cause of law, bent, twisted and reinterpreted international rules to suit the purposes of their political masters. Sands provides what is, perhaps, one of the most resounding critiques of these lawyers, writing that "The 'war on terrorism' has led many lawyers astray. This phoney 'war' has been used to eviscerate well-established and sensible rules of international law..."[36] He claims that the arguments and legal interpretations of whether or not the US is bound by particular treaties and international obligations have been made by "political appointees, many of whom had no real background in international law or were closely associated with a group of American academics known to be hostile to international law."[37] On this point Sands lays out special criticism for the former White House Counsel (and now, additionally, former Attorney General) Alberto Gonzales, the former Assistant Attorney-General Jay S. Bybee and the former Deputy Assistant Attorney-General John Yoo, who all had a role in "redefining" the administration's obligation to adhere to the Geneva Conventions and international treaties on torture. Rose argues that "at every location in the global war on terror, from Washington DC to Afghanistan, previous restraints on the treatment of prisoners was being reconsidered and in significant ways abandoned" by lawyers from all branches of the military and intelligence agencies.[38] These redefinitions and reclassifications of what constituted legal treatment of detainees, what obligations the US had to "detainees" as opposed to prisoners of war and what activities amounted to torture created a climate of legal confusion which seemed to suggest that suspected terrorists had no rights under international law and could be subjected to whatever treatment or abuse that was deemed to be prudent. The abuse at Abu Ghraib was therefore the tragic logical endpoint of this misleading legal strategy.

The systemic argument, then, rests on the idea that officials within the Bush administration pushed forward a legally (and morally) dubious interpretation of the law that was readily accepted as sound legal advice given the already sceptical view of international rules that the Bush administration had. This created a confused environment for military personnel on the ground where the Global War on Terror was being fought The administration had developed several categories of detainees—enemy prisoners of war proper, prisoners of war who were eligible for the protections of the Geneva Convention but failed to meet the criteria set out by the Conventions, "security detainees", ordinary criminals, insurgents, etc. Each group was entitled to a different set of rights or, alternatively, a different set of interrogation methods that could be used. As Supreme Court Justice Sandra Day O'Connor noted in *Hamdi et al v. Rumsfeld*, the Bush administration never actually set out a list of criteria determining the distinctions between the different categories.[39] In a situation where legal definitions and categories were in flux, it is not surprising that abuse took place. As Sands argues, "it seems pretty clear that the legal minds which created Bush's doctrine of pre-emption in the use of force and established the procedures at the Guantánamo detention camp led directly to an environment in which the monstrous images from Abu Ghraib could be created."[40]

However, criticism is not just directed towards the executive branch of the American government, but also towards the complacency of Congress, law-makers and even the media who allowed the Bush administration to "get away with it". In the same way that military leaders failed to control and curtail the actions of the Abu Ghraib prison guards through a lack of oversight and regulation, Sands argues that the US Congress did not engage with the issues until late in the day. He also accuses the US media of taking their eye off the ball or becoming "engaged in the kind of 9/11 coverage that made it impossible to give rules which might constrain American actions a decent hearing."[41] Although he notes that the allegations at Abu Ghraib began to alter the environment of unquestioning support for the Bush administration, Rose argues that the American responses to criticism over the War on Terror were marked with "complacency and insouciance".[42] Even after the fact, there was a failure of Congress to follow up on what happened at Abu Ghraib and to determine who knew and ordered what at which level. Seymour Hersh writes that in the wake of Abu Ghraib, "The problems weren't confronted, and no independent Committee investigation was authorized into the policies that led to Abu Ghraib." In fact, Senators who had pressed for further investigations into the matter came under pressure to cease their calls for an independent inquiry.[43]

This is what has led many of those arguing for systemic responsibility to claim that the reports and investigations carried out by the Department of Defense into the abuse at Abu Ghraib were a "whitewash". It is a virtually unanimous consensus from this perspective that Bush administration officials bear responsibility for the abuse at Abu Ghraib. Michael Byers goes so far as to argue that "Had Saddam ratified the ICC statute, the chief prosecutor would, quite properly, already be investigation the Abu Ghraib situation, with a view to possibly laying charges for command responsibility against the secretary of defense and president."[44]

Hersh writes that of the official inquiries into the abuse, none challenged the official Bush administration line that there was no high-level policy condoning or overlooking such abuse:

The buck always stops with the handful of enlisted Army Reservists...

It's a dreary pattern. A military report is released and, within a few days, a high-level general or admiral appears before the Senate Armed Services Committee...and reveals under questioning, that he has no mandate to investigate the responsibility, if any, of higher-ups such as President George W. Bush and Secretary of Defense Donald Rumsfeld.[45]

As Hersh sees it:

The legal and moral issue is not high-level knowledge of the specific events in the photographs–of course the President and his senior advisors did not know of the particular acts of insanity repeatedly taking place on the night shift at the prison. The question that never gets adequately asked or answered, though, is this: What did the President do *after* being told about Abu Ghraib?...

It's what was not done at that point that is significant. There is no evidence that President Bush, upon learning of the devastating conduct at Abu Ghraib, asked any hard questions of Donald Rumsfeld and his own aides at the White House...There was no evidence that they had taken any significant steps upon learning in mid-January of the Abu Ghraib abuses to review and modify the military's policy toward prisoners.[46]

Therefore, from this perspective, the abuse at Abu Ghraib prison originated from systemic sources: that is, problems related to the confusion generated by legal definitions and standards in constant flux, a willingness on the part of the administration to achieve its goals in the War on Terror at all costs including the violation of international law, poor leadership oversight from all levels (horizontal and vertical) within the US government and military, and deliberately dubious legal advice. In this way, the blame for Abu Ghraib lies at the top of the chain of command, rather than the bottom. According to this view with their emphasis on conditions on the ground, psychological factors and low-lying leadership culpability, the official reports on the abuse really amount to little more than a cover-up for the Bush administration and high ranking US officials.

For example, as Hersh questions in his book, why did a group of Army Reserve military policemen, most of them from small towns, torment their prisoners as they did, in a manner that was especially humiliating for Iraqi men? He postulates that such techniques were learned from special forces and intelligence operatives who were also at work at Abu Ghraib. Karpinski, in writing her side of the Abu Ghraib story, agrees indicating that the young soldiers who were involved:

...could not have had an inkling of President Bush's decision to exempt the terrorists of Afghanistan from the Geneva Conventions, permitting more extreme interrogation techniques that eventually leeched over into Iraq. They could have had no understanding of the conflicting and confusing rules for interrogation issued at various times... They had no part in General Miller's mission to 'Gitmo-ize' Abu Ghraib, introducing a tougher style of questioning. They had not studied Arab psychology, giving them the tools to humiliate security detainees without physically harming the great majority of them. While it's true that the 372nd MP Company was a patchwork outfit suffering like many Reserve unites from the ills of cross-levelling, sloppy training, and spotty leadership, the soldiers had demonstrated one consistent trait throughout their seven months of service in Iraq: They did as they were told...For the rest of my days I will believe that, at Abu Ghraib, these solders also were following orders when they humiliated and abused detainees.[47]

Hersh argues these trained figures "had been authorized by the Pentagon's senior leadership to act far outside the normal boundaries, the normal rules of engagement."[48] Such techniques, then, authorized by the top, were unsurprisingly adopted by the bottom of the command chain. The responsibility for passing these techniques is therefore directly linked to higher-ups.

Philippe Sands goes further–literally setting out a case for prosecution. He identifies six Bush administration lawyers as the "torture team" which enabled abuse to occur at Guantánamo and then spread to Afghanistan and Iraq: David Addington, General Counsel to Vice President Cheney, Jay Bybee, Assistant Attorney General, Doug Feith, former Undersecretary of Defense for Policy, Alberto Gonzales, Counsel to President Bush, William J. Haynes II, General Counsel to the Secretary of Defense, and John Yoo, Deputy Assistant Attorney General.

The techniques used...were the result of decisions and actions taken at the highest echelons of the Bush Administration. The senior lawyers and policy-makers deliberately decided to remove the protections of Geneva. They actively sought methods of interrogation that had been used by others on Americans, even if they were inconsistent with the minimum standards reflected in Common Article 3 of the Conventions. They conspired to create the impression that the process had started on the ground at Guantanamo. They caused to be prepared and then relied on grossly inadequate legal advice from the [Department of Justice], and then claimed they'd relied on other legal advice. They took steps to circumvent any legal advice that would have stopped the abuse, short-circuiting the normal decision-making process. These deliberate, concerted actions have all the hallmarks of a conspiracy, bringing those most closely associated into complicity with torture.[49]

Analysis: who is responsible? [50]

In the political and legal fallout from the scandal at Abu Ghraib, it is certainly possible to point to factors that probably did contribute to the situation on the ground, as well as a failure to plan adequately for the problems of post-war Iraq. That many of the troops did not have and were not provided with training in their duties, and that military doctrine did not take into consideration the circumstances that the military personnel at the prison found themselves confronting, is clear. Additionally, if the accounts of the conditions that both detainee and soldier found themselves in are accurate, it is certainly possible to argue that the environment at Abu Ghraib, with its poor supplies, understaffed personnel and constant risk of danger from shelling, probably was a factor in creating stressful conditions for those individuals stationed there.

Naturally, this does not excuse such sadistic behaviour. Certainly the troops of the 800th Military Brigade were not the only ones to face harsh circumstances in the war on terror. Then why did circumstances turn out as they did at Abu Ghraib? The photos of soldiers standing around and over hooded, beaten and terrified prisoners beg the question "how did this happen?"

One thing that the systemic and non-systemic views of Abu Ghraib have in common is the idea that there was a confused legal situation on the ground. According to the military reports, this stemmed from a lack of adequate training in the laws of war and US military doctrine and the inability to obtain training or resources in this area. Yet even some of the military reports, such as the Schlesinger Report, go further than this. Both the systemic and non-systemic theories agree that the confusing situation originated from the decisions made by the Bush administration since 2002.

A closer look at the timeline will make this clear. What was in place with regard to interrogation of prisoners of war before 9/11 was listed in *Army Field Manual 34–52* (on Intelligence Interrogation). This included a list of seventeen authorized interrogation methods.[51] In October 2002, authorities at Guantánamo requested approval for stronger interrogation techniques to counter "tenacious resistance" by some detainees.[52] On 2 December 2002, Secretary of Defense Donald Rumsfeld authorized sixteen additional techniques for use at Guantánamo.[53] However, the Navy General Council Alberto J. Mora raised concerns about these new techniques and on 15 January 2003 Rumsfeld rescinded the majority of the approved measures in the December 2002 authorization.[54]

At this time, Rumsfeld directed the Department of Defence General Counsel to establish a working group to study interrogation techniques. According to the Schlesinger Report, thirty-five techniques were reviewed and twenty-four were eventually recommended to the Secretary of Defense—although this was not shown to all members of the working group. On 16 April 2003, a list of approved techniques, strictly limited for use at Guantánamo, was secretly approved.[55]

Meanwhile, in Afghanistan, from the beginning of the War on Terror to the end of 2002, all forces used the *Field Manual* as a guide for interrogation. However, as the Schlesinger Report points out, the use of more aggressive interrogation methods on detainees appears to have been ongoing. In January 2003 a list of techniques being used in Afghanistan, including some not explicitly set out in the field manuals, was forwarded to the working group that had been set up by the Secretary of Defense. This included Special Operations Forces Operating Standard Operating Procedures. According to the Report, the 519th Military Intelligence Battalion, which was later sent to Iraq, assisted in the interrogations in support of the Special Operations Forces and was fully aware of their interrogation techniques.[56]

This, the Report states, made it clear that during this time "Interrogators and lists of techniques circulated from Guantanamo and Afghanistan to Iraq."[57] When the officer in charge prepared the draft interrogation guidelines, they were a near copy of the Special Forces Standard Operating Procedures. Techniques which had been approved for very particular circumstances in Guantánamo were now migrating and being applied elsewhere—outside Guantánamo's controlled conditions.

The situation was further confused when attempts were made to improve intelligence gathering from detainees. Two officers were sent to Abu Ghraib for this purpose. Major General Geoffrey Miller, who had been in charge at Guantánamo, was sent to Iraq to conduct an assessment of DoD counter-terrorism interrogations and detention operations. Additionally Captain Carolyn Wood of the 519th military intelligence battalion, who had spent time at the Bagram Collection Point in Afghanistan, was put in charge of interrogations.[58]

One report indicated that Miller, while at Guantánamo, had been responsible for putting a lot of pressure on military intelligence officers to "Get me results!" Given the demand post-9/11 for intelligence, Miller had "unleashed a lot of aggressive tactics."[59] According to the Schlesinger Report, when sent to Iraq, Miller brought with him the April 2003 approved guidelines for Guantánamo and gave them to the CJTF-7 as a possible model for the command-wide policy that he recommended should be established. At this time

Miller called for the military police and military police intelligence soldiers to work cooperatively in "setting the conditions" for interrogation. While previously military police had played a passive role in collecting intelligence, cooperation on this level had not yet been tried outside Camp Delta.

Most of the military reports indicate that Miller said his model was approved only for Guantánamo. However, CJTF-7, using reasoning from the President's argument that the Geneva Convention did not apply to "unlawful combatants", believed that additional, tougher measures were warranted "because there were unlawful combatants mixed in with Enemy Prisoners of War and civilian and criminal detainees."[60] On 14 September, 2003, Lt-General Sanchez signed a memorandum authorizing a dozen interrogation techniques beyond *Field Manual 34–52*–five beyond those approved for Guantánamo. CENTCOM, however viewed this policy as unacceptably aggressive, and on 12 October 2003 the authorization for interrogation techniques approved by CJTF-7 was rescinded.

Upon arrival at Abu Ghraib, Wood laid down procedures that had been established at Bagram, including, according to some reports, rewriting the interrogation policy and adding an extra nine techniques. When interviewed for the Fay/Jones Report, Wood claimed that these techniques had been approved by a lawyer and that she had been told her policies were "a good start" when visited by Miller's team in 2003.[61] Speaking about Wood, a military spokesperson indicated that the Bagram rules she had brought were modified to make sure the right restraints were in place. However, her techniques still included sleep and sensory deprivation, stress positions, dietary manipulation and the use of dogs.[62]

Clearly, this created a confusing situation. As the Schlesinger Report notes, "The existence of confusing and inconsistent interrogation technique polices contributed to the belief that additional interrogation techniques were condoned."[63] Again, the involvement of other government agencies in the collection of intelligence and treatment of detainees contributed to the belief that methods harsher than those found in *Field Manual 34–52* were allowed.[64] But even more confusing was the fact that where military personnel at Abu Ghraib did consult field manuals, they used versions that were out of date. The 1987 version of *Field Manual 34–52* authorized interrogators to use provision or restriction of all facilities such as light, heating, food, clothing, and shelter for detainees in interrogation. This was changed in the 1992 version of the Manual and again led to a variance of opinion as to what techniques were permissible. The lack of attention paid by commanders to these kinds of details led the Schlesinger Report to assert, "We cannot be sure how much the number and severity of abuses would have been curtailed had there been early and consistent guidance from higher levels."[65]

Given the length and detail in the reports (as well as the sheer number of them), it is hard to disagree with this assessment. It is obvious that there was serious confusion as to which law applied where and to whom. That a military reservist might become confused by this constant flux of rules seems very reasonable.[66] It also is clear that Miller's advice was very problematic for the Iraq theatre. When his model was applied outside the controlled Guantánamo environment it led to disaster. Guantánamo has a very low prisoner to guard ratio and is in a (very) remote area. Given the chaotic prison conditions of Abu Ghraib, the shortage of personnel, and the lack of training for applying the "advanced" techniques, the same approach, ethical or not, was bound to fail. What all of the military reports also tend to criticize is Miller's suggestion that the military police play a larger role in collecting intelligence by "setting favourable conditions". The Taguba, Schlesinger and Fay-Jones Reports argue that in the environment of Abu Ghraib, this was taken to be an excuse for abusive behaviour towards detainees.

In this way, it is fairly clear that there were mistakes and errors made as well as confusions propagated at many levels of the command chain. Given this chaotic state of affairs, it is difficult to assign blame in the way that systemic or non-systemic proponents seem to want. In some ways it seems as wrong-headed to suggest that these actions were solely the responsibility of low-ranking "sadistic" military personnel as to suggest that all blame should rest with President Bush for starting the war in the first place. Certainly, policy confusion was generated from the top, but it is also clear that individuals acted inappropriately and interpreted their orders in what must have been one of the worst ways possible.

Given the policy confusion, it is not that difficult to see why critics would want to start with the initial decision to reinterpret or redefine the laws of war. The argument presented in the last chapter suggested that it may be reasonable to reconsider (but not reject) the balance of liberty, law, freedoms and security in the context of an existential threat or nihilistic terrorism. However, the Bush administration did more than merely "reconsider" the laws of war. Instead, between 9/11 and the end of 2004, it was clear that the administration reinterpreted and redefined the rules every three to six months, and did so in a highly secretive and inconsistent manner. It is one thing to change the rules of the game when that game changes, it is entirely another thing when those rules change every few weeks.

Clearly, in this respect, senior officials are to blame for creating this initial confusion. Some of the "political appointee" lawyers in the Departments of Justice and Defense sought to challenge the restrictions that Vietnam and Watergate had placed on the powers of the president, especially in wartime. John Yoo argued that, after 9/11, all decisions on how to defend the country under the American Constitution "are for the President alone to make".[67] Arguments defending this authority were made with reference to the USA PATRIOT Act and, as we have seen, to the argument that America was fighting a new kind of war. Hence commitments to international law were significantly downplayed. Yet, what really seems to have been the driver of abuse was that after the rules had been broken, nothing substantial or concrete was put in place. Concerns of government and military lawyers over these new legal interpretations were overlooked and it appears that the way to disaster was paved. As even the Schlesinger report notes, the Secretary of Defense clearly did not make use of all of the legal advice open to him. In retrospect, he only used the legal advice that would get him what he wanted.

Interrogation of prisoners: a case study of ethics in war

The last chapter looked at whether a nation should consider the nature of the threat it faced when it applied the laws of war. US policies in Iraq can then be considered a case study of the results of tampering with the standard separation of the two, and so the arguments here have moved from the theoretical to the very practical. It has been argued that US policy in the area of the laws of war has taken the step of essentially re-linking the concepts of *jus ad bellum* and *jus in bello*. It has also been suggested that this does not have to be, as some international lawyers would argue, an immoral or entirely unreasonable argument, provided that such actions are subjected to open political debate and democratic oversight and unambiguous guidelines are put in place with certain fundamental guarantees. It is clear that this is precisely what did not take place in the case of the Bush administration and Abu Ghraib. If the end result of this process is Abu Ghraib, the potential for abuse and scandal is very high indeed.

Still, it is possible to argue that Abu Ghraib represents an example of what can happen rather than being a guaranteed certainty whenever occupations take place. It represents a worst-case scenario where righteous fury in soldiers (who become convinced that they are doing the "right thing") is unchecked and leaders fail to monitor the effects of their decision. It is the end point of the clichéd "slippery slope" on which nations may find themselves when they begin to tamper with the law in a reckless manner. In failing to have a set of concrete, easy to understand guidelines for its troops, in failing to enforce a code of conduct or standard operating procedures, and in failing to act when it was clear that the prison in Abu Ghraib was in serious legal and moral jeopardy, the US went down that slippery slope.

The growing insurgency in Iraq and the always pressing need for timely and useful intelligence in relation to the War on Terror were key considerations for the military and the Bush administration. This placed significant demands on individuals and interrogators on the ground. As the Schlesinger Report notes:

With the active insurgency in Iraq, pressure was placed on the interrogators to produce "actionable" intelligence... A number of visits by high-level officials to Abu Ghraib undoubtedly contributed to this perceived pressure... Despite the number of visits and the intensity of interest in actionable intelligence, however, the Panel found no undue pressure exerted by senior officials. Nevertheless, their eagerness for intelligence may have been perceived by interrogators as pressure.[68]

However, even the Schlesinger Report notes that detention operations, especially in the War on Terror, are not just for detaining prisoners of war to stop them returning to the battlefield, but also for the key purpose of intelligence gathering.[69] The role of intelligence gathering has been heavily emphasized by the Bush administration in this war. Yet, as the outcome of the war so far has demonstrated, it is one of those matters most subject to grey areas and legal violations when not carried out correctly.

One of the most interesting accounts of the US military in the war on terror in this regard has come from Chris Mackey, who served with the intelligence corps in Afghanistan from December 2001 until the summer of 2002.[70] During his time in Operation Enduring Freedom, Mackey supervised all military interrogations at Bagram airfield. In his book, he describes his training, the environment in which interrogations took place and the resistance offered by prisoners, and offers some reflection on the events he experienced and the subsequent controversies regarding US detention centres in Iraq.

The need to get intelligence from these prisoners posed moral dilemmas for the interrogators in Afghanistan in establishing exactly how far they could go. Mackey refers to the techniques that he had been taught in his interrogation training as "schoolhouse" and not at all effective against the new breed of prisoner who would swear, spit and threaten when confronted about their activities.

When we arrived in Afghanistan, I had an unshakable conviction that we should follow the rules to the letter...

But, as I realized now, the trouble was that the safe route was ineffective. Prisoners overcame [our] model almost effortlessly, confounding us not with clever cover stories, but with simple refusal to cooperate. They offered lame stories, pretended not to remember even the most basic of details, and then waited for the consequences that never really came.[71]

Therefore, argues Mackey, the interrogators began, incrementally, to use harsher means.[72] Later on this graduated to forcing detainees into stress positions. Reflecting on these experiences, Mackey writes: "Of course, these changes really amounted to minor tinkering with technique, tiny encroachments on the rules. But during the coming months in Bagram, a combination of forces would lead us–lead me–to make allowances that I wouldn't have even considered [earlier on]."[73]

What is striking about Mackey's account is that the decisions made were not taken lightly. Considerations of law, morality and necessity played a significant role when determining "how far to go". Mackey writes that he and his team "had been left largely on our own to sort out the ethical boundaries of our job."[74] This may then be an indication of where things may have also gone so horribly wrong in Abu Ghraib. In a section titled "Ethical Issues" the Schlesinger Report notes:

For the United States and other nations with similar value systems, detention and interrogation are themselves ethically challenging activities. Effective interrogators must deceive, seduce, incite and coerce in ways not normally acceptable for members of the general public....

In periods of emergency, and especially in combat, there will always be a temptation to override legal and oral norms for morally good ends. Many in Operations Enduring Freedom and Iraqi Freedom were not well prepared by their experience, education and training to resolve such ethical problems.[75]

The Report goes on to indicate that training had clearly failed in this regard and that a professional ethics programme addressing these situations would help equip them with "a sharper moral compass for guidance in situations often riven with conflicting moral objections."[76] In this way, the Report seems to be confident that improved ethical training could help improve the overall situation.[77]

However, increasingly there is another element in warfare–certainly in Operation Iraqi Freedom–that is posing serious challenges to the ability of military training and responsible command chains to put a stop to violations of the law of war: private military firms.

Private military firms

Although the trend has certainly been growing since the end of the Cold War, the 2003 Iraq war highlighted the role of Private Military Firms (PMFs) in contemporary warfare.[78] To support Operation Iraqi Freedom and combat the subsequent insurgency, PMFs have been contracted to provide everything from logistical support to food and services to armed security for humanitarian organizations and even high ranking officials like the former head of the Coalition Provisional Authority, Paul Bremer.

The sheer numbers of PMFs operating in Iraq are noteworthy alone, with the *Economist* referring to the conflict as "the first privatised war".[79] More than sixty firms employing more than 20,000 private personnel were estimated to be in Iraq by mid-2005. This amounts to roughly the same number of troops provided by all of the United States' coalition partners combined.[80] This means that at its peak the ratio of private contractors to US military personnel in the Gulf was roughly one to ten, ten times the ratio during the 1991 Gulf War.[81]

Yet the role of PMFs has also been highlighted for reasons other than numbers. PMFs have been involved in several controversies regarding the laws of war which have raised some serious questions regarding the increasing numbers of such firms in armed conflicts. PMFs, private actors who, for the bulk of the post-invasion period, were not (and to a large degree are still not) accountable to any military system of justice, have been accused of playing by their own rules, cowboy-like behaviour and "bringing a Wild West mentality to the streets of Baghdad".[82] Although many of the private contractors are involved in activities such as technical support for computers, mechanics or delivering mail, many (especially those involved in guard duties) have been involved in what would seem to be combat duties. Blackwater, one of the most high-profile PMFs operating in Iraq (and largely contracted out to the State Department), had 845 guards who fired their weapons in 195 incidents (according to Blackwater's count) between 2005 and October 2007. These incidents left an undetermined number of Iraqis dead and raise serious questions about the role of civilians in warfare and direct participation in hostilities.[83]

(Un)Accountability

One of the most controversial and complex issues resulting from the use of PMFs on such a large scale (and most significant for our purposes here) is accountability. When questions are put to PMFs for their actions, very often there is no one to give answers regarding their conduct and possible breaches of the law of war. Some PMFs, like Blackwater and CACI, refuse to give investigators or authorities information, arguing that their companies should be immune from legal processes because of jurisdiction or because they work at the behest of the US government.[84] Yet, given the increasingly controversial nature of the participation of PMFs in military operations, it is becoming clear that these are issues which need to be addressed. The reports coming out of the Abu Ghraib investigation revealed that PMFs had played a significant role in the abuse which took place. The Taguba Report goes so far as to cite two contractors of a Virginia based PMF, CACI, as partially responsible for what took place.[85]

Part of the problem is that PMFs have a very ambiguous status in both domestic and international law. This of course, relates back to the less savoury antecedents of PMFs, mercenaries. The first international legislation dealing with mercenaries came out of nineteenth century laws that were mostly concerned with implications for neutrality. A country that allowed its national territory to be used for recruitment or enlistment of mercenaries was deemed to be in support of a belligerent.[86] This principle was codified into the 1907 Hague Convention but was not a very strong one—certainly not for the purposes of any kind of regulation.

Serious attempts to do anything about the issue were not made until the 1960s and 1970s, after mercenaries became involved in various civil wars, wars of national liberation and coups in Africa. In December 1968, UN General Assembly Resolution 2465 was passed which designated mercenaries as outlaws. This position was further endorsed through subsequent resolutions concerned with colonialism.[87] In 1977 the Organization of African Unity (now known as the African Union) drafted the Convention of the OAU for the Elimination of Mercenarism in Africa. The Convention entered into force in 1985 and defines a mercenary as "anyone who, not a national of the State against which his actions are directed, is employed, enrols or links himself to a person, group or organization...which seeks political destabilization." As Sarah Percy point out, the Convention is not particularly useful in the modern context because it is only binding on African states and because the narrow definition in the Convention bears little resemblance to the wide range of roles that PMFs now play in conflict.[88]

The anti–mercenary sentiment was also encapsulated in the 1977 Additional Protocols to the Geneva Convention, which denied a mercenary the opportunity to be considered either a combatant or a prisoner of war. Yet the definition which was developed for the Protocols was highly controversial and so specific as to be practically useless. Article 47(2) defines a mercenary as any person who:

(a) is specially recruited locally or abroad in order to fight in an armed conflict;

(b) does, in fact, take a direct part in the hostilities;

(c) is motivated to take part in the hostilities essentially by the desire for private gain and, in fact, is promised, by or on behalf of a Party to the conflict, material compensation substantially in excess of that promised or paid to combatants of similar ranks and functions in the armed forces of that Party;

(d) is neither a national of a Party to the conflict nor a resident of territory controlled by a Party to the conflict;

(e) is not a member of the armed forces of a Party to the conflict; and

(f) has not been sent by a State which is not a Party to the conflict on official duty as a member of its armed forces.

In order for someone to be declared a mercenary, they must fulfil all of these criteria–leaving a definition that is full of loopholes. How, for example, could anyone ever demonstrate (much less prove in a court) that a person's motivation for fighting was "essentially" for financial reasons? Even the religious Taliban in Afghanistan typically fight for a combination of religious fanaticism and financial gain. As Geoffrey Best (somewhat colourfully) argues, anyone who manages to get prosecuted under this definition "deserves to be shot–and his lawyer [with him]".[89] Considering that almost any subsequent definitions have relied on this definition of a mercenary, regulation has mostly been left in the domestic sphere.

Yet only two countries have really attempted to draft legislation in this area—the US and South Africa—and even in these cases the legislation is weak.[90] As discussed in Chapter 3, attempts to prosecute civilians supporting US forces in Vietnam were unsuccessful. Yet, by the time of the 2003 Iraq War, there had been little done to remedy this gap in regulation.[91] The Uniform Code of Military Justice only covers transgressions by the US military and does not apply to civilians accompanying the forces overseas. The first recent attempt to address this gap was the 2000 Military Extraterritorial Jurisdiction Act (MEJA), which was enacted as a way to solve the problem of dealing with the crimes committed by civilians accompanying US armed forces abroad; this largely came about as a means to address criminal acts committed on US military bases by the spouses of military members.[92] In this way, the MEJA was intended to fill in a significant gap in the law with respect to US military facilities overseas, but with regard to PMFs, its provisions only applied to civilian contractors working for the US Department of Defense on US military bases in foreign countries. Therefore, when news about Abu Ghraib broke, the Act did not apply to contractors working for other US government departments or agencies (such as the Central Intelligence Agency), nor did it apply to US nationals working overseas for foreign governments or organizations. This was the case with Abu Ghraib, where the contractors involved in the alleged abuse of prisoners were employed by the Department of the Interior and therefore could not be prosecuted under the provisions of MEJA.[93]

In the wake of the Abu Ghraib scandal, the MEJA was amended in 2004 and now covers PMFs contracted by the Department of Defense or any federal agency supporting the "mission of the Department of Defense overseas". As Carney notes, it remains to be determined how "supporting the mission" will be interpreted in light of the many services that PMFs provide.[94] There are other uncertainties as well; the MEJA only applies to crimes that would incur a minimum of one year in prison–effectively excluding those crimes which may be considered misdemeanours. Acts such as humiliating a detainee or minor assault may therefore not come under the MEJA jurisdiction. Hence the usefulness of the MEJA to prosecute crimes such as those which occurred at Abu Ghraib may be limited.[95]

There are other pieces of legislation, such as the 1996 War Crimes Act, which may also play a role in prosecuting PMFs. However, since the Act only applies to US nationals, the many non-nationals employed by PMFs working for the US government remain unregulated. It has also been suggested that the Alien Tort Claims Act could provide a greater means of accountability over PMFs. Claims made under this Act, however, may only be for monetary damages rather than criminal prosecution.[96]

Regulation?

Given this history and this list of legal loopholes regarding the use of PMFs to support military operations, it is clear that many problems should have been apparent before 9/11. There were several incidents suggesting that the use of PMFs in Iraq on such a large scale could be problematic. In 1998 a Florida-based PMF, Airscan, coordinated an air strike which resulted in the accidental death of eighteen civilians, including nine children, in Colombia. In 2001, an

Alabama-based PMF, Aviation Development Corporation (ADC), contracted to the CIA accidentally shot down a small plane of missionaries and businessmen in Peru.[97] In neither case was anyone brought to account for their actions. In Bosnia and Kosovo, employees of the Virginia-based PMF DynCorp, who were fulfilling part of the US government's commitment to the peacekeeping operation there, were found to have committed statutory rape, abetted prostitution and accepted bribes. While none of the employees was ever charged in the incident, the "whistleblowers" who brought these actions to light were fired by the firm in retaliation.[98]

Yet, if problems regarding PMFs could have been anticipated before Abu Ghraib, why was nothing done? It is hard to say for certain, but there certainly seems to have been little political will to do much about the situation. There seems to have been a lack of foresight as to potential problems that could arise with switching government roles for contractors and a lack of a unified policy among government departments about what the role and limits of contractors should be (hence the differing policies between State, Interior, Defense and the CIA). Additionally, it might be due to the fact that the need to hire so many PMFs was not originally anticipated. As Brian Bennett argues in a report for *Time* magazine:

As with much of the occupation, the emergence of guns for hire among this contractor group was not part of the original plan. The number of contractors swelled, the insurgency grew, and the military was unable to provide adequate security for all of the civilian workforce. So companies like Blackwater began offering those services–at a high price–in the military's stead.[99]

Given this late development, it is not entirely surprising that legislation was not put in place.

But there are other reasons as to why regulations were lacking for PMFs operating in Iraq; as indicated above, regulation at either the domestic or the international level faces many difficulties of definition, jurisdiction and implementation. Domestically, there remain jurisdictional issues, and the fact that many of the PMF employees working for the US are not American or subject to US laws. Internationally, despite the plethora of PMFs working around the world, there is virtually no international law governing their behaviour. Even if regulation could be introduced, given the chaotic environment that PMFs tend to operate in, there would be tremendous difficulty monitoring their activities. But apart from the lack of a straightforward way to regulate PMFs, there has been little will to do so until recently. States require the services of PMFs and benefit from their services. PMFs free up personnel for combat or other more essential duties. They also are less of a liability if they are killed on the job—the death of a contractor generates far less media attention than that of a US soldier. As Percy argues, "Sustaining an unpopular war becomes easier if the state's own army is not suffering casualties and the burden of replacing troops is eased by the presence of a large number of contractors."[100]

Still, the role of PMFs in Abu Ghraib has thrust these issues into the spotlight. The inability to properly control or regulate PMFs contributed to the abuses which took place in the prison, and military investigations found that contractors from two PMFs, Titan and CACI, were involved in 36 per cent of the proven incidents of abuse.[101] The Fay-Jones Report listed six PMF employees who should be referred to the Justice Department for prosecution and another PMF employee who was "confused" about what constituted improper interrogation techniques.[102] However, there have been no arrests of or charges against any of the six PMF employees identified by these investigations (although the Justice Department still maintained that it did not consider the investigation closed by April 2006).[103] Why this is so is still not entirely clear—especially considering that the Army successfully prosecuted eleven soldiers involved in the Abu Ghraib scandal.[104] As Singer observes: "The only formal inquiry into PMF wrongdoing on the corporate level was conducted by CACI itself. CACI investigated CACI and, unsurprisingly, found that CACI had done no wrong."[105]

These controversies and the still somewhat unclear role that PMFs played at Abu Ghraib suggest that there are some serious gaps in the law that the US and the international community need to address, especially regarding accountability. Already, as mentioned above, there have been legislative changes—but there are still many loopholes for PMFs. This became very apparent in September 2007 when Blackwater employees were accused of opening fire on seventeen unarmed Iraqis. Even though there had been legislative steps made in the wake of Abu Ghraib, PMFs operating outside US military facilities had protection from prosecution granted under Order 17—a law which had been put in place by the Coalition Provisional Authority, giving PMFs in Iraq immunity for their actions. The provision, which had been in place since 2004, had long upset Iraqis who felt that it allowed PMFs to use excessive force with impunity.[106] However, the Iraqi government had not repealed the law prior to the September 2007 incident. In addition, Blackwater employees involved in the incident, interviewed by State Department officials (for whom Blackwater was working in this particular instance), say that they were given immunity for their statements. Although State Department officials said this did not mean that there would no charges brought against the employees, they admitted there was a loophole in the law suggesting that prosecution would be unlikely.[107]

Therefore, PMFs represent serious challenges to the laws of war in conflict zones like Iraq. While the law of war provides for soldiers and civilians, it still does not say much about PMFs. Because of the lack of regulation, it is fairly clear that there has been little attention paid to what kind of training these individuals have received, and probably none whatsoever to training in the laws of war. That the PMF employees at Abu Ghraib lacked proper training on the Geneva Conventions was one of the findings made in the Fay-Jones Report:

The necessity for some sort of standard training and/or experience is made evident by the statements of both contractor employees and military personnel... Likewise, numerous statements indicated that little, if any, training on Geneva Conventions was presented to contractor employees.... Prior to deployment, all contractor linguists or interrogators should receive training in the Geneva Conventions standards for treatment of detainees/prisoners. This training should include a discussion of the chain of command and the establishment of some sort of 'hotline' where suspected abuses can be reported in addition to reporting through the chain of command.[108]

There are also concerns that the clandestine manner in which PMFs operate dangerously blurs the line between civilian, soldier and NGOs. As Bjork and Jones argue:

In addition to the many private security company personnel who resemble threatening Hollywood figures, there are numerous security personnel moving around in unmarked vehicles, civilian clothes, with firearms held discretely in order to blend in with the general community, blurring perceptions to an even greater extent...

In a country where secret police as well as armed Ba'ath party death squads used to act in civilian clothes, it is not hard to see how these persons are perceived as military rather than as part of a group of contractors or aid workers...

This is worrying as it is precisely this perception held by many [Iraqis] that will ensure that attacks on non-military personnel continue.[109]

Given their unaccountability and the lack of a regulatory body or system of background checks or effective ability to prosecute individuals, it is clear that PMFs pose significant challenges for the laws of war in modern conflict. After Abu Ghraib and the September 2007 Blackwater shooting there have been some changes made; for example, following the latter incident, the Iraqi Government moved to repeal Order 17 and introduce new requirements for foreign security guards. The scandal also appears to have encouraged the Afghan authorities to act as well. In November 2007 they closed down the offices of Olympus, a UK-based PMF, in Afghanistan. This followed several high-profile controversies involving PMFs, including an incident where an employee of the US-based DynCorps slapped the Transport Minister in the face, and numerous car accidents. In addition, many PMFs in Afghanistan were set up by militia leaders and warlords who have simply set up shop as private firms selling "security services" rather than turn in their weapons.[110]

These are baby steps in regulating a fast growing industry that still seems to have a frontier mentality. Yet, despite all the controversies which surround them, PMFs appear to be emerging as a permanent fixture of warfare. Whereas the pre-9/11 Quadrennial Defense Review ("a strategic assessment of the future for the U.S. war machine") did not even contain the word "contractor", the 2006 version envisioned an even greater role for PMFs, integrating them into the US "total force" and ultimate war fighting capability.[111] Although Defense Secretary Robert Gates has been less enthusiastic in his support for PMFs than his predecessor, it was reported in July 2009 that these firms were being considered for a major role in providing services at forward operating bases in Afghanistan.[112]

But, even more important, even if the United States completely gave up its use of PMFs, it is still likely that companies such as Blackwater (which changed its name to Xe Services in late 2007) would remain in business because they have diverse client portfolios and because they have shown an ability to continually adapt to meet the various security needs and roles in a more nimble fashion than national militaries. Unless the US government takes steps to ensure that PMFs have appropriate training and understanding of the laws of war, and ends the system of weak regulation, more controversies like Abu Ghraib are very likely to occur.

Preventing atrocity in war

At Abu Ghraib, Iraqi prisoners found themselves the victims of some very serious abuse, and the US found itself in a highly embarrassing situation which, in a graphic manner, created serious doubts about its claim that all prisoners were being treated humanely. It has been the argument here that the wavering of the Bush administration with regard to the laws of war, its assessment that different laws applied in different places to different individuals at different times, and its failure to set in place a single set of guidelines for its troops created an environment whereby abuse was likely to occur. It has been further suggested that the involvement of PMFs in Abu Ghraib has also added to this confusion as to which rules apply where and whether or not those rules can be enforced.

However, what the situation in Abu Ghraib ultimately seems to amount to is that a group of soldiers felt that it was acceptable, or even proper, to carry out the actions which created the abuse scandal. These actions have been attributed to poor quality circumstances, harsh and dangerous living conditions, racism, or psychological factors. Inadequate training has also been mentioned by most of the reports investigating the abuse. Yet, it seems almost intuitive that soldiers would automatically regard such abuse as a violation of the principles of laws of war, or barring this, codes of basic decent behaviour. These actions were not committed in the "fog of war" or in the "heat of battle", circumstances which sometimes allow us to at least understand how atrocities may occur (if not excuse them).

What happened at Abu Ghraib seems to go beyond a failure of training into something more towards the core of the military code that democracies try to instil in their armies. Several authors who write about military training and the laws of war refer to this idea as the military "ethos" which is necessary in order for the laws of war to be instilled and maintained in the conduct of military activity.[113]

A military ethos can be described as an ethical culture embedded within everyday operations. This culture reflects the fundamental values and character peculiar to the military, and therefore the culture should reflect the way operations are conducted. The opposite should then hold true as well–that actions should reflect ethos. If respect for life and the principles of the laws of war is seen as a priority for the military and the society in which it is situated, respect for the laws of war needs to be cultivated within the military ethos.

Ethos advocates have set out a list of requirements in order for this approach to enforcing the laws of war to work. First, there need to be appropriate internal regulations and/or doctrine for a variety of issues.[114] This may be set out in field manuals, codes, rules and regulations that are geared towards everyday operations. These are set policies to which soldiers can refer to provide guidelines as to proper conduct.[115] Second, these guidelines and policies must be linked to training and become an integral part of the way soldiers are taught to perform their jobs. The training a soldier goes through is not categorized explicitly as law of war training, but instead as instruction in set doctrine or regulations.[116] If troops are taught to perform their tasks in accordance with military doctrine (which, in turn, is in accordance with the laws of war), the conduct of soldiers becomes ingrained and automatically compliant with international obligations. For example, soldiers taught not to pillage or attack innocent civilians follow these rules not because they are taught explicitly that this is part of an international treaty obligation, but because this is the way operations are conducted, period. Respect for civilians then becomes automatic. As Anthony E. Hartle writes of his experiences in Vietnam:

As a young lieutenant in [the military], I learned what it meant to function effectively and professionally.... I knew what was expected of me as a leader and as an officer. I knew the established procedures. When our [Vietnamese guide] suggested torturing the prisoner, I really did not give the matter a second thought. As I look back, I recognize that my reaction resulted from the training that I had received and my experience in the Army.[117]

Of course this is just one experience of one individual in a controversial war. However, the value of such a policy is maintained by those who train, teach and comment on the laws of war. Yet there is one more crucial requirement: that relating law to procedures and rules *must* be linked to common sense. Law embedded within procedures must make sense for the soldier told to carry out a specific operation. Training should be tailored to individual soldiers, consistent with their mission and responsibilities. The training should cover all of the circumstances that a particular soldier will be dealing with, but at the same time not overload that individual with complex international legislation. For example, for those members of the military whose job involves target selection, more complex training is needed than for someone whose job is more focused on logistics. In addition to this, as Charles Garraway argues, law within procedures should reflect reality and also reflect principles of proportionality. This then ensures that soldiers can look upon the rules as their ally in getting tasks done correctly, rather than as a restricting annoyance.[118]

However, what is also crucial is whether or not such training is insisted upon by higher-ups in the military and by political leaders—and there was a clear failure in this regard at Abu Ghraib. Political and military leaders can enforce and insist upon law of war training to be carried out. However, commanders of troops and soldiers also play a huge role in ensuring that the laws of war are embedded into training and are taken seriously, and that violations are followed up. As W. Hays Parks notes, "Commands promulgate directives and provide guides for law of war instruction while integrating law of war issues into training exercises at all levels."[119] Garraway also notes that while military lawyers are useful adjuncts in creating an ethos, the prime responsibility rests with the commanders:

History shows that leaders can be good or bad. If we want to instil in our soldiers an ethos of doing what is right, of moral integrity and obedience to the law, then it is to the commanders that we must look. Unless the commander is prepared to take his or her responsibilities in this field seriously, there is little chance of anyone else doing so.[120]

Like any topic necessary for soldiers to know in order to complete their job correctly, law of war training competes with other mandatory subjects in units that are busy returning from deployment, getting ready to go on a deployment, or on deployment.[121] Because there is considerable competition for training time, commanders must believe that law of war training is a necessary and important task for their troops, rather than another "box to tick".

Parks acknowledges that it is understandable that military commanders might view law of war training in this way–that it is natural to believe that soldiers of Western democracies will automatically behave in a way that will support human rights or that soldiers will instinctively "do the right thing". "Commanders and their soldiers undoubtedly tire of receiving law of war training because they do not believe they or members of their unit are capable of violating the law of war...[the] response was simple 'Marines don't do that.'"[122] Garraway agrees that this seems to be the consensus, arguing that "in many Western countries there is still a belief that our forces do inherently know 'what is right.'"[123]

Yet if the experiences of My Lai or Abu Ghraib demonstrate anything, it is that under the right (or more correctly, wrong) conditions soldiers will violate the laws of war. While it may seem natural to citizens or soldiers of a Western-style democracy that their soldiers would never commit atrocities, the very nature of war and violence is that they just might. Emphasis on law of war training is crucial and necessary to prevent abuse of the sort that happened in Iraq; or perhaps, putting it in a more ugly way, we need to put emphasis on the laws of war because we cannot trust human nature in war. Where actions are too easily justified as necessary or where pressures are intense, the laws of war can be very easily overlooked. Therefore, in terms of results, it is hoped that law of war training embedded into an ethos will result in a system where adherence to the laws of war becomes automatic, where soldiers refrain from torturing their prisoners not just because it is wrong, but also because it is contrary to what has been ingrained in their training. This training then needs to be emphasized in terms of comprehensive rules of engagement, discipline and command supervision.

The reports of the various investigations into Abu Ghraib are interesting in this respect. While Schlesinger ultimately concludes that what is needed is better doctrine regarding the new conditions that soldiers are facing (such as the working relationships between military police and military intelligence) and a "professional ethics program", he also states that:

Major service programs such as the Army's "core values" however fail to adequately prepare soldiers working in detention operations....

Core-values programs are grounded in organizational efficacy rather than the moral good. They do not address humane treatment of the enemy and non-combatants, leaving military leaders and educators an incomplete tool box with which to deal with "real-world" ethical problems.[124]

This seems to be suggesting that training can only take soldiers so far, that when conditions that go beyond training and pose ethical dilemmas, complex decisions will have to be made. Soldiers on the frontlines, who may not be the best educated, need references through which they can make ethical judgements. In this way, future training may have to make the ethical component more prominent.

While ethics training for soldiers may seem unrealistic as demands on soldiers' training time are already so high, the US military may be starting to take this approach seriously. In June 2006 it was announced that troops in Iraq were immediately to undertake a course on battlefield ethics after allegations were made that twenty-four unarmed civilians had been shot by Marines near Haditha. The course involves an explanation of "core warrior values" which included a slide show on ethical standards under fire. President Bush described the programme as "a reminder for troops in Iraq, or throughout our military, that there are high standards expected of them and that there are strong rules of engagement".[125] Marines in boot camp now get thirty-eight hours of values training, up from twenty-four. Lessons start off with the basics such as not to drink and drive, not to sleep on guard duty, etc., and then work up to more complex issues.[126]

It would appear that, in the wake of Abu Ghraib, military officials are taking such charges very seriously and are eager to be seen as responding quickly to allegations of war crimes. However, it also seems that the military is taking seriously the idea that it may need to contextualize its law of war training within a programme of ethics and moral values, in order to make such training more relevant and, perhaps, accessible to its personnel. And such a programme is still very much needed today–a report released in May 2007 suggested that 40 per cent of Marines and 55 per cent of soldiers would still not report a member of their unit for killing or wounding an innocent civilian. The same report indicated that only 38 per cent of Marines and 47 per cent of soldiers believed that non-combatants should be treated with dignity and respect. This lead the then US commander in Iraq, General David Petraeus, to suggest a "redoubling" of ethics education efforts where necessary.[127]

Is an ethics-training approach the way forward with regard to training? Certainly such an approach is not without risks and difficulties. The problem with an ethics approach is that the military is a system that has traditionally been and continues to be based on military drill and discipline. In this sense, an approach that encourages soldiers to "think" might cause more problems than it solved. If military personnel are trained so that they know how to act and respond in the heat of battle, an approach which encourages critical thinking at this same moment may be problematic. It sounds cruder than the reality of the situation, but there may be very good reasons why the military would not want its soldiers thinking too much when they come under fire. There is a case to be made for training in accordance with the laws of war which produces automatic responses. It may be that a blend of ethos and ethics is what is required to prevent future Hadithas and Abu Ghraibs.

The lessons of Iraq and Abu Ghraib?

It is clear from the investigations of what went wrong at Abu Ghraib that what took place was not solely a failure of training–though this can certainly be considered one of the causes. It was noted above that Western societies and militaries typically expect that their soldiers, when in a grey area, will be able to tell right from wrong and act in a manner that supports the values of the military and society from which they come. However, unless a sense of the rules is cultivated under high-pressure and stressful conditions, this is not what will occur. Human nature alone will not ensure that soldiers will "do the right thing". In this way, it may be more correct to say that what really happened at Abu Ghraib was a failure of ethos on many levels. The worst of human nature gave way in a stressful environment because individuals did not, or could not, seek out the rules. Commanders did not ensure that the proper procedures were in place and were being followed. Worse, they ignored indications that something was seriously wrong. Military superiors and, ultimately, the political administration neglected to ensure that commanders were doing their jobs, created an environment of legal confusion, and failed to provide a set of comprehensive and easy to follow guidelines for the troops in the field. The ethos–or the military culture which reinforces the rules in the conduct of its activities–was significantly altered in the wake and rush of 9/11 and did not long survive in the new conditions.

The addition of PMFs to this picture only serves as a serious complication, especially to the military ethos model. Many of the employees of private military firms are former soldiers of Western democracies. However, despite their ever increasing role in military operations, there is certainly no guarantee of the origins of a PMF's employees, or of the training they have received, especially regarding the law of war. Regulation may be one solution to this problem, but there are many difficulties standing in the way of such a development in the near future.[128] As for the firms themselves, they prefer a system of self-regulation (such as that which already exists in the form of security industry associations in the domestic security market). This would be a system relying essentially on a corporate social responsibility model whereby "reputable" companies would set standards to be voluntarily adhered to in the absence of domestic and international legislation. Certainly this is an interesting idea in the absence of a regulation regime, but as Clive Walker and Dave Whyte argue, this model does not really seem appropriate for an industry where companies are often established for one purpose–military or security services–and often disbanded after a tour of duty.[129]

Even if such a model were to be created, there is an additional problem–humanitarian organizations such as the ICRC have a very problematic relationship with PMFs and are reluctant to instruct them in the laws of war because of their questionable legal status and mercenary roots.[130] Recently, however, the ICRC seems to have come to the realization that PMFs are likely to remain a regular feature of current and future conflicts. (And this may be due to the fact that many NGOs are forced to use PMFs for protection when carrying out humanitarian operations.) In 2004, the ICRC announced that it would plan for "a more systematic approach focusing on companies operating in conflict situations or providing training and advice to armed forces" with regard to the law of war.[131] By 2007, the ICRC began a process of consultations with government experts on the role of PMFs in modern conflicts, culminating in the Montreux Document. The document, which is non-binding, lists seventy recommendations, derived from "good state practice". It also reaffirms the obligations of states to ensure that PMFs operate in line with the laws of war. Although not a fully fledged international treaty or regulatory regime, the document will, it is hoped, provide guidance as to what steps states should follow when they deploy PMFs to the field.

Yet, it is clear that the ICRC remains uncomfortable with the idea of working with PMFs, indicating that it is important to look at such agencies on a case by case basis in terms of legitimacy and that the "ICRC does not plan to take a position on the legitimacy of these private companies." The ICRC has called for states to play a larger role in terms of monitoring mercenary activity for violations committed by "individuals operating on or from their territory."[132] While this is certainly a step forward in terms of promoting the laws of war among PMFs, given the problems listed above regarding regulation, it will hardly solve the problems of accountability and enforcement of the law for countries where PMFs are deployed and those from which they are deployed.

For the US, a step forward was taken when a federal jury, under domestic legislation, indicted David Passaro, a contractor working for the CIA, for committing acts of torture in Afghanistan, claiming jurisdiction over US "diplomatic, consular, military or other US government missions or entities in foreign states, including buildings, parts of buildings, and land appurtenant or ancillary thereto or used for purposes of those missions or entities irrespective of ownership."[133] (Passaro was convicted in February 2007 and sentenced to eight and a half years in jail.) Still, this is just one case–and one where the US had jurisdiction because Passaro's actions took place on a US military base. Much of the legalities involved relate to whom the PMF was contracted to (which government department) and where. Additionally, at the time of writing, the Senate had just passed an amendment by Senator Al Franken to the Defense Appropriations Bill which would prohibit the Pentagon from using PMFs that oblige employees to take disputes to arbitration rather to court. The intention behind the amendment is that it would give employees access to courts in allegations of serious crimes such as rape and sexual assault.[134]

The question remains, then, what next for the laws of war in America? There seems to be an agreement in the literature, as argued previously, that My Lai was a wake-up call for the US military in the 1970s. As a result, there was an entire restructuring and reconceptualization of the way the laws of war were taught to soldiers. However, after 9/11, the security environment has not been very conducive to such a rethinking in a way that would strengthen adherence to America's international law of war obligations. It seems clear that in times of war, the pressure on a military's adherence to the laws of war is always downwards. While a descent down a slippery slope is by no means unavoidable (though accidents and at least some violations in warfare seem inevitable), in a permissive environment, with unclear law and an increasingly unstable ethos, the journey down that slope is going to be made that much quicker.

American leaders and military commanders have clearly paid a political cost for the scandal over Abu Ghraib and have indicated as much.[135] That the response to an alleged massacre at Haditha came swiftly and with the implementation of an ethics training programme after the allegations were made suggests that there have been lessons learned, although here too there have been difficulties.[136] That a legislative tug-of-war continues in the US government over detainee policy suggest that these lessons may only go so far.

Conclusion

In looking at the challenges posed to America's relationship with the laws of war through the controversy that came out of Abu Ghraib, the chapter has not spent much time looking at the actual insurgency and fighting that have been under way since the end of formal hostilities in Iraq. This is not to downplay the important issues that have arisen out of the conflict, but merely reflects the fact that the methods of fighting employed raise more or less traditional concerns regarding the laws of war—what weapons can be used, how the law of occupation applies, and the rights of insurgents are not new questions for the law of war.[137]

The scandal at Abu Ghraib prison, however, represents new challenges and questions—or at least old issues in a newer light. The full implications of America's rebalancing of its commitment to international law in the face of a new security threat, the changing and increasing role of PMFs (including their role in detention operations) and the need to address gaps in terms of training and military doctrine in the wake of the War on Terror have had a major impact on the way America's relationship with the law of war is conceived.

There have been several arguments put forward in this chapter. First, that the Bush administration's policies, which downplayed America's traditional commitment to the laws of war as they are—for the most part—internationally understood, failed to replace this commitment with anything concrete enough to withstand the pressures of the War on Terror. This resulted in a situation of confusion about which law applied. As a result, not only did soldiers completely fail to uphold the law, in some cases they felt they were doing the right thing through their abusive actions against prisoners. Second, related to this, the soldiers at Abu Ghraib failed to uphold the military ethos that training was designed to instil in them. This appears to be due to several causes. The training that they received was inadequate for the purposes of the mission as circumstances rapidly went beyond what soldiers had been prepared for. When faced with ethical dilemmas in an incredibly stressful environment, soldiers failed entirely to maintain proper conduct. In part this seems to be due to a failure of command responsibility, and a resulting environment of permissibility generated by legal confusions and lack of accountability. However, the increasing roles of PMFs seem to have only complicated this, as the training and accountability of PMFs involved in military operations remain undefined and unclear. There is substantial evidence to suggest that there was PMF involvement in what happened in Abu Ghraib and the 16 September Blackwater shooting incident, yet it appears there will be no prosecutions of the personnel involved.

Thus there is no one clear reason why Abu Ghraib occurred, but rather a considerable number of factors came together to generate the circumstances in which the abuse could take place. After taking away the stable foundation for conduct of operations in line with the laws of war (and prosecution where this does not happen) provided by international law, the Bush administration's failure to set and enforce standards of its own was an incredibly risky approach that may lay the foundation for further incidents like Abu Ghraib.

The implications of all of this suggest that America needs a serious reconsideration of and recommitment to its policies towards the laws of war. President Obama was quick to ensure that his administration made a break with the Bush policies by signing three executive orders that, as discussed in Chapter 4, ordered the closure of Guantánamo Bay, ordered a review of the status of all remaining prisoners in Guantánamo, and ordered all personnel to adhere to the *Army Field Manual* and the Geneva Convention. Speaking to the media who witnessed the signing of the orders on his first day in office, Obama said: "This is me following through on not just a commitment I made during the campaign, but I think an understanding that dates back to our founding fathers, that we are willing to observe core standards of conduct, not just when it's easy but also when it's hard."[138]

In the wake of these decisions there has been much debate, and criticism arguing that Obama's policies endanger the United States. However, it is clear that many major military officials believe that such policies make good sense, including General Petraeus, now chief of US Central Command. Speaking on the Obama administration's policies on the closure of Guantánamo and prohibition of "enhanced interrogation techniques", Petraeus was supportive. He indicated that closing Guantánamo in a "responsible manner... sends an important message to the world, as does the commitment of the United States to observe the Geneva Convention when it comes to the treatment of detainees."[139]

A few days later he was even clearer. After noting how Guantánamo had been used as a propaganda weapon against the United States and its goals in both Afghanistan and Iraq, Petraeus stated: "When we have taken steps that have violated the Geneva Conventions, we rightly have been criticized, so as we move forward I think it's important to again live our values, to live the agreements that we have made in the international justice arena and to practice those."[140]

It remains uncertain as to how successful the new administration will be in completing the tasks it has set out for itself. It seems, however, to have at least made a good start.

CONCLUSION

THE UNITED STATES AND THE FUTURE OF THE LAW OF WAR

Introduction

It has been over sixty years since the signing of the four Geneva Conventions in 1949. Since then, the way states wage war and engage in conflicts has undergone a dramatic change. This is partially due to rapid developments in technology which have enabled more accurate targeting and deadlier weapons. Because of this increasingly sophisticated machinery, the advance of the coalition in Operation Iraqi Freedom was the fastest recorded in world history. However, warfare has also changed in terms of *who* is doing the fighting. Large-scale national armies fighting set-piece battles on open fields have been replaced by guerrillas in the tropics, insurgents in Iraq or, perhaps saddest of all, child soldiers in Africa. Clearly, none of these groups was likely to have been in the minds of the negotiators in Geneva when they drafted the rules of the Conventions.

In the past sixty years the American armed forces, which have engaged in many of these post-World War II conflicts, have changed as well. The military has adapted from being a conscription-based force to being based entirely on enlisted volunteers. It is technologically superior to any other army on the planet, and although it is not the largest, it remains the strongest. In terms of the law of war, the US forces have increasingly taken matters seriously. The Uniform Code of Military Justice was developed, as was "operational law" after the mistakes of Vietnam. US weaponry allows for discriminate attacks and efforts are made to try to spare innocent civilian life wherever possible. Yet, as this study has demonstrated, adapting to pressures and changes involving the law of war has always been, and clearly remains, a challenge.

But the law of war itself has not remained a constant in the past sixty years. It has changed and developed–becoming increasingly more specific and complex. There are increasing pressures to blend "international humanitarian law" with human rights law. There are more non-governmental organizations concerned with, and seeking to monitor, the law of war in conflict situations than ever before.

This study has tried to examine developments in the approach of the United States to the laws of war, given these changes which have occurred in the nature of fighting and warfare, in its armed forces and in international law. In order to make these changes clear, it has advanced in a chronological fashion. Yet the interaction between these factors through the years makes apparent certain trends and "themes" in America's relationship with the law of war, and this concluding chapter will attempt to draw out some of the major themes of the preceding chapters to help provide a sense of the bigger picture. These include the issue of the role of ideology, a "dualistic tendency", implementation, and complications with the involvement of new actors. Because a project such as this cannot engage in all of the questions that may be raised, issues and problems which emerge, it will conclude by looking at areas for further research.

Ideology

In its simplest terms, ideology may perhaps be best understood as that which helps to take us from our ideas to understanding of issues. It forms the prism through which we view the world and ourselves in it. Ideology plays an important part in self-identification and in forming expectations. As such, ideology has a major impact on the way we behave and, it can be said, how states conduct their foreign policy.

A major claim of this work is that the United States, in its conduct of foreign policy, is greatly influenced by the idea of American exceptionalism. This is the idea of a powerful strand of thinking in the United States, that the republic is "exceptional" among nations, unique in the world for its founding values and for its way of life. While Chapter 2 discussed the impact of "Jacksonianism" on America's attitudes towards international law, American exceptionalism is strongly reflected in what Walter Russell Mead describes as "Wilsonianism".[1] This is a belief that both democracy and democratic institutions are good for America and the world as they promote domestic and international stability. He notes that Wilsonians, inspired by missionary-like zeal, are the ones who have sought to limit the scourge of war through anti-war movements, humanitarian activities (including the development of the laws of war) and international institutions. The spreading of American and democratic values is conceived as an important impediment to war.

But Wilsonians have also been driven by their desire to promote the "global triumph of democracy and the rule of law", as well as an American understanding of human rights abroad.[2] Where necessary, this translates into a desire to promote military intervention in countries like Cuba and the Philippines, with the idea of transforming these societies into American-style democracies. Max Boot usefully differentiates between "soft" and "hard" Wilsonians—the former being those who prefer to work multilaterally and with international institutions in their foreign policies, and the latter those who are willing to commit US military might to secure Wilsonian ideas.[3]

Yet what unites all Wilsonians is that they are inspired by American-exceptionalist conceptions of democracy and the rule of law. In this way, the American role in the world has manifested itself into a mission to promote and defend those values which are perceived as making the nation great. In the nineteenth century, this was a civilizing mission to the First Nations within its own borders and in the Philippines. In the twentieth century, this role translated into that of a defender of freedom against fascism, communism and, today, Islamic radicalism.

Clearly, such a world view and self-understanding are going to affect the way that America regards its enemies. In the eighteenth century, the wars over North America were fierce as developing Enlightenment restraints were challenged by the notion that only a complete solution would solve the colonists' problem of their safety on the continent. In these wars for complete security, cruelty to one's enemy was meted out with the aim of removing one's opponent and, in some cases, extracting revenge. In the nineteenth century, America attempted to bring its ideas of civilization to the First Nations and Filipinos. When these ideas were rejected and fighting began, employing methods that fell outside the American understanding of war, the results were bloody and brutal. Those who rejected America's mission in the world and its ideas, and conducted their fighting in ways that "civilized" nations did not recognize, were shown little mercy. It is not hard to draw parallels to America's engagements in the Vietnam War or the insurgency in Iraq. It appears that rejection of values and refusal to adhere to a set of expectations often influenced the restraints the US chose to impose on its fighting campaign.

This rejection matters more than either race or religion. While America's notion of civilization, the implications of this understanding and the practical results of its civilizing mission may today be characterized as racist, it would appear that the rejection of "civilized" values, including "civilized" warfare, rather than racial notions and conceptions, was of paramount importance for the way America's enemies were regarded. The campaign in Vietnam was carried out with much brutality on both sides. However, the Korean War, which fitted the classic model of interstate warfare far better than the conflict in Vietnam, saw the US treat the prisoners it had taken relatively well. The overall violence and bloodshed in Korea should, of course, not be underestimated. Yet, in many ways, that conflict, which fell into a recognized category of warfare, does not have the same notions of mayhem and savagery associated with it.

The US is not exceptional in being influenced in its worldview and behaviour by its ideology. Clearly the same may be said for every nation which needs to choose between priorities and engage with others politically. Rather, it is the ideology itself that makes America unique in the world. More often than not, there is an imperative that the United States should act in accordance with its ideological vision of itself. Surely this is true of the way it has interacted with international law, including the law of war. Treaties, which become the supreme law of the land, are not to be undertaken lightly, and those who sign on with the United States are expected to live up to their end of the bargain.

It does not necessarily follow that American exceptionalism automatically dictates a dislike of or disinclination towards international law. Rather, because the US sees itself as exceptional in its virtue, the United States will only sign those treaties to which it fully intends to adhere. It would violate America's view of itself to only partially implement a commitment that it had made. So, while one may be tempted to point out the differences between Democrat and Republican administrations (such as the differences between the administrations of George H.W. Bush and Bill Clinton, or Clinton and George W. Bush) it is clear that the ideological imperatives of exceptionalism have played a role in most American administrations regardless of political affiliation.[4] Although Clinton (often described as a "soft Wilsonian") may have been more willing to engage multilaterally, or with international institutions, when examined closely it is clear that his administration was not willing to bind itself to international law much more than its successor. For example, while Clinton did sign the Kyoto Protocol (fully aware that it would not pass in the Senate), it only gave lukewarm support to the ICC during its negotiations and the treaty was only signed at the very end of his presidency. He refused to sign the 1997 Landmine Treaty and did not take any steps to sign legislation such as the 1989 United Nations Convention on the Rights of the Child. In this way, differences between administrations may be differences in lip-service to the international community rather than substantial differences in attitude towards international law.

Dualistic tendencies

America's ideology can thus be said to give it a unique relationship as regards the laws of war and its enemies. The above argument suggests that American exceptionalism results in a set of understandings and expectations regarding international law and the laws of war. In terms of understandings, American administrations have tended to view international law as a binding contract which is not to be undertaken lightly. International law is signed and ratified because it matters, not because it "looks good" in either domestic or international circles. In this way America undertook its negotiations at The Hague and Geneva in the nineteenth and twentieth centuries very seriously, with a real commitment to the further development of international law. As discussed above, this was inspired by its liberal vision for the world, which included the rule of law and a desire to end or limit all wars.

On the other hand, such understandings results in an expectation that the other side will live up to its side of the bargain. In order to qualify for the restraints set out in the laws of war, enemies were expected to act within a set of boundaries of "civilized warfare". Where America's opponents failed to do so, they could expect little mercy. This helps to explain a "dualistic tendency" when it comes to America's implementation of the laws of war. The Confederate Army's actions fell within the set of understandings that the laws of war had set out, and hence Southern prisoners were treated relatively decently under the care of the Union Army. On the other hand, as seen in the first section of the book, the First Nations and Filipinos fell outside this understanding and were not afforded the same rights or restraints.

This "dualistic tendency", influenced by ideology, was also supported by the generally accepted notion of reciprocity as applicable to the laws of war in the nineteenth century. Under this notion, when opponents fail to live up to their obligations under the laws of war, they lose any protections or restraints that would otherwise be applied. However, after the Second World War and the signing of the 1949 Geneva Conventions, reciprocity began to lose its normative basis. Common Article 3 of the Conventions stated that parties would agree to treat their prisoners humanely, no matter how a conflict was characterized and what law applied. States were increasingly expected to apply the law in all circumstances. Thus, the "dualistic tendency" began to clash with the idea that some restraints were always applicable, no matter how enemies conducted their campaigns or what kind of conflict was being fought.

The events of Vietnam as relating to the laws of war can, perhaps, be explained by these conflicting ideas. The US applied Geneva Convention standards to the prisoners it captured in the conflict because it was seen as the morally correct course of action and politically prudent. However, the nature of the insurgency, which frustrated the US military, began to push for harsher tactics against an entrenched foe. As US soldiers became increasingly frustrated, some, albeit a small minority, took their frustrations out on those they could get their hands on–villagers and civilians who were seen as collaborating with the enemy. While such behaviour was never condoned, there was very little political will to prosecute those who were responsible for massacres like My Lai.

Implementation

However, the problems regarding implementation of the laws of war in Vietnam did illustrate a point to the US military: that when soldiers are untrained and poorly disciplined and fail to adhere to the laws of war, the results can be militarily disastrous. In the post-Vietnam era, military lawyers who had taken part in the conflict began a process that tried to impress this point on their military commanders. It was argued that enforcing the laws of war made good military sense. The Vietnam War demonstrated that units which were well disciplined and adhered to international standards and domestic codes of conduct were ultimately far more effective in accomplishing their missions.

Essentially, the principle was as old as Clausewitz's dictum on the "economy of force": effort wasted on pointless murder and pillage takes away from the overall effectiveness of a military campaign. If soldiers were trained to do their tasks in such a way as to automatically and fully implement the laws of war, the US military was more likely to complete its missions efficiently and effectively. Thus, the "re-branding" and "re-selling" of the laws of war back to the US military resulted in the development of "operational law". Conceived as a tool that would help commanders conduct their missions (rather than just restrict them), operational law would demonstrate its usefulness in the conduct of the 1991 Gulf War. In this way the military lawyers had proved that the laws of war were something more than an impractical list laid out by law-yers in Geneva; law, policy and effectiveness were essentially linked. Put sim-ply, following the laws of war almost always made good military sense.

So why was this view rejected after 9/11?

This work has tried to suggest why. It has looked at the Bush administra-tion's argument that the "War on Terror" placed the United States in a "new paradigm" of warfare which has required new thinking about issues such as the relation of law to policy, including policy towards the laws of war. The President required new and sweeping powers to defend the United States from attacks and these powers, it was argued, were granted by the Constitu-tion and authorized by Congress. They included the power to override inter-national law wherever and whenever necessary.

And it was clear that the Bush administration did think it was necessary. The need to prevent further attacks, to gather intelligence and to disrupt al-Qaida as much as possible meant that rights traditionally afforded to prisoners of war could not be given to those who were potentially so valuable for the fight against terrorism. While the Geneva Conventions allow for the ques-tioning of prisoners, the administration believed that their interrogations needed to go beyond this level, especially when facing fanatics willing to die for their cause. Because the President needed to protect the United States at any cost, the Geneva Conventions did not, and should not, apply to the War on Terror in Afghanistan.

Ultimately, when the Geneva standard was taken away, nothing firm was put in its place. As the War on Terror expanded to encompass Iraq, different sets of rules began to apply to different areas. One set of rules was set for Guantánamo Bay, another applied at Bagram Air Base and yet another in Iraq. Different sets of rules began to migrate from one area of operations to another. Guantánamo's rules, intended for its strict and isolated environment, were applied to the relative chaos of Abu Ghraib. It was under these confusing conditions that the opportunity for abuse at Abu Ghraib emerged.

In this way it can be argued that the link between law and policy holds; and this may be the strongest argument for the implementation of the laws of war. Where there is one clear standard, soldiers in a zone of conflict, already bur-dened with many pressing and demanding tasks, know what is expected of them. When this guidance is taken away, the confusion can lead to disaster. As has been acknowledged by the administration, nothing was served by Abu Ghraib, and a lot was lost.

New actors

Yet the nature of the threat, and those who impose this threat, should not be forgotten. The United States has typically faced difficulties in applying the laws of war when confronted with fighting that has fallen outside its understanding of "legitimate" warfare. The same may be said for when it has confronted new actors. As this work has tried to demonstrate, when confronted with the First Nations and Filipinos, who used tactics deemed "uncivilized", or with the style of guerrilla fighting in Vietnam, the US had difficulties in applying restraints on its fighting. Today, it is the tough Taliban fighters, determined insurgents and globally networked al-Qaida who pose challenges to the US military and comprise the threat to the United States. These are groups unlike any other enemy the US has faced, and again serious challenges have materialized as these new actors have emerged. But it is not only America's enemies that have posed difficulties in this regard. As argued in Chapter 5, the dramatic increase in the number of private military firms (PMFs) means that new problems of regulation and enforcement of the laws of war have arisen.

Arguably, the emergence of these new actors falls outside the concept of warfare that is implicit in the 1949 Geneva Conventions, and so insurgents, terrorists and PMFs have challenged both international law and the ability for the United States to implement it. This is not to say that there is no applicable law, but practically the tactics used by insurgents do create real difficulties when it comes to applying that law to a dangerous foe. A similar argument may be raised regarding the relatively unaccountable PMFs who also create their own separate challenges for law of war implementation. Given indications that these "new actors", in terms of war fighting, are here to stay, the problems that they pose, in terms of the US' ability to apply the laws of war, may become increasingly problematic. If these new actors are here to stay, how the US chooses to deal with them may have major significance for the way the laws of war are regarded, or applied, in the future.

Law as politics

Ultimately, one of the main aims of this thesis has been to demonstrate that the debate over America's relationship with the law of war is revealing about the way international law is viewed by both international relations specialists and international lawyers. Although the tendency has lessened within the last ten years, there is still an inclination for students of international relations to dismiss international law as ineffective or as a set of rules developed in times of peace which can be, and usually is, overlooked in times of crisis. International law is seen as stale rules of conduct drafted in boardrooms in New York and Geneva. Compared with the forceful and active world of international politics–wars, great powers, diplomacy–international law is, quite frankly, boring. It tells us nothing much about the way the world works, and never could, as international law can only be based on naïve idealism.

Most lawyers on the other hand tend to view international law as the final word on many matters of international politics. While there is always room for interpretation and arguments in front of international legal bodies on the matters of war, aggression and the rules of conduct in conflicts, there are set rules which bind states. These rules which control major international political actions are largely unambiguous and give little room for compromise no matter what the context. In writing on the relationship between law and the War on Terror, many international lawyers have done no more than provide lists of applicable law and how it applies–a "checklist" of items which states must follow if they are to act with any kind of legitimacy. Where international law is ignored, actions are to be condemned. To these international legal scholars legality is implicitly, if not explicitly tied to morality.

Of course, for the most part, these are exaggerated stereotypes, with a vast majority of individuals falling somewhere in between. But these stereotypes do point to a problem when looking at issues of international law and politics–the tendency to let one, either law or politics, dominate the other. That the relationship between the two is of necessity dynamic and intimate seems to be either ignored entirely or often bemoaned, by those who believe that law should guide politics or that politics should not be constrained by a dubious international community. The history of international law, and the law of war, makes clear that the interpretation, development and implementation of international law have been and always will be accomplished through the prism of international and, indeed, domestic politics.

Therefore, it is important to look not only at legal texts when faced with international developments, but also at the historical context, and the context of the law in its relationship to politics. Such an approach provides us better insight into our present predicaments and guides our interpretation of the law. While it would be wrong to chain ourselves to past understandings of the law, a full appreciation of how law relates to a particular situation will not occur unless we acknowledge the other forces at work, such as history and politics, that help to give us our present understandings.

In this way, the story of America and the laws of war is far less a legal than a political story, in the sense that it is about the governance of a particular area of international relations, the exercise of power and attempts to restrain it, and the various beliefs as to how, exactly, all of this should be accomplished. The role of politics has been central to the way the law of war has been implemented by the United States. Politics, influenced by both ideology and national priorities, determines how enemies of the United States have been viewed, regarded and treated. Politics influences the way that training is conducted and the laws of war are implemented, and ultimately how the law of war is perceived. In this way, a full understanding of how America has engaged with the laws of war is as much political as it is legal.

America and the laws of war after Iraq

At the time of this writing, it is not known how much longer the United States will be in Iraq and Afghanistan or engaged in the broader War on Terror. Obama has begun the process of withdrawal in Iraq but this is likely to be contingent on the stability of the country and the region as a whole. At the same time, while the Bush administration promised a long-term commitment to Iraq, falling domestic support for the conflict, a sense of fatigue in the military, and spiralling costs may curtail US military activity sooner rather than later. The effect of current and emerging threats, such as instability in the Middle East and a hostile and nuclear Iran and North Korea, may also have an effect on US military policy in the near future, or the effects of natural disasters (such as a Katrina-style hurricane) or instability close to the US homeland (such as the possibility that the ongoing crisis in Haiti may spill over into a refugee crisis) may also prompt changes in US military activity in the coming months or years.

The purpose of this section is not to speculate on where or how the US will be involved in conflicts around the globe, but only on how such changes may or may not prompt changes in US policies towards the law of war in the future. What can be expected of the way the US will engage with the laws of war after Iraq? Given the recent past and the challenges ahead, there is plenty of opportunity for ongoing research into this complex relationship.

One scenario may be that after the scandals and controversies over the prison at Guantánamo Bay's Camp Delta, the death of prisoners at Bagram Air Base in Afghanistan, the abuse at Abu Ghraib, and allegations of war crimes at Haditha in Iraq, US military lawyers or the Department of Defense may take an approach to the laws of war like that of their post-Vietnam predecessors. In this, a post-Vietnam model scenario, military lawyers, unsatisfied with what they have seen regarding the implementation of the laws of war in America's current military engagements, might argue and push for new approaches of looking at and implementing and adhering to the law of war—not just because it is the "right thing to do", but so that operations continue to run smoothly and controversies which take away from the purpose of a mission (such as the above-mentioned scandals) are avoided. This would require a new generation of so-called "activist-lawyers" to emerge in the Department of Defense who would again argue their case for operational law, one consistent legal policy and the role of lawyers in the war room. Such a shift might entail what otherwise might be referred to as a "second legal revolution" or "renaissance" within the US military.

On the other hand, the experiences regarding the politics of the law of war in the War on Terror may provoke the opposite response despite whatever speeches President Obama may make. If there is a perception that the law of war prompted difficulties and frustrations in US military operations, or if the task of implementing the law of war leaves a bitter taste in the mouths of soldiers and commanders, there may be a great deal of resistance or hostility to the general idea of the law of war in combat. If the whole principle behind operational law is that it helps to make operations run smoother, and if that is no longer considered to be the case by US military personnel, suggested improvements or a full implementation of the law of war may be rejected. Attitudes towards the law of war within the Department of Defense should therefore remain an area of research for those interested in America's relationship with the law of war.

This second, "rejection" scenario would be aided by a continued or increased acceptance of the neo-conservative/new sovereigntist critique of international law. If such a position attracts a sympathetic ear or even explicit approval within US governments in the future, there would be even greater pressure to reject the development of international law, especially in the areas of human rights and the law of war. Such an approach, which has been recently advocated by Dick Cheney, would mark an increasing tendency to base arguments regarding international law on political and moral grounds rather than legal arguments based on legal interpretation. It is probably too extreme to suggest that such an approach would result in the US withdrawing from the 1949 Geneva Conventions or the 1984 United Nations Convention Against Torture. However, it may mean a downplaying of the significance of such international legislation (perhaps going beyond the "quaint" remarks of Alberto Gonzales), a clear indication that the relevant current international treaties (such as the Ottawa Convention to ban landmines or the Convention on the Rights of the Child) will not be ratified or even presented to the Senate for ratification, and a refusal of the US to participate in the drafting of further treaties of this nature.

The actual course of US policies towards the law of war in the future is still uncertain, although it will probably fall somewhere between these two scenarios. A second legal revolution may not be necessary in so far as what seems to be required is maintaining US military doctrine in *all* situations, rather than the "mixed bag" approach mandated by the current administration. And, as has been argued here, the reluctance of the US to be seen as totally disregarding international rules will probably prevent a full-on "rejection" approach to the law of war.

What then may remain significant for the debate over the direction of US policies are arguments relating to linking purpose and tactics in fighting the War on Terror. As was argued in Chapter 4, an increasing tendency for certain US legal scholars as well as Bush administration officials to justify the means employed on the basis of the political and moral imperatives to win the War on Terror essentially involves re-linking *jus ad bellum* and *jus in bello*–a reversal of the legislative history of the last 160 years and customary trends of at least the last two centuries. While this may seem an issue of semantics or even political and moral rhetoric, there are serious practical implications to the question. The need to win the War on Terror has already caused many in the US government and in America to rethink the rules on torture, and such an approach has clear implications for how issues like extraordinary rendition and the treatment of prisoners of war are handled in future conflicts. As Cheney argued in May 2009:

And to call [the enhanced interrogation program] torture is to libel the dedicated professionals who have saved American lives, and to cast terrorists and murderers as innocent victims. What's more, to completely rule out enhanced interrogation methods in the future is unwise in the extreme. It is recklessness cloaked in righteousness, and would make the American people less safe...

For all the partisan anger that still lingers, our administration will stand up well in history–not despite our actions after 9/11, but because of them.[5]

Nor is it clear that the change in administrations will make a difference to this debate. The Democratic President Bill Clinton demonstrated that, when push came to shove, he was willing to go against international legal opinion, and it is fairly clear that Democrats or "soft Wilsonians" are not willing to sacrifice perceived American political and security interests in the name of international law. The debate here frequently crosses domestic political lines with many Democrats voting for the USA PATRIOT Act, and Republicans such as Senator John McCain speaking out against torture. Perhaps, then, the only thing which is clear is that the role of politics, ideology and perceptions of national imperatives will continue to have an effect on how the laws of war are considered and implemented by the United States and its military.

The law of war in the future

The issues highlighted in this study point to several questions regarding the future for the law of war. Perhaps the most blatant of these has been whether or not the law of war will survive beyond the War on Terror and if so, in what form? In a speech on the need to reexamine the laws of war, one commentator stated:

Historically, of course, laws have always been adapted to better suit the times. When they have become out-dated, or less relevant, or less applicable to the realities of the day they have been modified or changed. This is true of all laws, domestic or international...

...since some change is less perceptible, more incremental, the balance between considerations such as obligation and entitlement, and freedom and security needs to be continually reviewed and, where necessary, re-forged. If we act differently today from how we behaved yesterday, it is not necessarily wrong. Indeed it may be wrong not to. We owe it to ourselves, to our people, to our forces and to the cause of international order to constantly reappraise and update the relationship between our underlying values, the legal instruments which apply them to the world of conflict, and the historical circumstances in which they are to be applied, including the nature of that conflict.[6]

The remarks did not come from the Bush administration or a neo-conservative think-tank but from the then British Secretary of State for Defence, an elected MP of the Labour Government. In his speech, entitled "Twenty-first Century Warfare–Twentieth Century Rules", he went on to question whether or not society was adequately convinced that it was protected from the threat of international terrorism under the current frameworks of domestic and international law.

What the speech demonstrates is that many of the questions and issues currently affecting America and international law also affect and stir other countries around the world. The way that America chooses to answer these quandaries will naturally affect the way the rest of the world perceives such issues. However, it is fair to say that the way the rest of the world answers the same challenges will probably also affect the United States.

Do we need new thinking on the laws of war? As suggested in Chapter 4, the issue was raised long before the War on Terror began. The issue was raised, practically, in the Kosovo campaign. Today, the argument that we need new rules to combat a new breed of networked international terrorists is the main moral and political justification for the Bush administration's policies on Guantánamo Bay and interrogation.

Despite the outrage of human rights organizations, humanitarians and activists, these arguments are not incomprehensible. It can only be natural that when presented with a conflict that is, if only in size and scale, unprecedented, the rules and restrictions that apply are put under some scrutiny. Should we compromise the safety of our troops, or even our societies, for the rights of terrorists? Should the West really engage in a war with one hand tied behind its back, against an enemy who holds the very idea of restraint in disdain?

The premise of the question is, of course, whether the law of war is the restraint which keeps the one hand tied behind the back. As argued above, this is not necessarily the case. Rather, the law of war is a tool which may be used to facilitate operations to help them go smoother. Because the law of war imposes both duties and rights on combatants, regarding the law as only a set of restrictions and restraints is a mischaracterization.

Perhaps, then, what we need is not so much "new thinking" about the law of war in the War on Terror, but a return to "old thinking". Old thinking in this context refers to the approach that was outlined by the "activist lawyers" in the 1980s but also resonates with the approach taken in 1949. Old thinking recognizes that the law gives both rights and responsibilities to combatants and acknowledges that law which gives one side a distinct advantage is unworkable. In other words, defenders have an obligation not to base themselves in or near civilian areas and then expect that the other side will refrain from attacking. Additionally, old thinking emphasizes the need to keep the rules as simple and straightforward as possible for military personnel–not to over-complicate the law of war with new and increasingly specific or complex regulations. However, keeping the rules simple also mean sticking to one policy–approaches which seek to apply different sets of rules to different areas of operation (or even in the same area) result in confusion and misunderstandings. Having one approach and sticking to it helps to keep things clear in confusing and dangerous situations and, crucially, it helps to prevent the abuse that occurred in Abu Ghraib.

Yet, what is key about "old thinking", especially when compared to arguments for "new thinking" on the law of war, is the belief that the law of war can be flexible and be applied to unfamiliar and unprecedented situations. Where the "new game, new rules" argument tends to look upon our current law as outdated or no longer appropriate for the War on Terror, old thinking looks for parallels and ways that our current law can apply in such a way that political and military imperatives can still be met.

As he sets out to look at the applicable law in the war on terror, Christopher Greenwood (now a judge at the International Court of Justice) notes that much of the controversy over the American approach to the War on Terror

...has its roots in the fact that the events of 11 September–a terrorist attack of unprecedented savagery, apparently carried out by a shadowy organization operating outside the control of any state–did not fit easily within any of the obvious categories of international law. To some observers, the attack can only be regarded as an entirely new phenomenon falling wholly outside the existing framework of international law... For the members of that school of thought, a challenge on this scale of a non-state actor to the one superpower calls for an entirely new thinking about the nature of international law. There is much substance in this argument, but does not help to answer the immediate questions about what law is applicable now. The fact that the events of 11 September may demonstrate a need to re-examine some of the assumptions on which the international legal system rests does not mean that those events occurred in a legal vacuum.[7]

Thus, questions about new thinking and old thinking are clearly an interesting area for further research. However, the point being made in this short discussion is that even where there is not a perfect fit between events and international law, this does not mean that there are no conventions to govern a particular operation or conflict. Custom and norms provide rules and surely most, if not all, circumstances in the War on Terror can draw on at least one parallel from past conflicts or emergencies. In this way, our current law is flexible and is more adaptable than has been considered by many academics, politicians and even international lawyers. Ideas about precedent and finding ways to make the law work were the goals of "activist lawyers" in the post-Vietnam military context. A return to this kind of old thinking may then be more useful than finding and agreeing on alternatives in a fractured, post-9/11 world.

Conclusion: putting it all together

The executive orders which Obama signed on his first day in office at least seem to indicate that he is committed to policies under which the War on Terror will be fought in line with international legal standards but also, as he put it, in line with American values:

The Framers who drafted the Constitution could not have foreseen the challenges that have unfolded over the last 222 years. But our Constitution has endured through secession and civil rights, through World War and Cold War, because it provides a foundation of principles that can be applied pragmatically; it provides a compass that can help us find our way. It hasn't always been easy. We are an imperfect people. Every now and then, there are those who think that America's safety and success requires us to walk away from the sacred principles enshrined in this building. And we hear such voices today. But over the long haul the American people have resisted that temptation. And though we've made our share of mistakes, required some course corrections, ultimately we have held fast to the principles that have been the source of our strength and a beacon to the world.[8]

After all, Barack Obama is also an American exceptionalist.

Yet applying Obama's first orders in this domain has already proven to be a logistical nightmare. Few nations are willing to cooperate with the United States in harbouring former inmates and there are few countries to which such individuals could be sent where they could live relatively free of the risk of torture. Within the United States, the idea that Guantánamo detainees could be sent to face trial on US soil sent convulsions through the US public, media and Congress in the spring of 2009. The hysteria that Guantánamo Bay can still provoke several years after its establishment shows how it lies at the nexus of a sensitive and difficult debate about balancing security and values. It is likely that the debates over the issued discussed in this book will not end with the Obama administration.

Prisoners of war and prisoners in war–the central case study of this book–also represent a contradiction of sorts. Captured, they are removed from war and yet remain in it. During the First and Second World Wars, POWs on both sides frequently felt that it was their duty to try to escape. Part of the success attributed to "the Great Escape" is that it temporarily distracted German units and provided a major propaganda coup for the Allies. However, in the War on Terror, the fear is that the struggle also remains ongoing for the detainees in orange jumpsuits–deemed murderous terrorists who are biding their time before they strike at US targets. The difficulties of such a dilemma are a central focus of this book.

And yet, the story of prisoners of war in American conflicts is more complex than this. POWs spend months, if not years, behind barbed wire–or worse–during their time in captivity. For the American public, unlike the rows of crosses at Arlington, they are living symbols of the sacrifices of war. What then can we learn from this history?

As the source material for this book shows, much has already been written about prisoners of war and much of this has been in the context of the War on

Terror. While the vast majority of this has concentrated on the United States, a comparison with other countries would probably demonstrate that very few militaries which have engaged in conflict in the last century have particularly clean hands when it comes to prisoners and the laws of war. In the second half of the twentieth century, one need only think of the French in Algeria or the British in Malaysia, Kenya and Aden. Even more recently, one would probably not wish to be a prisoner taken by the Russians in Chechnya or a Uighur taken by the Chinese.

Yet America, despite its complexities, is also an easy target in a way, because it wears its ideas and ideologies on its national sleeves. It is a nation whose Constitution and institutions profess a distinct set of American values which are particular but also universal. Additionally, as it is militarily and politically engaged throughout the world it is easier to see its global impact on international legal issues. Therefore, drawing on the previous chapters, the final section of this work has tried to highlight the issues surrounding the United States and the politics of the law of war in a thematic manner. In doing so it has attempted to demonstrate that when it comes to these issues there are no clear separating lines. The major themes that run through this study all relate and engage with one another. It is impossible to speak of a dualistic tendency or implementation without reference to ideology.

The overall project has also tried to emphasize the need for a hybrid approach to study these issues. The role of law in politics and the nature of politics in law need to be considered and examined. A political account which too easily dismisses the effect of international law and a shallow reading and analysis of a legal text tell us very little of how America engages with the law of war in modern conflicts.

Ultimately, this study has tried to tell a story about how America has engaged with the law of war and why it chose to act in a particular manner. It has done so in the hope that interested individuals will be able to draw lessons and, perhaps, better understand where the United States stands in relation to the law of war today and why. Such an understanding remains important because, despite its current pressures, America remains the world's only superpower and is likely continue in this role for at least the next few decades. As such it is reasonable to estimate that the US will remain militarily engaged, if only in the defence of its own territory. The dilemmas America faces in terms of the law of war are therefore likely to remain important to us all for the foreseeable future.

If the past is any indication, it is likely that America's relationship with the law of war will continue to change because of the effect of ideology, national tendencies and politics. America has an effect on international law and international law has an effect on America, and this certainly includes the law of war. After all, it has been said that the law of war has been written in the blood of past conflicts—and much of this blood, it may be said, has been American.

APPENDIX A

INTERROGATION TECHNIQUES REQUESTED BY THE COMMANDER OF THE US SOUTHERN COMMAND FOR USE AT GUANTÁNAMO BAY. MEMO DATED 25 OCTOBER 2002

On 2 December 2002, Secretary of Defense Donald Rumsfeld approved all of the techniques in Category I and II and the fourth technique in Category III.

This permission was rescinded on 15 January and a working group was set up to assess the legal, policy and operational issues relating to the interrogation of detainees.

Category I

1. Yelling at Detainee
2. Techniques of Deception
a. Multiple interrogator techniques
b. Interrogator identity. The interviewer may identify himself as a citizen of a foreign nation or as an interrogator from a country with a reputation for harsh treatment of detainees.

Category II techniques

1. The use of stress positions (like standing), for a maximum of four hours.
2. The use of falsified documents or reports.
3. Use of isolation facility for up to thirty days. Requests must be made to through the OIC[1], Interrogation Section, to the Director, Joint Interrogation Group (JIG). Extensions beyond the initial thirty days must be approved by the Commanding General. For selected detainees, the OIC,

Interrogation Section will approve all contacts with detainee, to include medical visits of non-emergent nation.

4. Interrogating the detainee in an environment other than the standard interrogation booth.
5. Deprivation of light and auditory stimuli.
6. The detainee may also have a hood placed over his head during transportation and questioning. The hood should not restrict breathing in any way and the detainee should be under direct observation when hooded.
7. The use of twenty-hour interrogations.
8. Removal of all comfort items (including religious items).
9. Switching the detainee from hot rations to MREs².
10. Removal of clothing.
11. Forced grooming (shaving of facial hair, etc).
12. Using detainee individual phobias (such as fear of dogs) to induce stress.

Category III techniques

1. The use of scenarios designed to convince the detainee that death or severely painful consequences are imminent for him and/or his family.
2. Exposure to cold weather or water (with appropriate medical monitoring).
3. Use of a wet towel dripping water to induce the misperception of suffocation.
4. Use of mild, non-injurious physical contact such as grabbing, poking in the chest with the finger, and light pushing.

APPENDIX B

INTERROGATION TECHNIQUES APPROVED BY SECRETARY OF DEFENSE DONALD RUMSFELD FOR USE AT GUANTÁNAMO BAY AFTER REVIEW BY A WORKING GROUP IN THE DEPARTMENT OF DEFENSE. MEMO DATED 16 APRIL 2003.

Techniques A-Q: from Field Manual 34-52

A. Direct: Asking straightforward questions.

B. Incentive/removal of incentive: Providing a reward or removing a privilege, beyond those that are required by the Geneva Conventions.

C. Emotional love: Playing on the love a detainee has for an individual or a group.

D. Emotional hate: Playing on the hatred a detainee has for an individual or a group.

E. Fear up harsh: Significantly increasing the fear level in a detainee. (This is generally interpreted as yelling or throwing things but not touching the detainee.)

F. Fear up mild: Moderately increasing the fear level in a detainee.

G. Reduced fear: Reducing the fear level in a detainee.

H. Pride and ego up: Boosting the ego of a detainee.

I. Pride and ego down: Attacking and insulting the ego of a detainee, not beyond the limits that would apply to a prisoner of war. (Caution given that this may violate Article 17 of the Third Geneva Convention and consideration on these grounds should be given prior to application of this technique.)

J. Futility: Invoking the feeling of futility in a detainee.

K. We know all: Convincing a detainee that the interrogator already knows the answer to the question he is asking.

L. Establish your identity: Convincing a detainee that the interrogator has mistaken him for someone else.

M. Repetition approach: Continuously repeating the same question to a detainee within interrogation periods of normal duration.

N. File and dossier: Convincing a detainee that the interrogator has a damning and inaccurate file that must be fixed.

O. Mutt and Jeff: Pairing a friendly interrogator with a harsh one.

P. Rapid fire: Questioning in rapid succession without allowing detainee to answer.

Q. Silence: Staring at a detainee to encourage discomfort.

Techniques which go beyond Field Manual 34–52 and require "Further implementation guidance"

R. Change of scenery up: Removing a detainee from the standard interrogation setting–generally to a more pleasant location, but not to a worse one.

S. Change of scenery down: Moving a detainee from the standard interrogation setting to one less comfortable, but not one that would constitute a substantial change in environmental quality.

T. Dietary manipulation: Changing the diet of a detainee, but with no intended deprivation of food or water and without an adverse cultural or medical effect. e.g., hot rations to MREs.

U. "Environmental manipulation": Altering the environment to create moderate discomfort (e.g., adjusting temperature or introducing an unpleasant smell). Conditions would not be such that they would injure a detainee. Detainee would be accompanied by an interrogator at all times. [Caution: Based on court cases in other countries, some nations may view application of this technique in certain circumstances to be inhumane. Consideration of these views should be given prior to use of this technique.]

V. Sleep adjustment: Adjusting the sleeping times of a detainee (e.g., reversing sleep cycles from night to day.) This technique is NOT sleep deprivation.

W. False Flag: Convincing the detainee that individuals from a country other than the United States are interrogating him.

X. Isolation: Isolating a detainee from other detainees while still complying with the basic standards of treatment.[1]

NOTES

INTRODUCTION: THE POLITICS OF THE LAWS OF WAR

1. Anthony Swofford, *Jarhead: A Soldier's Story of Modern War*, London: Scribner, 2003, pp. 157–8. The debate to which Swofford is referring is one over how 0.50 calibre weapons could be used in conflict. There was concern that the 0.50 calibre rifle, used against a human target, would cause wounds that were considered excessive and in contravention of the laws of war. The determination of the legality of weapons is a very complex issue but a useful discussion looking at the history, the current issues and the way the US currently conducts legal review of weapons can be found in Donna Marie Verchio, "Just Say No! The SIRUS Project: Well-Intentioned but, Unnecessary and Superfluous", *Air Force Law Review*, Vol. 51, 2001, pp. 183–228. Also see the article by W. Hays Parks, "Means and Methods of Warfare", *George Washington International Law Review*, Vol. 38 No. 3, 2006. pp. 511–39.
2. "President Bush and Prime Minister Tony Blair of the United Kingdom participate in Joint Press Availability" 25 May 2006. Available online at: http://www.whitehouse.gov/news/releases/2006/05/20060525-12.html
3. This also goes for targeting issues discussed during examination of the 1990s. While the link may not appear obvious, the assumption is that the discussions of the relevance of the laws of war (the set of laws in which the rules governing the treatment of prisoners of war are contained) were significant as they later had an effect on how the laws were applied after 9/11.
4. However, as Adam Roberts and Richard Guelf note: "The term 'international humanitarian law' could be seen as implying that the laws of war have an exclusively humanitarian purpose, when their evolution in fact reflected various practical concerns of states and their armed forces on ground other than those which may be considered humanitarian". Adam Roberts and Richard Guelff, *Documents on the Laws of War*, Third Edition, Oxford University Press, 1999. p. 2.
5. Cited in Geoffrey Best, *Humanity in Warfare: The Modern History of the International Law of Armed Conflicts*, London: Methuen & Co. Ltd., 1980, p. 49.
6. During Napoleon's march to Moscow it had pretty much been expected that troops would be able to live off the land as they marched to victory. When this did not pan out as expected and villages were swarmed with hungry and half starved

243

troops, the result for the inhabitants was usually devastation. See Adam Zamoyski, *1812: Napoleon's Fatal March on Moscow*, London: Harper Perennial, 2004.

7. For example, see Jeremy Rabkin, *Law Without Nations: Why Constitutional Government Requires Sovereign States*, Princeton University Press, 2005. This work will examine these arguments in Chapter 4.

8. Michael Howard, "*Tempermenta Belli*: Can War Be Controlled" in Michael Howard, ed. *Restraints on War: Studies in the Limitation of Armed Conflict*, Oxford University Press, 1979, p. 1.

9. Colum Lynch, "U.N. sexual abuse alleged in Congo", *Washington Post*, 16 December 2004; Page A26, available online at: http://www.washingtonpost.com/wp-dyn/articles/A3145–2004Dec15.html. Also see Brian Ross, David Scott and Rhonda Schwartz, "U.N. sex crimes in Congo", ABC News, 10 February 2005, available online at: http://abcnews.go.com/2020/UnitedNations/story?id= 489306&page=1; BBC News, "UN sexual allegations double", 6 May 2005, available online at: http://news.bbc.co.uk/2/hi/americas/4521481.stm.

10. See Wesley K. Clark, *Waging Modern War: Bosnia, Kosovo and the Future of Conflict*, Oxford: Public Affairs, 2001 and Ivo H. Daalder and Michael E. O'Hanlon, *Winning Ugly: NATO's War to Save Kosovo*, Washington: Brookings Institute Press, 2000.

11. For a presentation of the law relating the War on Terror see Helen Duffy, *The 'War on Terror' and the Framework of International Law*, Cambridge University Press, 2005, and Dominic McGoldrick, *From '9–11' to the 'Iraq War 2003': International Law in an Age of Complexity*, Portland: Hart Publishing, 2004.

12. See Michael Byers, *War Law: International Law and Armed Conflict*, London: Atlantic Books, 2005; Philippe Sands, *Lawless World: America and the Making and Breaking of Global Rules*, London: Allen Lane, 2005.

13. Sands, *Lawless World*, p. 205. Also see, Philippe Sands, *Torture Team: Uncovering War Crimes in the Land of the Free*, London: Penguin Books, 2009. That the softcover version of the book includes the phrase "Updated with major new prosecutorial material" suggests that Sands is not afraid to wear his cause (and apparently that of international law) on his sleeve.

14. Byers, *War Law*, p. 155.

15. E.H. Carr, *The Twenty Year's Crisis 1919–1939: An Introduction to the Study of International Relations*, Basingstoke: Palgrave, 2001, p. 159.

16. Rabkin, *Law Without Nations?*, p. 268.

17. Hersh Lauterpacht, "The Limits of the Operation of the Laws of War", *British Yearbook of International Law*, Volume 30, 1953, pp. 206–43.

1. CULTURE OR CARNAGE? THE LAWS OF WAR IN THE FIRST WARS OF THE REPUBLIC 1750–1860

1. This book will refer to the aboriginal peoples of North America as First Nations. However, where it has cited other authors, it will use the terms that they employ in their books.

2. For a good survey, see Christopher Hibbert, *Red Coats and Rebels: The War for America 1770–1781*, London: Penguin Books, 2001.

3. Henry Wheaton, *Elements of International Law: The Literal Reproduction of the Edition of 1866*, ed. Richard Henry Dada Jr., ed. George Grafton Wilson, Oxford: The Clarendon Press, 1936, pp. 368–71.

4. During this period the Navy operated under the "Rules and Regulation of the Navy of the United Colonies", which was put in place on 28 November 1775. The name was later changed to the Articles for the Government of the Navy in 1799. See John D. Cooke, "Introduction: Fiftieth Anniversary of the Uniform Code of Military Justice Symposium Edition", *Military Law Review*, Vol. 165, September 2000, pp. 1–20, pp. 2–3.

5. Edmund M. Morgan, "The Background of the Uniform Code of Military Justice," *Military Law Review*, Vol. 28, April 1965, pp. 17–35.

6. Cooke, "Introduction", p. 4.

7. Cooke, "Introduction", p. 3.

8. William T. Sherman, *Journal of the Military Service Institute of the United States*, Vol. 132, 1880. Cited in George S. Prugh, Jr., "Observations on the Uniform Code of Military Justice: 1954 and 2000", *Military Law Review*, Vol. 165, September 2000, pp. 21–41. p. 30.

9. There were changes made in 1786, 1806, 1874, 1917. The future Presidents Thomas Jefferson and John Adams were made members of one of the first committees set the task of revising the military code of 1775 but made no substantial changes. As Morgan notes, even the Articles enacted in 1916 were only a rearrangement and a reclassification without much alteration in substance. See Morgan, "The Background of the Uniform Code of Military Justice", pp. 17–18.

10. Francis Jennings notes that the conflict has been called the first world war. See Francis Jennings, *Empire of Fortune: Crown, Colonies, and Tribes in the Seven Years War in America*, New York: W.W. Norton & Company, 1988, p. 6.

11. This was the British General Amherst's suggestion to Colonel Henry Bouquet, who agreed to do so during Pontiac's Rebellion in the end stages of the war and discussed below. Although it is not clear that the germ plan was ever executed, smallpox would decimate the First Nations population shortly thereafter. Starkey notes that while biological warfare was not addressed in eighteenth century treaties on the laws of war, poisoned weapons were condemned specifically. As with other aspects of the war, the law regulating European conduct frequently fell silent as the different cultures collided. See Starkey, *European and Native American Warfare, 1675–1815*, London: UCL Press, 1998, pp. 106–7; Jennings, *Empire of Fortune*, pp. 447–8.

12. John Shy, "The American Military Experience: History and Learning", *Journal of Interdisciplinary History*, Vol. 1 No. 2 (Winter 1971), pp. 205–8, p. 212.

13. Armstrong Starkey, "Paoli to Stony Point: Military Ethics and Weaponry During the American Revolution", *The Journal of Military History*, Vol. 58 No 1 (Jan. 1994), pp. 7–27. p. 17.

14. Ian K. Steele, "When Worlds Collide: The Fate of Canadian and French Prisoners Taken at Fort Niagara, 1759", *Journal of Canadian Studies*, Vol. 39 No. 3, 2005, pp. 9–39. p. 9.

15. Steele, "Hostage-taking", pp. 63–5. Of course there were demands for such good treatment. Washington was to secure the return of all French and Canadian prisoners within two and a half months and two officers serving with Washington, Jacob Van Braam and Robert Stobo, volunteered to be hostages for fulfilment of the bargain. However, as the British refused to release French prisoners taken, on account of the failure of the French to control the First Nations warriors, they were never released. Instead, they found fame as prisoners of war, particularly Stobo who bravely or foolishly sneaked a map of the defences of Quebec City to the British that was eventually captured by the French. Both prisoners were put on trial for spying and while Van Braam was acquitted, Stobo was found guilty and sentenced to death–although this order was suspended by the French government. Stobo tried to escape several times and eventually succeeded in May 1759. He was eventually awarded a pension for his efforts and time served as a prisoner. Anderson tells the story of the two prisoners in Fred Anderson, *Crucible of War: The Seven Years' War and the Fate of Empire in British North America, 1754–1766*, London: Faber and Faber, 2000, pp. 351–2.

16. Cited in Steele, "Hostage-taking", p. 66.

17. Steele, "Hostage-taking", pp. 66–9.

18. Thomas S. Abler, "Scalping, Torture, Cannibalism and Rape: An Ethnohistorical Analysis of Conflicting Cultural Values in War", *Anthropologica*, Vol. 34 No 1, 1992, pp 3–20. p. 9.

19. Abler, "Scalping", pp. 13–15.

20. Daniel K. Richter, "War and Culture: The Iroquois Experience", *The William and Mary Quarterly*, Vol. 40 No. 4 (October 1983), pp. 528–59. p. 535.

21. Richter, "War and Culture", p. 536.

22. Armstrong Starkey, *European and Native American Warfare 1675–1815*, London: UCL Press, 1998. p. 19

23. Given the success that was possible when First Nations tactics were adopted or modified to blend with European ways of war, Starkey is critical of the failure of the Anglo-Americans (and later Americans) to learn the lessons of the wars fought throughout the seventeenth and eighteenth centuries and the reluctance to adopt such tactics. After all, although the Canadians were outnumbered on the continent, their willingness to adopt much of the First Nations way of warfare made them a very deadly force. Yet, as Wayne Lee recognizes, the "persistent fear of European enemies" rather than just the First Nations tribes was an important factor here. See Wayne E. Lee, "Early American Ways of War: A New Renaissance, 1600–1815", *The Historical Journal*, Vol. 44 No. 1 (March 2001), pp. 269–89. p. 274.

24. Starkey, *European and Native American Warfare*, p. 123. Starkey cites Francis Jennings, *Empire of Fortune: Crowns, Colonies, and Tribes in the Seven Years War in America*, New York: W.W. Norton, 1988. p. 198.

25. Starkey, *European and Native American Warfare*. All of chapter two is useful here, pp. 17–35. The quote is from p. 26.

26. Starkey, *European and Native American Warfare*, pp. 28–30. Starkey goes on to note that attitudes towards life and death and the "unnatural act of killing" had effects in other areas that we would now normally recognize as part of the mod-

ern laws of war. Warriors about to go on a raid would avoid women so as to avoid the "unnatural mix of their warlike state with the woman's life force". This, Starkey suggests, to a large extent, prevented the rape and sexual molestation of prisoners.

27. Richter, "War and Culture", pp. 529–32.
28. Starkey, *European and Native American Warfare*, pp. 29–30
29. Richter notes that the beating of women and children prisoners was rare. "War and Culture", p. 533.
30. Abler, "Scalping", pp. 9–11. Abler notes that gruesome torture was not unknown to Europeans, and cites the case of the assassin of William of Orange who was tortured for eighteen days in 1584. However, what was shocking to the Europeans was the degree to which entire communities participated in the violence. Whereas torturers and executioners were "professionals" within their communities, all ages and sexes took turns at tormenting a prisoner. p. 12.
31. Starkey, *European and Native American Warfare*, p. 14.
32. Stephen Brumwell, *Redcoats: The British Soldiers and the War in the Americas, 1755–1763*, Cambridge University Press, 2002, p. 99.
33. Anderson, *Crucible of War*, London: Faber and Faber Limited, 2000. pp. 286–7. Brumwell argues, however, that the average British soldier was not ignorant of the concept of their rights and frequently protested when they were being violated. See *Redcoats*, pp. 127–36.
34. Brumwell, *Redcoats*, pp. 100–12; Anderson, *Crucible of War*, p. 287.
35. On tensions between the colonists, the British government and army see J. Alan Rogers, "Colonial Opposition to the Quartering of Troops During the French and Indian War", *Military Affairs*, Vol. 34 No. 1, (February 1970), pp. 7–11.
36. Anderson, *Crucible of War*, p. 103.
37. Brumwell, *Redcoats*, pp. 179–83.
38. Brumwell, *Redcoats*, p. 183.
39. Shy, "The American Military Experience", p. 214.
40. Starkey, *European and Native American Warfare*, p. 86.
41. Jan Grabowski, "French Criminal Justice and Indians in Montreal, 1670–1760", *Ethnohistory*, Vol. 43 No. 3 (Summer 1996), pp. 405–29.
42. Grabowski, "French Criminal Justice", pp. 406–7.
43. Brumwell, *Redcoats*, p. 183.
44. Starkey, *European and Native American Warfare*, pp. 101–2.
45. Anderson, *Crucible of War*, pp. 135–6.
46. Anderson, *Crucible of War*, pp. 155–6.
47. Anderson, *Crucible of War*, pp. 187–9.
48. Anderson, *Crucible of War*, pp. 189–90.
49. Steele, *Betrayals*, p. 85.
50. Anderson, *Crucible of War*, p. 191.
51. Anderson, *Crucible of War*, p. 192.
52. Jennings, *Empire of Fortune*, p. 317. Steele notes that this was a meaningful status to Montcalm–that there had to have been some effort made in the name of honour in order to deserve full rights. He notes that Montcalm did not give the sur-

rendered Oswego garrison full rights "because of its lame defense". Steele, *Betrayals*, p. 109.

53. Anderson, *Crucible of War*, pp. 195–6.

54. Steele, *Betrayals*, p. 117.

55. Steele, *Betrayals*, p. 119.

56. Anderson, *Crucible of War*, p. 198. Jennings suggests that "It is impossible to be certain of the number killed in this horror." He writes that among the dead no one counted the Black servants, First Nations allies of the British, women or children. *Empire of Fortune*, p. 319. However, Steele argues that since the Europeans regarded Blacks as property, the First Nations did too and as such "they were treated better than the witnesses presumed." Steele, *Betrayals*, p. 116. He also notes that in the aftermath of the massacre only around 10 of 80 women made it to Fort Edwards. p. 123.

57. Steele, *Betrayals*, p. 119.

58. Anderson, *Crucible of War*, pp. 198–9. Steele writes that Montcalm had proposed that the First Nations who had taken part in the massacre should be imprisoned for subordination. Steele, *Betrayals*, p. 131.

59. Steele, *Betrayals*, p. 131.

60. Anderson, Crucible of War, p. 196.

61. Fred Anderson and Andrew Cayton, *The Dominion of War: Empire and Conflict in America, 1500–2000*, London: Atlantic Books, 2005. p. 124.

62. Anderson, *Crucible of War*, p. 199.

63. Even though they turned out in smaller numbers in 1758, Montcalm chose not to employ what warriors he did have against the British and Anglo-American forces. In 1759, despite a significant turnout, they were not able to save the French at the Plains of Abraham as the war had come to be dominated by European regulars fighting in conventional battles. MacLeod, "Microbes and Muskets", p. 55. Jon William Parmenter writes that the western First Nations tribes sent more warriors to assist in the last-ditch effort against the British as a part of their factional diplomatic strategy (or "play-off" system) that sought to balance their interests with that of the British and the French. See John William Parmenter, "Pontiac's War: Forging New Links in the Anglo-Iroquois Covenant Chain, 1758–1766", *Ethnohistory*, Vol. 44 No. 4 (Autumn, 1997), pp. 617–54). p. 621.

64. Anderson, *Crucible of War*, p. 199.

65. Steele, *Betrayals*, pp. 145–7.

66. Anderson, *Crucible of War*, p. 344. Anderson notes that by this time scalping was an activity engaged in by regular troops and sanctioned by Wolfe himself against "Indians" or Canadians "dressed like Indians". p. 788, fn. 1 Chapter 36.

67. Jennings, *Empire of Fortune*, p. 420.

68. Steele, "When Worlds Collide", p. 11.

69. Ibid.

70. Steele, "When Worlds Collide", pp. 12–15.

71. Steele, "When Worlds Collide", p. 14.

72. Historians suggest that Pontiac's role in leading the conflict has been traditionally exaggerated and that the "resistance" involved many tribes as a kind of pan-First

Nations movement. As a result, there was never any unified command and chiefs vied with one another for prestige. See, for example, Jennings, *Empire of Fortune*, pp. 442–53.

73. Anderson, *Crucible of War*, p. 466.
74. Jennings, *Empire of Fortune*, p. 447.
75. Anderson, *Crucible of War*, p. 542.
76. Anderson, *Crucible of War*, pp. 542–5.
77. Anderson, *Crucible of War*, p. 617.
78. Ian K. Steele, *Guerrillas and Grenadiers: The Struggle for Canada, 1689–1760*, Toronto: The Ryerson Press, 1969.
79. Starkey, *European and Native American Warfare*, pp. 80–1. However, although the warfare that took place during these seventy years was cruel, violent and possibly medieval, particularly regarding prisoners of war, Steele reminds us that it is important to keep things in perspective. During a raid by the French Canadians and First Nations warriors at Deerfield, Massachusetts against an Anglo-American settlement, sixty-five persons were slaughtered. In the same year, around the little Danube town of Benheim more than 100,000 men fought and nearly half of them died. Steele, *Guerrillas*, p. 11. Starkey writes that 40–50 inhabitants were killed and 109 prisoners were taken, of whom twenty died of exposure or were killed during the demanding return march to Canada through deep snow. Stories were told of one woman being killed because she could not keep up, but also of captors providing the prisoners with Indian snow shoes and constructed sleds to carry the children and the wounded. *European and Native American Warfare*, p. 91.
80. Shy, "American Military Experience", pp. 213–14.
81. Shy, "American Military Experience", p. 214.
82. Shy, "American Military Experience", pp. 215–16.
83. Higginbotham, "The Early American Way of War", p. 262.
84. Lee, "Early American Ways of War", p. 286. This was a style of warfare that had been waged in Europe which incorporated many minor operations of raid, ambush, reconnaissance and security that complemented operations, waged by troops with a variety of "exotic" titles: pandours, croats, hussars, freikorps, jaegers, chasseurs, etc. In this sense, though bloody, the irregular activity is probably better understood as falling within the tradition of Roman Legions and the writings of the French marshal Maurice de Saxe than that of the First Nations. As the provincials and militia who made up much of Washington's forces would not be disciplined enough to stand up to the British and their Hessian auxiliaries in a formal battle, guerrilla forces were used to deny the British control of the countryside. See Andrew J. Birtle, "The Origins of the Legion of the United States", *The Journal of Military History*, Vol. 67, No. 4, October 2003. pp. 1249–61; Fred Anderson and Andrew Cayton, *The Dominion of War: Empire and Conflict in America 1500–2000*, London: Atlantic Books, 2005. p. 167.
85. Higginbotham, "The Early American Way of War", p. 254.
86. Starkey, *European and Native American Warfare*, p. 135.
87. Don Higginbotham, *The War of American Independence: Military Attitudes, Policies and Practice, 1763–1789*, Boston: Northeastern University Press, 1983.

88. Starkey, "Paoli to Stony Point", p. 11.

89. See Starkey, "Paoli to Stony Point".

90. And they were virtually all "he". Throughout the eighteenth and nineteenth centuries there are some notable exceptions. Families including women prisoners were sometimes kidnapped by first Nations Tribes. According to Fooks, US pensions bureau files indicate that at least two women were awarded pensions for injuries sustained while serving as private soldiers during the Revolutionary War and the US Civil War. See Herbert C. Fooks, *Prisoners of War*, Federalsburg: The J.W. Stowell Printing Co., 1924, p. 68.

91. A brief but interesting account of the experiences of these officers and the towns they were foisted on can be found in Laura L. Becker, "Prisoners of War in the American Revolution: A Community Perspective", *Military Affairs*, Vol. 46 No. 4, December 1982, pp. 169–73.

92. See Philip Raniet, "British Recruitment of Americans in New York During the American Revolution", *Military Affairs*, Vol. 88 No. 1 January 1984, pp. 26–8.

93. Geoffrey Best, *Humanity in Warfare: The Modern History of the International Law of Armed Conflicts*, London: Methuen & Co., 1980. p. 109.

94. William E.S. Flory, *Prisoners of War: A Study in the Development of International Law*, Washington: American Council on Public Affairs, 1942, p. 17. He also notes that during the Revolution Congress declared that being a prisoner was "a restraint of honour only"–not a punishment for a crime. p. 41.

95. Starkey, "Paoli to Stony Point", pp. 16–17.

96. Starkey, "Paoli to Stony Point", pp. 7–8. Also see Christopher Hibbert, *Redcoats and Rebels: The War for America: 1770–1781*, London: Penguin Books, 2001, pp. 158–9.

97. Starkey, "Paoli to Stony Point", p. 8.

98. Starkey, "Paoli to Stony Point", p. 19.

99. Hibbert, *Redcoats and Rebels*, pp. 262–3.

100. Hibbert, *Redcoats and Rebels*, pp. 280–1.

101. Starkey, "Paoli to Stony Point", p. 23.

102. Starkey, "Paoli to Stony Point", p. 24.

103. Jane Mayer invokes this example to suggest that there is a long history of humane warfare in the United States which the Bush administration ignored. One can understand (and even be sympathetic to) the larger argument that Mayer is trying to make. However, there can be no question that citing this one example is a gross simplification of both the American Revolutionary War and the American tradition of warfare. See Jane Mayer, *The Dark Side: The Inside Story of How the War on Terror Turned Into A War on American Ideals*, New York: Anchor Books, 2008, pp. 8–9 and 83–4. See also, for example, Alex Markel, "Will Terrorism Rewrite the Laws of War?" National Public Radio, 6 December 2005. Available online at: http://www.npr.org/templates/story/story.php?storyId=5011464. Lyman H. Butterfield argues that the relatively good treatment given to the Hessians was largely a practical decision to encourage desertion. See "Psychological Warfare in 1776: The Jefferson-Franklin Plan to Cause Hessian Desertions", *Proceedings of the American Philosophical Society*, Vol. 94 No. 3, 1950,

pp. 233–41. Additionally, after capture, there was no guarantee that treatment was always going to be fully humane. Becker suggests that once prisoners were billeted in towns around the colonies, local residents treated them with suspicion and sometimes open animosity. See Becker, "Prisoners of War in the American Revolution", pp. 170–1.

104. Catherine M. Prelinger, "Benjamin Franklin and the American Prisoners of War in England during the American Revolution", in *The William and Mary Quarterly*, 3rd Ser., Vol. 32, No. 2. April 1975. pp. 261–94. Also see Fooks, *Prisoners of War*, pp. 271–2. Apparently this was an issue that came up during the various cases of Guantánamo detainees arguing for *habeas corpus* rights. The incident was submitted as evidence of a historical example where prisoners of war had been given *habeas* rights–presumably the prisoners would have to have had the rights in order for the North Act to take them away. Conversation with US State Department employee, December 2007.

105. This is the position taken by Flory, *Prisoners of War*, p. 17; Ranlet, "British Recruitment", p. 26–8; David L. Sterling, "American Prisoners of War in New York: A Report by Elias Boudinot", *The William and Mary Quarterly*, 3rd Ser., Vol. 13 no. 3 (July 1956), pp. 376–93. pp. 376–9. Still, it is clear that not everyone in the British government was pleased at the treatment of the American prisoners. Stories of brutality on the part of British jailors "produced a vehement response from members of the British opposition. On the day before Christmas, 1777 a committee to relieve the American prisoners was organized, and within fifteen days £3,700 was raised for distribution." Prelinger, "Benjamin Franklin", p. 264.

106. Apparently, in addition to the poor state many prisoners were in upon their arrival, many of the Americans in Britain had to deal with the corruption of the guards and agents in whose charge they found themselves. The US emissary, Thorton, noted that these individuals short-weighed the rations, watered the beer and served beef spoiled by maggots. See Prelinger, "Benjamin Franklin", p. 269. Francis Abell supports this conclusion and cites an unnamed London newspaper which records the "real cause of their ill-treatment": "[the Americans] penury and distress was undoubtedly great and was much marked by the *fraud and cruelty of those who were entrusted with their government, and the supply of their provisions.*" In this way, Abell is suggesting that some of the suffering inflicted on the Americans was not a deliberate policy, but was due to fraud committed by those who were supposed to look after them. This may be being a bit too generous to the British government. The newspaper article goes on to say that a subscription was taken up to "remedy the evil". See Francis Abell, *Prisoners of War in Britain 1756–1815: A Record of their Lives, Their Romance and Their Sufferings*, Oxford University Press, 1914, p. 48.

107. Ranlet suggests that of 405 Americans captured after the disastrous invasion of Canada in 1775, 111 enlisted–although apparently some of the new recruits tried to desert. Having had this success, the policy was later used on prisoners in New York. Ranlet, "British Recruitment", p. 26. Prelinger indicates that at the Old Mill prison in Plymouth, 54 Americans out of a prisoner population of

approximately 330 had entered British service by January 1778. Prelinger, "Benjamin Franklin", p. 275. According to Olive Anderson, in the first six months of 1781 there were eighty-two volunteers out of 400 prisoners (even though prisoner exchanges were being made at this time). See Olive Anderson, "British Governments and Rebellion at Sea", *The Historical Journal*, Volume III No. I, 1960. pp. 56–84. Note 57 p. 63.

108. Elias Boudinot was the "suitable person" appointed by Washington to report on the conditions of American prisoners. A copy of his report may be found in Sterling, "American Prisoners of War in New York". His agent, Lewis Pintard, a New York merchant, moved back into the city to attempt to lessen the sufferings of the prisoners and stayed in that role until 1781. See Ranlet, "British Recruitment". In addition, John Thorton was sent to Britain as an American envoy to report on the conditions of the prisoners and to distribute relief where possible. Prelinger, "Benjamin Franklin", p. 266.

109. Anderson, "British Governments and Rebellion at Sea", p. 272.

110. Ranlet, "British Recruitment", p. 27.

111. Betsey Knight, "Prisoner Exchange and Parole in the American Revolution", *The William and Mary Quarterly*, 3rd Ser., Vol. 48 No. 2 (April 1991), pp. 201–2. p. 206.

112. Knight, "Prisoner Exchange", pp. 211–12. While on parole, officers were forbidden to do any sort of work associated with the war effort which would have given them some sort of regular pay.

113. Knight, "Prisoner Exchange", p. 205. Knight cites numbers from Boudinot who indicated that officers on parole on Long Island were boarded at $2 per week. At one point, Boudinot indicated that the United States owed £7,000 for the board of officers there as well as £15,000 in unspecified expenses. Note 15, p. 205.

114. See Knight, "Prisoner Exchange", p. 212; Prelinger, "Benjamin Franklin", p. 271; and Ranlet, "British Recruitment", p. 26.

115. Ranlet, "British Recruitment", pp. 26–7.

116. Prelinger, "Benjamin Franklin", p. 271. Anderson agrees–see Anderson, "British Governments and Rebellion at Sea", p. 63.

117. Prelinger, "Benjamin Franklin", p. 271.

118. Prelinger, "Benjamin Franklin", p. 272 and pp. 276–82.

119. Prelinger, "Benjamin Franklin", p. 271. On Howard, Prelinger cites Olive Anderson, "Treatment of Prisoner of War in Britain during the American War of Independence", *Bulletin of the Institute of Historic Research*, XXVIII, 1955. p. 76.

120. Knight, "Prisoner Exchange", p. 207. According to Knight there are no records of the total number exchanged, but that there was great confusion as states made deals without regard to the overall prisoner situation. In January 1780, Congress passed a resolution which 'recommended' that no states make these exchanges.

121. See Flory, *Prisoners of War*, and Fooks, *Prisoners of War*.

122. Text of these treaties from Yale University's Avalon Project. Available online at: http://www.yale.edu/lawweb/avalon/avalon.htm.

123. However, the United States would continue to have trouble with the "Barbary Pirates" for some time yet. In several instances, Americans were taken hostage and made slaves. In some cases the government would ransom them, but realizing that this could become a profitable business, the Americans soon took to gunboat diplomacy to rescue its citizens and prevent harm from coming to them. See Max Boot, *The Savage Wars of Peace: Small Wars and the Rise of American Power*, New York: Basic Books, 2002, especially Chapter 1 on the Barbary Wars 1801–5 and 1815.

124. Ralph Robinson, "Retaliation for the Treatment of Prisoners in the War of 1812", *The American Historical Review*, Vol. 49 No. 1, October 1943, pp. 65–70. p. 65.

125. Jonathan Vance, *Objects of Concern: Canadian Prisoners of War Throughout the Twentieth Century*, Vancouver: UBC Press, 1994. p. 9.

126. Vance, *Objects of Concern*, pp. 9–11.

127. Vance, *Objects of Concern*, p. 11. The incident is described in more detail in Robinson, "Retaliation", pp. 65–70.

128. Vance, *Objects of Concern*, p. 11.

129. Ibid.

130. Robinson, "Retaliation", p. 66.

131. Robin F. Fabel, "Self-Help in Dartmoor: Black and White Prisoners in the War of 1812", *Journal of the Early Republic*, Vol. 9 No. 2, Summer 1989, pp. 165–90. p. 160.

132. Fabel, "Self-Help in Dartmoor", p. 166.

133. Fabel argues that some Americans were clamped in irons aboard ships when they claimed POW status and forced, at pistol point, to participate in operations against American ships. Others were apparently flogged. Still, Fabel argues that most captains generally honoured claimes for transfers. See Fabel, "Self-Help in Dartmoor", pp. 174–5. Abell notes that this had been the US practice since 1755 but had ended after the American War of Independence. Still, it was apparently brought back during the War of 1812 despite the fact that the British Navy was desperate for manpower. See Abell, *Prisoners of War in Britain*, p. 84 and Fabel, p. 174.

134. Fabel indicates that there were 6,553 American prisoners held at Dartmoor through the course of the war. Commissioned officers were paroled and were allowed to live privately in nearby villages. Fabel, "Self-Help in Dartmoor", p. 166 and p. 170.

135. See Abell, *Prisoners of War in Britain*, p. 254. Abell recounts an incident where the understandably upset US prisoners had to be persuaded not to give Beasley a mock trial and burn him in effigy. They proceeded to do so a few days later. Fabel also indicates that Beasley "seems to have had an appetite for London life." He apparently visited Dartmoor only once in 1813–and then only to tell the prisoners that he had no power to do anything, nor any funds to do it with. See Fabel, "Self-Help in Dartmoor", p. 173. In fairness, however, it needs to be said that both Abell and Fabel note that many a US prisoner made life harder for himself by gambling. See Abell pp. 82–3 and Fabel p. 173. However, such

behaviour was frowned upon and in some cases, it was outlawed by the prisoners themselves. Abell p. 86.

136. Abell, *Prisoners of War in Britain*, p. 249.

137. Fabel, "Self-Help in Dartmoor", pp. 176–7.

138. Both Abell and Fabel cite Benjamin Waterhouse's account of his time as a prisoner of war for a description of the system. Benjamin Waterhouse, *Journal of a Young Man of Massachusetts*, Boston, 1816.

139. Abell, *Prisoners of War in Britain*, p. 254.

140. Anderson and Cayton, *Dominion of War*, p. 133.

141. James H. Merrell, "Amerindians and the New Republic" in Jack P. Greene and J. R. Pole eds, *A Companion to the American Revolution*, Malden: Blackwell Publishers Inc., 2000. pp. 413–18.

142. Merrell, "Amerindians and the New Republic", p. 413.

143. Jeremy Black, *War for America: The Fight for Independence 1775–1783*, Phoenix Mill: Sutton Publishing, 2001, p. 35.

144. The most (in)famous incident was the alleged murder and scalping of Jane McCrea at the hands of a band of First Nations warriors while she was travelling to meet her fiancé. Although many facts were and remain unclear about the incident, the Americans used this as a chance to confirm the cruel and unjust nature of the British who had persuaded the First Nations tribes to attack innocent civilians. As Starkey argues, "It could be claimed that a government which resorted to such barbaric practices had ceded legitimate authority." Starkey, *European and Native American Warfare*, p. 111. The incident is also noted in Black, *War for America*, p. 36.

145. Merrell, "Amerindians", p. 414.

146. Merrell, "Amerindians", pp. 16–17.

147. Merrell, "Amerindians", pp. 17–18.

148. Early on in the war General Isaac Brock did this at Detroit to encourage the Americans to surrender–which they did without a fight. Starkey notes that this raises "the interesting moral question of the responsibility of officers who knowingly employed warriors who they knew would violate European standards." *European and Native American Warfare*, p. 102.

149. Starkey, *European and Native American Warfare*, p. 160.

150. J. Mackay Hitsman, *The Incredible War of 1812: A Military History*, University of Toronto Press, 1965.

151. Boot, *The Savage Wars of Peace*, p. xvi. The post-1812 situation is dealt with in the next chapter.

152. See Theodore J. Crackel, *West Point: A Bicentennial History*, Lawrence: University Press of Kansas, 2002. Especially chapters 4 and 5.

153. Abell, *Prisoners of War in Britain*, p. 91. The comment was made by a British officer who, though exasperated with the American prisoners in his charge, indicated that he could not help liking them. Shortland, a despised British official at Dartmoor, indicated similar sentiments: "I never saw or ever read or heard of such a set of Devil-daring, God-provoking fellows, as these same Yankees. I had rather have the charge of 5,000 Frenchmen, than 500 of these sons of lib-

erty; and yet I love the dogs better than I do the d———d frog-eaters." p. 258.
Perhaps not too much should be drawn from these remarks, but they do demonstrate that the common language and culture that the Americans and British shared did have an influence on attitudes towards the enemy.

154. James M. McCaffrey, *The Army of Manifest Destiny: The American Soldier in the Mexican War, 1846–1848*, New York University Press, 1992. p. 139

155. Flory, *Prisoners of War*, p. 18.

156. Stories surrounding the fate of those at the Alamo vary. In accordance with Santa Anna's order, all of the defenders were killed. Whether or not there were any prisoners of war, however, seems to be of some debate. Some suggest that there were approximately seven prisoners taken at the Alamo, with some accounts suggesting that American legend Davy Crocket was among them. These prisoners were then killed for having taken part in the battle. Whether or not the legend is true does not take away from the fact that Santa Anna's order against giving quarter and the idea that he had murdered prisoners were seen as inhumane and an example of the injustice of the Mexicans in Texas and in the United States. According to Waddy Thompson, the American envoy to Mexico before the war, Santa Anna claimed that he had "seven different times summoned them to surrender, and offered them quarter, which he would have taken the risk and responsibility of granting, but that they refused to accept it, and fought to the last and died gloriously." Thompson did not claim to endorse this argument but thought it interesting to present in his memoirs of Mexico. See Waddy Thompson, *Recollections of Mexico*, New York: Wiley and Putnam, 1847.

157. Interestingly, Santa Anna himself was captured and became a prisoner of war after this battle. Many of the Texans who captured him wanted to execute him then and there, but cooler heads prevailed and he was held prisoner until an agreement was reached on the status of Texas and his return to Veracruz. While held in Texas, however, he was not always treated well and was, at one point, put in chains, which led him to attempt suicide. He was revived by the efforts of an American doctor whose son, in what must be one of history's more bizarre twists of fate (if true), later became a prisoner of war. The son was freed by Santa Anna for his father's efforts. Thompson notes the story in his *Recollections*, pp. 75–6.

158. Sam W. Haynes, *Soldiers of Misfortune: The Somervell and Mier Expeditions*, Austin: University of Texas Press, 1990. p. 78.

159. Haynes, *Soldiers of Misfortune*, p. 78.

160. It seems harsh, but Haynes offers an explanation: that while the one-in-ten or *diezmo* seems shockingly unfair today, the Mexican government took the view that the sentence was an act of clemency—especially as the prisoners had killed five Mexican soldiers while making their escape. Haynes, *Soldiers of Misfortune*, p. 119. Rather than prisoners being selected at random, 176 beans were placed into a jar—159 white and seventeen black. Those soldiers who picked black beans were given a last meal and a chance to write a letter home, and promptly executed.

161. Flory, *Prisoners of War*, p. 34. Flory cites Francis Wharton, *A Digest of the International Law of the United States*, 1886 Vol 3, p. 332.

162. Haynes, *Prisoners of Misfortune*, p. 125

163. Thompson, *Recollections*, p. 74. This account is, of course, his own recounting of his conversation with Santa Anna, but can still probably be seen as indicative of the position of the US government on the matter.

164. Thompson, *Recollections*, pp. 92–4.

165. Charles L. Dufour, *The Mexican War: A Compact History 1846–1848*, New York: Hawthorn Books Inc. 1968. p. 16.

166. Cited in Dufour, *The Mexican War*, p. 47.

167. Dufour, *The Mexican War*, p. 200.

168. Stephen A. Carney, *The Occupation of Mexico: May 1846–July 1848*, Washington: US Army Center of Military History, 2005. p. 28.

169. Carney, *The Occupation of Mexico*, pp. 27–8.

170. But this does not mean that everyone took Scott's views. Territory under the control of General Taylor, who was apparently content not to give his volunteers diversions to occupy their time, apparently suffered from crimes against Mexicans to a much greater extent–as discussed below.

171. McCaffrey, *The Army of Manifest Destiny*, pp. 106–7.

172. McCaffrey, *The Army of Manifest Destiny*, pp. 107–8.

173. McCaffrey, *The Army of Manifest Destiny*, pp. 109–10.

174. McCaffrey, *The Army of Manifest Destiny*, pp. 124–5. Carney refers to a similar incident where a soldier was able to get off charges of theft through bribing the witnesses and judge. *The Occupation of Mexico*, p. 28.

175. McCaffrey, *The Army of Manifest Destiny*, pp. 123–7.

176. McCaffrey, *The Army of Manifest Destiny*, p. 127.

177. Carney, *The Occupation of Mexico*, pp. 17–18.

178. Pedro Santoni, "The Failure of Mobilization: The Civic Militia of Mexico in 1846", *Mexican Studies/Estudios Mexicanos*, Vol. 12 No. 2, 1996. pp. 169–94. p. 186. Santoni provides a good account of the state of the forces the Americans faced in 1846 and their inability to organize themselves better.

179. Bruno S. Frey and Heinz Buhofer, "Prisoners and Property Rights", *Journal of Law and Economics*, Vol. 31 No. 1, 1988, pp. 19–46. p. 41. Frey and Buhofer cite Charles Murphy, "Prisoners of War: Repatriation or Internment in Wartime", in *US POWs in South East Asia* 479 (US Congress, Committee on Foreign Affairs 1971).

180. George S. Prugh, Jr., "The Code of Conduct for the Armed Forces" in *Columbia Law Review*, Vol. 56 No. 5, 1956, pp. 678–707. n. 54 p. 691.

181. See Richard Blaine McCornack, "The San Patricio Deserters in the Mexican War", *The Americas*, Vol. 8 No. 2, 1951, pp. 131–42. He notes that the title "Irish Deserters" was a misnomer "but Riley and the other leaders seem to have stamped their nationality upon the whole outfit for posterity." p. 89

182. Edward S. Wallace, "The Battalion of Saint Patrick in the Mexican War", *Military Affairs*, Vol. 14, No. 2, 1950, pp. 84–91. pp. 85–7. Wallace notes that of the deserters not a single one was from the volunteers, even though one third of them were Catholic.

183. McCornack, "The San Patricio Deserters", p. 137. See also Wallace, "Battalion of Saint Patrick", p. 87.

184. Wallace, "Battalion of Saint Patrick", p. 88.

185. McCornack, "The San Patricio Deserters", p. 140.

186. Wallace, "Battalion of Saint Patrick", p. 88.

187. Wallace, "Battalion of Saint Patrick", p. 89.

188. McCornack, "The San Patricio Deserters", pp. 138–9 and Wallace, "Battalion of Saint Patrick", p. 90.

189. Wallace, "Battalion of Saint Patrick", p. 87.

190. Thompson, *Recollections of Mexico*, p. vi.

2. 'MANIFEST' HUMANITARIANS: THE UNITED STATES, INTERNATIONAL LAW AND MODERN WARFARE 1860–1950

1. William B. Hesseltine, "The Propaganda Literature of Confederate Prisons", *The Journal of Southern History*, Vol. 1 No. 1, 1953, pp. 56–66. p. 57.

2. Ibid.

3. David Williams, *A People's History of the Civil War: Struggles for the Meaning of Freedom*, New York: The New Press, 2005. p. 236.

4. For an account of life at Libby Prison, see Frank L. Byrne, "Libby Prison: A Study in Emotion", *The Journal of Southern History*, Vol. 24 No. 4, 1958. pp. 430–44.

5. For an account of the propaganda campaign see Hesseltine, "Propaganda Literature".

6. Hesseltine, "Propaganda Literature", p. 59.

7. Cited in Williams, *A People's History*, p. 340. King was writing in the context of describing attempts by slaves to covertly assist the Union soldiers.

8. Williams, *A People's History*, p. 239.

9. Byrne, "Libby Prison", pp. 437–8.

10. Hesseltine, "Propaganda Literature", p. 59.

11. Williams, *A People's History*, pp. 236–9.

12. Geoffrey Best, *War and Law Since 1945*, Oxford University Press, 1997. p. 41.

13. Caroline Moorehead, *Dunant's Dream: War, Switzerland and the History of the Red Cross*, London: HarperCollins, 1999. 37.

14. Moorehead, *Dunant's Dream*, p. 37.

15. Text found at Yale University's *Avalon Project: Documents in Law, History and Diplomacy*. Available online: http://www.yale.edu/lawweb/avalon/avalon.htm.

16. Best, *Humanity in Warfare*, p. 156.

17. Ibid.

18. Williams, *A People's History*, pp. 366–7.

19. Williams, *A People's History*, p. 367.

20. Although there is relevance in terms of the Bush administration's policies and the justifications employed to defend them, there is not enough space to go into the impact of Lincoln's policies on civilians in this work. See Daniel A. Farber, *Lincoln's Constitution*, University of Chicago Press, 2003. On Lincoln's and FDR's decisions in a contemporary context, see Jack Goldsmith, *The Terror Presidency:*

Law and Judgment Inside the Bush Administration, New York: W.W. Norton & Company, 2007.

21. Editorial Comment, "The Red Cross in Civil Wars", *The American Journal of International Law*, Vol. 5, No. 2, 1911. pp. 438–40. p. 439.
22. Fooks, *Prisoners of War*, p. 15. More on manifest destiny will be discussed below.
23. International Committee of the Red Cross, "Declaration Respecting Maritime Law. Paris, 16 April 1856", Available online: http://www.icrc.org/ihl.nsf/INTRO/105?OpenDocument.
24. Letter from Eugene Schuyler to Secretary of State Fish, 14 December 1874. [No. 55] Foreign Relations of the United States, *United States Department of State Executive Documents Printed by Order of the House of Representatives. 1875–'76: Vol. II (1875–1876)*, pp. 1022–4.
25. Ibid.
26. John Hay, "Instructions to the American Delegates to the Hague Conferences", as reprinted in: *World Peace Foundation Pamphlet Series*, Vol. III No. 4, April 1913. p. 5.
27. Andrew D. White, *The First Hague Conference*. Boston: The World Peace Foundation, 1912.
28. White, *The First Hague Conference*, pp. 0–76. In a letter to von Bülow reprinted in the book, White refers to the fact that even the Conservative Churches in America were praying for success, and in the very next paragraph warns von Bülow that failure would play into the hands of the French Socialists. By the end of the Conference von Bülow did "come around" and eventually became proud of the accomplishments at The Hague. Koskenniemi argues that it was Professor Philip Zorn's influence that convinced von Bülow. (Zorn was a member of the German delegation to the conference who, prior to his attendance, said that international law was not real law but merely treaties subject to the will of states.) See *The Gentle Civilizer of Nations: The Rise and Fall of International Law 1870–1960* Cambridge University Press, 2001. p. 8. This would complement the account by White who claimed to have debated with Zorn and "seemed to impress him". Zorn then returned to Berlin with a member of the American delegation who helped to change the Chancellor's mind. According to Koskenniemi, von Bülow would claim that the initial German scepticism had been caused by inflated expectations of the Conference. *Gentle Civilizer of Nations*, p. 212.
29. Cited in Francis Wharton, *A Digest of International Law of the United States*, Volume III, Washington: Government Printing Office, 1886. p. 326.
30. Peter Maguire, *Law and War: An American Story*, New York: Columbia University Press, 2001. p. 5.
31. Maguire, *Law and War*, p. 6. Of course it is possible to overdo the uniqueness of the American approach. The French republican tradition and the British sense of liberty were also deemed compatible with Empire. Additionally, all of these empires saw themselves as undertaking a civilizing mission in their engagements abroad.
32. Maguire, *Law and War*, p. 9.

33. Reginald Horseman, *Expansion and American Indian Policy, 1783–1812*, Norman: University of Oklahoma Press, 1992. p. 83.
34. Horseman, *Expansion and American Indian Policy*, p. 89.
35. Richard H. Dillon, *North American Indian Wars*, Wigston: Magna Books, 1983. p. 64.
36. Dillon, *North American Indian Wars*, p. 251.
37. Maguire, *Law and War*, p. 21.
38. Maguire, *Law and War*, p. 32.
39. Boot, *The Savage Wars of Peace*, p. 39.
40. Boot, *The Savage Wars of Peace*, p. 38.
41. Stanley Karnow, *In Our Image: America's Empire In the Philippines*. New York: Random House, 1989. p. 100.
42. The Additional Articles, which were intended to enlarge the scope of the original 1864 Geneva Convention had never come into force.
43. Karnow, *In Our Image*, p. 75.
44. Karnow, *In Our Image*, pp. 128–9.
45. Karnow, *In Our Image*, p. 109. Interestingly, Beveridge would later go on to be an isolationist within the Senate. In this speech, he echoed the sentiments of another advocate of the war with Spain, Theodore Roosevelt, who played a large role in pushing for the conflict and who also would go on to advocate an isolationist stance for the US.
46. Karnow, *In Our Image*, p. 160.
47. Karnow, *In Our Image*, p. 140.
48. Brian McAllister Linn, *The US Army and Counterinsurgency in the Philippine War 1899–1902*, Chapel Hill: The University of North Carolina Press, 1989. p. 16.
49. Karnow, *In Our Image*, p. 178.
50. Linn, *The US Army and Counterinsurgency*, p. 17.
51. Boot, *The Savage Wars of Peace*, p. 283.
52. Karnow, *In Our Image*, p. 172.
53. Karnow, *In Our Image*, p. 179
54. Linn, *The US Army and Counterinsurgency*, p. 25.
55. Maguire, *Law and War*, p. 60.
56. David L. Fritz, "Before the 'Howling Wilderness': The Military Career of Jacob Hurd Smith, 1862–1902", *Military Affairs*, Vol. 43 No. 4, December 1979. pp. 186–90.
57. Maguire, *Law and War*, p. 37.
58. Karnow, *In Our Image*, p. 179.
59. Maguire, *Law and War*, p. 63. Waller admitted to the killings, claiming that they were justified by General Smith's orders and the laws of war. Waller was found not guilty and sentenced only to a loss of pay. Maguire argues that Secretary Root wanted to use Waller as a scapegoat but Waller was able to successfully to defend himself by producing Smith's written orders and witnesses. Waller was thus able to implicate Smith. See the discussion of the rather sensational trial, pp. 62–6. The courts-martial of Waller and Smith are also discussed in Fritz, "Before the 'Howling Wilderness'".

60. Maguire, *Law and War*, p. 63.

61. Linn, *The US Army and Counterinsurgency*, p. 24.

62. Ibid.

63. Maguire, *Law and War*, p. 42.

64. Walter Russell Mead, *Special Providence: American Foreign Policy and How It Changed the World*, New York: Alfred A. Knopf, 2001.

65. Mead, *Special Providence*, p. 226.

66. Mead, *Special Providence*, p. 246.

67. Mead, *Special Providence*, pp. 246–52.

68. Mead, *Special Providence*, p. 252. And the same could be said about why the Germans were seen as honourable and the Japanese were not.

69. Mead, *Special Providence*, p. 259.

70. Mead, *Special Providence*, p. 255.

71. Maguire, *Law and War*, p. 63. Then again Mead also points out that Jacksonianism held less sway over New York and East Coast populations than over the more populist and "folk" oriented populations in other parts of the country. See Mead's discussion *Special Providence*, pp. 226–7.

72. Letter from Mr Hay to Mr Choate, 16 October 1900, [No. 468], *United States Department of State/Papers Relating to the Foreign Relations of the United States, with the Annual Message of the President Transmitted to Congress December 2, 1902 (1902)*, p. 463. The correspondence over ensuring adequate treatment and repatriation, included in this volume, would go on for another two years.

73. The invitation was turned down by the UK and Germany–the former was distracted by wars in South Africa and China (called "experiments" in the correspondence) while the latter did not think it would be in a position to be represented at a conference at the time. A 1904 conference was suspended at the outbreak of the Russo-Japanese War.

74. Elihu Root, "Instructions to the American Delegates to The Hague Conference, 1907" 31 May 1907. *United States Department of State/Papers Relating to the Foreign Relations of the United States with the Annual Message of the President Transmitted to Congress December 3, 1907. (In two parts) Part II (1907)*. pp. 1128–39.

75. Philip C. Jessup, *Elihu Root: Volume II 1905–1937*, New York: Dodd, Mead & Company, 1938. p. 70.

76. Richard W. Leopold, *Elihu Root and the Conservative Tradition*, Boston: Little, Brown and Company, 1954.

77. See Article I, 1899 Hague Convention (II) with Respect to the Laws and Customs of War on Land and its annex: Regulations concerning the Laws and Customs of War on Land. The first "instructions" might be considered General Orders 100 as mentioned above. In addition, a volume on "official treaties", *Military Law and Precedents*, was published by Colonel William Winthrop in 1886, and later revised and enlarged in a second edition in 1895. Information from the files of W. Hays Parks.

78. Telegram from Lansing to Stovall, 24 April 1918 [No. 1800], *United States Department of State Papers Relating to the Foreign Relations of the United States,*

1918. Supplement 2, The World War, Washington: US Government Printing Office, 1918. p. 48.

79. Telegram from Polk to Stovall, 10 August 1918, [No. 2430], *United States Department of State Papers relating to the foreign relations of the United States, 1918. Supplement 2, The World War*, Washington: US Government Printing Office, 1918. p. 34.

80. Telegram from Stovall to the Secretary of State, 30 September 1918, [No. 4968], *United States Department of State Papers Relating to the Foreign Relations of the United States, 1918. Supplement 2, The World War*, Washington: US Government Printing Office, 1918. pp. 49–50.

81. Telegram from Lansing to Stovall, 2 November 1918 [No 3259], *United States Department of State Papers Relating to the Foreign Relations of the United States, 1918. Supplement 2, The World War*, Washington: US Government Printing Office, 1918. pp. 50–1. Article 24 of the 1906 Geneva Convention states: "The provisions of the present Convention are obligatory only on the Contracting Powers, in case of war between two or more of them. The said provisions shall cease to be obligatory if one of the belligerent Powers should not be signatory to the Convention." Text from ICRC website: http://www.icrc.org/ihl.nsf/WebART/180-170025?OpenDocument.

82. American concerns are laid out in a letter to the German government sent via the American ambassador in Spain. Telegram from Lansing to Joseph E. Willard, 28 January 1918 [850], *United States Department of State Papers Relating to the Foreign Relations of the United States, 1918. Supplement 2, The World War*, Washington: US Government Printing Office, 1918. pp. 19–21.

83. For examples, see the letter to the German government mentioned in note 9. Reciprocity was also invoked over the issue of allowing prisoners to be interviewed without guards present: Lansing to the Swiss Minister [No. 160], *United States Department of State Papers Relating to the Foreign Relations of the United States, 1918. Supplement 2, The World War*, Washington: US Government Printing Office, 1918, p. 25. Interestingly, when the Austrian government announced that the death penalty would be inflicted upon any allied aviator who dropped political manifestos, the United States announced that it could not consent to retaliate by executing Austrian officers out of reciprocity. The letter did note that the Austrian policy would "invite extreme measures to prevent its continuance". Telegram from Lansing to the Ambassador in France [No. 5801], *United States Department of State Papers Relating to the Felations of the United States, 1918. Supplement 2, The World War, 1918*, Washington: US Government Printing Office, 1918. p. 786.

84. Note from Secretary of State Lansing to the Secretary of War, 17 April 1918, *United States Department of State Papers Relating to the Foreign Relations of the United States, 1918. Supplement 2, The World War*, Washington: US Government Printing Office, 1918. pp. 55–6.

85. Chandler P. Anderson, "Agreement Between the United States and Germany Concerning Prisoners of War", *The American Journal of International Law*, Vol. 13 No. 1, 1919, pp. 97–101. pp. 98–9.

86. Anderson "Agreement", p. 99.
87. James Wilford Garner, *International Law and the World War*, London: Longmans, Green and Co., 1920. p. 21.
88. But the issue of the treatment that Allied prisoners of war faced did not immediately go away. In fact, in Article 228 of the Treaty of Versailles, the German Government recognized "the right of the Allied and Associated Powers to bring before military tribunals persons accused of having committed acts in violation of the laws and customs of war". A list of such individuals was presented to the German Government in February 1920. However, given post-war politics, Germany argued that handing these individuals over to be tried in a foreign court would cause a political crisis. It was subsequently agreed that the responsibility for the prosecution of the accused would be left to the German Government. With evidence submitted by the British, four individuals were eventually put on trial, found guilty and sentenced to imprisonment. See Green Haywood Hackworth, *Digest of International Law: Volume VI Chapters XIX-XXI*, Washington: United States Government Printing Office, 1943. pp. 279–80.
89. Exceptions to this include the Treaty relating to the Use of Submarines and Noxious Gases in Warfare (1922 Washington Treaty), an attempt to draft "Rules concerning the Control of Wireless Telegraphy in Time of War and Air Warfare" in 1922–23, the Protocol for the Prohibition of the Use of Asphyxiating, Poisonous or Other Gases, and of Bacteriological Methods of Warfare (aka the 1925 Geneva Gas Protocol), and the Convention on Maritime Neutrality (1928 Havana Convention). Of these the Geneva Gas Protocol is the most significant and remains in force today. The 1922 Washington Treaty never came into force after France refused to ratify the agreement, and the 1928 Havana Convention largely duplicated the law that was already to be found in the 1907 Hague Convention.
90. Memorandum by Mr Rollin R. Winslow, Division of Western European Affairs, 5 June 1929, *United States Department of State Papers Relating to the Foreign Relations of the United States, 1929: Volume I (1929)*, Washington: United States Government Printing Office, 1929. p. 317.
91. Flory, *Prisoners of War*, p. 23.
92. Telegram from the Ambassador in the Soviet Union Steinhardt to the Secretary of State, 9 August 1941 [No. 1458], *United States Department of State/Foreign Relations of the United States Diplomatic Papers, 1941. General, The Soviet Union,Volume I (1941)*, Washington: US Government Printing Office, 1941. pp. 1005–6. Interestingly, the Soviet Union also protested against Article 9 of the 1929 Conventions which stated that "Belligerents shall as far as possible avoid bringing together in the same camp prisoners of different races or nationalities." According to Soviet officials, this was against the Soviet Constitution which prohibited discrimination on grounds of race. Considering that the Stalinist government was not exactly known for its humanity, this was probably a ploy to avoid application of the Convention. Still, it is interesting that Soviet officials raised this issue–something that had frequently been the complaint of white

American POWs in previous wars including the War of 1812 and the First World War.

93. Telegram from the Secretary of State to the Ambassador in the Soviet Union, 7 November 1941 [1199], *United States Department of State/Foreign Relations of the United States Diplomatic Papers, 1941. General, The Soviet Union Volume I (1941).* pp. 1009–10; Telegram from the Secretary of State to the Chargé in the Soviet Union, 9 December 1941 [1271] Same Volume, pp. 1017–18.

94. See the Telegrams from Hull to the Chargé in Switzerland, 18 December 1941 [No. 331] and 13 January 1942 [No. 83], *United States Department of State/ Foreign Relations of the United States Diplomatic Papers, 1942. General; the British Commonweath; the Far East Volume I (1942)*, Washington: US Government Printing Office, 1942. pp. 792–4.

95. Telegram from the Secretary of State to the Minister in Switzerland, 12 December 1942 [2814], *United States Department of State/Foreign Relations of the United States Diplomatic Papers, 1942. General; the British Commonwealth; the Far East Volume I (1942).* pp. 832–9.

96. S.P. Mackenzie, "The Treatment of Prisoners of War in World War II", *The Journal of Modern History*, Vol. 66 No. 3, 1994. pp. 487–520. p. 516.

97. See James J. Weingartner, "The Malmédy Massacre Prosecution and Idaho Law Alumnus Colonel Burton Ellis: A Warning of the Difficulties in Administering Justice to a Defeated Enemy", *Michigan State Journal of International Law*, Vol. 13 No 1, 2005. pp. 63–78. Weingartener's article explains the aftermath of the massacre after the war had ended. American prosecutors would go on to prosecute seventy-four defendants in the case. However, the subsequent trial demonstrated some flaws in the way the Americans handled post-war justice when it came to prisoners. In order to get evidence, American investigators employed "psychological stratagems" which included confronting suspects with false witnesses and "mock trials" where hooded suspects were brought into a darkened courtroom-like setting where they may have been led to believe that they were on trial for their lives. The prosecutors subsequently denied that any form of physical coercion had been used to get the statements which were used to obtain convictions. However, such methods violated the 1929 Geneva Conventions forbidding method of coercion which had been used to get confessions under Article 63. In addition the trials used hearsay evidence, which was forbidden in American courts-martial–the standard by which the trials needed to be carried out according to the laws of war. Because of this, the Germans convicted of the "Malmédy Massacre" had their convictions overturned.

98. See Arnold P. Krammer, "German Prisoners of War in the United States", *Military Affairs*, Vol. 40 No. 2, 1976. pp. 68–73; MacKenzie, "Treatment of Prisoners", pp. 490–1. Krammer offers an overview of the set-up and running of the camps.

99. Krammer, "German Prisoners of War", pp. 70–1.

100. Arnold Krammer, "Japanese Prisoners of War in America", *The Pacific Historical Review*, Vol. 52 No. 1, 1983. pp. 80–1.

101. Krammer, "Japanese Prisoners", pp. 81–4.

102. Goldsmith, *The Terror Presidency*, p. 50. Goldsmith provides a useful overview of the case and comments on its contemporary relevance in light of the Bush administration's policy of using military commissions to try terrorists.

103. *Ex parte Quirin* (63 S. Ct. 2 87 L. Ed. 3 [1942])

104. See *Ex parte Quirin*. To support this conclusion, the Court cited the 1907 Hague Conventions, as well as the military manuals of Britain and Germany and the writings of several international legal scholars.

105. Goldsmith, *The Terror Presidency*, p. 52.

106. A useful summary of Bush's 2001 proposal and *Ex parte Quirin* can be found in Christopher M. Evans, "Terrorism on Trial: The President's Constitutional Authority to Order the Prosecution of Suspected Terrorists by Military Commission", *Duke Law Journal*, Vol. 51 No. 6, 2002. pp. 1831–56.

107. Goldsmith, *The Terror Presidency*, pp. 50–3.

108. Krammer, "Japanese Prisoners", p. 70.

109. Ibid. Not discussed here, however, are the over 100,000 Japanese civilians and Japanese-American citizens who were detained during the Second World War out of fear that they were a potential fifth column. This detention, now widely regarded as unjustified, was upheld by the Supreme Court in 1944. I have chosen not to discuss this issue as it falls outside the subject of prisoners of war and more into the issue of civilian internment. This is not to downplay the significance of civilian internment, but has more to do with the consideration of the length of this work.

110. Krammer, "Japanese Prisoners", p. 68.

111. Cited in Mackenzie, "Treatment of Prisoners", p. 517.

112. Krammer, "Japanese Prisoners", pp. 69–70.

113. Krammer, "Japanese Prisoners", p. 72 and p. 74. According to Kramer, there were two interrogation centres during the War: at Fort Hunt near Washington and Byron Hot Springs near San Francisco. Given the descriptions of eight-foot high fences, barred windows and heavy gates for an incredibly secretive intelligence-gathering operation, one cannot help but think of modern comparisons with Guantánamo Bay. Still, if the records that Krammer looks at are accurate, there were several key differences between the two. First, at no time did the government try to reclassify the Japanese prisoners as anything other than POWs. This would have been very hard to do, given the way the Japanese had been caught and given that, for the most part, they qualified under the Geneva and Hague Treaties. Second, interrogations "were generally conducted in an informal atmosphere" in interviews that lasted from forty-five minutes to an hour. These interviews were conducted at a rate of two or three each day for a week or more. In this way, they seem to be a contrast to an apparently much harsher Guantánamo regime.

114. Mackenzie, "Treatment of Prisoners", p. 514.

115. Gary Solis, "Obedience to Orders: History and Abuses at Abu Ghraib Prison", *Journal of International Criminal Justice*, Vol. 2. No. 4, 2004. pp. 988–98. p. 991. Solis notes, the International Military Tribunals concluded that the true

test was not whether or not the manifestly illegal order existed, but whether moral choice was in fact possible.

116. Moorehead, *Dunant's Dream*, pp. 530–8.

117. Eva-Maria Stolberg, "Yalta Conference", in *Encyclopedia of Prisoners of War and Internment*. ed. Jonathan F. Vance, Santa Barbara: ABC-CLIO, 2000. pp. 345–5. See also Anne Applebaum, *Gulag: A History of the Soviet Camps*, London: Penguin Books Limited, 2004. Rafael Zagovec notes, of the approximately 1.8 million prisoners eventually repatriated to the USSR, 150,000 were sentenced to six years of forced labour for "aiding the enemy". Almost all of the other former POWs experienced hostility enabled by Josif Stalin's infamous Order 270 which labelled all Red Army soldiers who allowed themselves to be captured alive as "traitors to the motherland". "World War II–Eastern Front" in *Encyclopedia of Prisoners of War and Internment*. ed. Jonathan F. Vance, Santa Barbara: ABC-CLIO, 2000. pp. 329–33.

118. Richard D. Wiggers, "Forcible Repatriation" in *Encyclopedia of Prisoners of War and Internment*, ed. Jonathan F. Vance, Santa Barbara: ABC-CLIO, 2000. pp. 100–2.

119. However, Cathal J. Nolan points out that the Soviets were holding 60,000 US POWs and US policy developed out of a concern to get these prisoners back. This, of course, might not have happened if the US did not force the Russians back to the Soviet Union. See Cathal J. Nolan, "Americans in the Gulag: Detention of US Citizens by Russia and the Onset of the Cold War, 1944–9", *Journal of Contemporary History*, Vol. 24 No. 4 (October 1990), 523–45.

120. Nolan, "Americans in the Gulag", p. 526.

121. This view was backed by the senior American military officer in Russia, Major General John R. Deane Nolan, "Americans in the Gulag", pp. 526–7.

122. Nolan cites Russell Buhite, "Soviet/American Relations and the Repatriation of Prisoners of War, 1945", *Historian*, May 1973, pp. 385–6. "Americans in the Gulag", p. 527 and note 15, p. 542.

123. Nolan, "Americans in the Gulag", p. 530.

124. Nolan, "Americans in the Gulag", p. 531.

125. Nolan, "Americans in the Gulag", p. 534.

126. Best, *War and Law Since 1945*, pp. 89–91.

127. Best, *War and Law Since 1945*, p. 109.

128. Best, *War and Law Since 1945*, p. 110–11.

129. Jean S. Pictet, ed. *Commentary: III Geneva Convention Relative to the Treatment of Prisoners of War*, Geneva: International Committee of the Red Cross, 1960. p. 413.

130. Pictet, *Commentary*, p. 415.

131. Best, *War and Law since 1945*, pp. 137–8.

132. Text found in Pictet, *Commentary*, p. 423.

133. Other countries which made similar reservations were: Albania, Bulgaria, the Byelorussian Soviet Socialist Republic, the People's Republic of China, Czechoslovakia, the German Democratic Republic, Hungary, the Democratic People's Republic of Korea, Poland, Rumania, the Ukrainian Soviet Socialist Republic

and the People's Republic of Vietnam. List found in Pictet, *Commentary*, p. 423.

134. Cooke, "Introduction", p. 7.

135. For an account of the attempts at reform at the beginning of the twentieth century, see Morgan, "The Background of the Uniform Code of Military Justice". Morgan was the protégé of one of the main voices for reform, General Samuel T. Ansell. Morgan recounts how Ansell's push for reform was rejected by a hostel military establishment.

136. Solis, "Obedience to Orders", p. 991. Solis notes that this had actually been the US policy until the 1914 manual on the laws of war was published which "ignored previous military and civilian case law of the previous 110 years." The 1944 version of the Field Manual reversed the 1914 Manual. pp. 990–1. The US law of war manual was revised twice during the Second World War, in 1940 and 1944.

137. Cooke, "Introduction", p. 7.

138. It was at first named the National Military Establishment in 1947, but this was changed in 1949–apparently because of the unfortunate acronym of "NME".

139. Gary Solis, *Marines and Military Law in Vietnam: Trial by Fire*, Washington: History and Museums Division Headquarters, U.S. Marine Corps, 1989. p. 6. It should also be pointed out that the 1948 Elson Act sought to amend the Articles of War in a way that answered a lot of the criticism of the US system of military justice. However, Forrestal saw that a continued system of separated branches of law for the different services was contrary to the unification of the armed services. Also see Cooke, "Introduction", p. 7.

140. Solis, "Obedience to Orders", p. 994.

141. This, notes Cooke, proved to be a formidable task for the judge advocates of the day. "Introduction", p. 8.

142. The six articles of the Code of Conduct are: (1) I am an American, fighting in the forces which guard my country and our way of life. I am prepared to give my life in their defence. (2) I will never surrender of my own free will. If in command, I will never surrender the members of my command while they still have the means to resist. (3) If I am captured, I will continue to resist by all means available. I will make every effort to escape and aid others to escape. I will accept neither parole nor special favours from the enemy. (4) If I become a prisoner of war, I will keep faith with my fellow prisoners. I will give no information or take part in any action which might be harmful to my comrades. If I am senior, I will take command. If not, I will obey the lawful orders of those appointed over me, and will back them up in every way. (5) When questioned, should I become a prisoner of war, I am required to give only name, rank, service number, and date of birth. I will evade answering further questions to the utmost of my ability. I will make no oral or written statements disloyal to my country and its allies or harmful to their cause. (6) I will never forget that I am an American, fighting for freedom, responsible for my actions, and dedicated to the principles which made my country free. I will trust in my God and in the United States of America.

143. However, it is important to remember that the laws of war do allow for detaining powers to ask and question their prisoners, but restrict their ability to bribe and, more importantly for the welfare of POWs, torture is forbidden. As A.P.V. Rogers has argued, "There seems to be a popular misconception... that you cannot interrogate prisoners of war. This is not so. Prisoners of war are often a valuable source of military intelligence and there is nothing in the Geneva Prisoner of War Convention that prohibits questioning them. However, under Article 17, they are not obliged to answer questions (only to give their name, rank and date of birth) and no torture, coercion, threats, insults, or unpleasant disadvantageous treatment may be used to secure information from them. The situation is no different in the case of people classified as illegal combatants. They can be questioned but if they refuse to answer question, basic human rights standards prevent torture, inhuman or degrading treatment." Letter published in the *Independent*, 31 January 2002. A.P.V. Rogers, *Law on the Battlefield*, second edition. Manchester: Jurispublishing, Manchester University Press, 2004. p. 55–6. Also see Article 17 of the Geneva Convention relative to the treatment of Prisoners of War.

3. LEGAL REVOLUTION: AMERICA AND THE LAWS OF WAR AFTER VIETNAM

1. Army Field Manual 27–10 18 July 1956. Those working on the manual were only given a few weeks to fully update the previous version issued in 1914 (updated in 1918) in order to reflect the changes and developments that came with US ratification of the 1949 Geneva Conventions. Produced under strict time and resource constraints, the 1956 version stripped out the footnotes of previous versions. While understandable given the circumstances, this in effect removed the history and context which explained the law, US practice and provided examples of application of the law. The 1956 version was subsequently updated in 1976 after the Vietnam War but did not change the approach taken. Other services, particularly Navy and the Air Force, went on to develop their own law of war doctrines. The US Department of Defense is currently working on a new Law of War Manual, with an expected release in 2010. When produced, it will reflect the approach taken in earlier manuals and incorporate explanations and footnotes. It will also apparently be the document to which all service manuals will be expected to comply.

2. Seymour M. Hersh, *Chain of Command: The Road from 9/11 to Abu Ghraib*, New York: HarperCollins Publishers, 2005.

3. Steven Keeva, "Lawyers in the War Room", *American Bar Association Journal*, December 1991. pp. 52–9. p. 52.

4. Keeva, "Lawyers in the War Room", p. 52.

5. The Son Thang massacre occurred on the night of 19 February 1970 where a Marine night patrol killed sixteen women and children in a Vietnamese hamlet. See Gary Solis, *Son Thang; An American War Crime*, New York: Bantam, 1998.

6. Gary Solis, *Marines and Military Law in Vietnam: Trial by Fire*, Washington: History and Museums Division Headquarters, U.S. Marine Corps, 1989. p. 14. As George Prugh notes, "The United States has never relinquished jurisdiction over its armed forces during combat; to do so in Vietnam would have been as unprecedented as it would have been impractical. During World War II, for example, the United States kept jurisdiction over U.S. troops in the United Kingdom." *Law at War: Vietnam 1964–1973*, Washington: Department of the Army, 1975. p. 89.

7. Solis, *Marines and Military Law in Vietnam*, p. 14.

8. Ibid., p. 14.

9. Prugh, *Law at War*, p. 87.

10. Prugh, *Law at War*, pp. 89–90.

11. Frederic L. Borch, *Judge Advocates in Combat: Army Lawyers in Military Operations from Vietnam to Haiti*, Washington: Office of the Judge Advocate General and Center of Military History United States Army, 2001. pp. 22–3. Also see Prugh, *Law at War*, pp. 109–10.

12. Borch, *Judge Advocates in Combat*, p. 23.

13. Ibid. As Borch notes, Article 2 of the UCMJ permits the courts-martial of civilians "accompanying an armed force in the field." However, that provision applied only in "time of war", and it was unclear whether the fighting in Vietnam even constituted a war.

14. Solis, *Marines and Military Law*, pp. 99–100. Solis cites a letter from then Major General George S. Prugh to Brigadier General Edwin H. Simmons dated 29 December 1988. Available in the comment folder of the Marines and Military Law in Vietnam file at the Marine Corps Historical Division. Solis also notes that there were many in the US embassy who felt that it was "politically unacceptable" to have Americans prosecuted by the Vietnamese. Solis, *Marines and Military Law in Vietnam*, p. 99.

15. The article states that "In time of war, persons serving with or accompanying an armed force in the field" are subject to certain provisions of the UCMJ.

16. Prugh, *Law at War*, pp. 109–10.

17. The case of problems over jurisdiction regarding private military firms is discussed in Chapter 5.

18. Prugh, *Law at War*, p. 62.

19. It was the position of the International Committee of the Red Cross (ICRC) that the NLF was bound by the Geneva Conventions (or at least the customary law listed under Common Article 3) as it comprised nationals of a state whose government had ratified the Conventions. However, the NLF argued that it was not bound by the Conventions because it had not taken part in their negotiations. See Geoffrey Best, *Law and War Since 1945*, Oxford University Press, 1994. p. 364. A legal justification of this argument was put forward in an anonymous note in the Harvard Law Review, "The Geneva Convention and the Treatment of Prisoners of War in Vietnam", in Richard Falk, ed., *The Vietnam War and International Law*, Vol. 2, Princeton University Press, 1969. pp. 398–415.

20. Prugh, *Law at War*, p. 63.

21. William Hays Parks, "The Law of War Advisor", *JAG Journal*, Vol. 31, Summer 1980, pp. 1–52. pp. 13–17.

22. Parks, "The Law of War Advisor", p. 14. According to Parks, tribunals consisted of three officers who, insofar as practical, were familiar with the Geneva Conventions. At least one member of the tribunal was to be a judge advocate.

23. Prugh, *Law at War*, p. 62.

24. Borch, *Judge Advocates in Combat*, p. 11.

25. Borch, *Judge Advocates in Combat*, p. 11.

26. Ibid. Borch and Prugh note that this resulted in Viet Cong captives often being placed in the same prisons as common criminals and political prisoners. Prugh, *Law at War*, p. 64.

27. Borch, *Judge Advocates in Combat*, p. 12.

28. There are several good accounts of the treatment received by Americans held in Vietnam. One of the best is written by perhaps the most famous of the American POWs, US Senator John McCain, *Faith of My Fathers*, New York: Random House, 1999.

29. For example, see Solis, *Marines and Military Law in Vietnam*, p. 2.

30. Borch, *Judge Advocates in Combat*, pp. 5–6.

31. Borch, *Judge Advocates in Combat*, pp. 10–13.

32. See Prugh, *Law at War*–especially chapters 2 and 3 for detail on the advice given to South Vietnam and attempts to improve respect for the rule of law, pp. 15–39.

33. Borch, *Judge Advocates in Combat*, p. 16.

34. Prugh notes, "The soldier's first introduction to the Geneva Conventions was during basic training, where he received two hours of formal instruction, followed by a test, the results of which were noted on his record." *Law at War*, p. 74.

35. Prugh, *Law at War*, p. 75.

36. Card found in Appendix H of Prugh, *Law at War*.

37. Prugh, *Law at War*, pp. 75–6.

38. Message cited in Solis, *Marines and Military Law in Vietnam*, p. 34. Interestingly, Krulak's son, Charles C. Krulak, a retired Marine and commandant of the Marine Corps 1995–99, would speak out against the mistreatment of prisoners and the use of torture in 2009. See, Charles C. Krulak and Joseph P. Hoar, "Fear was no excuse to condone torture", *Miami Herald*, 11 September 2009. Available online at: http://www.miamiherald.com/opinion/other-views/story/1227832.html

39. Message cited in Solis, *Marines and Military Law in Vietnam*, p. 34.

40. Prugh, *Law at War*, p. 74

41. Borch, *Judge Advocates in Combat*, p. 22.

42. There have been several books on the massacre at My Lai already published, and so the argument will not go into the details of the event. For an account of the incident by the reporter who broke the story, see Seymour M. Hersh, *Cover-Up: The Army's Secret Investigation of the Massacre at My Lai 4*, New York: Random House, 1972. See also Michael Bilton and Kevin Sim, *Four Hours in My Lai: a War Crime and its Aftermath*, London: Viking, 1992.

43. Famously, despite receiving a life sentence for the massacre, Calley was released from jail by Nixon and only served three and a half years of house arrest.

44. Guenter Lewy, *America in Vietnam*, New York: Oxford University Press, 1978. pp. 328–9.

45. Parks, "The Law of War Advisor", pp. 13–14.

46. Lewy, *America in Vietnam*, p. 234.

47. Prugh, *Law at War*, p. 107.

48. On "Project 100,000" and its effects, see Solis, *Marines and Military Law*, especially pp. 73–4. Also Kelly M. Greenhill, "Don't dumb down the Army", *New York Times*, 17 February 2006, p. A23; Lewy discusses the matter in his book, *America in Vietnam*, p. 331.

49. W. Hays Parks, "Crimes in Hostilities", *Marine Corps Gazette* LX, no. 9 (September 1976), pp. 38–9. p. 38.

50. Lewy, *America in Vietnam*, p. 330.

51. Ibid.

52. See Prugh, *Law at War*, pp. 99–102 for a discussion of these difficulties as well as Solis, *Marines and Military Law in Vietnam*, pp. 48–51.

53. Department of the Army, "Report of the Department of the Army Review of the Preliminary Investigations into the My Lai Incident", Washington: Department of the Army, 1970. (Herein referred to as the "Peers Report".) See "Findings and Recommendations".

54. See Hersh, *Cover-Up*, p. 42. Hersh cites correspondence between General Bruce Palmer and General Harold K. Johnson, Army Chief of Staff, in May 1968.

55. W. Hays Parks, "The United States Military and the Law of War: Inculcating an Ethos", *Social Research*, Vol. 69 No 4 (Winter 2002), pp. 981–1015. p. 984.

56. Parks, "The United States Military", p. 984.

57. Prugh, *Law at War*, p. v.

58. Lewy, *America in Vietnam*, p. 234.

59. Ibid.

60. Lewy, *America*, p. 268.

61. Lewy, *America*, p. 366. "Body count" refers to a measure of "success" of US forces in Vietnam. As confusion over the goals of the war grew, body counts–the number of individuals (presumably enemy forces) killed in an encounter–were presented to the public to demonstrate progress in the conflict. Unfortunately, or perhaps predictably, anyone killed in a skirmish, whether a member of the Viet Cong or a civilian, was reported as part of this body count. See Scott Sigmund Gartner and Marissa Edson Myers, "Body Counts and 'Success' in the Vietnam and Korean Wars", *Journal of Interdisciplinary History*, Vol. 25 No. 3, Winter 1995. pp. 377–95. Interestingly, Gartner and Myers note that "body counts" were also used in Korea, although the term is normally associated with the Vietnam War.

62. Lewy, *America*, p. 369.

63. See US Department of Defense, Directive 510077 "Department of Defense Law of War Program", 5 November 1974. There were several updates of this directive, in 1979 and in 1998. The most recent update is the US Department of Defense

Directive 2311.01E, "Department of Defense Law of War Program" of 9 May 2006. The 2006 updates reflect some of the controversies which came out of the War on Terror and the Iraq War which will be discussed in Chapters 4 and 5.

64. Parks, "The United States Military", pp. 985–6. See also W. Hays Parks, "The Gulf War: A Practitioner's View", *Dickinson Journal of International Law*, Vol. 10 No. 3, 1991–92. pp. 393–423, pp. 396–7. n. 29.

65. Parks, "The Gulf War", pp. 408–9.

66. The sources of this section are heavily dependent on books and articles written by individuals in or formerly in the military. It would seem that there has not been much research done on the development of operational law from a non-military perspective. One exception might be the work of critical legal scholars who claim that international legal institutions are moulded to serve the interests of dominant states, such as Thomas W. Smith, "The New Law of War: Legitimizing Hi-Tech and Infrastructural Violence", *International Studies Quarterly*, Vol. 46, 2002. pp. 355–74. See also Chris af Jochnick and Roger Normand, "The Legitimation of Violence: A Critical History of the Laws of War", *Harvard International Law Journal*, Vol. 35 No. 1, 1994. pp. 49–95; and Roger Normand and Chris af Jochnick "The Legitimation of Violence: A Critical Analysis of the Gulf War." *Harvard International Law Journal*, Vol. 35 No. 2, 1994. pp. 387–416. Smith argues that operational law, or the "new law of war", serves to merely legitimize violence rather than restrain it. "The new law of war burnishes hi–tech campaigns and boosts public relations, even as it undercuts customary limits on the use of force and erodes distinctions between soldiers and civilians." p. 356. Naturally, these arguments are very controversial and not typically accepted among law of war scholars who tend to work on the assumption that the law operates on the basis of protecting lives rather than serving state interests. af Jochnick and Normand do present a compelling case for arguing that the law of war has typically been the servant of state interests. However, it only seems to make sense that states would only sign on to those international agreements that were in some way compatible with their long term interests, given that states rarely act out of purely altruistic motives. In this sense, the argument presented by af Jochnick and Normand may be original–but ultimately of questionable use in terms of understanding the politics of the law of war. While the critical argument may make more sense when applied to targeting issues, its line of reasoning does not seem to adequately explain US attempts to implement the law of war in Korea or Vietnam in terms of policies towards prisoners of war. Therefore the critique of the critical legal scholars will not be given much attention in this work–especially as the focus of this work is not on the legitimation of violence.

67. Borch, *Judge Advocates in Combat*, p. 51.

68. Ibid.. It should be noted here that Borch is referring specifically to the Army JAGs, but it would be fair to say that this went for the entire Corps.

69. Borch, *Judge Advocates in Combat*, p. 62.

70. Parks, "The Gulf War", p. 397. Parks notes that many of the restrictions were put in place not because of the law, but because of political decisions or because of a mistaken belief that certain actions would violate the laws of war. Parks expands

on this argument in W.H. Parks, "Rolling Thunder and the Law of War", *Air University Review*, Vol XXXIII No. 2, 1982 and "Linebacker and the Law of War", *Air University Law Review*, XXXIV No. 2, 1983.

71. The term "activist lawyers" is borrowed from Parks, "The Gulf War", p. 400.

72. Parks, "The Gulf War", p. 394. On operational law see, David E. Graham, "Operational Law (OPLAW)–A Concept Comes of Age", *The Army Lawyer*, July 1987, pp. 9–10. Graham and Parks define the concept in very similar terms.

73. Parks, "The Gulf War", p. 398.

74. Graham, "Operational Law", p. 9.

75. Although Parks notes that the law of war remained the foundation for the operational law programme. "The Gulf War", p. 398.

76. William Eckhardt argues that an approach which teaches the law of war as a set of "positives" instead of "negatives" is more effective. Therefore, instead of instructing troops "Do not kill civilians", lawyers would tell troops "Marines fight only enemy combatants." See William George Eckhardt, "Lawyering for Uncle Sam When He Draws His Sword", *Chicago Journal of International Law*, Vol. 4, 2003. pp. 431–44; especially note 23, p. 440.

77. Borch, *Judge Advocates in Combat*, p. 318.

78. Parks, "The Gulf War", p. 398.

79. Parks, "The Gulf War", p. 399.

80. Borch, *Judge Advocates in Combat*, pp. 62–3.

81. Borch, *Judge Advocates in Combat*, p. 62. Incidentally, in Urgent Fury, Army lawyers determined that the Geneva Conventions applied and that all persons captured should be treated as prisoners of war. p. 66.

82. Borch, *Judge Advocates in Combat*, p. 65.

83. Stuart Taylor, "Treatment of prisoners is defended", *New York Times*, 29 October 1983. p. 7.

84. United Press International, "Grenada denies Amnesty International charges", 24 November 1983. The telegram was sent after the Prisoner of War camp had already been closed.

85. Borch, *Judge Advocates in Combat*, p. 66. Many of the captured Cubans claimed that they were not soldiers but construction workers. The US government replied that it was not at war with Cuba, but that the Cubans had willingly engaged in combat and had engaged in hostilities. See Taylor, "Treatment of Prisoners".

86. Mark Whitaker, Ron Moreau and Linda R. Prout, "The Battle for Grenada", *Newsweek*, 7 November 1983.

87. UPI, "100 Cuban Prisoners Return from Grenada", *New York Times*, 6 November 1983, p. 18. Interestingly, the US Senate adopted a non-binding resolution urging President Reagan to refuse to return Cuban POWs in Cuba unless Fidel Castro took back Cuban criminals who were allowed to come to the United States during a 1980 boatlift and who were being held in US prisons. However, such a step would have been illegal under the Geneva Conventions which prohibit the taking of hostages, in addition to their various repatriation provisions.

88. Editorial, "Remember Grenada?", *New York Times*, 15 December 1983, p. 30.

89. George Worme, "Red Cross complains about Richmond Hill prison conditions", United Press International, 2 December 1983. The ICRC, sticking with its policy of confidentiality, refused to comment on the report.

90. Editorial, "Remember Grenada?"

91. Borsch, *Judge Advocates in Combat*, p. 72.

92. Most of the law of the conflict's legalities surrounded three issues. First, the confusing legal status of the conflict; this was important for whether or not the Geneva Conventions would apply. (The Army lawyers determined that it did regardless.) Second, a mental hospital was bombed in the course of the campaign (it was unmarked, so that the Army judge advocate determined that there was no law of war violation). Third, there was the treatment of Cuban diplomats caught in the conflict.

93. Borsch, *Judge Advocates in Combat*, p. 68.

94. Marc L. Warren, "Operational Law–A Concept Matures", *Military Law Review*, Vol. 152, 1996, pp. 33–73. See pp. 37–40.

95. Borsch, *Judge Advocates in Combat*, pp. 68–9.

96. Borsch, *Judge Advocates in Combat*, p. 81.

97. Borsch, *Judge Advocates in Combat*, p. 81.

98. Eckhardt, "Lawyering for Uncle Sam", pp. 433–4. See also the Goldwater-Nichols Department of Defense Reorganization Act of 1986. Pub L. No. 99–433. The Act reorganized the command structure of the US military.

99. Borsch, *Judge Advocates in Combat*, pp. 95–6. Borch outlines five major concerns that were dealt with in advance. First, the issue of armed civilians accompanying the Panama Defense Forces; second, the circumstances under which civilian aircraft could be targeted; third, indirect fire in populated areas; fourth, the regulation of air-to-ground attacks in populated areas; and finally, the treatment of individuals captured or detained during hostilities. (Again it was determined that under the ROE all of those detained would be treated as Prisoners of War.) See Borch, *Judge Advocates in Combat*, pp. 96–7.

100. Eckhardt, "Lawyering for Uncle Sam", p. 440. However, one cannot help but wonder if this is an overstatement of the case. Given the history so far explored in this work, it is clear that the military appears to have claimed rather than reclaimed the law of war in terms of its implementation.

101. Dana Priest, "Captured Panamanians pose test of changing rules on POWs", *Washington Post*, 31 December 1989.

102. Priest, "Captured Panamanians". Quote from Staff Judge Advocated Wallace.

103. See Reuters, "Prisoner-of-war camp in Panama nearly full", *The Toronto Star*, 3 January 1990 and Scott Wallace, "Tent city prisoners await 'habeas grabus' process: The US has 15,000 Noriega troops behind wire and is sorting them into the good and the bad", *The Guardian*, 3 January 1990.

104. Borch, *Judge Advocates in Combat*, pp. 103–5.

105. This is dealt with under Chapter III "Penal and Disciplinary Sanctions" of the Third Geneva Convention.

106. See Borch, *Judge Advocates in Combat*, pp. 113–14. A similar incident would occur in Iraq when US Marines were videotaped shooting and killing an injured

Iraqi lying on the floor. See MSNBC, "U.S. probes shooting at Fallujah mosque: Video shows Marine killing wounded Iraqi" 16 November 2004. Available online: http://www.msnbc.msn.com/id/6496898

107. Americas Watch, "The Laws of War and the Panama Invasion", cited in Jim Lobe, "Panama: America's Watch cites U.S. violations of laws of war", Inter-Press Service 10 May 1990.

108. This section draws on material previously written by the author. See Stephanie Carvin, "Caught in the Cold: International Humanitarian Law and Prisoners of War During the Cold War", *Journal of Conflict and Security Law*, Vol. 11 No. 1, 2006. pp. 67–92.

109. Common Article 3 States: "In the case of armed conflict not of an international character occurring in the territory of one of the High Contracting Parties, each party to the conflict shall be bound to apply, as a minimum, the following provisions:

1. Persons taking no active part in the hostilities, including members of armed forces who have laid down their arms and those placed hors de combat by sickness, wounds, detention, or any other cause, shall in all circumstances be treated humanely, without any adverse distinction founded on race, colour, religion or faith, sex, birth or wealth, or any other similar criteria.

    To this end the following acts are and shall remain prohibited at any time and in any place whatsoever with respect to the above-mentioned persons:

    (a) Violence to life and person, in particular murder of all kinds, mutilation, cruel treatment and torture;

    (b) Taking of hostages;

    (c) Outrages upon personal dignity, in particular, humiliating and degrading treatment;

    (d) The passing of sentences and the carrying out of executions without previous judgment pronounced by a regularly constituted court affording all the judicial guarantees which are recognized as indispensable by civilized peoples.

2. The wounded and sick shall be collected and cared for.

    An impartial humanitarian body, such as the International Committee of the Red Cross, may offer its services to the Parties to the conflict.

    The Parties to the conflict should further endeavour to bring into force, by means of special agreements, all or part of the other provisions of the present Convention.

    The application of the preceding provisions shall not affect the legal status of the Parties to the conflict."

110. Ingrid Detter, *The Law of War*, Second Edition. Cambridge University Press, 2000. pp. 199–202. Detter notes that extending the Convention to internal wars could be done through a "literary interpretation construed regardless of the intention of the drafters" to consolidated resistance movements and to guerrillas. R.R. Baxter writes that the Geneva Conference of 1949 was "well aware of the problem implicit in the existence of guerilla and partisan warfare and seemed

to be under the impression that it had dealt with it in satisfactory fashion." Baxter, however, argues that this clearly was not the case. "So-called 'unprivileged belligerency'": spies, guerillas and saboteurs" in *British Yearbook of International Law*, Vol. XXVIII, 1952. pp. 336–7. Cited in Keith Suter, *An International Law of Guerilla Warfare: The Global Politics of Law Making*, London: Frances Pinter, 1984. pp. 13–14. Suter agrees, arguing that the 1949 Geneva Diplomatic Conference did not "deal satisfactorily with the status of a guerilla in an international conflict." p. 14.

111. This includes a series of General Assembly resolutions on issues such as "Respecting Human Rights in Armed Conflicts", "Protection of Journalists Engaged in Dangerous Missions in Areas of Armed Conflicts", and the "Basic Principles for the Protection of Civilian Populations in Armed Conflicts", as well as a series of UN Secretary-General's reports on human rights in armed conflict.

112. Suter, *An International Law of Guerrilla Warfare*, p. 80. Suter's book provides a good overview of the build up to and events at the Geneva Diplomatic Conference. Bothe, Partsch and Solf agree that by this point "a certain division of labour" had developed between the UN and the ICRC and the latter took on the task of drafting the concrete proposals. See Michael Bothe, Karl Joseph Partsch and Waldemar A. Solf, *New Rules for Victims of Armed Conflicts: Commentary on the Two 1977 Protocols Additional to the Geneva Conventions of 1949*, The Hague: Martinus Nijhoff, 1982.

113. Suter, *An International Law of Guerrilla Warfare*, pp. 98–9.

114. Suter, *An International Law of Guerrilla Warfare*, pp. 99–101.

115. David Forsythe, "Legal Management of Internal War: The 1977 Protocol on Non-International Armed Conflicts", *American Journal of International Law*, Vol. 72 No. 2, 1978. pp. 272–95.

116. The participation of the national liberation groups in the full deliberations marked a major difference in the Conference from the others that had taken place. Various international organizations were also represented in an observer status. See Adam Roberts and Richard Guelff, *Documents on the Laws of War*, Third Edition, Oxford University Press, 2000. p. 419. Such groups included the Palestine Liberation Organization and the African National Congress which, besides international recognition, also demanded full POW status for their captured personnel on account of what they felt to be the justness of their cause.

117. Christopher Greenwood, "A Critique of the Additional Protocols to the Geneva Conventions of 1949" in Christopher Greenwood, *Essays on War in International Law*, London: Cameron, May 2006. pp. 201–24. p. 206.

118. Suter, *An International Law of Guerrilla Warfare*, p. 78.

119. For a critical look at what happened at the Diplomatic Conference, including the politics involved in the negotiations, Keith Suter, *An International Law of Guerrilla Warfare*. Also useful is W. Hays Parks, "Air War and the Law of War", *Air Force Law Review*, Vol. 32 No. 1, 1990. pp. 1–225. While the focus of the article is on Air War and targeting, there are quite lengthy sections on the history of the laws of war, the Diplomatic Conference, the US Review of the 1977

Protocols and reasons for the US ultimately rejecting them. Best, on the other hand, argues that the politicization of the conference may be overstated. "The difference between 1949 and 1974–7 is not, as some anguished complaints about the latter alleged, that humanitarian legislation had become politicized. Indeed, the proceedings were in some ways highly political but... that was nothing new. The making of international law of war always had been political... What from one angle could be presented as 'the reaffirmation and development of IHL', from another angle had more attractiveness as a project to de-Westernize the law of war." Geoffrey Best, *War & Law Since 1945*, Oxford University Press, 1994. p. 415.

120. Israel voted against for reasons that are, perhaps, fairly obvious.
121. Forsythe, "Legal Management of Internal War", p. 279.
122. Detter, *The Law of War*, p. 202.
123. Bothe *et al.*, *New Rules for Victims of Armed Conflicts*, p. 605; Forsythe, "Legal Management of Internal War", pp. 278–82.
124. Bothe *et al.*, *New Rules for Victims of Armed Conflicts*, p. 605.
125. Quoted in Bothe *et al.*, *New Rules for Victims of Armed Conflicts*, pp. 606–7.
126. David P. Forsythe, *The Humanitarians*, Cambridge University Press, 2005. pp. 92–3.
127. Best, *War & Law*, p. 417.
128. George H. Aldrich, "New Life for the Laws of War", *American Journal of International Law*, Vol. 75 No. 4, October 1981. pp. 764–783.
129. George H. Aldrich, "Some Reflections on the Origins of the 1977 Geneva Protocols", in Christophe Swinarski ed., *Studies and Essays on International Humanitarian Law and Red Cross Principles in Honour of Jean Pictet*, Hague: Martinus Nijhoff, 1984. pp. 129–37.
130. Aldrich, "Some Reflections" pp. 130–2 and Aldrich, "New Life for the Laws of War", p. 766.
131. Aldrich, "New Life for the Laws of War" p. 768.
132. Aldrich, "New Life for the Laws of War" p. 770. Of course, as Aldrich points out, there were exceptions made for spies, mercenaries and guerrillas who take advantage of their apparent civilian status and conceal their weapons heading into an attack.
133. Parks, "The Gulf War", p. 398.
134. Parks, "The Gulf War", p. 399.
135. Douglas J. Feith, "Law in the Service of Terror—The Strange Case of the Additional Protocol", *The National Interest*, No. 1, 1985; Douglas J. Feith, "'International Responses', in Uri Ra'anan *et al* eds, *Hydra of Carnage, International Linkages of Terrorism*, Lanham, MD: Lexington Books, 1986; and Douglas Feith, "Protocol I: Moving Humanitarian Law Backwards", *Akron Law Review*, Vol. 19, pp. 531–5.
136. How far Feith was able to influence the eventual decision is not entirely clear. Speaking confidentially, one Department of Defense employee who participated in the process indicated that the legal review concluded would have put the US in a position to ratify both Protocols (with the proper reservations put in place,

akin to those of other Western countries). However, Feith, upon taking up his position in the DoD, indicated to the lawyers that the US would not be signing the Protocols–period. This, apparently, put an end to finding ways to make ratification possible and the military lawyers overseeing the process felt free to criticize Protocol I as much as they could. That Feith was the Under Secretary for Defense in the first George W. Bush Administration in 2001–5 makes his views particularly interesting for this work.

137. "Message to the Senate Transmitting a Protocol to the 1949 Geneva Conventions" 29 January 1987. The speech is available online at the website of the Ronald Reagan Presidential Library, http://www.reagan.utexas.edu/archives/speeches/1987/012987B.HTM.

138. The author expects this to remain true even with "less hostile" administrations, like the Obama administration. This is mostly due to the difficulty of ratification posed by the Senate, which has been hostile to international treaties including the Convention on the Rights of the Child. Ideological opposition to international law, as well as concerns over sovereignty that grew in the 1980s and 1990s, will be discussed in Chapter 4.The US position was considered to have been summed up in Michael J. Matheson, "The United States Position on the Relation of Customary Law to the 1977 Protocols Additional to the 1949 Conventions", *American University Journal of International Law and Policy*, 1987. pp. 419–31. Still, as late as 2005 there was some confusion as to whether or not Matheson was speaking in an official capacity. Regardless of whether or not it was an official statement, it seems to reflect current US practice. Aldrich's disappointment with the decision is made clear in a follow-up to his "Some Reflections" article where he states: "Looking back from 1997, I deeply regret that 20 years ago I did not press, within the executive branch of my government, for prompt submission of the Protocols to the Senate of the United States for advice and consent for their ratification. All but a very few provisions had been adopted in Geneva with the complete support of both the U.S. State and Defense Departments, and I believe President Carter and Secretary Vance would have endorsed them. I failed to realize that, with the passage of time, those in both Departments who had negotiated and supported the Protocols would be replaced by skeptics and individuals with a different political agenda." George H. Aldrich, "Comments on the Geneva Conventions", *International Review of the Red Cross* No. 320, October 1997. pp. 508–10.

139. The term is borrowed from Françoise J. Hampson, "Means and Methods of Warfare in the Conflict in the Gulf", in *The Gulf War 1990–91 in International and English Law*, ed. Peter Rowe. London: Routledge, 1993. pp. 108–10. p. 108.

140. Christopher Greenwood, "Customary International Law and the First Geneva Protocol of 1977 in the Gulf Conflict" in *The Gulf War 1990–91 in International and English Law*, ed. Peter Rowe. London: Routledge, 1993. pp. 63–88, p. 64.

141. Greenwood, "Customary International Law", p. 65.

142. On 13 February 1991, there was an attack on the Amiriya bunker which resulted in 400 civilian deaths. The United States Air Force commanders who ordered the attack argued that the bunker had previously been used in the Iran-Iraq war for military purposes and that they did not suspect that this had changed. The Americans maintained that the structure housed a command and control centre, from which military radio communications had been monitored for two or three weeks. Some information here from Greenwood, "Customary International Law".

143. Michael Wines, "After the War: P.O.W's; Ex–P.O.W's Offer Accounts of Terror and Torture in Iraq", *The New York Times*, 15 March 1991. p. 1.

144. See *The Sunday Times*, "The humbling of Saddam Hussein", 3 March 1991; Guy Gugliotta, "U.S. forces battle Iraqi tanks on eve of cease-fire talks", *Washington Post*, 3 March 1991, p. A1.

145. Philip Stephens, "The Gulf War; troops prepare to care for prisoners by the thousand", *Financial Times*, 28 January 1991. p. 3.

146. Edward Cody, "Friendly persuasion–stick, then carrot; torrent of leaflets promise embattled Iraqis 'Arab hospitality' if they surrender", *Washington Post*, 7 February 1991. p. A21.

147. William Branigin, "Defectors called sign of air attacks' toll; Allied generals say strikes on Iraqi troops causing deprivations, shattering morale", *Washington Post*, 9 February 1991.

148. Peter Rowe, "Prisoners of War in the Gulf Arena" in *The Gulf War 1990–91 in International and English Law*, ed. Peter Rowe, London: Routledge, 1993. pp. 188–204. p. 197.

149. Rowe, "Prisoners of War in the Gulf Arena", p. 198.

150. Michael R. Gordon, "After the war; G.I.'s, facing a moral quandary, try to aid Iraqis", *New York Times*, 2 April 1991. p. 1.

151. Peter Rowe, "Prisoners of War in the Gulf Arena", p. 203.

152. David Garratt, "The Role of Legal Advisors in the Armed Forces," in *The Gulf War 1990–91 in International and English Law*, ed. Peter Rowe. London: Routledge, 1993. p. 59. Garratt notes that this was partly due to the wider responsibilities of US legal advisers.

153. Keeva, "Lawyers in the War Room", p. 52. Of course not everyone agreed. Critical lawyers and scholars had a range of complaints and allegation against the campaign and its toll on civilians: first, that the attacks were disproportionate; second, that the Coalition's definition of what constituted a "military" target was too loose and operationalized at the expense of civilian lives; third, that while the laws of war may take targeting into consideration, they do not take into account the after-effects–some of which were catastrophic for civilians; fourth, that while the allies might claim due diligence for any mistakes made, they also might be held to a higher standard of conduct; and fifth, that the *jus ad bellum* was used to create a more permissible environment for the *jus in bello* which allowed so much carnage to take place. In particular, critical studies of the war argue that the significant problem with its conduct was that proportionality and necessity were measured such a way as to dismiss the long-term effects of the

bombing campaign. Judith Gardam largely argues, "The majority of civilian casualties appear to be the result of targeting objectives which, although apparently serving a military purpose, and thus a legitimate military objective, were also directed at facilities integral to the survival of the civilian population... It appears, therefore, that it is not so much the direct casualties during the attack that are the most problematic, but rather the longer term casualties." In other words, the targeting of a military objective might have been technically legal, but the horrific after-effects suggest it was not or should not have been. Judith G. Gardam, "Non-combatant Immunity and the Gulf Conflict", *Virginia Journal of International Law*, Vol. 32, 1992. pp. 13–836. p. 832. Also see Normand and af Jochnick, "The Legitimation of Violence"; Smith, "The New Law of War".

154. Keeva, "Lawyers in the War Room", pp. 52–3.
155. Cited in af Jochnick and Normand, "A Critical Analysis of the Gulf War", p. 409. It should be pointed out that both organizations remained critical over certain aspects of the bombing campaign.
156. Of course, the word "violation" seems to suggest a deliberate plan to infringe upon the law of war. However, the term is here used to also encompass accidents which may happen in the fog of war where no one is necessarily to blame.
157. Warren, "Operational Law", p. 35.
158. Carl von Clausewitz, *On War*, ed. and trans. Michael Howard and Peter Paret, University Press, 1976. p. 624.
159. US Department of Defence, "Conduct of the Persian Gulf War: Final Report to Congress", Washington: Department of Defence, April 1992. p. 624. Interestingly, the Report was authored under the supervision of the future Vice President Richard Cheney, who was the Secretary of Defense during the First Gulf War.
160. Parks, "The United States Military and the Law of War", p. 7.
161. Ibid.
162. For a discussion on operations other than war, see Warren, "Operational Law", especially pp. 41–8 and pp. 51–7. Also, for a slightly partial look at the law in operations other than war, see the chapters on Haiti and Somalia in Borch, *Judge Advocates in Combat*. In his efforts to praise the efforts of judge advocates, Borch tends to paint a picture that must be a little rosier than the reality in both operations. For example, in his Somalia chapter Borch barely mentions the Battle of Mogadishu which took place on 3–4 October 1994, which saw eighteen US military personnel killed as well as hundreds of Somali dead and thousands wounded. The situation was certainly a mess–politically if not legally.
163. Warren, "Operational Law", pp. 58–61.
164. Anthony Zinni, "The SJA in Future Operations", *Marine Corps Gazette*, February 1996. pp. 15–17.
165. Cited in Sean D. Murphy ed., *United States Practice in International Law: Volume 1: 1999–2001*, Cambridge University Press, 2002. p. 369.

4. JUST CAUSE AND JUST MEANS? LINKING THE PURPOSE AND TACTICS OF WAR AFTER 9/11

1. A modified part of this chapter appeared in Stephanie Carvin, "Linking Purpose and Tactics: America and the Reconsideration of the Laws of War During the 1990s", *International Studies Perspectives*, Vol. 9 No. 2, May 2008, pp. 128–43.

2. Julie A. Mertus, *The United Nations and Human Rights: A Guide for a New Era*, London: Routledge, 2005. p. 8.

3. Cassese, *International Law*, p. 396.

4. Cassese, *International Law*, p. 404. Cassese notes that this point of view can be supported by the *Tadič (Decision on Interlocutory Appeal)* decision by the International Criminal Tribunal for the former Yugoslavia, which noted "the impetuous development and propagation in the international community of human rights doctrines... had brought about significant changes in international law..." Cited in Cassese, 404, note 2. The International Court of Justice made a similar decision in the *Nuclear Weapons case*, arguing that the protection of human rights does not cease in times of war, except for some provisions that may be derogated from in a time of national emergency as defined under Article 4 of the International Covenant of Civil and Political Rights. Jean-Marie Henckaerts and Louise Doswald-Beck, *Customary International Humanitarian Law*, Volume 1: Rules, Cambridge University Press, 2005. p. 301.

5. For a critique of merging the laws of war with human rights law, see Yoram Dinstein, *The Conduct of Hostilities under the Law of International Armed Conflict*, Cambridge University Press, 2004; additionally, René Provost illustrates the problems of merging the two areas of law in René Provost, *International Human Rights and Humanitarian Law*, Cambridge Studies in International and Comparative Law, Cambridge University Press, 2002. For a look at the issue in the wake of allegations after the exposure of the Haditha incident, see Mackubin Thomas Owens, "Men@War: Hadithah in context", *National Review Online*, 30 May 2006. http://article.nationalreview.com/?q=MGFjZGFhZGJjYWM0NTJlM2IzMjAxM2I4NDEwYWM5NWI; There has also been much discussion about this issue in the UK where the line between human rights and the laws of war has been even further blurred. See Michael Smith. "Iraq battle stress worse than WWII", *The Sunday Times*, 6 November 2005; and Thomas Harding, "Britain's Armed Forces 'under legal siege'", *Daily Telegraph*, 15 July 2005. http://www.telegraph.co.uk/news/main.jhtml;jsessionid=UCQBOHAGB0MNPQFIQMFCM5WAVCBQYJVC?xml=/news/2005/07/15/nforces15.xml.

6. For a discussion of attempts to ensure protections for POWs in Cold War conflicts, see Stephanie Carvin, "Caught in the Cold: International Humanitarian Law and Prisoners of War During the Cold War", *Journal of Conflict and Security Law*, Vol. 11 No. 1, 2006. pp. 67–92.

7. The discussion of legal issues here is brief. Much has been written on the legal aspects of the Kosovo campaign. Some useful sources include: Adam Roberts, "Nato's 'Humanitarian War' over Kosovo", *Survival*, Vol. 41 No. 3, 1999. pp. 102–23; Andru E. Wall, *Legal and Ethical Lessons of NATO's Kosovo Cam-*

paign, International Law Studies Volume 78, Newport, RI: Naval War College, 2002; Nicholas J. Wheeler, "Chapter 8: The Kosovo Bombing Campaign" in Christian Reus-Smit ed., *The Politics of International Law*, Cambridge University Press, 2004. Also see the series of articles published in the *American Journal of International Law*, Vol. 93 No. 4, Oct., 1999; the special section in *International and Comparative Law Quarterly*, Vol. 49 no. 4, 2000, including Vaughan Lowe, "Legal Issues Arising in the Kosovo Crisis"; "Special issue: The Kosovo Crisis and International Humanitarian Law", *International Review of the Red Cross*, No. 837, March 2000.

8. See, for example "NATO grapples with 'war by committee'", CNN, 19 April 1999, http://www.cnn.com/US/9904/19/war.by.committee/and "Nato leadership splits revealed", BBC News, 9 March 2000, http://news.bbc.co.uk/1/hi/world/europe/671420.stm.

9. Daalder and O'Hanlon, *Winning Ugly*, p. 118.

10. For a discussion of this, see Nicholas J. Wheeler, "The Kosovo Bombing Campaign" in Christian Reus-Smit ed. *The Politics of International Law*, Cambridge University Press, 2004, pp. 189–216. Wheeler points out,"What makes this dispute so fascinating is that there was agreement on the legal rules that should be applied, but disagreement over the correct application of the rules." p. 191.

11. Lieutenant General Michael Short, USAF (Retired), "Operation Allied Force from the Perspective of the NATO Air Commander" pp. 19–26 in Andru E. Wall, *Legal and Ethical Lessons of NATO's Kosovo Campaign*, International Law Studies Volume 78, Newport, RI: Naval War College, 2002. p. 25.

12. Short, "Operation Allied Force", p. 20.

13. Ivo H. Daalder and Michael E. O'Hanlon, *Winning Ugly: NATO's War to Save Kosovo*, Washington: Brookings Institute Press, 2000. p. 4. This raises issues relating to discrimination which will be discussed below.

14. Daalder and O'Hanlon, *Winning Ugly*, pp. 105–6. See also James E. Baker, "Judging Kosovo: The Legal Process, the Law of Armed Conflict and the Commander in Chief", pp. 7–26 in Wall, *Legal and Ethical Lessons of NATO's Kosovo Campaign*. Baker servers as the Special Assistant to the President and Legal Adviser to the National Security Council during Operation Allied Force.

15. Short, "Operation Allied Force", p. 24.

16. Clark, *Waging Modern War*, p. 426. However, Clark goes on to add, "We paid a price in operational effectiveness by having to constrain the nature of the operation to fit within the political and legal concerns of NATO member nations, but the price brought significant strategic benefits that future political and military leaders must recognize." p. 430. Clark was also a fairly strong advocate for a NATO role in Afghanistan, claiming that US political and military leaders had learned the wrong lesson from the Kosovo campaign and his book. See Gen. Wesley Clark "An Army of One?" *Washington Monthly*, September 2002. Available online: http://www.washingtonmonthly.com/features/2001/0209.clark.html.

17. Clark, *Waging Modern War*, p. 434.

18. Adam Roberts, "The Law of War After Kosovo", in Wall, *Legal and Ethical Lessons of NATO's Kosovo Campaign*. pp. 401–32. p. 420.

19. Text of the *Final Report to the Prosecutor by the Committee Established to Review the NATO Bombing Campaign Against the Federal Republic of Yugoslavia* is available at: http://www.un.org/icty/pressreal/nato061300.htm.

20. Judith A. Miller, "Commentary", in Wall, *Legal and Ethical Lessons of NATO's Kosovo Campaign*. pp. 107–12. pp. 111–12.

21. David B. Rivkin, Jr. and Lee A. Casey, "The Rocky Shoals of International Law, *The National Interest*, Winter 2000/2001.

22. Jesse Helms, "American Sovereignty and the UN", *The National Interest*, Winter 2000/2001.

23. John Bolton, "The Global Prosecutors: Hunting War Criminals in the Name of Utopia", *Foreign Affairs*, Vol. 78 No. 1, 1999. pp 157–64. pp. 158–9. For his critique of the ICC, see John R. Bolton, "Courting Danger: What's Wrong with the International Criminal Court", *The National Interest*, Winter 1998/1999.

24. David P. Forsythe, "The United States and International Criminal Justice", *Human Rights Quarterly*, 24 (2002), pp. 974–91. p. 975.

25. Forsythe, "The United States and International Criminal Justice", p. 975. For some of the exceptionalist critics of international law, the only law that could or should matter is treaty law which is acknowledged as part of US law in the Constitution. For others, any form of international law is necessarily vague and fuzzy and, because it lacks any form of enforcement, is not real law.

26. Peter J. Spiro, "The New Sovereigntists: American Exceptionalism and Its False Prophets", *Foreign Affairs*, Vol. 79 No. 6, November/December 2000. pp. 9–15.

27. Spiro, "The New Sovereigntists"

28. In particular, New Sovereigntists argue with post-modern thinkers on sovereignty and realists such as Stephen Krasner (and his book *Sovereignty, Organized Hypocrisy*, Princeton University Press, 1999).

29. Jeremy Rabkin, *Law Without Nations: Why Constitutional Government Requires Sovereign States*, Princeton University Press, 2005. p. 68

30. Rabkin, *Law Without Nations*, p. 255.

31. Jack L. Goldsmith and Eric A. Posner, *The Limits of International Law*, Oxford University Press, 2005. Also see the collection of essays, "The New York University-University of Virginia Conference on Exploring the Limits of International Law" *Virginia Journal of International Law*, Vol. 44 No. 1, Fall 2003.

32. Robert Bork, "The Limits of International Law", *The National Interest*, Winter 1989/1990. pp. 1–10.

33. John Bolton, "Is There Really "Law" in International Affairs?", *Transnational Law and Contemporary Problems*, Vol. 10 No. 1, 2000. pp. 1–48. pp. 4–5.

34. See the signing statement made by Clinton, "Statement by the President" 31 December 2000. Available online at the National Archive and Records Administration's Clinton Materials Project Virtual Library Publications, http://clinton6.nara.gov/2000/12/2000–12–31–statement-by-president-on-signature-the-icc-treaty.html.

35. Although it should be noted that during its first year in office the Obama administration has been significantly less hostile to the ICC than the Bush administration. See AFP, "Under Obama, US drops hostility to ICC: experts", 22 March 2009. In addition, there was some speculation in the autumn of 2009 that the Obama administration would soon issue a statement of policy regarding the ICC. While this is still likely to be a far cry from the United States becoming a party to the Rome Statute (or even submitting it to Congress), it may widen the scope for more cooperation with the Court.

36. Andru Wall, *Legal and Ethical Lessons of NATO's Kosovo Campaign*, Newport, RI: Naval War College, 2002.

37. Ruth Wedgwood, "Propositions on the Law of War after the Kosovo Campaign" pp. 433–41 in Wall, *Legal and Ethical Lessons of NATO's Kosovo Campaign*, pp. 434–5.

38. Wedgwood, "Propositions on the Law of War", p. 434.

39. Where Wedgwood would draw the line is not exactly clear as she does not specify a limit in her argument, other than to mention "the limits of basic humanity" mentioned in the cited quotation. Wedgwood, "Propositions on the Law of War", p. 434.

40. Wedgwood, "Propositions on the Law of War", pp. 434–5.

41. For discussions about the ethics of fighting the "supreme emergency" faced by Great Britain in 1940, see one of the most famous arguments by Michael Walzer, *Just and Unjust Wars: A Moral Argument with Historical Illustrations*, Third Edition, New York: Basic Books, 2000. See especially the chapter on "Supreme Emergency", pp. 251–68. It is interesting to consider the implications for the discussion here. Walzer is clear that he is writing about a threat that poses an imminent danger and a nature that can be seen as "as evil objectified in the world" and how this may defend the adoption of extreme measures. He is clear that "the danger must be of an unusual and horrifying kind", which, although a common enough description in wartime, refers to a situation whereby a country is fighting for national survival. Although it would be wrong to downplay the significance of the 9/11 attacks, asserting that the United States is (or was) in a war of national survival of the kind that Walzer is describing is problematic (although, as discussed later in the chapter, this would still seem to be the position of many former Bush administration officials). In this way, the argument here has chosen not to look at Walzer's "supreme emergency" doctrine. However, for an interesting discussion of Walzer's arguments in light of the War on Terror, see Nicholas J. Wheeler, "Dying for Enduring Freedom: Accepting Responsibility for Civilian Casualties in the War against Terrorism" *International Relations*, Vol. 16 No. 2, 2002. pp. 205–25.

42. Wade Mansell, "Goodbye to All That? The Rule of Law, International Law, the United States and the Use of Force", *Journal of Law and Society*, Vol. 31 No 4, December 2004. pp. 433–56. p. 437.

43. This is a point that should certainly not be overlooked. A chorus of opposition has come from both sides of the political fence; Democrats such as Dianne Feinstein and Patrick Leahy and Republicans such as Senator John McCain, Senator

John Warner and Senator Chuck Hagel would all raise concerns over US detainee policy. See the Floor Statement of Senator Patrick Leahy, "Guantanamo Bay Has Become A Blot And A Black Hole" 13 June 2005. Available online: http://leahy. senate.gov/press/200506/061305.html and "McCain Statement on Detainee Amendments" 5 October 2005. Available online: http://mccain.senate.gov/ index.cfm?fuseaction=NewsCenter.ViewPressRelease&Content_id=1611 for a summary of the arguments against Guantánamo on both political sides. Former Clinton official have also spoken out against the treatment of detainees. For example, David J. Scheffer, who was the former US Ambassador at Large for War Crimes Issues in the Clinton administration, has spoken out against the Bush administration's arguments. See his letter in *Foreign Affairs*, "Court Order" November/December 2001, and comments made in Neil A. Lewis, "Broad use of harsh tactics is described at Cuba base", *New York Times*, 17 October 2004. Available online at: http://www.nytimes.com/2004/10/17/politics/17gitmo.html?e x=1255665600&en=67208a988fb44907&ei=5090&partner=kmarx and his criticism of the Bush administration's policies regarding the military commissions at Guantánamo: David Scheffer, "Why Hamdan is Right about Conspiracy Liability" *Jurist: Legal News and Research*, 30 March 2006. Available online: http:// jurist.law.pitt.edu/forumy/2006/03/why-hamdan-is-right-about-conspiracy.php. Additionally, former Secretary of State Madeline Albright has questioned the policies regarding Guantánamo Bay. See William Douglas, "President Bush meets ex–secretaries of state, defense to discuss Iraq", Knight Ridder/Tribune Information Services, 12 May 2006 and Suzanne Goldenberg, "Guantanamo's day of reckoning in supreme court", *The Guardian*, 29 March 2006. Available online: http://www.guardian.co.uk/guantanamo/story/0,,1741825,00.html. Human Rights First has compiled a list of quotes from leaders speaking out against Guantánamo available online: http://www.humanrightsfirst.org/us_law/etn/ misc/call_commish.asp. NGOs, especially Amnesty International and Human Rights Watch, have both set up special monitoring sections on their website and have repeatedly condemned Bush administration policies. See Amnesty's site at: http://web.amnesty.org/pages/guantanamobay-index–eng and Human Rights Watch's site at: http://hrw.org/doc/?t=usa_gitmo.

44. James E. Baker, "Judging Kosovo", p. 18.

45. As of the autumn of 2009 there were approximately 221 detainees at Guantánamo Bay–down from a peak of 775. However, it should be remembered that the US is also holding a large number of prisoners in Afghanistan. Additionally, during the Bush administration the United States kept a number of detainees in facilities (frequently dubbed "secret prisons") throughout the world, possibly including Eastern Europe. In this sense the true number of detainees kept during operations in the war on terror remains unknown. By the end of the Bush administration officials had begun to work to reduce the numbers of prisoners at Guantánamo through repatriation programmes–complicated by the (perhaps ironic) requirement that the individuals would not be tortured by the countries to which they were returned. In addition, many of the home countries of the Guantánamo detainees did not want them returned. This process has been continued and, to a

certain extent, sped up by the Obama administration and the numbers of detainees continues to decline.

46. "DoD News Briefing—Secretary Rumsfeld and Gen. Myers", 11 January 2002. Available at: http://www.defenselink.mil/transcripts/2002/t01112002_t0111sd. html. It should be noted that the term "unlawful combatant", although not in the Geneva and Hague Conventions, has been used for at least a century. Some critics suggest that any use of the term is purposely and deliberately vague so as to escape international legal obligations. Cassese argues that this category can only be accepted for descriptive purposes: "it cannot be admitted as an intermediate category between combatants and civilians. In particular, it would be contrary to the law of war to hold that this category embraces persons who may be considered neither as legitimate belligerents nor as civilians... and are therefore deprived of any rights." Cassese, *International Law*, p. 409.

47. Bolton was the Undersecretary of State for Arms Control and International Security and became the US Ambassador to the United Nations in August 2005. Wedgwood was appointed by Rumsfeld to the Defense Policy Board. She is also the US member of the United Nations Human Rights Committee and a member of the US Secretary of State's Advisory Committee for International Law. Yoo worked for the Justice Department's Office of Legal Counsel from 2001–3 and has subsequently returned to academia.

48. "Guards and Reserves 'Define Spirit of America': Remarks by the President to Employees at the Pentagon." 17 September, 2001. Available at: http://www. whitehouse.gov/news/releases/2001/09/20010917–3.html.

49. Memo from the US Department of Justice Office of the Legal Counsel written by John Yoo, then Deputy Assistant Attorney General, "Memorandum Opinion for Timothy Flanigan, the Deputy Counsel to the President" on "The President's Constitutional Authority to Conduct Military Operations Against Terrorists and Nations Supporting Them", 25 September 2001. Issues relating to presidential/ executive powers as they relate to international law will be discussed later on in the chapter. Arguments about executive power are outlined throughout this chapter, but in keeping with the international laws of war theme, the focus is more geared towards the New Sovereigntist critique.

50. 107th Congress, Authorization for the Use of Military Force, 18 September 2001. Public Law 107–40 [S. J. RES. 23].

51. Statement of Daniel J. Dell'Orto, Principal Deputy General Counsel, Department of Defense; Major General Thomas J. Romig, Judge Advocate General of the Army; Major General Jack L. Rives, Acting Judge Advocate General of the Air Force; Rear Admiral James E. McPherson, Judge Advocate General of the Navy; Brigadier General Kevin M. Sandkuhler, Staff Judge Advocate to the Commandant of the United States Marine Corps Before the Senate Arms Services Committee Subcommittee on Personnel Military Justice and Detention Policy, 14 July 2005.

52. See the judgement in *ex parte Quirin*, 317 U.S. 1 (1942).

53. See Statement of Daniel Dell'Orto *et al.*, 14 July 2005. Such commissions are appealing because the rules on evidence are much less demanding and they can

help protect classified and sensitive information. They have been used throughout American history, including the 1942 *ex parte Quirin* case. Yet there is a striking, more recent, comparison which can be made here. Perhaps one of the most interesting stories coming out of Kosovo in relation to the laws of war was the case of the Nis bus bombers. On 16 February 2001, a bus was blown-up by a group of Kosovar-Albanians resulting in the death of eleven Serbs. Four individuals were eventually detained for the incident. However, three out of four of the individuals thought to have been guilty were linked to the crime only by sensitive intelligence information–information that NATO officials did not want to have brought out in an open court. The arrested were eventually transferred into US custody at Camp Bondsteel, but languished in prison for months as authorities debated exactly how the case could be prosecuted while protecting intelligence sources. Eventually UNMIK (the United Nations Interim Administration in Kosovo) decided to create a Detention Review Commission of three international judges (from the US, UK and Germany) with security clearance to determine the case in a closed courtroom. According to the UNMIK spokeswoman Susan Manuel: "This is sensitive information which sources will not release as evidence in courts. This judicial review panel will decide based on the information presented to them, whether further detention by executive order is warranted... According to the regulation which set up this special panel, the Commission has seven days to render its decision on further detention...The commission's decision will not be subject to appeal." Ultimately the court found that there was reason to detain the suspects for a further ninety days by which time charges were to be brought against them in a civilian court. However, without access to the intelligence in which to charge or convict the individuals involved, they were set free by Kosovo's Supreme Court. The parallels of this case with Guantánamo are striking–right down to the orange jumpsuits the detainees were allegedly wearing. However, there was very little outcry in this case with regard to the rights of the prisoners, NATO or UN policies. Perhaps this was because the court only extended detention for a further ninety days or because the Detention Review Commission was composed of judges from different NATO countries. Still, the fact that the court went ahead with little outcry is interesting. However, because the incident deals with NATO and the UN rather than the US, and because the issue was relatively non-controversial, this work will not engage in a further discussion of these matters. The author feels that pointing out the similarities in these cases suggests an area of potential future comparison or research. For more information on these rather unknown events, see UNMIK-OSCE-EU-UNHCR Press Briefing, 20 September 2001. Available online: http://www.unmikonline.org/press/2001/trans/tr240901.html.

54. Memo from the US Department of Justice Office of the Legal Counsel, John Yoo and Robert J. Delahunty. "Memorandum For William J. Haynes II General Counsel, Department of Defense", 9 January 2002.

55. "Memorandum for William J. Haynes II General Counsel, Department of Defense", 9 January 2002. The conclusion did go on to say that "Nonetheless, we also believe that the President as Commander-in-Chief, has the constitutional

authority to impose the customary laws of war on both the al Qaeda and Taliban groups and the U.S. Armed Forces."

56. Memo from the US Department of Justice Office of Legal Council, Jay S. Bybee, the then Assistant Attorney General, "Memorandum for Alberto R. Gonzales Counsel to the President, and William J. Haynes II, General Counsel of the Department of Defense Re: Application of Treaties and Laws to al Qaeda and Taliban Detainees" 22 January 2002.

57. Gonzales' memo can be found online at Michael Isikoff "Memos Reveal War Crimes Warning", *Newsweek*, 19 May 2004, http://msnbc.msn.com/id/4999734/.

58. "Fact Sheet: Status of Detainees at Guantanamo", 7 February 2002. Available at: http://www.whitehouse.gov/news/releases/2002/02/20020207–13.html.

59. Article 4 of the Third Geneva Convention reads:

A. Prisoners of war, in the sense of the present Convention, are persons belonging to one of the following categories, who have fallen into the power of the enemy:

  (1) Members of the armed forces of a Party to the conflict, as well as members of militias or volunteer corps forming part of such armed forces.

  (2) Members of other militias and members of other volunteer corps, including those of organized resistance movements, belonging to a Party to the conflict and operating in or outside their own territory, even if this territory is occupied, provided that such militias or volunteer corps, including such organized resistance movements, fulfill the following conditions:

  (a) that of being commanded by a person responsible for his subordinates;
  (b) that of having a fixed distinctive sign recognizable at a distance;
  (c) that of carrying arms openly;
  (d) that of conducting their operations in accordance with the laws and customs of war.

  (3) Members of regular armed forces who profess allegiance to a government or an authority not recognized by the Detaining Power.

  (4) Persons who accompany the armed forces without actually being members thereof, such as civilian members of military aircraft crews, war correspondents, supply contractors, members of labour units or of services responsible for the welfare of the armed forces, provided that they have received authorization, from the armed forces which they accompany, who shall provide them for that purpose with an identity card similar to the annexed model.

  (5) Members of crews, including masters, pilots and apprentices, of the merchant marine and the crews of civil aircraft of the Parties to the conflict, who do not benefit by more favourable treatment under any other provisions of international law.

  (6) Inhabitants of a non-occupied territory, who on the approach of the enemy spontaneously take up arms to resist the invading forces, without

having had time to form themselves into regular armed units, provided they carry arms openly and respect the laws and customs of war.

B. The following shall likewise be treated as prisoners of war under the present Convention:

(1) Persons belonging, or having belonged, to the armed forces of the occupied country, if the occupying Power considers it necessary by reason of such allegiance to intern them, even though it has originally liberated them while hostilities were going on outside the territory it occupies, in particular where such persons have made an unsuccessful attempt to rejoin the armed forces to which they belong and which are engaged in combat, or where they fail to comply with a summons made to them with a view to internment.

(2) The persons belonging to one of the categories enumerated in the present Article, who have been received by neutral or non-belligerent Powers on their territory and whom these Powers are required to intern under international law, without prejudice to any more favourable treatment which these Powers may choose to give and with the exception of Articles 8, 10, 15, 30, fifth paragraph, 58–67, 92, 126 and, where diplomatic relations exist between the Parties to the conflict and the neutral or non-belligerent Power concerned, those Articles concerning the Protecting Power. Where such diplomatic relations exist, the Parties to a conflict on whom these persons depend shall be allowed to perform towards them the functions of a Protecting Power as provided in the present Convention, without prejudice to the functions which these Parties normally exercise in conformity with diplomatic and consular usage and treaties.

C. This Article shall in no way affect the status of medical personnel and chaplains as provided for in Article 33 of the present Convention.

60. This argument was set out in a White House press release "Fact Sheet: Status of Detainees at Guantanamo" 7 February 2002. Available online at: http://www.whitehouse.gov/news/releases/2002/02/20020207–13.html.

61. The term "New Paradigm" is taken from Jane Mayer. See Jane Mayer "The Hidden Power: The legal mind behind the White House's war on terror", *The New Yorker*, 3 July 2006. pp. 44–55.

62. Memo from the US Department of Justice Office of Legal Counsel, Jay S. Bybee, then Assistant Attorney General, "Memorandum for William J. Haynes II, General Counsel, Department of Defense Re: Potential Legal Constraints Applicable to Interrogations of Persons Captured by U.S. Armed Forces in Afghanistan", 26 February 2006. *Miranda* warnings are given to suspects in police custody in the United States before they are asked any questions. The warnings are given as a way to protect an individual's right against self-incrimination. Reminding suspects of their "right to remain silent" was seen as problematic by those who wanted to gather information from suspects. For more information on *Miranda* warnings see, the US Supreme Court decision in *Miranda v. Arizona* 384 U.S. 436 (1966).

63. Memo from the US Department of Justice Office of Legal Council, Jay S. Bybee, Assistant Attorney General, "Memorandum for Alberto R. Gonzales Counsel to

the President Re: Standards of Conduct for Interrogation under 18 U.S.C. §§ 2340–2340A. Dated 26 February 2002.

64. Letter from the US Department of Justice Office of Legal Counsel to the Honourable Alberto R. Gonzales, Counsel to the President. 1 August 2002. In Article 8(2)(ii) the ICC Statue prohibits "Torture or inhuman treatment, including biological experiments". Yoo was trying to determine if the ICC would be able to prosecute interrogators for their actions. He claimed that Article 8 of the Rome Statue only applied to those protected by the Geneva Conventions but could not guarantee that the ICC, a "rogue prosecutor" or other countries would see the legal argument the same way.

65. See Appendix A. These memos and their timeline will be discussed in greater detail in Chapter 5.

66. An outline of the US argument was provided by the White House Press Secretary on 14 November 2005. Available online at: http://www.defenselink.mil/news/Jan2006/d20060215legalbasis.pdf

67. Scott Shane, "Waterboarding used 266 times on 2 suspects", *New York Times*, 19 April 2009. Available online at: http://www.nytimes.com/2009/04/20/world/20detain.html

68. That there were many within the government who were concerned with the interpretations of the laws of war being put forward by the administration has been made clear through discussions with officials in the research done by the author. One former State Department official confirmed that State was largely kept in the dark as to the debates going on. It was only after the advice had been asked for and received that internal concerns were raised about the detainee policies. This was also the view of a Department of Defense employee (familiar with, and to a certain extent present during, the events of this period) who felt that one of the biggest failings of the Bush administration officials was a failure or refusal to ask for help and advice on the law of war from the experts at DoD. This sentiment has also been noted by many news reports. See Jane Mayer, "The Memo", *The New Yorker*, 27 February 2006 and John Barry, Michael Hirsh and Michael Isikoff, "The roots of torture", *Newsweek* 24 May 2005. Available online at: http://www.msnbc.msn.com/id/4989481/.

69. See Colin Powell's memo of 26 January 2002 to Counsel to the President and Assistant to the President for National Security Affairs, "Draft Decision Memorandum for the President on the Applicability of the Geneva Convention to the Conflict in Afghanistan". Also see the memo from William H. Taft, IV to the Counsel to the President, "Comments on Your Paper on the Geneva Convention", 2 February 2002.

70. Colin Powell's memo of 26 January 2002.

71. For example, there is an interesting point here to be made regarding "extraordinary rendition" which received much publicity during the Bush administration but actually began under the Clinton administration. In the 1990s, the CIA "extraordinarily rendered" individuals suspected in engaging in radical Islamic terrorist activities to foreign countries. If the foreign country had a record of torture, the administration would seek a "guarantee" that the state would not

engage in acts of torture so that the action would comply with the United Nations Convention Against Torture. For more information on this programme, see Stephen Grey, *Ghost Plane: The Untold Story of the CIA's Secret Rendition Programme*, London: Hurst/St. Martin's Press, 2006. Also, see the 2007 PBS Frontline Program, *Extraordinary Rendition* and accompanying website available here: http://www.pbs.org/frontlineworld/stories/rendition701/ Grey argues that there were certain differences between the Clinton administration and Bush administration when it came to rendition policies. First (at least initially), the worst torturing countries (like Syria) were off limits. Second, whereas the Clinton administration geared its programme towards intelligence gathering, the Bush administration used rendition to disrupt terrorist activities. This work does not deal extensively with rendition, not because it is an unimportant issue, but because it is a large and complex issue that falls outside the main theme of prisoners of war, and because of length concerns.

72. See, for example, Jeremy Rabkin, "After Guantanamo: The War Over the Geneva Conventions", *The National Interest*, Summer 2002.

73. Jack Goldsmith left after disagreeing with the 2002 memorandum on torture and the assertion of executive authority in related issues. He is widely considered to have led a small group of lawyers in the administration in a quiet revolt against what he considered the constitutional excesses of the legal policies embraced by White House officials—particularly over the so-called torture memos. He tells his side of the story in his book, Jack Goldsmith, *The Terror Presidency: Law and Judgment Inside the Bush Administration*, New York: W.W. Norton & Company, Inc. 2007. Levin, who was the acting head of the Office of Legal Council after the departure of Goldsmith, soon took a job as legal adviser at the National Security Council after he agreed with Goldsmith's opinions on interrogation techniques and presidential power. More on Goldsmith's argument will be discussed below.

74. Neal Katyal, "Counsel, Legal and Illegal", *The New Republic*, 5 November 2007. p. 37.

75. Legal arguments here are based upon the following: Michael Byers, *War Law: International Law and Armed Conflict*, London: Atlantic Books, 2005; Antonio Cassese, *International Law*, Second Edition, Oxford University Press, 2005; Yoram Dinstein, *The Conduct of Hostilities*; Helen Duffy, *The 'War on Terror' and the Framework of International Law*, Cambridge University Press, 2005; Forsythe, *The Humanitarians*, Cambridge University Press, 2005.; and Sands, *Lawless World: American and the Making and Breaking of Global Rules*, London: Allen Lane, 2005..

76. Although ultimately rejecting AP I, Ronald Reagan indicated that there were "sound elements" to the Protocols which the US would work with its allies to implement in conflict. See his "Message to the Senate Transmitting a Protocol to the 1949 Geneva Conventions," 29 January 1987. Accessible on the Ronald Reagan Presidential Library Website: http://www.reagan.utexas.edu/archives/speeches/1987/012987B.HTM.

77. It should be pointed out that this has been a very contentious issue within the humanitarian and laws of war community since before 9/11. In the case of

Afghanistan Dinstein argues that the Taliban did not meet the criteria for POW status because they were not in uniform and did not have an identifiable mark; Cassese argues that this is irrelevant in modern customary law. See Dinstein, *The Conduct of Hostilities*, pp. 47–8 and Cassese, *International Law*, pp. 405–10. Although the United States has not ratified API for reasons outlined in the previous chapter, many lawyers argue that it is a clear statement of the principles of customary law relating to the treatment of prisoners of war, in which case the United States would be bound by the provisions.

78. Duffy, *The 'War on Terror' and the Framework of International Law*, p. 243; see also note 143 on the same page.
79. Spiro, "The New Sovereigntists", pp. 9–16.
80. Rabkin, "After Guantanamo".
81. Duffy, *The "War on Terror"*, p. 2.
82. Rabkin, "After Guantanamo".
83. For example, see Rabkin's chapter "The Human Rights Crusade" in *Law Without Nations*, or Bolton's *Foreign Affairs* article, "The Global Prosecutors".
84. Jeremy Rabkin quoted in Spiro, "The New Sovereigntists".
85. Rabkin, "After Guantanamo".
86. Short, "Operation Allied Force", p. 26.
87. In 2002 there were 428 judge advocates in the Marine Corps alone compared with 102 in the UK, 100 in Canada, 90 in Australia and 17 in New Zealand. W. Hays Parks, "The United States Military and the Law of War: Inculcating an Ethos", *Social Research*, Vol. 69 No. 4, Winter 2002. pp. 981–1015. p. 989.
88. Parks, "The United States Military", pp, 983–4.
89. United States Department of Defense, *Final Report to Congress: Conduct of the Persian Gulf War*, Washington: Department of Defense, 1992. p. 624.
90. See for example, John Barry, Michael Hirsch and Michael Isikoff, "The roots of torture", *Newsweek*, 17 May 2004. Available online at: http://msnbc.msn.com/id/4989422/. This also reflects the attitude expressed by several current and retired military officials when confidentially interviewed on the issue. The debate's paper trail has largely been captured in paper and published in Karen J. Greenberg and Joshua L. Dratel eds, *The Torture Papers: The Road to Abu Ghraib*, Cambridge University Press, 2005.
91. For example, in the continuing battles over military tribunals, several Department of Defense lawyers have continually argued, against the position of the Bush administration, that suspected terrorists should be tried according to the standards set in the UCMJ which are internationally respected. See the testimony of the Senate Armed Services Committee, "To continue to receive testimony on the future of military commissions in light of the Supreme Court decision in Hamdan v. Rumsfeld", 2 August 2006. Available online at: http://armed-services.senate.gov/e_witnesslist.cfm?id=2032. *Hamdan v. Rumsfeld* will be dealt with later in the chapter. Also see Anne Plummer Flaherty, "Gonzales Holds Line on Terror Detainees", Associated Press, 2 August 2006.
92. The Counter Insurgency manual and subsequent strategy adopted by the United States to combat the Iraqi insurgency explicitly links the laws of war to successful

operations. The manual, FM 3–24 published in 2006, goes into extensive detail as to the treatment of detainees and strongly warns against abuse in all circumstances. For an overview of the manual and counter-insurgency strategy developed in response to the Iraqi Insurgency, see, Thomas Ricks, *The Gamble: General David Petraeus and the American Military Adventure in Iraq, 2006–2008*, New York: Penguin Press, 2009.

93. "Vice President Cheney Delivers Remarks at the 56th Annual Alfred E. Smith Memorial Foundation Dinner" 18 October, 2001. Available at: http://www.whitehouse.gov/vicepresident/news-speeches/speeches/vp20011018.html.

94. "Excerpt: Rumsfeld Says Taliban to Blame for Casualties" 29 October, 2005. Excerpt available online at: http://bangkok.usembassy.gov/news/press/2001/nrot113.htm.

95. "Richard B. Cheney, "Remarks by Richard B. Cheney", 21 May 2009. Available online at: http://www.aei.org/speech/100050. An individual who was working at a senior level in the Bush White House during the first two years of the administration confirmed that most, if not all, of the officials believed that a second attack was imminent. The policies undertaken were therefore based on this assumption and the perceived need to keep America safe at virtually all costs. Interview in Washington, October 2009. This perhaps raises the question whether the approach taken regarding international law was based more on expediency rather than being a theoretical attack on international law. However, given the inclusion of New Sovereigntists in the administration, the nature of the opinions issued and the ideological positions taken within them, it seems clear that expediency and ideology were not mutually exclusive in terms of decision making regarding the prisoners.

96. There is actually some dispute as to who originated the phrase–Justice Jackson or Justice Goldberg. Most citations of the cliché usually refer to Justice Jackson in *Terminiello v. City of Chicago* (1949). See "The "Suicide Pact" Mystery: Who coined the phrase? Justice Goldberg or Justice Jackson?" David Corn, Slate.com, 4 January 2002. Available at http://slate.msn.com/id/2060342/.

97. Ruth Wedgwood, "Propositions on the Law of War after the Kosovo Campaign", pp. 433–41.

98. Michael Ignatieff, *The Lesser Evil: Political Ethics in an Age of Terror*, Edinburgh University Press, 2004. p. 1.

99. Ignatieff, *The Lesser Evil*, p. vii.

100. Ignatieff, *The Lesser Evil*, pp. 8–9.

101. Ignatieff, *The Lesser Evil*, p. 12.

102. Ignatieff, *The Lesser Evil*, p. 14.

103. Ignatieff, *The Lesser Evil*, p. 16.

104. Ignatieff, *The Lesser Evil*, p. 18.

105. Ignatieff, *The Lesser Evil*, pp. 14–15.

106. This point was made by Ronald Steel in his harsh criticism of Ignatieff's book in the *New York Times*, 25 July 2004.

107. Conor Gearty, "Legitimising Torture—with a Little Help", *Index on Censorship* issue 1/05. Available online at: http://www.indexonline.org/en/news/articles/

2005/1/international-legitimising-torture-with-a-li.shtml. Apparently, by Rumsfeldians, Gearty is implying individuals who are "distinguished by their determination to permit, indeed to encourage, the holding of suspected 'terrorists' or 'unlawful combatants'... in conditions which make torture, inhuman and degrading treatment well-nigh situationally inevitable." Given the nuances of Ignatieff's argument, it is certainly a provocative description.

108. Gearty, "Legitimizing Torture".

109. Ignatieff, *The Lesser Evil*, pp. 139–40. This argument can also be found online at the Kennedy School of Government website: http://www.ksg.harvard.edu/news/opeds/2004/ignatieff_torture_ft_051504.htm.

110. Ignatieff, *The Lesser Evil*, p. 138. Ignatieff recently defended himself against the criticisms of Steel's review of *The Lesser Evil* in the *New York Times*, arguing that Steel has mischaracterized his intentions.

111. Ignatieff, *The Lesser Evil*. See in particular the chapter titled "The Temptations of Nihilism", pp. 112–44.

112. Ignatieff, *The Lesser Evil*, p. 165.

113. Ignatieff, *The Lesser Evil*, p. 14.

114. Ignatieff, *The Lesser Evil*, p. 17.

115. Ron Suskind, *The One Percent Doctrine: Deep Inside America's Pursuit of Its Enemies Since 9/11*, London: Simon & Schuster UK Ltd, 2006. p. 42.

116. Michael Ignatieff, "The Lesser Evil", Letter published in the *New York Review of Books* 15 August 2004. Ignatieff was responding to Ronald Steel's criticism of *The Lesser Evil* that had been published in the *Review* on 25 July 2004.

117. Dell'Orto, "Hearing on the Supreme Court's Decision in Hamdan v. Rumsfeld".

118. Mayer, "The Hidden Power", p. 44.

119. See Goldsmith, *The Terror Presidency*.

120. 109–359 109th Congress, Making Appropriations for the Department of Defense for the Fiscal Year Ending September 30, 2006 and for Other Purposes. 18 December 2005 (H.R. 2863, Title X). (Also referred to as the Detainee Treatment Act.)

121. Mayer, "The Hidden Power", p. 55. Specifically, the signing statement read: "The executive branch shall construe these sections in a manner consistent with the constitutional authority of the President." The text of the signing statement is available online at: http://www.whitehouse.gov/news/releases/2005/12/20051230–8.html.

122. Three important cases to go to the Supreme court were *Rumsfeld v. Padilla* (124 S. Ct. 2711 [2004]), *Hamdi v. Rumsfeld* (124 S. Ct. 2633 [2004]) and *Rasul v. Bush* (124 S. Ct. 2686 [2004]). In *Padilla*, a US born citizen was held on the suspicion of a plot to detonate a "dirty bomb", without trial or access to a lawyer. It is arguably the least important case. The Supreme Court side-stepped the issue at hand and rejected Padilla's petition because it had been filed in the wrong district. Padilla continued to challenge his designation as an "enemy combatant" and rather than face continued legal battles at the Supreme Court which it might lose, the Bush administration eventually dropped the enemy combatant

designation and charged Padilla with charges relating to criminal conspiracy. He was found guilty in August 2007. In *Hamdi*, a US citizen was captured on the battlefield and brought to Guantánamo Bay where his lawyers argued that, as a US citizen, Hamdi was entitled to the protections of the US Constitution. The Court ruled that the US government could detain a combatant who had joined a wartime enemy of the United States, but that this did not nullify a citizen's constitutional protection. Hamdi therefore had the right to a lawyer, to challenge his designation as an enemy combatant. In September 2004, Hamdi was released to Saudi Arabia on the condition that he give up his US citizenship. In *Rasul*, a UK citizen asserted that he had the right to have the US court system determine whether or not he was rightfully imprisoned. The Court decided that although the US did not exercise full sovereignty over Guantánamo Bay, the detainees were held under full US jurisdiction and therefore had the right to challenge their detentions. Interestingly, Rasul and another UK suspect were released from US custody back to the UK three months before the Supreme Court decision was made. Given this poor success rate, it is clear that the US government has turned to releasing suspects rather than face continuous Court challenges that are seen as risky and possibly undermining the administration's position even further.

123. *Hamdan v. Rumsfeld* (126 S. Ct. 2749 [2006]).
124. See the decision in *Hamdan v. Rumsfeld*, (126 S. Ct. 2749 [2006]).
125. Steven Bradbury, "Statement of Steven G. Bradbury Acting Assistant Attorney General, Office of Legal Counsel, Department of Justice, Before the Committee on the Judiciary United States Senate Concerning the Supreme Court's Decision in Hamdan v. Rumsfeld" 11 July 2006. Available online at: http://judiciary.senate.gov/testimony.cfm?id=1986&wit_id=5505.
126. Daniel Dell'Orto, "Statement of Daniel J. Dell'Orto Principal Deputy General Counsel, Office of General Counsel U.S. Department of Defense, Before the Committtee on the Judiciary United States Senate Hearing on the Supreme Court's decision in Hamdan v. Rumsfeld" 11 July 2006. Available online at: http://judiciary.senate.gov/testimony.cfm?id=1986&wit_id=5506.
127. It should be noted that the application of Common Article 3 applies only to those detainees being held by the Department of Defense. Detainees being held around the world by other US government agencies (such as the CIA) do not benefit from this protection.
128. Scott Shane, David Johnston and James Risen, "Secret U.S. endorsement of severe interrogations", *New York Times*, 3 October 2007. p. 1.
129. Shane *et al.*, "Secret U.S. endorsement"
130. See David S. Cloud and Sheryl Gay Stolberg, "White House bill proposes system to try detainees", *New York Times*, 25 July 2006.
131. However, when the administration appealed to the (then) newly established Court of Military Commission Review, it won. Proceedings against Omar Khadr and Salim Ahmed Hamdan resumed in November and December 2007.
132. See *Boumediene v. Bush* (128 S. Ct. 2229 [2008]).

133. The results were mixed. While in October a federal court ordered the release of 17 Chinese Uighurs. The administration appealed against the decision and their release was put on hold. Additionally, the US District Court for the District of Columbia orders five of six men seized in Bosnia and Herzegovina. The six individuals remained in custody and one was the first to have his *habeas* petition ruled on after the decision in *Boumediene*. Some information here from Amnesty International, "Guantánamo Bay–Timeline", 9 January 2009. Available online at: http://www.amnesty.org.au/guantanamo/comments/20057/.

134. Marc Santora, "3 Top Republican Candidates Take a Hard Line on the Interrogation of Detainees" *New York Times*, 3 November 2007. Available online: http://www.nytimes.com/2007/11/03/us/politics/03torture.html

135. See Amnesty International,"Obama Breaks Major Campaign Promise as Military Commissions Resume, Says Amnesty International" 15 May 2009. Available online at: http://www.amnestyusa.org/document.php?id=ENGUSA20090 515003; American Civil Liberties Union, "Obama Administration To Revive Fatally Flawed Military Commissions" 15 May 2009. Available online at: http://www.aclu.org/safefree/detention/39601prs20090515.html

136. Interestingly, Goldsmith then says that these changes are not unimportant. Rather, packaging and rhetoric can make a huge difference and this is where the Bush administration got it wrong. See Jack Goldsmith, "The Cheney Fallacy", *The New Republic*, 18 May 2009. Available online at: http://www.tnr.com/politics/story.html?id=1e733cac-c273–48e5–9140–80443ed1f5e2

137. See *Wazir, et al. v. Gates, et al.* 29 June 2009, US District Court for the District of Columbia, Civil Action No. 06–1697. The court dismissed the case.

5. FAILURE OF AN ETHOS? OPERATION IRAQI FREEDOM, AMERICA AND ABU GHRAIB

1. See, for example Michael N. Schmitt, "Conduct of Hostilities During Operational Iraqi Freedom: An International Humanitarian Law Assessment", 6 *Yearbook of International Humanitarian Law*, 2003. pp. 73–110.

2. NGOs critiqued the US for the decapitation strikes aimed at the Iraqi leadership on 20 March 2003 and for the use of cluster munitions. During the campaign, Amnesty International argued for "an immediate moratorium on the use of cluster bombs by US/UK forces and on other weapons that are inherently indiscriminate or otherwise prohibited under international humanitarian law". See Amnesty International "Iraq: Civilians under fire" AI Index: MDE14/071/2003, 8 April 2003. Available online at: http://web.amnesty.org/library/Index/ENGMDE1407 12003; Also see Human Rights Watch, "Background on International Humanitarian Law, War Crimes and the War in Iraq" Available online: http://www.hrw.org/press/2003/12/ihl-qna.htm. Human Rights Watch concluded "U.S.-led Coalition forces took precautions to spare civilians and, for the most part, made efforts to uphold their legal obligations. Human Rights Watch nevertheless identified practices that led to civilian casualties in the air war, ground war, and post-conflict period." Additionally, HRW argued that the Coalition did not investigate thor-

oughly enough the reasons why civilians had been killed in some circumstances. See Human Rights Watch, "Off Target: The Conduct of the War and Civilian Casualties in Iraq" December 2003. Available online: http://www.hrw.org/reports/2003/usa1203/.

3. For an overview of Operation Iraqi Freedom and the subsequent challenges that Iraq has faced, see the summary by Steve Bowman, "Iraq: U.S. Military Operations" Congressional Research Service, Library of Congress, Updated 23 January 2006. Available online: http://fpc.state.gov/documents/organization/25375.pdf.

4. US Department of Defense News Briefing "DoD News Briefing—Mr. Di Rita and Gen. Abizaid" 16 July 2003. http://www.defenselink.mil/transcripts/2003/tr20030716-0401.html.

5. A good and brief summary of the law of belligerent occupation, Michael N. Schmitt, "The Law of Belligerent Occupation", Crimes of War Project, 15 April 2003. Available online: http://www.crimesofwar.org/special/Iraq/news-iraq5.html.

6. Adam Roberts, "Transformative Military Occupation: Applying the Laws of War and Human Rights", *American Journal of International Law*, Vol. 100 No. 3, July 2006. pp. 580–622.

7. "Final Report of the Independent Panel to Review DoD Detention Operations Inspection" (The Schlesinger Report), August 2004. Cited in Karen J. Greenburgh and Joshua L. Dratel eds, *The Torture Papers: The Road to Abu Ghraib*. Cambridge University Press, 2005. p. 921.

8. Perhaps the one of the most critical of all of the accounts of the failures of Bush administration policies regarding Iraq is from Michael Gordon and Bernard Trainor, *Cobra II: The Inside Story of the Invasion and Occupation of Iraq*, London: Atlantic Books, 2006. Also see the remarks of a former Senior Adviser to the Coalition Provisional Authority in Baghdad, Larry Diamond, "What Went Wrong in Iraq", *Foreign Affairs*, Vol. 83 No. 5, September/October 2004. As Diamond argues, "Contemptuous of the State Department's regional experts who were seen as too "soft" to remake Iraq, a small group of Pentagon officials ignored the elaborate postwar planning the State Department had overseen through its 'Future of Iraq' project, which had anticipated many of the problems that had emerged after the invasion."

9. Janis Karpinski, *One Woman's Army: The Commanding General of Abu Ghraib Tells Her Story*, New York: Miramax Books, 2005. p. 208.

10. Col. Henry Nelson, "AR 15–16 Investigation–Allegations of Detainee Abuse at Abu Ghraib: Psychological Assessment" Annexed to "Article 15–16 Investigation of the 800th Military Police Brigade" (The Taguba Report), March 2004. Cited in Karen J. Greenburgh and Joshua L. Dratel eds, *The Torture Papers: The Road to Abu Ghraib*. Cambridge University Press, 2005. pp. 448–9.

11. Re-designated Multi–National Force-Iraq and Multi–National Corps-Iraq on 15 May 2004.

12. "Final Report of the Independent Panel to Review DoD Detention Operations" (the Schlesinger Report), Cited in Karen J. Greenburgh and Joshua L. Dratel eds,

The Torture Papers: The Road to Abu Ghraib. Cambridge University Press, 2005. pp. 908–86. p. 944.

13. The major reports on the abuse are: MG Miller Report, "Assessment of Interrogation & Detention Operations in Iraq" (September 2003); MG Ryder Report, "Assessment of Detention & Corrections Operations in Iraq" (November 2003); BG Jacoby Report, "Inspection of Detainee Operation & Facilities in Afghanistan" (July 2004); Mikolashek Report, "Department of the Army, The Inspector General–Detainee Operations Inspection" (July 2004); MG Taguba Report, "Article 15–16 Investigation of the 800th Military Police Brigade" (July 2004); Schlesinger Report, "Final Report of the Independent Panel to Review DoD Detention Operations" (August 2004); Fay/Jones Report "Investigation of Intelligence Activities at Abu Ghraib/Investigation of the Abu Ghraib Prison and 205th Military Intelligence Brigade, LTG Anthony R Jones/Investigation of the Abu Ghraib Detention Facility and 205th Military Intelligence Brigade, MG George R. Fay" (August 2004); BG Formica "Investigation Into Abuse (SOF) on Arabian Peninsula" (November 2004); Church Report "Review of Policy, Doctrine, Gaps & Seams" (February 2005).

14. Although all of these documents are available online through the DoD website, I have accessed them through an edited collection of papers, reports and memos regarding Abu Ghraib. Karen J. Greenberg and Joshua L Dratel, *The Torture Papers: The Road to Abu Ghraib.* Cambridge University Press, 2005. Page numbers will therefore refer to this collection. This section has chosen not to look at the MG Ryder Report as it deals more with the overall problems of the prison system in the autumn of 2003 rather than the abuse directly. Certainly the Ryder Report should be taken as a document which forewarned of many of the problems that occurred. Other reports not discussed here are the Jacoby Report and the Formica Report, which were not released to the public until June 2006. The Jacoby Report was mainly concerned with the treatment of Afghan detainees and the Formica Report with detainees held in Iraq by Special Forces. Both reports essentially agree with the points made by the others–that there were serious faults in training and oversight and that many of the actions taken (such as feeding prisoners only bread and water for eighteen days) constituted abuse. Both reports also suggest problems with oversight and generally support the findings and recommendations of the above mentioned reports. The Church Report, which investigated all Department of Defense detainee operations, has still not been fully released. However, an executive summary, again mostly supporting the contentions of the other reports, was presented to the public.

15. Nelson, "Psychological Assessment", Annex to the Taguba Report, p. 448.

16. Schlessinger Report, p. 934.

17. Taguba Report, p. 419.

18. Mikolashek Report, p. 665.

19. Taguba Report, pp. 411–2.

20. Mikolashek Report, pp. 664–5.

21. For example, see the Schlesinger Report, p. 909.

22. Mikolashek Report, p. 635.

23. Mikolashek Report, p. 636.

24. These include C. Haney, W.C. Banks and P.G. Zimbardo, "Interpersonal Dynamics in a Simulated Prison", *International Journal of Criminology and Penology*, 1973, 1, pp. 69–97; and the work of Dr. Robert Jay Lifton who has argued that ordinary people can experience a "socializing to evil", especially in a war environment. Schlesinger Report, Appendix G, "Psychological Stresses", pp. 970–2. For his part, Lifton appears to agree, at least regarding the role of medical personnel in the War on Terror, writing: "We know that medical personnel have failed to report to higher authorities wounds that were clearly caused by torture and that they have neglected to take steps to interrupt this torture. In addition, they have turned over prisoners' medical records to interrogators who could use them to exploit the prisoners' weaknesses or vulnerabilities. We have not yet learned the extent of medical involvement in delaying and possibly falsifying the death certificates of prisoners who have been killed by torturers." Lifton, Robert Jay, "Doctors and Torture" *New England Journal of Medicine*, Vol. 315 No 5, 2004. pp. 415–16.

25. Taguba Report, p. 438.

26. Taguba Report, p. 443.

27. Mikolashek Report, p. 656.

28. Taguba Report, p. 439.

29. Schlesinger Report, p. 915.

30. Mikolashek Report–see the Foreword, p. 632. The Report specifically defines an issue as "systemic" if it can be found horizontally across many various types of units, or vertically through many command levels from squad through division or higher level. In this way, the Report argues that the abuse should be considered "isolated events". p. 652.

31. Schlesinger Report, p. 924.

32. Of course there are many books from which one could chose to demonstrate this point. In order to make a concise argument, four books dealing with international law and the War on Terror were chosen that were published in 2004–5. Two are by journalists (Seymour M. Hersh, who played a role in bringing the Abu Ghraib scandal to light, and David Rose, a British journalist who travelled to Guantánamo and who was writing shortly after the scandal emerged) and two lawyer/ academics (Philippe Sands and Michael Byers). This is, naturally, an arbitrary decision, and allegations that the responsibility for the torture lies with the Bush administration are not limited to these books. Even in her relatively descriptive book on the role of international law in the War on Terror, Helen Duffy, an international law and human rights advocate, notes that "In light of the parallel allegations arising from Guantanamo Bay, Iraq, Afghanistan and elsewhere, others have emerged as to these practices revealing a systemic policy of either encouraging, purporting to justify or turning a blind eye, to such abuse." Helen Duffy, *The 'War on Terror' and the Framework of International Law*, Cambridge University Press, 2005. p. 268. Still, it is the assertion here that a basic summary of the arguments put forward by this "group" may be gathered by looking at these texts.

33. It is fair to say that most of these works start from an anti–war/anti–Bush perspective. Virtually all of the authors listed here agree that the Iraq War was illegal under international law and that Bush administration policies were as wrong as they were dangerous. The works cited here should be understood in this context.

34. Philippe Sands, *Lawless World: America and the Making and Breaking of Global Rules*, London: Allen Lane, 2005. p. 221.

35. David Rose: *Guantánamo: America's War on Human Rights*, London: Faber and Faber, 2004.

36. Sands, *Lawless World*, p. 205.

37. Sands, *Lawless World*, p. 229.

38. Rose, *Guantánamo*, pp. 90–2.

39. Specifically, she argued in the majority opinion: "The threshold question before us is whether the Executive has the authority to detain citizens who qualify as "enemy combatants." There is some debate as to the proper scope of this term, and the Government has never provided any court with the full criteria that it uses in classifying individuals as such."

40. Sands, *Lawless World*, p. 221.

41. Sands, *Lawless World*, pp. 229–30.

42. Rose, *Guantánamo*, p. 10.

43. Seymour M. Hersh, *Chain of Command: The Road from 9/11 to Abu Ghraib*, New York: HarperCollins, 2005. pp. 66–8. Hersh argues that Senator John Warner, a Republican, Bush supporter and chairman of the Armed Services committee, as one of these antagonists. Warner, a former Marine, was upset at the mistreatment of prisoners. However, within a few weeks of his calls for a full accounting of what happened, Warner began to backtrack under "a lot of pressure" to protect national security.

44. Michael Byers, *War Law: International Law and Armed Conflict*, London: Atlantic Books, 2005. p. 145.

45. Hersh, *Chain of Command*, p. 369.

46. Hersh, *Chain of Command*, pp. 372–4.

47. Karpinski, *One Woman's Army*, pp. 207–8. Of course it is important to read this quote with the understanding that Karpinski's book is written for the purpose of clearing her name in the scandal. It also fails to answer the question as to why the soldiers did not recognize that such orders were patently illegal. In this way, Karpinski's book comes out of the military, but tends to fall on the "systemic" side of the debate. Interestingly, Karpinski's assertions both complement and contradict the testimony given by the soldiers charged with their participation in Guantánamo, discussed below. Many of the soldiers did argue that they were acting under orders, but many of them also admitted to knowing what they did was wrong at the time. Certainly they should have known that obeying an illegal order is a violation of the Uniform Code of Military Justice.

48. Hersh, *Chain of Command*, p. 373.

49. Philippe Sands, *Torture Team: Uncovering War Crimes in the Land of the Free*, London: Penguin Books Ltd., 2009. p. 293.

50. There is a third argument which could be raised here: that there is a long-standing tradition of the United States engaging in torture, particularly in the period from the 1960s to the 1980s. Indeed there is a lengthy tradition of literature that is dedicated to documenting certain incidents, including activities by the CIA and its contractors around the world, during the Vietnam War for example, and the training of militaries in Latin American and Indochina in means and methods of warfare contrary to the law of armed conflict. See, for example, Ruth Blakeley, *State Terrorism and Neoliberalism: The North in the South*, London: Routledge, 2009 and "Still Training to Torture? US Training of Military Forces from Latin America", *Third World Quarterly*, Vol. 27 No. 8, 2006. pp. 1439–61; Lisa Haugaard, "Textbook Repression: US Training Manuals Declassified", *Covert Action Quarterly*, vol. 61 (1997), pp. 1–9; Michael McClintock, *Instruments of Statecraft*, New York: Pantheon Books, 1992. Noam Chomsky is a constant critic in this tradition. See particularly, Noam Chomsky and Edward Herman, *The Washington Connection and Third World Fascism: The Political Economy of Human Rights*, Boston: South End Press, 1979 and *Postwar Indochina and the Reconstruction of Imperial Ideology. The Political Economy of Human Rights*, Nottingham: Spokesman, 1979. In this sense, the abuses in Abu Ghraib and Guantánamo could be seen as part of a longer standing tradition of US engagement in illegal practices rather than as a product of certain debates and practices in the 1990s, running through to the decision of the Bush Administration between 2001 and 2009 (particularly as regards the outsourcing of torture). In short, this literature is sceptical of the idea that the US engaging in torture was an aberration from "normal" US policies. I am very grateful to a reviewer for reminding me of this particular argument. However, this book does not engage in this critique for several reasons. First, the aim of the book is to look at prisoners in wars rather than detainees in CIA covert operations. In other words, it is primarily concerned about military operations where the Department of Defense played a large role in actual war-fighting rather than in the smaller, clandestine operations. In this sense, I have aimed to situate the book (to the best of my abilities) through the perspective of the DoD and the average soldier on the ground when taken prisoner and in taking prisoners. The book, rightly or wrongly, makes a *de facto* distinction between the two "types" of detainee. First, because covert operations, while possibly violating various US statutes including those on torture, may not have amounted the level of an "armed conflict"–at which point the Geneva Conventions would come into play. This relates to a second point, that such operations should be covered by international/domestic human rights law and not the laws of war. In this sense people captured in such operations, although prisoners, fall outside the scope of the book.

51. See Techniques A-Q listed in Appendix B

52. This is the term of the Schlesinger report, p. 910.

53. See Appendix A

54. For an interview with the Mora and an account of the internal debate within the Pentagon, see Jane Mayer, "The Memo: How an internal effort to ban the abuse

and torture of detainees was thwarted", *The New Yorker*, 20 February 2006. http://www.newyorker.com/fact/content/articles/060227fa_fact

55. For a list of the techniques, see Appendix B.

56. Schlesinger Report, p. 911.

57. Ibid.

58. In much of the critical literature on this, it is often said that Miller was deliberately sent to "Gitmo-ize" the prisons. See Hersh, *Chain of Command*, p. 31 and Rose, *Guantánamo*, p. 82. This would concur with the quote from the Schlesinger report quoted above.

59. Jane Mayer, "The experiment", *The New Yorker*, 11 July 2005. Mayer is citing a US military intelligence officer.

60. Schlesinger Report, p. 912.

61. Emily Bazelon and Dahlia Lithwick, "What is Torture?", *Slate Magazine*, 19 June 2006.

62. Duncan Campbell and Suzanne Goldenberg, "They said this is America... if a soldier orders you to take off your clothes, you must obey", *The Guardian*, 23 June 2004.

63. Schlesinger Report, p. 912.

64. Schlesinger Report, p. 921.

65. Schlesinger Report, p. 926.

66. A survey of the legal defences presented by those charged with abuse at Abu Ghraib is telling as to whether these individuals felt their actions were legal. At his court-martial, Charles Graner argued that the abuse was carried out at the behest of military intelligence officers and that he was following orders. However, Graner seems to have known that the activities being carried out were illegal, stating in his testimony, "A lot of it was wrong, a lot of it was criminal." Kate Zernike, "Ringleader in Iraqi prisoner abuse is sentenced to 10 years" *New York Times*, 15 January 2005, p. 12. Graner also acknowledged that the abuse was in direct violation of the law of war: "I know the Geneva Conventions, better than anyone else in my company. And we were called upon to violate the Geneva Conventions." T.R. Reid, "Graner gets 10 years for abuse at Abu Ghraib", *Washington Post*, 16 January 2005, p. A01. Lynndie England's defence rested on the fact that she was an overly compliant person who participated in the detainee abuse to please her then boyfriend, Graner–even though she knew the actions were wrong. "England sentenced to 3 years for prison abuse" MSNBC, 28 September 2005. Available online: http://www.msnbc.msn.com/id/9492624/; T.A. Badger, "Jury deliberations expected in Lynndie England's Abu Ghraib abuse case" Associated Press, 26 September 2005. Ivan Frederick indicated that he knew his actions were wrong, but that when he brought up the matter with his military commanders he was instructed to do as he was told. At his court-martial, Frederick came "to the conclusion that his actions broke the law" and pleaded guilty to charges of maltreating detainees, conspiracy to maltreat detainees, dereliction of duty and wrongfully committing an indecent act. Hugh Williamson, "Charges likely for two officers" *Financial Times*, 25 August 2004. Tony Paterson, "Soldier will admit role in Abu Ghraib abuse" *The Independent*, 24 August, 2004. Tim Reid, "Abu Ghraib abuser

jailed for 8 years", *The Times*, 22 October 2004, p. 4. Armin J. Cruz also pleaded guilty to the abuse on similar grounds, indicating that he knew his actions were wrong, and Specialist Cruz said, "There's no way to justify it." Norimitsu Onishi, "Military specialist pleads guilty to abuse and is jailed" *New York Times*, 11 September 2004; "US soldier pleads guilty in Iraq detainee abuse scandal" Agence France Presse, 11 September 2004. Jeremy Sivits, the first soldier charged with abuse at Abu Ghraib, testified that while some of his colleagues at the jail indicated that their actions were ordered or condoned by military intelligence, but he did not believe them. James Drummond, "Court martial sentences US soldier to year in jail for abusing Iraqi prisoners", *Financial Times*, 20 May 2004, p. 9. Specialist Sabrina Harman also argued that she knew the abuse was wrong but apparently felt "powerless to stop the sadistic activities when her superiors— Colonel Thomas Pappas, commander of military intelligence at the prison, and Lieutenant Colonel Steven Jordan, head of Abu Ghraib's interrogation centre– knew what was going on." "Hearing of US soldier accused of posing with Iraqi corpse raises questions", Agence France Presse, 25 June 2004. In this way, the individuals charged seemed to have realized that the activities they were doing were wrong and illegal but carried them on for different reasons. Those who argued that they had been given directions from their superiors claimed to have been rebuked when they brought up the issue of abuse. Therefore it seems that none of the individuals believed that their actions were legal, but that some may have been operating under the impression that they were either allowed or forced to carry out the abuse regardless of the law, and that the abuse was considered permissible.

67. Quoted in Mayer, "The Memo".
68. Schlesinger Report, p. 940.
69. Schlesinger Report, p. 917.
70. Chris Mackey and Greg Miller *The Interrogators: Task Force 500 and America's Secret War Against Al Qaeda*, New York: Back Bay Books, 2005. "Chris Mackey" is a pseudonym.
71. Mackey and Miller, *The Interrogators*, p. 288.
72. Although Mackey maintains that the interrogators remained well aware of their obligations under the Geneva Conventions. In an interview, Mackey added that at no time did anyone tell them that the Geneva Conventions did not apply. Interview with author via phone 11 March 2006.
73. Mackey and Miller, *The Interrogators*, p. 287.
74. Mackey and Miller, *The Interrogators*, p. 471.
75. Schlesinger Report, pp. 974–5. (Appendix H)
76. Schlesinger Report, p. 975.
77. More on training will be discussed at the end of the chapter.
78. There is some controversy over what PMFs should be called. Frequently one can find references to "Private Military Companies" (PMCs) or "Private Security Companies" (PSCs) in the literature. P.W. Singer, who has written several articles and a book on the phenomenon, argues that "firm" implies a broader context and "thus encompass the overall industry rather than just a subsector, but is also more

theoretically grounded, pointedly drawing from the business economics 'theory of the firm' literature." See P.W. Singer, "Corporate Warriors: The Rise of the Private Military Industry and its Ramifications for International Security." *International Security*, Vol. 26 No. 2, Winter 2001/2, pp. 186–220. pp. 186–7, note 2. Avant argues that the Iraq war is the latest manifestation of "a two decade long trend". See Deborah Avant, "Private Security Companies", *New Political Economy*, Vol. 10 No 1, March 2005. pp. 121–31. p. 122. Additionally, it should be noted that while the term "PMF" can apply to all contractors (from those supplying parts to those preparing food through those actually guarding diplomats and embassies), this section will focus on those groups which provide "security" and, as the international legal terminology would have it, may at times take a "direct part in hostilities".

79. *Economist*, "Military Industrial Complexities" 29 March 2003, p. 56.
80. P.W. Singer, "Outsourcing War: Understanding the Private Military Industry", *Foreign Affairs*, Vol. 84 No. 2, March/April 2005, pp. 119–32. Singer notes that this may imply that the "coalition of the willing" might be more aptly described as the "coalition of the billing".
81. Cited in P.W. Singer, "War, Profits, and the Vacuum of Law: Privatized Military Firms and International Law", *Columbia Journal of Transnational Law*, Vol. 42 No. 2, Spring 2004, pp. 521–50. p. 523.
82. Brian Bennett, "Outsourcing the War", *Time*, 26 March 2007. pp. 36–40. See also, Rod Norland and Mark Hosenball, "Blackwater is Soaked", *Newsweek*, 15 October 2007. p. 30. The article includes an interview with an anonymous colonel who recounts an incident where Blackwater guards drew their guns on American soldiers after a car accident in 2006.
83. Statistics from John M. Broder and David Johnston, "U.S. military will supervise security firms", *New York Times*, 31 October 2007. p. 1. On PMFs and legal issues surrounding direct participation, see Michael N. Schmitt, "Humanitarian Law and Direct Participation in Hostilities by Private Contractors or Civilian Employees", *Chicago Journal of International Law*, Vol. 5 No. 2, 2005. pp. 511–46. This issue will be raised below.
84. See Josh White, "Judge allows Abu Ghraib lawsuit against contractor", *Washington Post*, 7 November 2007 and Broder and Johnston, "U.S. military will supervise security firms".
85. Mr Steven Stephanowicz, with CACI, was cited for giving false statements to investigators and for allowing MPs who were not trained in interrogation techniques to facilitate interrogations by "setting conditions" which were not authorized. As the report states: "He clearly knew his instructions equated to abuse." Taguba Report, pp. 442–3. Another CACI employee, Mr John Israel, was also cited for giving false testimony. Taguba concludes that along with some of the other military personnel that were charged, Stephanowicz and Israel were "either directly or indirectly responsible for the abuses at Abu Ghraib." Taguba Report, p. 443.
86. Christopher Kinsey, "Challenging International Law: a Dilemma of Private Security Companies", *Conflict, Security & Development*, Vol. 5 No. 3, December 2005. pp. 269–93. p. 271.

87. Interestingly, this marked a significant move away from the idea that states were responsible for policing their own population's mercenary activities, towards individual criminal liability. Kinsey, "Challenging International Law", p. 273. On this point Kinsey also cites James Taulbee,"Myths, Mercenaries and Contemporary International Law", *California Western International Law Journal*, Vol. 15 No. 2, pp. 339–63. These developments and resentment over the participation of private military forces in African conflicts led to several declarations on mercenary activities.

88. Sarah Percy, *Regulating the Private Security Industry*, Adelphi Paper 384, London: International Institute for Strategic Studies, 2006. pp. 41–2.

89. Geoffrey Best, *Humanity in Warfare: The Modern History of the International Law of Armed Conflict*, p. 328 note 83.

90. As the argument here is concentrating on the US, other attempts at regulation will be ignored. Information on South Africa's legislation as well as any other relevant legislation put forward by (mostly) Western states is usefully summarized in Annex B of the Green Paper on mercenaries published by the UK government in 2002. HC577 *Private Military Companies: Options for Regulation* 12 February 2002. Foreign and Commonwealth Office, London: The Stationery Office. See also Percy, *Regulating the Private Security Industry*, pp. 30–2.

91. But even then, there were problems before Vietnam. Problems regarding jurisdiction over civilians may be said to go as far back as 1956, when the Supreme Court ruled in *Reid v. Covert* that the military could not try civilians using courts-martial, as these tribunals did not meet the guarantees in the Fifth and Six Amendments to the US Constitution regarding due process and rights of the accused. Heather Carney, "Prosecuting the Lawless: Human Rights Abuses and Private Military Firms", *George Washington Law Review*, Vol. 74 No. 2, 2006. pp. 317–44. p. 331.

92. Carney, "Prosecuting the Lawless", p. 331.

93. Percy, *Regulating the Private Security Industry*, pp. 28–9.

94. Carney, "Prosecuting the Lawless", p. 332.

95. Ibid.; Percy, *Regulating the Private Security Industry*, p. 29. One might also consider certain US regulations for PMFs under the International Traffic in Arms Regulations (ITAR). This provides for licensing within the US of PMFs in cases where their contracts involve arms transfers. Yet the licensing procedures have been described as "idiosyncratic". The input that the Defense and State Departments have regarding the licensing processes varies from case to case and neither companies nor independent observers have clear guidelines as to how the process works. Additionally, if the contract is worth less than US $50 million, any US military firm can work without notifying Congress. Many contracts already fall under this category and larger ones are easily broken up. Finally, as Singer points out, once a contract is awarded, there is little to no follow-up by the US government, or any other agency, to monitor the firms or their activities. On this point Singer cites Deborah D. Avant, "Privatizing Military Training", *Foreign Policy in Focus*, May 2000. Singer, "War, Profits and the Vacuum of Law", pp. 538–9.

96. See the discussion in Carney, "Prosecuting the Lawless", p. 333. The Alien Torts Claims Act as a possible means of regulation is also discussed in Tina Garmon, "Domesticating International Corporate Responsibility: Holding Private Military Firms Accountable under the Alien Tort Claims Act", *Tulane Journal of International and Comparative Law*, Vol. 11 No. 1, 2003. pp. 325–54; Nathaniel Stinnett, "Regulating the Privatization of War: How to Stop Private Military Firms From Committing Human Rights Abuses", *Boston College International and Comparative Law Review*, Vol. 28 No. 1, 2005. pp. 212–23. pp. 217–18.

97. See Julian Borger and Martin Hodgson, "A plane is shot down and the US proxy war on drug barons unravels" *The Guardian*, 2 June 2001.

98. Singer, "War, Profits and the Vacuum of Law", p. 538.

99. Bennett, "Outsourcing the War".

100. Percy, *Regulating the Private Security Industry*, p. 17. Percy cites Avant's research that in the *New York Times* in 2004 there were forty articles about casualties among regular troops for everyone on private security personnel.

101. Singer, "Outsourcing War".

102. These individuals are listed as *CIVILIAN-05, CACI employee*; *CIVILIAN-10, Translator, Titan employee*; *CIVILIAN-11, Interrogator, CACI employee*; *CIVILIAN-16, Translator, Titan employee*; *CIVILIAN-17, Interpreter, Titan employee*; *CIVILIAN-21, Interrogator, CACI employee*. The individual who was 'confused' is listed as *CIVILIAN-20, CACI employee*. See the Fay-Jones Report pp. 1122–5.

103. Mark Benjamin, "No justice for all" Salon.com, 14 April 2006. Available online at: http://www.salon.com/news/feature/2006/04/14/contractor/.

104. Benjamin, "No justice for all". Those prosecuted include: Spc. Megan Ambuhl, 372nd M.P. Co.; Spc. Armin J. Cruz Jr., 325th M.I. Battalion; Sgt. Javal S. Davis, 372nd M.P. Co.; Pfc. Lynndie England, 372nd M.P. Co.; Staff Sgt. Ivan Frederick II, 372nd M.P. Co.; Cpl. Charles A. Graner Jr., 372nd M.P. Co.; Spc. Sabrina Harman, 372nd M.P. Co.; Spc. Roman Krol, 325th M.I. Battalion Spc. Jeremy Sivits, 372nd M.P. Co.; Sgt. Santos Cardona, 320th M.P. Co.; Sgt. Michael J. Smith, 523rd M.P. Detachment. Also, in April 2006 Lt. Col. Steven L. Jordan became the first officer to face charges associated with the prison scandal. Most of the higher ranking officers, such as Karpinski, have faced non-judicial punishment.

105. Singer, "Outsourcing War".

106. Alissa J. Rubin, "Iraqi cabinet votes to end security firms' immunity", *New York Times*, 31 October 2007. p. 10.

107. See, Karen DeYoung, "Immunity jeopardizes Iraq probe", *Washington Post*, 30 October 2007, p. A01. Broder and Johnston, "U.S. military will supervise security firms",

108. Fay-Jones Report, pp. 1052–6.

109. Kjell Bjork and Richard Jones, "Overcoming Dilemmas Created by the 21st Century Mercenaries: Conceptualising the Use of Private Security Companies in Iraq", *Third World Quarterly*, Vol. 26 No. 4, 2005. pp. 777–96. Of course,

whether or not they look like "Hollywood figures", attacks on civilians in conflict zones (unless they are directly participating in hostilities) are illegal.

110. Jon Boone, "Blackwater scandal revives efforts on reforms", *Financial Times*, 2 November 2007. p. 6. However, the article goes on to suggest that the high level of corruption in Afghanistan will make cleaning up the industry–which is "a long way behind the regulatory regime that exists in Iraq"–very difficult. Yet an important difference is that most security companies in Iraq are owned and operated by foreigners.

111. Bennett, "Outsourcing War".

112. Walter Pincus, "Military weighs private security on front lines: firm could have broad protection authority in Afghanistan", *Washington Post*, 26 July 2009. Available online at: http://www.washingtonpost.com/wp-dyn/content/article/2009/07/25/AR2009072501738.html. Although the scale of use, and whether or not this plan would even come to fruition, were not clear at the time of writing.

113. I here refer to two authors and commentators on the laws of war: W. Hays Parks and Charles Garraway–both of whom have practiced as military lawyers specializing in the laws of war. Both of them comment on the importance of military ethos in a special issue of *Social Research* on "International Justice, War Crimes and Terrorism: The U.S. Record". See Charles H.B. Garraway, "Training: The Whys and Wherefores" and "The United States Military and the Law of War: Inculcating an Ethos", *Social Research* Vol. 69 No. 4 (Winter 2002), pp. 949–62 and pp. 981–1015 respectively.

114. Parks, "The United States Military and the Laws of War", p. 982.

115. Military manuals became a controversial issue in 2006 when it was announced that portions of an updated manual on the treatment of detainees would include a classified section on interrogation methods. Although it was announced that the techniques listed in that section would comply with the Geneva Conventions, some officials within the Department of Defense were reported as being concerned over this development as it would "send the wrong message", although others argued that it was necessary to keep techniques secret in the War on Terror. Human rights activists and some members of Congress also spoke out against having a classified section of the manual. In June 2006, Pentagon officials announced that plans to include a classified section would be dropped. The new manual on "Human Intelligence Collector Operations" (Army Field Manual 2–22.3) was released on 7 September 2006.

116. Parks, "The US Military and the Law of War", pp. 982–3.

117. Anthony E. Hartle, "Atrocities in War: Dirty Hands and Noncombatants" *Social Research* Vol. 69 No. 4 (Winter 2002), pp. 963–79. p. 964.

118. Garraway, "Training", pp. 954–7.

119. Parks, "The US Military and the Law of War", p. 994.

120. Garraway, "Training", pp. 955–6.

121. Parks, "The US Military and the Law of War", pp. 996–7.

122. Parks, "The US Military and the Law of War", p. 997.

123. Garraway, "Training", p. 951.

124. Schlesinger Report, p. 975.

125. Julian Borger, "US troops ordered to undergo ethical training after killing of Iraqi civilians", *The Guardian*, 2 June 2006. Available online: http://www.guardian.co.uk/Iraq/Story/0,,1788643,00.html; Ned Parker, "US orders coalition troops to take lessons in the ethics of battlefield" *The Times*, 2 June 2006. Available online: http://www.timesonline.co.uk/article/0,,7374–2207570,00.html; Hamza Hendawi, "U.S. Troops in Iraq to Get Ethics Training" CBS News, 1 June 2006. Available online: http://www.cbsnews.com/stories/2006/06/01/ap/world/mainD8HVL8EO3.shtml
Cited in Borger, "US Troops ordered to undergo ethical training".

126. Thomas Watkins, "US Marine Corps works on battlefield ethics after civilian deaths overseas", *Associated Press*, 14 July 2007.

127. *Boston Globe*, "An erosion of battlefield Ethics", 10 May 2007. p. A14. Indeed, the importance that Petraeus put on ethics is apparent from the *Counter Insurgency Manual* he helped to produce, published in 2006. Hoping to help the officers in the army "get it", the manual directly and explicitly links ethical behaviour and protection of the civilian population to the success of the COIN operation. On Petraeus' thinking and the process behind designing the COIN manual, see Thomas E. Ricks, *The Gamble: General David Petraeus and the American Military Adventure in Iraq 2006–2008*, New York: Penguin Press, 2009. (Especially Chapter 2.)

128. This was certainly the opinion of the UK Green Paper on the subject which looks at different regulating options. See "Private Military Companies, Options for Regulations", pp. 20–7.

129. Clive Walker and Dave Whyte, "Contracting Out War? Private Military Companies, Law and Regulation in the United Kingdom", *International and Comparative Law Quarterly*, Vol. 54, July 2005, pp. 651–90. p. 665.

130. Although by its own admission, the ICRC has used PMFs when operating in "exceptional cases and exclusively for the protection of premises". See "The ICRC to expand contacts with private military and security companies", ICRC website, http://www.icrc.org/Web/Eng/siteeng0.nsf/html/63HE58 4 August 2004.

131. ICRC "The ICRC to expand contacts with private military and security companies".

132. Ibid. These sentiments were further echoed in an ICRC press release, "Private military/security companies "acknowledge humanitarian law obligations", 27 November 2006. Available online: http://www.icrc.org/web/eng/siteeng0.nsf/html/private-military-companies-interview-271106?opendocument

133. Human Rights Watch, "Q&A: Private Military Contractors and the Law", http://hrw.orgenglish/docs/2004/05/05iraq8547_txt.htm 5 May 2004. Human Rights Watch indicates that this law is Title 18, section 7(9)(A) of the U.S. Code.

134. The amendment follows a high-profile case of Jamie Leigh Jones who claimed that she was drugged and raped by several employees of KBR in Iraq and, after

making the allegations, was put under guard in a shipping container with a bed and warned by the company that if she left Iraq for medical treatment, she would be out of a job. Leigh eventually sued to be granted access to the courts. On the case see, Brian Ross, Maddy Saur and Justin Roodab, "Victim: Gang-Rape Cover-Up by U.S., Halliburton/KBR", *ABC News*, 10 December 2007. Available online at: http://abcnews.go.com/Blotter/story?id=3977702&page=1&page=1; Chris McGreal, "Rape case to force US defence firms into the open", *Guardian*, 15 October 2009. http://www.guardian.co.uk/world/2009/oct/15/defence-contractors-rape-claim-block.

135. See the remarks of President Bush at a press conference in May 2005 where he indicates that Abu Ghraib is one of his biggest regrets about the Iraq invasion: "President Bush and Prime Minister Tony Blair of the United Kingdom participate in Joint Press Availability" 25 May 2006. Available online at: http://www.whitehouse.gov/news/releases/2006/05/20060525-12.html

136. Yet, despite the swift condemnation once the scandal came to light, there have still been problems with prosecuting the Marines who were involved in the incident. By November 2007, prosecutors had spent over a year putting a case together. However, one report indicated that "the evidence is contradictory, the forensic analysis is limited and almost all the witnesses have an obvious bias or prejudice." Quoted from Dan Ephron, "Haditha unraveled", *Newsweek*, 29 October 2007. p. 36. Part of the difficulty was that the investigation began only after the story broke in the papers, several months after the incident. This has rendered forensic and ballistic evidence virtually impossible to obtain (as well as the fact that the victim's families have not allowed investigators to exhume the bodies of those killed). Aside from the amount of time that elapsed between the killings and the beginning of the investigation, some of these problems have to do with the general difficulties of trying to conduct a murder investigation in a war zone–particularly one where insurgents hide among civilians. Eight Marines were eventually charged in the Haditha killings, making it the largest investigation arising out of the Iraq war so far. However, of these individuals, six have had their charges dropped and a seventh has been acquitted. As of writing, the sole remaining defendant in the case is squad leader Staff Sgt. Frank D. Wuterich, who does not at present have a court-martial scheduled. See Raymond Whitaker, "US Marines on trial for Iraq atrocity", *Independent on Sunday*, 21 October 2007. p. 32; Elliot Spagat, "Murder charge dropped in Iraqi detainee killing" *Associated Press*, 29 September 2009. See also the account of the incident and difficulties with the investigation in Ricks, *The Gamble*, pp. 1–8.

137. New and significant challenges in these areas are actually being felt by the UK, America's main ally, since the UK High Court of Justice ruled that certain human rights laws and treaties applied to areas under British control.

138. Jake Tapper, Jan Crawford-Greenburg and Huma Khan, "Obama Order to Shut Gitmo, CIA Detention Centers", ABC News, 22 January 2009. Available online at: http://abcnews.go.com/Politics/LawPolitics/story?id=6707095&page=1

139. Radio Free Europe/Radio Liberty, "Transcript: RFE/RL Interviews U.S. Central Command Chief, General David Petraeus", 24 May 2009. Available online at:

http://www.rferl.org/content/transcript_RFERL_Interviews_US_Central_
Command_Chief_General_David_Petraeus/1738626.html

140. Fox News, "General Petraeus discusses interrogation techniques, closing Gitmo
and Iran" 29 May 2009. No transcript available but video clip is available online
at: http://www.foxnews.com/video2/video08.html?maven_referralObject=545
7154&maven_referralPlaylistId=&sRevUrl=http://www.foxnews.com/
livedesk/.

CONCLUSION: THE UNITED STATES AND THE FUTURE OF THE LAW OF WAR

1. Walter Russell Mead, *Special Providence: American Foreign Policy and How it
Changed the World*, New York: Alfred A. Knopf, 2001. See the discussion in Chapter Five. Mead argues that although "Wilsonianism" takes its name from President
Woodrow Wilson, its origins are much older than his presidency. Instead, he looks
back to the American missionaries who, for the most part, believed in universal
values. As he writes: "Wilsoniansim is a universal, not a particular, ideal. That is,
no races, individuals, countries, or cultures are in principle excluded from the
Wilsonian vision of a world of peaceful democracies treating one another with
respect.... All nations an all peoples are assumed to be, or at least capable of becoming, equal." p. 169.

2. Mead, *Special Providence*, p. 172.

3. Max Boot, "What the Heck is a 'Neocon'?" *Opinion Journal*, 30 December 2002.
Available online: http://www.opinionjournal.com/editorial/feature.html?id=
110002840. As Boot argues, "Advocates of [hard Wilsonianism] embrace Woodrow Wilson's championing of American ideals but reject his reliance on international organizations and treaties to accomplish out objectives."

4. The foreign policy of the Nixon administration, clearly influenced by the *Realpolitik* of Henry Kissinger, being a possible exception.

5. "Richard B. Cheney, "Remarks by Richard B. Cheney", 21 May 2009. Available
online at: http://www.aei.org/speech/100050.

6. Rt Hon. Dr John Reid MP, Secretary of State for Defence, "Twenty-first Century
Warfare–Twentieth Century Rules", Banqueting House, Royal Palace of Whitehall,
3 April 2006. Whether or not this accurately reflects the opinion of Ministry of
Defence lawyers is, of course, unclear.

7. Christopher Greenwood, "International Law and the 'War against Terrorism'"
International Affairs, Vol. 78, No. 2, 2004, pp. 301–17. p. 301.

8. In making the case for national security in line with American values, Obama did
not invoke the Geneva Convention or international law. Barack Obama, "Remarks
by the President on National Security", 21 May 2009. Available online at: http://
www.whitehouse.gov/the_press_office/Remarks-by-the-President-On-National-
Security-5-21-09/.

APPENDIX A

1. Officer in charge.
2. "Meals Ready to Eat".

APPENDIX B

1. A lengthy guidance note here indicates that this technique requires detailed implementation instructions and that this technique has generally not known to be used for interrogation purposes for longer than thirty days. Additionally, the note specifies that this technique may be in violation of Article 13, 14, 34 and 126 of the Geneva Conventions which outline guidance on acts of intimidation, respect for the person, standards of treatment, etc.

BIBLIOGRAPHY

Abell, Francis. *Prisoners of War in Britain 1756–1815: A Record of their Lives, Their Romance and Their Sufferings*, Oxford University Press, 1914.

Abler, Thomas S. "Scalping, Torture, Cannibalism and Rape: An Ethnohistorical Analysis of Conflicting Cultural Values in War", *Anthropologica*, Vol. 34 No. 1, 1992. pp 3–20.

af Jochnick, Chris and Roger Normand. "The Legitimation of Violence: A Critical History of the Laws of War", *Harvard International Law Journal*, Vol. 35 No. 1, 1994. pp. 49–95.

Aldrich, George H. "New Life for the Laws of War", *American Journal of International Law*, Vol. 75 No. 4, October 1981. pp. 764–83.

———— "Some Reflections on the Origins of the 1977 Geneva Protocols", in Christophe Swinarski, ed. *Studies and Essays on International Humanitarian Law and Red Cross Principles in Honour of Jean Pictet*, Hague: Martinus Nijhoff Publishers, 1984. pp. 129–37.

———— "Comments on the Geneva Conventions", *International Review of the Red Cross*, No. 320, October 1997. pp. 508–10.

Alter, Jonathan. "Time to Think about Torture", *Newsweek*, 5 November 2001.

American Journal of International Law, "The Red Cross in Civil Wars", Editorial Comment, Vol. 5 No. 2, 1911. pp. 438–40.

Anderson, Chandler P. "Agreement Between the United States and Germany Concerning Prisoners of War", *The American Journal of International Law*, Vol. 13 No. 1, 1919, pp. 97–101.

Anderson, Fred. *Crucible of War: The Seven Years' War and the Fate of Empire in British North America, 1754–1766*, London: Faber and Faber, 2000.

———— and Andrew Cayton, *The Dominion of War: Empire and Conflict in America, 1500–2000*, London: Atlantic Books, 2005.

Anderson, Olive. "British Governments and Rebellion at Sea", *The Historical Journal*, Volume III No. I, 1960. pp. 56–84.

Applebaum, Anne. *Gulag: A History of the Soviet Camps*, London: Penguin Books Limited, 2004.

Avant, Deborah D. "Privatizing Military Training", *Foreign Policy in Focus*, May 2000.

———"Private Security Companies", *New Political Economy*, Vol. 10 No 1, March 2005. pp. 121–31.

Baker, James E. "Judging Kosovo: The Legal Process, the Law of Armed Conflict and the Commander in Chief", pp. 7–26 in Andru E. Wall, *Legal and Ethical Lessons of NATO's Kosovo Campaign*, International Law Studies Volume 78, Newport, RI: Naval War College, 2002.

Bazelon, Emily and Dahlia Lithwick. "What is Torture?", *Slate Magazine*, 19 June 2006.

Becker, Laura L. "Prisoners of War in the American Revolution: A Community Perspective", *Military Affairs*, Vol. 46 No. 4, December 1982, pp. 169–73.

Benjamin, Mark. "No justice for all" Salon.com, 14 April 2006. Available online at: http://www.salon.com/news/feature/2006/04/14/contractor/.

Best, Geoffrey. *Humanity in Warfare: The Modern History of International Law of Armed Conflicts*, London: Methuen & Co., 1980.

——— *War and Law Since 1945*, Oxford University Press, 1994.

Bilton, Michael and Kevin Sim. *Four Hours in My Lai: a War Crime and its Aftermath*, London: Viking, 1992.

Birtle, Andrew. "The Origins of the Legion of the United States", *The Journal of Military History*, Vol. 67 No. 4, October 2003. pp. 1249–61.

Bjork, Kjell and Richard Jones. "Overcoming Dilemmas Created by the 21st Century Mercenaries: Conceptualising the Use of Private Security Companies in Iraq", *Third World Quarterly*, Vol. 26 No. 4, 2005. pp. 777–96.

Black, Jeremy. *War for America: The Fight for Independence 1775–1783*, Phoenix Mill: Sutton Publishing, 2001.

Bolton, John R. "Courting Danger: What's Wrong with the International Criminal Court", *The National Interest*, Winter 1998/1999.

——— "The Global Prosecutors: Hunting War Criminals in the Name of Utopia", *Foreign Affairs*, Vol. 78 No. 1, 1999. pp. 157–64.

——— "Is There Really "Law" in International Affairs?", *Transnational Law and Contemporary Problems*, Vol. 10 No. 1, 2000. pp. 1–48.

Boot, Max. *The Savage Wars of Peace: Small Wars and the Rise of American Power*, New York: Basic Books, 2002.

——— "What the Heck is a 'Neocon'?" *Opinion Journal*, 30 December 2002. Available online: http://www.opinionjournal.com/editorial/feature.html?id=110002840.

Booth, Ken. *The Kosovo Tragedy: The Human Rights Dimension*, London: Frank Cass Publishers, 2000.

——— and Tim Dunne eds. *Worlds in Collision*, Basingstoke: Palgrave Macmillan, 2002.

Borch, Frederic L. *Judge Advocates in Combat: Army Lawyers in Military Operations from Vietnam to Haiti*, Washington: Office of the Judge Advocate General and Center of Military History United States Army, 2001.

Bork, Robert. "The Limits of International Law", *The National Interest*, Winter 1989/1990. pp. 1–10.

Bothe, Michael; Partsch, Karl Joseph and Solf, Waldemar A., *New Rules for Victims of Armed Conflicts: Commentary on the Two 1977 Protocols Additional to the Geneva Conventions of 1949*, The Hague: Martinus Nijhoff publishers, 1982.

Bowman, Steve. "Iraq: U.S. Military Operations", Congressional Research Service, Library of Congress, Updated 23 January 2006. Available online: http://fpc.state.gov/documents/organization/25375.pdf.

Brumwell, Stephen. *Redcoats: The British Soldiers and the War in the Americas, 1755–1763*, Cambridge University Press, 2002.

Byers, Michael. *Custom, Power and the Power of Rules: International Relations and Customary International Law*, Cambridge University Press, 1999.

——— ed. *The Role of Law in International Politics: Essays in International Relations and International Law*, Oxford University Press, 2000.

——— War Law: International Law and Armed Conflict, London: Atlantic Books, 2005.

Byrne, Frank L. "Libby Prison: A Study in Emotion", *The Journal of Southern History*, Vol. 24 No. 4, 1958. pp. 430–44.

Carney, Heather. "Prosecuting the Lawless: Human Rights Abuses and Private Military Firms", *George Washington Law Review*, Vol. 74 No. 2, 2006. pp. 317–44.

Carney, Stephen A. *The Occupation of Mexico: May 1846–July 1848*, Washington: U.S. Army Center of Military History, 2005.

Carr, E.H. *The Twenty Year's Crisis 1919–1939: An Introduction to the Study of International Relations*, Basingstoke: Palgrave, 2001.

Carvin, Stephanie. "Caught in the Cold: International Humanitarian Law and Prisoners of War During the Cold War", *Journal of Conflict and Security Law*, Vol. 11 No. 1, 2006. pp. 67–92.

Cassese, Antonio. *International Law*, Second edition. Oxford University Press, 2005.

——— ed. *The Rome Statute for an International Criminal Court: A Commentary*, Oxford University Press, 2002.

Clark, Wesley K. *Waging Modern War: Bosnia, Kosovo and the Future of Conflict*, Oxford: Public Affairs, 2001.

——— "An Army of One?" *Washington Monthly*, September 2002. Available online: http://www.washingtonmonthly.com/features/2001/0209.clark.html.

Clausewitz, Carl von. *On War*, ed. and trans. Michael Howard and Peter Paret, Princeton University Press, 1976.

Cooke, John D. "Introduction: Fiftieth Anniversary of the Uniform Code of Military Justice Symposium Edition", *Military Law Review*, Vol. 165, September 2000. pp. 1–20.

Corn, David. "The "Suicide Pact" Mystery: Who coined the phrase? Justice Goldberg or Justice Jackson?", Slate.com, 4 January 2002.

Crackel, Theodore J., *West Point: A Bicentennial History*, Lawrence: University Press of Kansas, 2002.

Daalder, Ivo H. and Michael E. O'Hanlon. *Winning Ugly: NATO's War to Save Kosovo*, Washington: Brookings Institute Press, 2000.

Detter, Ingrid. *The Law of War*, Second Edition. Cambridge University Press, 2000.

Dershowitz, Alan. "Is There a Torturous Road to Justice?" *Los Angeles Times*, 8 November 2001.

Diamond, Larry. "What Went Wrong in Iraq", *Foreign Affairs*, Vol. 83 No. 5, September/October 2004.

Dinstein, Yoram. *The Conduct of Hostilities under the Law of International Armed Conflict*, Cambridge University Press, 2004.

Duffy, Helen. *The 'War on Terror' and the Framework of International Law*, Cambridge University Press, 2005.

Dufour, Charles L. *The Mexican War: A Compact History 1846–1848*, New York: Hawthorn Books Inc. 1968.

Dillon, Richard H. *North American Indian Wars*, Wigston: Magna Boods, 1983.

Eckhardt, William George. "Lawyering for Uncle Sam When He Draws His Sword", *Chicago Journal of International Law*, Vol. 4, 2003. pp. 431–44.

Ethics and International Affairs. "Roundtable: The New War–What Rules Apply?" Vol. 16 No. 1, pp. 1–26, 2002.

Fabel, Robin F. "Self-Help in Dartmoor: Black and White Prisoners in the War of 1812", *Journal of the Early Republic*, Vol. 9 No. 2, Summer 1989, pp. 165–90.

Falk, Richard, ed. *The Vietnam War and International Law*, Vol. 2. Princeton University Press, 1969.

Feith, Douglas J. "Law in the Service of Terror—The Strange Case of the Additional Protocol", *The National Interest*, No. 1, 1985.

———— "International Responses", in Uri Ra'anan *et al.* eds. *Hydra of Carnage, International Linkages of Terrorism*, Lanham, MD: Lexington Books, 1986.

———— "Protocol I: Moving Humanitarian Law Backwards", *Akron Law Review*, Vol. 19, 1986. pp. 531–5.

Flory, William E.S. *Prisoners of War: A Study in the Development of International Law*, Washington: American Council on Public Affairs, 1942.

Fooks, Herbert C. *Prisoners of War*, Federalsburg: The J.W. Stowell Printing Co., 1924.

Frey, Bruno S. and Heinz Buhofer. "Prisoners and Property Rights", *Journal of Law and Economics*, Vol. 31 No. 1, 1988. pp. 19–46.

Fritz, David L. "Before the 'Howling Wilderness': The Military Career of Jacob Hurd Smith, 1862–1902", *Military Affairs*, Vol. 43 No. 4, December 1979, pp. 186–90.

Forsythe, David P. "Legal Management of Internal War: The 1977 Protocol on Non-International Armed Conflicts", *American Journal of International Law*, Vol. 72 No. 2, 1978. pp. 272–95.

———— "The United States and International Criminal Justice", *Human Rights Quarterly*, 24 (2002). pp. 974–91.

———— *The Humanitarians*, Cambridge University Press, 2005.

Garmon, Tina. "Domesticating International Corporate Responsibility: Holding Private Military Firms Accountable under the Alien Tort Claims Act", *Tulane Journal of International and Comparative Law*, Vol. 11 No. 1, 2003. pp. 325–54.

Garner, James Wilford, *International Law and the World War*, London: Longmans, Green and Co., 1920.

Garratt, David. "The Role of Legal Advisors in the Armed Forces" in *The Gulf War 1990–91 in International and English Law*, ed. Peter Rowe, London: Routledge, 1993.

Garraway, Charles H.B. "Training: The Whys and Wherefores", *Social Research*, Vol. 69 No. 4, Winter 2002, pp. 949–62.

Gartner, Scott Sigmund and Marissa Edson Myers. "Body Counts and 'Success' in the Vietnam and Korean Wars", *Journal of Interdisciplinary History*, Vol. 25 No. 3, Winter 1995. pp. 377–95.

Gearty, Conor. "Legitimising Torture—with a Little Help", *Index on Censorship* Issue 1/05, 2005.

Gordon, Michael and Bernard Trainor. *Cobra II: The Inside Story of the Invasion and Occupation of Iraq*, London: Atlantic Books, 2006.

Grabowski, Jan. "French Criminal Justice and Indians in Montreal, 1670–1760", *Ethnohistory*, Vol. 43 No. 3 (Summer 1996). pp. 405–29.

Goldsmith, Jack L. and Eric A. Posner. *The Limits of International Law*, Oxford University Press, 2005.

Goldsmith, Jack. *The Terror Presidency: Law and Judgment Inside the Bush Administration*, New York: W.W. Norton & Company, Inc. 2007.

Graham, David E. "Operational Law (OPLAW)–A Concept Comes of Age", *The Army Lawyer*, July 1987. pp. 9–10.

Green, L.C. *Essays on the Modern Laws of War*, Second Edition, New York: Transnational Publishers, Inc., 1998.

Greenberg, Karen J. and Joshua L. Dratel eds, *The Torture Papers: The Road to Abu Ghraib*, Cambridge University Press, 2005.

Greene, Jack P. and J.R. Pole eds. *A Companion to the American Revolution*, Malden: Blackwell Publishers Inc., 2000. pp. 413–18.

Greenwood, Christopher. "Customary International Law and the First Geneva Protocol of 1977 in the Gulf Conflict" in *The Gulf War 1990–91 in International and English Law*, ed. Peter Rowe, London: Routledge, 1993. pp. 63–88.

———— "International Law and the 'War against Terrorism'", *International Affairs*, Vol. 78 No. 2, 2004. pp. 301–17.

———— *Essays on War in International Law*, London: Cameron May 2006.

Grey, Stephen. *Ghost Plane: The Untold Story of the CIA's Secret Rendition Programme*, London: Hurst, 2006.

Gutman, Roy and David Rieff, eds. *Crimes of War: What the Public Should Know*, New York: W.W. Norton and Company, 1999.

Hackworth, Green Haywood. *Digest of International Law: Volume VI Chapters XIX-XXI*, Washington: United States Government Printing Office, 1943. pp. 279–80.

Hampson, Françoise J. "Means and Methods of Warfare in the Conflict in the Gulf", in *The Gulf War 1990–91 in International and English Law*, ed. Peter Rowe, London: Routledge, 1993.

Haney, C., C. Banks and P. Zimbardo. "Interpersonal Dynamics in a Simulated Prison", *International Journal of Criminology and Penology*, No. 1, 1973. pp. 69–97.

Hartle, Anthony E. "Atrocities in War: Dirty Hands and Noncombatants", *Social Research*, Vol. 69 No. 4, Winter 2002. pp. 963–79.

Hay, John. "Instructions to the American Delegates to the Hague Conferences", as reprinted in: *World Peace Foundation Pamphlet Series*, Vol. III No. 4, April 1913.

Haynes, Sam W. *Soldiers of Misfortune: The Somervell and Mier Expeditions*, Austin: University of Texas Press, 1990.

Hartigan, Richard. *The Forgotten Victim: A History of the Civilian*, Chicago: Precedent, 1982.

Helms, Jesse. "American Sovereignty and the UN", *The National Interest*, Winter 2000/2001.

Henckaerts, Jean-Marie and Louise Doswald-Beck. *Customary International Humanitarian Law, Volume 1: Rules*, Cambridge University Press, 2005.

Hersh, Seymour M. *Cover-Up: The Army's Secret Investigation of the Massacre at My Lai 4*, New York: Random House, 1972.

——— *Chain of Command: The Road from 9/11 to Abu Ghraib*, New York: HarperCollins Publishers, 2005.

Hesseltine, William B. "The Propaganda Literature of Confederate Prisons", *The Journal of Southern History*, Vol. 1 No. 1, 1953. pp. 56–66.

Hibbert, Christopher. *Red Coats and Rebels: The War for America 1770–1781*, London: Penguin Books Ltd, 2001.

Higginbotham, Don. *The War of American Independence: Military Attitudes, Policies and Practice, 1763–1789*, Boston: Northeastern University Press, 1983.

Hitsman, J. Mackay. *The Incredible War of 1812: A Military History*, University of Toronto Press, 1965.

Hoge, James F. and Gideon Rose, eds. *How Did This Happen? Terrorism and the New War*, New York: HarperCollins Publishers, 2001.

——— *War on Terror: Updated and Expanded*, New York: Council on Foreign Relations, 2003.

——— *Understanding the War on Terror*, New York: Council on Foreign Relations, 2005.

Horseman, Reginald. *Expansion and American Indian Policy, 1783–1812*, Norman: University of Oklahoma Press, 1992.

Howard, Michael. "*Tempermenta Belli*: Can War Be Controlled" in Michael Howard, ed. *Restraints on War: Studies in the Limitation of Armed Conflict*, Oxford University Press, 1979.

Human Rights Watch. "'No Blood, No Foul': Soldiers' Accounts of Detainee Abuse in Iraq", *Human Rights Watch*, Vol. 18 No. 3(G), July 2006. Available online: http://hrw.org/reports/2006/us0706/us0706web.pdf.

Hunter, Charles E. "The Delaware Nativist Revival of the Mid-Eighteenth Century", *Ethnohistory*, Vol. 18 No. 1 (Winter 1971). pp. 39–49.

Ignatieff, Michael. *Virtual War: Kosovo and Beyond*, Toronto: Viking, 2000.

———— *The Lesser Evil: Political Ethics in an Age of Terror*, Edinburgh University Press, 2004.

———— "The Lesser Evil", Letter published in the *New York Review of Books*, 15 August 2004.

Jennings, Francis. *Empire of Fortune: Crown, Colonies, and Tribes in the Seven Years War in America*, New York: W.W. Norton & Company, 1988.

Jessup Philip C. *Elihu Root: Volume II 1905–1937*, New York: Dodd, Mead & Company, 1938.

Johnson, James Turner and John Kelsay eds. *Cross, Crescent and Sword: the Justification and Limitation of War in Western and Islamic Tradition*, New York, Greenwood Press, 1990.

Johnson, James Turner. *The Holy War Idea in Western and Islamic Traditions*, University Park, Pa.: Pennsylvania State University Press, 1997.

Judah, Tim. *Kosovo: War and Revenge*, New Haven: Yale Nota Bene, 2000.

Karnow, Stanley. *In Our Image: America's Empire in the Philippines*, New York: Random House, 1989.

Karpinski, Janis. *One Woman's Army: The Commanding General of Abu Ghraib Tells Her Story*, New York: Miramax Books, 2005.

Keeva, Steven. "Lawyers in the War Room", *American Bar Association Journal*, December 1991. pp. 52–9.

Kinsey, Christopher. "Challenging International Law: a Dilemma of Private Security Companies", *Conflict, Security & Development*, Vol. 5 No. 3, December 2005. pp. 269–93.

Knight, Betsey. "Prisoner Exchange and Parole in the American Revolution", *The William and Mary Quarterly*, 3rd Ser., Vol. 48 No. 2 (April 1991). pp. 201–22.

Koskenniemi, Martti. *The Gentle Civilizer of Nations: The Rise and Fall of International Law 1870–1960*, Cambridge University Press, 2001.

———— "The Politics of International Law", *European Journal of International Law*, Vol. 1 No. 1. 1990.

Krammer, Arnold P. "German Prisoners of War in the United States", *Military Affairs*, Vol. 40 No. 2, 1976. pp. 68–73.

———— "Japanese Prisoners of War in America", *The Pacific Historical Review*, Vol. 52 No. 1, 1983.

Lammers, Stephen. "Approaches to Limits on War in Western Just War Discourse", in James Turner Johnson and John Kelsay eds, *Cross, Crescent and Sword: the Justification and Limitation of War in Western and Islamic Tradition*, New York: Greenwood Press, 1990.

BIBLIOGRAPHY

Lauterpacht, Hersh. "The Limits of the Operation of the Laws of War", *British Yearbook of International Law*, Volume 30, 1953. pp. 206–43.

Leopold, Richard W. *Elihu Root and the Conservative Tradition*, Boston: Little, Brown and Company, 1954.

Lewy, Guenter. *America in Vietnam*, New York: Oxford University Press, 1978.

Lifton, Robert Jay. "Doctors and Torture", *New England Journal of Medicine*, Vol. 315 No. 5, 2004. pp. 415–16.

Linn, Brian McAllister. *The US Army and Counterinsurgency in the Philippine War 1899–1902*, Chapel Hill: The University of North Carolina Press, 1989.

Lowe, Vaughan. "Legal Issues Arising in the Kosovo Crisis", in "Special Issue: The Kosovo Crisis and International Humanitarian Law", *International Review of the Red Cross*, No. 837, March 2000.

Mackenzie, S.P. "The Treatment of Prisoners of War in World War II", *The Journal of Modern History*, Vol. 66 No. 3, 1994. pp. 487–520.

Mackey, Chris and Greg Miller. *The Interrogators: Task Force 500 and America's Secret War Against Al Qaeda*, New York: Back Bay Books, 2005.

MacLeod, D. Peter "Microbes and Muskets: Small Pox and the Participation of the Amerindian Allies of New France in the Seven Years' War", *Ethnohistory*, Vol. 39 No. 1 (Winter 1992). pp. 42–62.

Maguire, Peter. *Law and War: An American Story*, New York: Columbia University Press, 2001.

Mandelbaum, Michael. "A Perfect Failure", *Foreign Affairs*, Vol. 98 No. 5, 1999.

Mansell, Wade. "Goodbye to All That? The Rule of Law, International Law, the United States and the Use of Force", *Journal of Law and Society*, Vol. 31 No. 4, December 2004. pp. 433–56.

Matheson, Michael J. "The United States Position on the Relation of Customary Law to the 1977 Protocols Additional to the 1949 Conventions", *American University Journal of International Law and Policy*, 1987. pp. 419–31.

Mayer, Jane. "The Experiment", *The New Yorker*, 11 July 2005.

——— "The Memo", *The New Yorker*, 27 February 2006.

——— "The Hidden Power: The legal mind behind the White House's war on terror", *The New Yorker*, 3 July 2006. pp. 44–55.

——— *The Dark Side: The Inside Story of How the War on Terror TurnediInto a War on American Ideals*, New York: Anchor Books, 2008.

McCaffrey, James M. *The Army of Manifest Destiny: The American Soldier in the Mexican War, 1846–1848*, New York University Press, 1992.

McCain, John. *Faith of My Fathers*, New York: Random House, 1999.

McCornack, Richard Blaine. "The San Patricio Deserters in the Mexican War", *The Americas*, Vol. 8 No. 2, 1951. pp. 131–42.

McGoldrick, Dominic. *From '9–11' to the 'Iraq War 2003': International Law in an Age of Complexity*, Portland: Hart Publishing, 2004.

Mckeogh, Colm. *Innocent Civilians: The Morality of Killing in War*, Basingstoke: Palgrave Macmillan, 2002.

Mead, Walter Russell. *Special Providence: American Foreign Policy and How it Changed the World*, New York: Alfred A. Knopf, 2001.

Merrell, James H. "Amerindians and the New Republic" in Jack P. Greene and J.R. Pole eds. *A Companion to the American Revolution*, Malden: Blackwell Publishers Inc., 2000. pp. 413–8.

Mertus, Julie A. *The United Nations and Human Rights: A Guide for a New Era*, London: Routledge, 2005.

Miller, Judith A. "Commentary", in Andru E. Wall, *Legal and Ethical Lessons of NATO's Kosovo Campaign*, International Law Studies Volume 78, Newport, RI: Naval War College, 2002. pp. 107–12.

Moorehead, Caroline. *Dunant's Dream: War, Switzerland and the History of the Red Cross*, London: HarperCollins, 1999.

Morgan, Edmund M. "The Background of the Uniform Code of Military Justice", *Military Law Review*, Vol. 28, April 1965.

Murphy, Sean D. ed. *United States Practice in International Law: Volume 1: 1999–2001*, Cambridge University Press, 2002.

Nash, William L. "The Laws of War: A Military View", *Ethics and International Affairs*, Vol. 16 No. 1, 2002.

Nolan, Cathal J. "Americans in the Gulag: Detention of US Citizens by Russia and the Onset of the Cold War, 1944–9", *Journal of Contemporary History*, Vol. 24 No. 4, October 1990. pp. 523–45.

Normand, Roger and Chris af Jochnick "The Legitimation of Violence: A Critical Analysis of the Gulf War", *Harvard International Law Journal*, Vol. 35 No. 2, 1994. pp. 387–416.

Onuf, Nicholas. "Do Rules Say What they Do? From Ordinary Language to International Law", *Harvard International Law Journal*, Vol. 26 No. 2, 1985.

Owens, Mackubin Thomas. "Men@War: Hadithah in context", *National Review Online*, 30 May 2006. Available online at: http://article.nationalreview.com.

Parks, W. Hays. "Crimes in Hostilities", *Marine Corps Gazette* LX, No. 9, September 1976. pp. 38–9.

———— "The Law of War Advisor", *JAG Journal*, Vol. 31, Summer 1980. pp. 1–52.

———— "Rolling Thunder and the Law of War" *Air University Review*, Vol. XXXIII No. 2, 1982 and "Linebacker and the Law of War", *Air University Law Review*, Vol. XXXIV No. 2, 1983.

———— "Air War and the Laws of War", *Air Force Law Review*, Vol. 32, 1990. pp. 1–225.

———— "The Gulf War: A Practitioner's View", *Dickinson Journal of International Law*, Vol. 10 No. 3, 1991–92. pp. 393–423.

———— "The United States Military and the Law of War: Inculcating an Ethos", *Social Research*, Vol. 69 No 4, Winter 2002. pp. 981–1015.

———— "The ICRC Customary Law Study: A Preliminary Assessment", *American Society of International Law Proceedings*, Vol. 99, 2005.

———— "Means and Methods of Warfare", *George Washington International Law Review*, Vol. 38 No. 3, 2006. pp. 511–39.

BIBLIOGRAPHY

Parmenter, John William. "Pontiac's War: Forging New Links in the Anglo-Iroquois Convenant Chain, 1758–1766", *Ethnohistory*, Vol. 44 No. 4 (Autumn, 1997). pp. 617–54.

Percy, Sarah. *Regulating the Private Security Industry*, Adelphi Paper 384, London: International Institute for Strategic Studies, 2006.

Pictet, Jean S. ed. *Commentary: III Geneva Convention Relative to the Treatment of Prisoners of War*, Geneva: International Committee of the Red Cross, 1960.

Prelinger, Catherine M. "Benjamin Franklin and the American Prisoners of War in England during the American Revolution", *The William and Mary Quarterly*, 3rd Ser., Vol. 32 No. 2, April 1975. pp. 261–94.

Provost, René. *International Human Rights and Humanitarian Law*, Cambridge Studies in International and Comparative Law, Cambridge University Press, 2002.

Prugh, George S. Jr. "The Code of Conduct for the Armed Forces", *Columbia Law Review*, Vol. 56 No. 5, 1956. pp. 678–707.

———— *Law at War: Vietnam 1964–1973*, Washington: Department of the Army, 1975.

———— "Observations on the Uniform Code of Military Justice: 1954 and 2000", *Military Law Review*, Vol. 165, September 2000. pp. 21–41.

Rabkin, Jeremy. "After Guantanamo: The War Over the Geneva Conventions", *The National Interest*, Summer 2002.

———— *Law Without Nations: Why Constitutional Government Requires Sovereign States*, Princeton University Press, 2005.

Ramsey, Paul. *War and the Christian Conscience: How Shall Modern War be Conducted Justly*, Durham, NC: Duke University Press, 1961.

Raniet, Philip. "British Recruitment of Americans in New York During the American Revolution", *Military Affairs*, Vol. 88 No. 1, January 1984.

Reus-Smits, Christian ed. *The Politics of International Law*, Cambridge University Press, 2004.

Richter, Daniel K. "War and Culture: The Iroquois Experience", *The William and Mary Quarterly*, Vol. 40 No. 4 (October 1983). pp. 528–59.

Ricks, Thomas E. *The Gamble: General David Petraeus and the American Military Adventure in Iraq, 2006–2008*, New York: Penguin Press, 2009.

Rivkin Jr., David B. and Lee A. Casey. "The Rocky Shoals of International Law" *The National Interest*, Winter 2000/2001.

Roberts, Adam. "Nato's 'Humanitarian War' over Kosovo", *Survival*, Vol. 41 No. 3, 1999. pp. 102–23.

———— "The Law of War After Kosovo", in Andru E. Wall, *Legal and Ethical Lessons of NATO's Kosovo Campaign*, International Law Studies Volume 78, Newport, RI: Naval War College, 2002. pp. 401–32.

———— "Transformative Military Occupation: Applying the Laws of War and Human Rights", *American Journal of International Law*, Vol. 100 No. 3, July 2006. pp. 580–622.

Roberts, Adam and Richard Guelff. *Documents on the Laws of War*, Third Edition, Oxford University Press, 1999.

Robinson, Ralph. "Retaliation for the Treatment of Prisoners in the War of 1812", *The American Historical Review*, Vol. 49 No. 1, October 1943, pp. 65–70.

Rogers, A.P.V. *Law on the Battlefield*, Second Edition, Manchester University Press, 2004.

Rogers, J. Alan. "Colonial Opposition to the Quartering of Troops During the French and Indian War", *Military Affairs*, Vol. 34 No. 1 (February 1970), pp. 7–11.

Rose, David. *Guantánamo: America's War on Human Rights*, London: Faber and Faber, 2004.

Rowe, Peter. *The Gulf War 1990–91 in International and English Law*, ed. Peter Rowe, London: Routledge, 1993. pp. 188–204.

———— "Prisoners of War in the Gulf Arena" in *The Gulf War 1990–91 in International and English Law*, ed. Peter Rowe, London: Routledge, 1993. pp. 188–204.

Russell, Frederick H. *The Just War in the Middle Ages*, Cambridge University Press, 1975.

Sands, Philippe. *Lawless World: American and the Making and Breaking of Global Rules*, London: Allen Lane, 2005.

———— *Torture Team: Uncovering War Crimes in the Land of the Free*, London: Penguin, 2009.

Santoni, Pedro. "The Failure of Mobilization: The Civic Militia of Mexico in 1846", *Mexican Studies/Estudios Mexicanos*, Vol. 12 No. 2, 1996. pp. 169–94.

Schabas, William. *An Introduction to the International Criminal Court*, Cambridge University Press, 2001.

Scheffer, David. "Why Hamdan is Right about Conspiracy Liability", *Jurist: Legal News and Research*, 30 March 2006. Available online: http://jurist.law.pitt.edu/forumy/2006/03/why-hamdan-is-right-about-conspiracy.php

Scheffer, David J. "Court Order", Letter published in *Foreign Affairs*, November/December 2001.

Schmitt, Michael N. "Conduct of Hostilities During Operation Iraqi Freedom: An International Humanitarian Law Assessment", *6 Yearbook of International Humanitarian Law*, 2003, pp. 73–110.

———— "The Law of Belligerent Occupation", Crimes of War Project, 15 April 2003. Available online: http://www.crimesofwar.org/special/Iraq/news-iraq5.html.

———— "Targeting and Humanitarian Law: Current Issues", *34 Israel Yearbook on Human Rights*, 2004, pp. 59—104.

———— "Humanitarian Law and Direct Participation in Hostilities by Private Contractors or Civilian Employees", *Chicago Journal of International Law*, Vol 5 No. 2, 2005. pp. 511–46.

Schwarzenberger, Georg. *A Manual of International Law*, 5th Edition. London: Stevens & Sons Limited, 1967.

Shearer, David. "Outsourcing War", *Foreign Policy*, Issue 112, Fall 1998.

BIBLIOGRAPHY

———— *Private Armies and Military Intervention*, Adelphi Paper 316, Oxford University Press for the International Institute for Strategic Studies, 1998.

Short, Michael. "Operation Allied Force from the Perspective of the NATO Air Commander" pp. 19–26 in Andru E. Wall, *Legal and Ethical Lessons of NATO's Kosovo Campaign*, International Law Studies Volume 78, Newport, RI: Naval War College, 2002.

Shy, John, "The American Military Experience: History and Learning", *Journal of Interdisciplinary History*, Vol. 1 No. 2 (Winter 1971), pp. 205–28.

Singer, P.W. "Corporate Warriors: The Rise of the Private Military Industry and its Ramifications for International Security." *International Security*, Vol. 26 No. 2, Winter 2001/2, pp. 186–220.

———— "War, Profits, and the Vacuum of Law: Privatized Military Firms and International Law", *Columbia Journal of Transnational Law*, Vol. 42 No. 2, Spring 2004, pp. 521–50.

———— "Outsourcing War: Understanding the Private Military Industry", *Foreign Affairs*, Vol. 84, No. 2. March/April 2005, pp. 119–32.

Slaughter, Anne-Marie. "International Law and International Relations Theory: A Dual Agenda", *American Journal of International Law*, Vol. 87 No. 2, 1993.

Slaughter, Anne-Marie and Stepan Wood. "International Law and International Relations Theory: A New Generation of Interdisciplinary Scholarship", *American Journal of International Law*, Vol. 92 No. 3, 1998.

Smith, Thomas W. "The New Law of War: Legitimizing Hi–Tech and Infrastructural Violence", *International Studies Quarterly*, Vol. 46 No. 3, 2002. pp. 355–74.

Smyth, Frank. "The Gulf War" in *Crimes of War: What the Public Should Know*, eds Roy Gutman and David Rieff, New York: W.W. Norton and Company, 1999. pp. 162–8.

Social Research, "International Justice, War Crimes and Terrorism: The U.S. Record". Vol. 69 No. 4, Winter 2002.

Solis, Gary. *Marines and Military Law in Vietnam: Trial by Fire*, Washington: History and Museums Division Headquarters, U.S. Marine Corps, 1989.

———— "Obedience to Orders: History and Abuses at Abu Ghraib Prison", *Journal of International Criminal Justice*, Vol. 2 No. 4, 2004. pp. 988–98.

Spiro, Peter J. "The New Sovereigntists: American Exceptionalism and Its False Prophets", *Foreign Affairs*, Vol. 79 No. 6, November/December 2000. pp. 9–15.

Stafford Smith, Clive, *Bad Men: Guantánamo Bay and the Secret Prisons*, London: Weidenfeld & Nicholson, 2007.

Starkey, Armstrong. *European and Native American Warfare 1675–1815*, London: UCL Press, 1998.

———— "Paoli to Stony Point: Military Ethics and Weaponry During the American Revolution", *The Journal of Military History*, Vol. 58 No 1 (Jan. 1994), pp. 7–27.

Steele, Ian K. "When Worlds Collide: The Fate of Canadian and French Prisoners Taken at Fort Niagra, 1759", *Journal of Canadian Studies*, Vol. 39 No. 3, 2005.

———— "Hostage-taking 1754: Virginians vs Canadians", *Journal of the Canadian Historical Association*, Vol. 16 No. 1, 2005. pp. 49–73.

——— *Betrayals: Fort William Henry and the "Massacre"*, Oxford University Press, 1990.

——— *Guerrillas and Grenadiers: The Struggle for Canada, 1689–1760*, Toronto: The Ryerson Press, 1969.

Sterling, David L. "American Prisoners of War in New York: A Report by Elias Boudinot", *The William and Mary Quarterly*, 3rd Ser., Vol. 13 No. 3, July 1956. pp. 376–93.

Stinnett, Nathaniel. "Regulating the Privatization of War: How to Stop Private Military Firms from Committing Human Rights Abuses", *Boston College International and Comparative Law Review*, Vol. 28 No. 1, 2005. pp. 212–23.

Stolberg, Eva-Maria. "Yalta Conference", in *Encyclopedia of Prisoners of War and Internment*. ed. Jonathan F. Vance, Santa Barbara: ABC-CLIO, 2000. pp. 345–6.

Suskind, Ron. *The One Percent Doctrine: Deep Inside America's Pursuit of Its Enemies Since 9/11*, London: Simon & Schuster UK Ltd, 2006.

Suter, Keith. *An International Law of Guerilla Warfare: The Global Politics of Law Making*, London: Frances Pinter, 1984.

Swofford, Anthony. *Jarhead: A Soldier's Story of Modern War*, London: Scribner, 2003.

Taulbee, James. "Myths, Mercenaries and Contemporary International Law", *California Western International Law Journal*, Vol. 15 No. 2. pp. 339–63.

Thompson, Waddy. *Recollections of Mexico*, New York: Wiley and Putnam, 1847.

United States Department of State, *United States Department of State Executive Documents Printed by Order of the House of Representatives. 1875–'76: Vol. II (1875–1876)*, Washington: U.S. Government Printing Office, 1875–1876.

——— *United States Department of State/Papers Relating to the Foreign Relations of the United States, with the Annual Message of the President Transmitted to Congress December 2, 1902 (1902)*, Washington: U.S. Government Printing Office, 1902.

——— *United States Department of State/Papers Relating to the Foreign Relations of the United States with the Annual Message of the President Transmitted to Congress December 3, 1907. (In two parts) Part II (1907)*, Washington: U.S. Government Printing Office, 1907.

——— *United States Department of State Papers Relating to the Foreign Relations of the United States, 1918. Supplement 2, The World War*, Washington: U.S. Government Printing Office, 1918.

——— *United States Department of State Papers Relating to the Foreign Relations of the United States, 1929: Volume I (1929)*, Washington: United States Government Printing Office, 1929.

——— *United States Department of State/Foreign Relations of the United States Diplomatic Papers, 1941. General, The Soviet Union, Volume I (1941)*, Washington: U.S. Government Printing Office, 1941.

——— *United States Department of State/Foreign Relations of the United States Diplomatic Papers, 1942. General; the British Commonweath; the Far East Volume I (1942)*, Washington: U.S. Government Printing Office, 1942.

BIBLIOGRAPHY

Van Deventer, Henry W. "Mercenaries at Geneva", *American Journal of International Law*, Vol. 70 No. 4, October 1976. pp. 811–16.

Vance, Jonathan F. *Objects of Concern: Canadian Prisoners of War Throughout the Twentieth Century*, Vancouver: UBC Press, 1994.

——— ed. *Encyclopedia of Prisoners of War and Internment*. Santa Barbara: ABC-CLIO, 2000.

Verchio, Donna Marie. "Just Say No! The SIrUS Project: Well-Intentioned but, Unnecessary and Superfluous", *Air Force Law Review*, Vol. 51, 2001. pp. 183–228.

Virginia Journal of International Law, "The New York University-University of Virginia Conference on Exploring the Limits of International Law", Vol. 44 No. 1, Fall 2003.

Walker, Clive and Dave Whyte. "Contracting Out War? Private Military Companies, Law and Regulation in the United Kingdom", *International and Comparative Law Quarterly*, Vol. 54, July 2005. pp. 651–90.

Wall, Andru E. *Legal and Ethical Lessons of NATO's Kosovo Campaign*, International Law Studies Volume 78, Newport, RI: Naval War College, 2002.

Wallace, Edward S. "The Battalion of Saint Patrick in the Mexican War", *Military Affairs*, Vol. 14 No. 2, 1950. pp. 84–91.

Walzer, Michael. *Just and Unjust Wars: A Moral Argument with Historical Illustrations*, Third Edition, New York: Basic Books, 2000.

Warren, Marc L. "Operational Law–A Concept Matures", *Military Law Review*, Vol. 152, 1996. pp. 33–73.

Wedgwood, Ruth. "Propositions on the Law of War after the Kosovo Campaign", pp. 433–41 in Andru E. Wall, *Legal and Ethical Lessons of NATO's Kosovo Campaign*, International Law Studies Volume 78, Newport, RI: Naval War College, 2002.

Weingartner, James J. "The Malmédy Massacre Prosecution and Idaho Law Alumnus Colonel Burton Ellis: A Warning of the Difficulties in Administering Justice to a Defeated Enemy", *Michigan State Journal of International Law*, Vol. 13 No 1, 2005. pp. 63–78.

Wharton, Francis. *A Digest of International Law of the United States*, Volume III, Washington: Government Printing Office, 1886.

Wheaton, Henry. *Elements of International Law: The Literal Reproduction of the Edition of 1866*, Richard Henry Dada Jr.,ed. and George Grafton Wilson, ed., Oxford: The Clarendon Press, 1936.

Wheeler, Nicholas J. "Dying for Enduring Freedom: Accepting Responsibility for Civilian Casualties in the War against Terrorism", *International Relations*, Vol. 16 No. 2, 2002. pp. 205–25.

——— "The Kosovo Bombing Campaign" in Christian Reus-Smit ed., *The Politics of International Law*, Cambridge University Press, 2004.

White, Andrew D. *The First Hague Conference*. Boston: The World Peace Foundation, 1912.

Wiggers, Richard D. "Forcible Repatriation" in *Encyclopedia of Prisoners of War and Internment*, ed. Jonathan F. Vance, Santa Barbara: ABC-CLIO, 2000. pp. 100–2.

Williams, David. *A People's History of the Civil War: Struggles for the Meaning of Freedom*, New York: The New Press, 2005.

Zagovec, Rafael. "World War II–Eastern Front" in *Encyclopedia of Prisoners of War and Internment*, ed. Jonathan F. Vance, Santa Barbara: ABC-CLIO, 2000. pp. 329–33.

Zamoyski, Adam. *1812: Napoleon's Fatal March on Moscow*, London: Harper Perennial, 2004.

Zinni, Anthony. "The SJA in Future Operations", *Marine Corps Gazette*, February 1996. pp. 15–17.

News Stories

Agence France Presse. "Under Obama, US drops hostility to ICC: experts" 22 March 2009.

——— "US soldier pleads guilty in Iraq detainee abuse scandal", 11 September 2004.

——— "Hearing of US soldier accused of posing with Iraqi corpse raises questions", 25 June 2004.

Badger, T.A. "Jury deliberations expected in Lynndie England's Abu Ghraib abuse case", Associated Press, 26 September 2005.

Barry, John, Michael Hirsch and Michael Isikoff. "The roots of torture", *Newsweek*, 17 May 2004. Available online at: http://msnbc.msn.com/id/4989422/

BBC News. "Nato leadership splits revealed", 9 March 2000. Available online at: http://news.bbc.co.uk/1/hi/world/europe/671420.stm.

——— "UN sexual allegations double", 6 May 2005. Available online at: http://news.bbc.co.uk/2/hi/americas/4521481.stm

——— "Guantanamo pair's charges dropped", 5 June 2007. Available online: http://news.bbc.co.uk/1/hi/world/americas/6720315.stm

Bennett, Brian. "Outsourcing the war", *Time*, 26 March 2007. pp. 36–40.

Boone, Jon. "Blackwater scandal revives efforts on reforms", *Financial Times*, 2 November 2007.

Borger, Julian. "US troops ordered to undergo ethical training after killing of Iraqi civilians" *The Guardian*, 2 June 2006. Available online: http://www.guardian.co.uk/Iraq/Story/0,,1788643,00.html

Borger, Julian and Martin Hodgson. "A plane is shot down and the US proxy war on drug barons unravels" *The Guardian*, 2 June 2001. p. 3.

Boston Globe, "An erosion of battlefield Ethics", 10 May 2007. p. A14.

Boyle, Jon. "Europe 'actively participated' with CIA prisons" Reuters UK, 7 June 2006, Available online at: http://today.reuters.co.uk/news/newsArticle.aspx?type=topNews&storyID=2006-06-07T100214Z_01_L07492816_RTRUKOC_0_UK-SECURITY-CIA-PRISONS.xml

Branigin, William. "Defectors called sign of air attacks' toll; Allied generals say strikes on Iraqi troops causing deprivations, shattering morale", *Washington Post*, 9 February 1991.

BIBLIOGRAPHY

Broder, John M. and David Johnston, "U.S. military will supervise security firms", *New York Times*, 31 October 2007. p. 1.

Campbell, Duncan and Suzanne Goldenberg. "They said this is America… if a soldier orders you to take off your clothes, you must obey", *The Guardian*, 23 June 2004.

Cloud, David S. and Sheryl Gay Stolberg. "White House bill proposes system to try detainees", *New York Times*, 25 July 2006. p. 1.

CNN. "NATO grapples with 'war by committee'", 9 April 1999. Available online at: http://www.cnn.com/US/9904/19/war.by.committee.

Cody, Edward. "Friendly persuasion–stick, then carrot; torrent of leaflets promise embattled Iraqis 'Arab hospitality' if they surrender", *Washington Post*, 7 February 1991. p. A21.

Douglas, William. "President Bush meets ex–secretaries of state, defense to discuss Iraq" Knight Ridder/Tribune Information Services, 12 May 2006.

Drummond, James. "Court martial sentences US soldier to year in jail for abusing Iraqi prisoners", *Financial Times*, 20 May 2004. p. 9.

Economist. "Military industrial complexities", 29 March 2003. p. 56.

Ephron, Dan. "Haditha unraveled", *Newsweek*, 29 October 2007. p. 36.

Goldenberg, Suzanne. "Guantanamo's day of reckoning in Supreme Court", *The Guardian*, 29 March 2006. Available online: http://www.guardian.co.uk/guantanamo/story/0,,1741825,00.html.

Glaberson, William. "New detainee rights weighed in plans to close Guantánamo", *New York Times*, 4 November 2007. Available Online: http://www.nytimes.com/2007/11/04/us/nationalspecial3/04gitmo.html?_r=1&ref=todayspaper&oref=slogin.

Gordon, Michael R. "After the War; G.I.'s, facing a moral quandary, try to aid Iraqis", *New York Times*, 2 April 1991. p. 1.

Greenhill, Kelly M. "Don't dumb down the Army" *New York Times*, 17 February 2006. p. A23.

Gugliotta, Guy. "U.S. forces battle Iraqi tanks on eve of cease-fire talks", *Washington Post*, 3 March 1991, p. A1.

Harding, Thomas. "Britain's armed forces 'under legal siege'", *Daily Telegraph*, 15 July 2005. http://www.telegraph.co.uk/news/main.jhtml;jsessionid=UCQBOHAGB0MNPQFIQMFCM5WAVCBQYJVC?xml=/news/2005/07/15/nforces15.xml.

Hendawi, Hamza. "U.S. troops in Iraq to get Ethics training", CBS News, 1 June 2006. Available online: http://www.cbsnews.com/stories/2006/06/01/ap/world/mainD8HVL8EO3.shtml

Katyal, Neal. "Counsel, legal and illegal", *The New Republic*, 5 November 2007.

Krulak, Charles C. and Joseph P. Hoar, "Fear was no excuse to condone torture", *Miami Herald*, 11 September 2009. Available online at: http://www.miamiherald.com/opinion/other-views/story/1227832.html

Lewis, Neil A. "Broad use of harsh tactics is described at Cuba Base", *New York Times*, 17 October 2004. Available online at: http://www.nytimes.com/2004/10/17/

politics/17gitmo.html?ex=1255665600&en=67208a988fb44907&ei=5090&pa rtner=kmarx.

Lobe, Jim. "Panama: America's Watch cites U.S. violations of laws of war", Inter-Press Service 10 May 1990.

Lynch, Colum. "U.N. sexual abuse alleged in Congo" *Washington Post*, 16 December 2004. p. A26. Available online at: http://www.washingtonpost.com/wp-dyn/articles/A3145–2004Dec15.html.

McGreal, Chris. "Rape case to force US defence firms into the open", *The Guardian*, 15 October 2009. http://www.guardian.co.uk/world/2009/oct/15/defence-contractors-rape-claim-block

MSNBC. "England sentenced to 3 years for prison abuse", 28 September 2005. Available online: http://www.msnbc.msn.com/id/9492624/

New York Times. "Remember Grenada?", 15 December 1983, p. 30.

Norland, Rod and Mark Hosenball. "Blackwater is soaked", *Newsweek*, 15 October 2007. p. 30.

Onishi, Norimitsu. "Military specialist pleads guilty to abuse and is jailed", *New York Times*, 11 September 2004. p. 9.

Parker, Ned. "US orders coalition troops to take lessons in the ethics of battlefield", *The Times*, 2 June 2006. Available online: http://www.timesonline.co.uk/article/0,,7374–2207570,00.html.

Paterson, Tony. "Soldier will admit role in Abu Ghraib abuse", *The Independent*, 24 August 2004. p. 23.

Pincus, Walter. "Military weighs private security on front lines: firm could have broad protection authority in Afghanistan", *Washington Post*, 26 July 2009. Available online at: http://www.washingtonpost.com/wp-dyn/content/article/2009/07/25/AR2009072501738.html

Plummer Flaherty, Anne. "Senators skeptical of tribunal plans" Associated Press, 2 August 2006.

Priest, Dana. "Captured Panamanians pose test of changing rules on POWs", *Washington Post*, 31 December 1989.

———— "CIA holds terror suspects in secret prisons: debate is growing within agency about legality and morality of overseas system set up after 9/11", *Washington Post*, 2 November 2005, Page A1. Available online at: http://www.washingtonpost.com/wp-dyn/content/article/2005/11/01/AR2005110101644.html.

Reid, Tim. "Abu Ghraib abuser jailed for 8 years", *The Times*, 22 October 2004, p. 4.

Reid, T.R. "Graner gets 10 years for abuse at Abu Ghraib", *Washington Post*, 16 January 2005. p. A01.

Reuters. "Prisoner-of-war camp in Panama nearly full", *The Toronto Star*, 3 January 1990.

Reynolds, Maura. "Messages conflict on detainee trials", *Los Angeles Times*, 14 July 2006. p. A22.

Ross, Brian, David Scott and Rhonda Schwartz. "U.N. sex crimes in Congo" *ABC News*, 10 February 2005. Available online at: http://abcnews.go.com/2020/UnitedNations/story?id=489306&page=1.

BIBLIOGRAPHY

Ross, Brian and Richard Esposito. "Sources tell ABC News top Al Qaeda figures held in secret CIA prisons: 10 out of 11 high-value terror teaders subjected to 'enhanced interrogation techniques'", ABC News, 5 December 2005. Available online at: http://abcnews.go.com/WNT/Investigation/story?id=1375123.

Ross, Brian, Maddy Saur and Justin Roodab. "Victim: gang-rape cover-up by U.S., Halliburton/KBR", ABC News, 10 December 2007. Available online at: http://abcnews.go.com/Blotter/story?id=3977702&page=1&page=1.

Santora, Marc. "Three top Republican candidates take a hard line on the interrogation of detainees", *New York Times*, 3 November 2007. Available online: http://www.nytimes.com/2007/11/03/us/politics/03torture.html

Smith, Michael. "Iraq battle stress worse than WWII", *The Sunday Times*, 6 November 2005. p. 1.

Spagat, Elliot. "Murder charge dropped in Iraqi detainee killing", Associated Press, 29 September 2009.

Stephens, Philip. "The Gulf War; troops prepare to care for prisoners by the thousand", *Financial Times*, 28 January 1991. p. 3.

Sunday Times, The. "The humbling of Saddam Hussein", 3 March 1991.

Taylor, Stuart. "Treatment of prisoners is defended", *New York Times*, 29 October 1983. p. 7.

United Press International. "100 Cuban prisoners return from Grenada", *New York Times*, 6 November 1983. p. 18.

———— "Grenada denies Amnesty International charges", 24 November 1983.

Wallace, Scott. "Tent city prisoners await 'habeas grabus' process: The US has 15,000 Noriega troops behind wire and is sorting them into the good and the bad", *The Guardian*, 3 January 1990.

Watkins, Thomas. "US Marine Corps works on battlefield ethics after civilian deaths overseas", Associated Press, 14 July 2007.

Westhead, James. "Planning the US 'long war' on terror" BBC News, 10 April 2006. Available online at: http://news.bbc.co.uk/1/hi/world/americas/4897786.stm.

Whitaker, Mark, Ron Moreau and Linda R. Prout. "The battle for Grenada", *Newsweek*, 7 November 1983.

Whitaker, Raymond. "US Marines on trial for Iraq atrocity", *Independent on Sunday*, 21 October 2007. p. 32.

White, Josh. "Judge allows Abu Ghraib lawsuit against contractor", *Washington Post*, 7 November 2007.

Williamson, Hugh. "Charges likely for two officers", *Financial Times*, 25 August 2004. p. 5.

Wines, Michael. "After the War: P.O.W.'s; ex–P.O.W.'s offer accounts of terror and torture in Iraq", *The New York Times*, 15 March 1991.

Worme, George. "Red Cross complains about Richmond Hill prison conditions", *United Press International*, 2 December 1983.

Zavis, Alexandra. "Rise of guns-for-hire in Iraq creates regulatory quandary", *Associated Press*, 8 May 2006.

Zernike, Kate. "Ringleader in Iraqi prisoner abuse is sentenced to 10 years", *New York Times*, 15 January 2005, p. 12.

Zernike, Kate and Sheryl Gay Stolberg. "Detainee rights create a divide on Capitol Hill", *New York Times*, 10 July 2006. p. 1

Floor Statements/Press Releases

Gonzales, Alberto. "Statement of the Attorney General Before the Armed Services Committee, United States Senate, Concerning Legislation in Response to Hamdan v. Rumsfeld", 2 August 2006. Available online: http://armed-services.senate. gov/statemnt/2006/August/Gonzales%2008–02–06.pdf.

Leahy, Patrick. "Guantanamo Bay Has Become A Blot And A Black Hole", 13 June 2005. Available online: http://leahy.senate.gov/press/200506/061305.html

McCain, John. "McCain Statement on Detainee Amendments", 5 October 2005. Available online at: http://mccain.senate.gov/index.cfm?fuseaction=NewsCenter. ViewPressRelease&Content_id=1611.

United States Department of Defense. "DoD News Briefing—Secretary Rumsfeld and Gen. Myers", 11 January 2002. Available online at: http://www.defenselink. mil/transcripts/2002/t01112002_t0111sd.html.

United States Department of Defense. "DoD News Briefing—Mr. Di Rita and Gen. Abizaid" 16 July 2003. Available online at: http://www.defenselink.mil/ transcripts/2003/tr20030716–0401.html.

United States Department of Defense. "The Legal Basis for Detaining Al Qaida and Taliban Combatants", 14 November 2005. Available online at: http://www.de-fenselink.mil/news/Jan2006/d20060215legalbasis.pdf.

United States Department of State. "Excerpt: Rumsfeld Says Taliban to Blame for Casualties", 29 October 2005. Excerpt available online at: http://bangkok.usembassy. gov/news/press/2001/nrot113.htm.

White House. "Guards and Reserves 'Define Spirit of America': Remarks by the President to Employees at the Pentagon." 17 September 2001. Available at: http:// www.whitehouse.gov/news/releases/2001/09/20010917–3.html.

White House. "Vice President Cheney Delivers Remarks at the 56th Annual Alfred E. Smith Memorial Foundation Dinner", 18 October 2001. Available at: http:// www.whitehouse.gov/vicepresident/news-speeches/speeches/vp20011018.html.

White House. "Fact Sheet: Status of Detainees at Guantanamo", 7 February 2002. Available at: http://www.whitehouse.gov/news/releases/2002/02/20020207–13. html.

Government Reports

United States

United States Department of the Army. "Report of the Department of the Army Review of the Preliminary Investigations into the My Lai Incident", Washington: United States Department of the Army, 1970. (AKA "The Peers Report")

BIBLIOGRAPHY

United States Department of Defense. "Conduct of the Persian Gulf War: Final Report to Congress", Washington: Department of Defence, April 1992.

——— Quadrennial Defense Review Report, 6 February 2006. Available online at: http://www.defenselink.mil/qdr/report/Report20060203.pdf.

White House. "The National Security Strategy of the United States", September 2002. Available online at: http://www.whitehouse.gov/nsc/nss.pdf.

——— "Progress Report on the Global War on Terror", September 2003. Available online at: http://www.whitehouse.gov/homeland/progress/.

United Kingdom

Foreign and Commonwealth Office. "HC577 Private Military Companies: Options for Regulation" 12 February 2002. Foreign and Commonwealth Office, London: The Stationery Office.

Reports from other organizations

Final Report to the Prosecutor by the Committee Established to Review the NATO Bombing Campaign Against the Federal Republic of Yugoslavia, Available online at http://www.un.org/icty/pressreal/nato061300.htm.

Websites Used in Research

Amnesty International: http://www.amnesty.org.

Avalon project: Documents in Law, History and Diplomacy, Yale University: http://www.yale.edu/lawweb/avalon/

Coalition for the International Criminal Court: http://www.iccnow.org.

International Committee of the Red Cross: http://www.icrc.org

International Criminal Court: http://www.un.org/law/icc.

Human Rights First: http://www.humanrightsfirst.org.

Human Rights Watch: http://www.hrw.org.

Ronald Reagan Presidential Library, http://www.reagan.utexas.edu/.

United States Senate Committee on Armed Services: http://armed-services.senate.gov.

United States Senate Committee on the Judiciary: http://judiciary.senate.gov.

INDEX

Adams, John Quincy: Secretary of State, 72
Afghanistan, 187, 197; and CIA, 217; Invasion of (2001), 2; Operation Enduring Freedom, 4, 139, 189, 201; presence of PMFs, 210; prisoners from, 9, 14; Taliban, 152–4, 156, 164, 205
Amherst, Field Marshall Jeffrey: campaign against First Nations of North America, 34
Al Qaida, 5, 153, 156, 164, 227–8; 9/11 attacks, 7, 152, 154, 156; members of, 154, 171

Baker, James E.: background of, 149
Belgium, 83
Blair, Tony: administration of, 10–11
Bolton, John, 146; background of, 147
Bonaparte, Napoleon, 7; military campaigns of, 6, 55
Brussels Declaration (1874), 70; and Lieber Code, 69; failure of, 71
Bush, George H. W.: administration of, 147, 224; and Noriega, Manuel, 123
Bush, George W., 152; administration of, 3, 10–11, 14, 68, 146, 148, 150–1, 153, 155–9, 166, 168, 171–2, 174, 176–8, 180, 184–5, 187, 191, 195, 199, 210, 224, 230, 233; and Guantánamo Bay, 163, 234; and War on

Terror, 157, 163, 175, 191, 201, 227; Invasion of Iraq (2003), 3, 183; legal arguments of, 153; USA PATRIOT Act (2001), 158–9, 200, 233

Campbell, Colonel William: and Virginia Militia, 40
Canada, 28; and Catholicism, 20; and France, 27, 31–2; Quebec City, 32; Somali torture scandal (1994), 8
Central Intelligence Agency (CIA), 207; alleged waterboarding of suspects, 155; and Afghanistan, 217; contractors working for, 206, 217; custody of terrorist suspects, 173; operation of 'black sites', 175
Cheney, Dick, 163, 179; blocking of Philbin, Philip promotion, 157; defence of Terrorist Surveillance Program, 164; ideology of, 231–2
Clausewitz, Carl von: *On War*, 134–5, 226
Clinton, Bill, 232; administration of, 9, 143, 156, 224; signed ICC Statute (2000), 148, 224; signed Kyoto Protocol, 224
Cold War: and Non-Aligned Movement, 127; chilling of, 96; end of, 149, 203
Confederate States of America, 66; Andersonville Prison, 65; and First

DATE DUE